China's New Consumers

The mesmerising potential of 1.3 billion customers has long constituted 'a magic market' for foreign entrepreneurs who once again are queuing to take advantage of China's fast-growing economy and rapidly changing society. Now, to counter a growing reliance on the markets of the world for exports, China's government too has turned to developing its own domestic markets by placing the expansion of domestic demand high on the nation's agenda. This book explores China's consumer revolution over the past three decades and shows a continuing cycle leading to excess supply and disappointing demand, at the centre of which lies the exaggerated expectations of China's new consumers.

Elisabeth Croll details the livelihoods and lifestyles of China's new and evolving social categories who, divided by wealth, location and generation, have both benefited from and been disadvantaged by the past two decades of reform and rapid economic growth. Given that consumption is about so much more than shopping and spending, this book focuses on the perceptions, priorities and concerns of China's new consumers which are an essential part of any contemporary narrative about China's domestic market. Documenting the social consequences of several decades of rapid economic growth and the new interest in 'all-round' social development, *China's New Consumers* will be of value to students, entrepreneurs and a wide variety of readers who are interested in social trends and concerns in China today.

Elisabeth Croll is Professor of Chinese Anthropology at the School of Oriental and African Studies, University of London. For the past 30 years, she has undertaken field studies and written widely on social development issues in contemporary China.

China's New Consumers

Social development and domestic demand

Elisabeth Croll

Routledge
Taylor & Francis Group

LONDON AND NEW YORK

First published 2006
by Routledge
2 Park Square, Milton Park, Abingdon, Oxon OX14 4RN

Simultaneously published in the USA and Canada
by Routledge
270 Madison Ave, New York, NY 10016

Routledge is an imprint of the Taylor & Francis Group, an informa business

© 2006 Elisabeth Croll

Typeset in Baskerville by
HWA Text and Data Management, Tunbridge Wells
Printed and bound in Great Britain by
Antony Rowe Ltd, Chippenham, Wiltshire

British Library Cataloguing in Publication Data
A catalogue record for this book is available from the British Library

Library of Congress Cataloging-in-Publication Data
A catalog record for this book has been requested

ISBN10: 0–415 41123–8 (hbk)
ISBN10: 0–415–41124–6 (pbk)

ISBN13: 978–0–415–41123–3 (hbk)
ISBN13: 978–0–415–41124–0 (pbk)

'... accelerating the growth of consumption is of vital importance to stimulating domestic demand, so as to attain the objectives of building a well-off society in an all-round way to the benefit of well over a billion people ...'

China's Foreign Trade (Beijing), February 2003

Contents

Preface

There is a 'China Story' or a 'China Speech' which, punctuated by a rush of statistics, stretched adjectives and breath-taking anecdotes, emphasises certain key features of today's fast-changing China and its globalised role. As international headlines have it 'The Dragon Awakes', 'The Giant Grows' and 'Everywhere the China Effect' – in global markets, in global commodity transfers and on global energy prices. More often than not, the twenty-first century is labelled a 'Chinese Century' for such is the 'phenomenal', 'high-flying' or 'supersonic' speed of economic growth that China is often said to have taken but a short march to super-power status and is expected to be the world's largest economy by 2025. A lot of money is chasing this China Story. The sheer scale of foreign direct investment has been unprecedented as transfixed foreign investors in the grip of 'China Fever' queue to pump hundreds of billions of dollars into the economy in the hope of sharing in the returns. China, the 'Hungry Dragon' is widely reported to have a 'voracious thirst' or a 'galloping demand' for energy and an 'unending appetite' for raw materials – consuming two-fifths of the world's cement, a third of its coal, a quarter of its steel and more copper, tin, aluminium, lead or any other metal – so straining supply and pushing up the world's commodity prices to new highs. In Europe and North America, it is not so much a matter of an 'oil shock' as a 'China Shock'. China is also an export-driven economy and, as it takes a growing share of the international market, it is expected to overtake America as the world's top exporter by the end of the decade. Already China's 'soaring' or 'surging' trade surplus with the USA has generated a clamour for protection across the political spectrum in Congress and country-wide. China, described as the 'Workshop of the World', manufactures the largest proportions of DVDs, televisions and other 'Made in China' products which flood the world's stores, driving prices down. China, as the world's largest source of cheap labour, is feared to have lured or to be about to lure jobs away from other countries as manufacturers take advantage of 'the China Price' which over much of the business world has become synonymous with 'the lowest price possible'.

Lastly, and perhaps most importantly, in a global retail sector that is sluggish, it is the mesmerising potential of 1.3 billion customers which constitutes the 'magic market', 'the mother of all new markets' or 'the biggest market for everything'. Whether it be about cars, mobile phones, diamonds or foreign students, China not only promises to be 'the market of the future' but 'China is the Future'. There is no question that China's economic transformation represents one of the most rapid and sustained of the past century or that China is of growing international economic and political importance and, behind the dramatic headlines, astute correspondents, commentators and analysts have regularly documented the many dimensions of the 'China Story' for their readers. In the past year or so, this 'China Story' has generated both hope and fear: a fear of China's rising power and economic hegemony alongside the hope that China's population will provide a limitless market amounting to millions of new customers. It is an old dream that China's market will make fortunes for foreign entrepreneurs and this book is about the revival of those dreams and the ways in which they generate patterns of supply and demand that so often lead to disappointed hopes of China's new consumers. This study explores this oft-repeated pattern which begins with initial demand and high profits, is followed by exaggerated expectations of the market and then excess supply, falling profits and some disillusionment – until next time. This book suggests that it is the exaggerated expectations which are pivotal to this cycle, the breaking of which requires further understanding of a paradox that has long puzzled foreign entrepreneurs. This paradox derives from the contrast between the mesmerising numbers who make up the China market and the repeated shortfalls in expected numbers of customers for fashion, accessories, durables and other goods or services. This book attempts to explore this pattern and paradox by focusing attention on a dimension that is so often missing from the China Story. An essential part of any contemporary narrative about China's domestic market are the perceptions, priorities and concerns of the different social categories that make up China's present-day population. In emphasising the needs and aspirations of China's new and potential consumers and their own expectations, this study complements the very interesting and insightful business-oriented books on China's billion customers which have been published in recent years.

It is also the general aim of this book to add a social dimension to the very many fine economic and political studies of contemporary China. This study sets out to document both the social consequences of several decades of rapid economic growth and today's new interest in 'all-round' social development, secure livelihoods and quality lifestyles. To this end, it examines the livelihoods and lifestyles of the main social categories divided by wealth, generation and location and the ways in which each group has both benefited from and been disadvantaged by reform and rapid economic growth. There is much here on the socio-political tensions and problems which preoccupy China's government and populace alike. More specifically, this book charts the policies and analyses the generation of and growth in domestic demand (neixu) which places the consumer at the centre of China's own political and economic agenda. To counter a growing reliance on the markets of the world for their exports, the government has turned to developing China's own domestic market and to encouraging consumption among the different categories of China's population. Some time ago and in the back of one of Beijing's many taxis, I came across this ditty perhaps written with a hint of Orientalist irony: 'China is the biggest market in the world, We are all Chinese, We must help this market'. In recent years the domestic market and increasing domestic demand have moved to the top of the national agenda, however this study focuses less on demand in the wider sense at the macro-level and more on demand for goods and services at the micro-level. It also uses the term 'domestic' in two senses: one to refer to internal demand at the national level and the other to denote the ways in which extended families, households and individuals look to foster their own domestic well-being and create new lifestyles. The lifestyle concept has been widely deployed in China as both a measure of development, a policy-goal or as an instrument of development as well as a means of constructing and confirming personal identities and social difference.

If expectations around China abound, so too do expectations within China. These focus on improved livelihood opportunities, new life-spaces, goods and the comfortable lifestyles that match those of the middle classes elsewhere in China or abroad. Such expectations are now widespread in the countryside and in the city, among the rich and the poor and among the young and the old. In the age of reform, the luxury of dreaming is less bound by income, location or age, for to dream is the stuff of movies, novels and paintings, television stories and advertisements, billboards and above all shop windows. Such is the interest in life-spaces, lifestyles and shopping that originally I wanted the title to include a reference to one of my favourite shops in Beijing, Life-Shop (Shehui Fangdian), much as the concept of 'life-shopping' has been developed elsewhere to denote the tendency of the young to experiment through a shopping-style search for the ideal relationship, a satisfying job and the most fulfilling lifestyle. However, for reasons that will become clear throughout the study, this concept is only appropriate for the everyday practices of a small but well-publicised minority of China's new consumers. Indeed another idea for the book's title was *The Handbag and the Hoe* for in China today there still as many wielding the hoe as choosing the handbags featured on the cover. Nevertheless it can be argued that over recent decades there has been a consumer revolution made up of three phases and that consumption has newly offered possibilities for self-definition, social aspiration and political legitimation.

In keeping with my own training as an anthropologist, this study takes a holistic approach which defines consumption as an everyday material and social practice in which the acquisition of goods fulfils a wide range of personal and social functions. Consumers too, as everyday persons, have other identities which also play a major part in determining their motivation to spend and means to shop and acquire. It is because consumption is about so much more than shopping and spending and as much about consumer confidence, perceptions and aspirations that this is a wide-ranging study embracing the many social trends and social problems that concern China's existing – and potential – new consumers. Their concerns include widening disparities, rising service costs, environmental degradation, corruption and the incidence of unrest. In keeping with anthropological practice, this book focuses not so much on economic statistics at the macro-level or the quantitative, although these are included where they add to the narrative. It has become commonplace in studies of contemporary China to note that there is much debate around the accuracy or not of macro- and local-level statistics and, in keeping with this caveat, I want to note that the ones used in the text are intended to illustrate common trends rather than to be definitive in detail. Others are more qualified than I to discuss the grey shades of data and my own preference for the significant human-interest story chosen because it too represents a trend that will become evident throughout the text. In leaning towards the qualitative, the micro-level and an exploration of local or everyday familial and individual practices and purchases, this study is based on both my own long years of field studies and on those of others. My own field studies of China's social development date back to the 1970s and began with investigations of the women's movement, marriage, food consumption, the family, gender, birth control, the single child, the elderly, the village, the urban neighbourhood and many other topics to do with social development in both city and countryside. In terms of domestic demand, the genesis of this study began with my own early studies of consumption including both 'The Family Rice Bowl: Food and Domestic Consumption in China' published in 1983 and a shorter piece entitled 'Desires and Destinies: Confucianism and the Rise of Consumption in China' which was published in the late 1990s. The interest in this topic is borne of my own thirty years of study and field experience in China as a social anthropologist conducting investigations in many different regions of China for a wide variety of development agencies and for my own academic studies. It also has to be said that I have spent many hours happily perusing the shops and markets in various parts of the country. Although this study has an anthropological and sociological bias, it is not based on the study of a single field-site rather it draws on a wide range of varied field experiences across China. This study owes much to the observations and research of others in academia and in the media both within and outside China. I am very grateful to fellow-academics in Europe, North America and China from a variety of disciplines in the social sciences and humanities who have undertaken numbers of nuanced and insightful documentary and field studies over the years. I have also drawn on and woven threads from a wide range of sources for this broad and very contemporary study which has a focus but is also the sum of China's 30 years of reform and change. In this respect, I also owe an enormous debt to the insightful commentaries by the correspondents and feature writers of *The Economist*, the *Far Eastern Economic Review*, the *Financial Times*, the *Guardian*, the *Independent*, the *International Herald Tribune*, *Newsweek*, the *Observer*, *Time*, *The Times*, the *Sunday Times* and the *China Quarterly Chronicle*. Their reports have been most helpful in providing a wide variety of local reports and individual interviews well beyond the reach of any single author. These have been fully referenced in the end-notes for each chapter.

Finally, I would like to acknowledge the help of many institutions and individuals including that of the School of Oriental and African Studies which has provided the facilities and support for my academic studies over many years. I would like to express my appreciation formally – to colleagues, friends and family for their collegiality, interest and fun times in London, China, France and Australia. My special thanks to editors Stephanie Rogers and Helen Baker at Routledge and to the anonymous reviewers whose thoughtful comments were most helpful. It is my hope that the broad and evolving canvas presented here will add a dimension to existing studies and be of value to the wide variety of audiences who are now interested in the many facets of social development and domestic demand in China today. While this book was being written, social development as well as domestic demand has moved to the centre of the political agenda in China. Indeed, just as this book goes to press, I attended two conferences. In London, presentations at a conference on 'China and Globalisation' suggested that the best way China could help the global economy was to increase domestic demand. At the second, during a conference on 'China's Social Policy' in Beijing, many an intervention declared that 'raising domestic demand was a matter of domestic urgency'.

Elisabeth Croll
London
February 2006

1 Introduction

Highlighting demand in development

This study was stimulated by the coincidence of two recent and major policy shifts in China: the new emphasis on domestic demand and a more inclusive definition of development to include the social. Just before the turn of the twenty-first century and since, there has been an emerging consensus in China around the importance of consumption-led growth or developing domestic demand or an internal market which has been designated variously as a 'new source', the 'new impetus' or the 'main engine' for China's long-term economic growth. In 1998 a new Five Year Plan advocated 'giving full play to the advantages of our domestic markets which are large and have great potential'.[1] A year later, Zhu Rongji, China's then Premier, openly acknowledged that the greatest of China's economic problems was 'lack of demand at home'.[2] In 2002, at the Fifth Session of the National People's Congress, China's Premier designated expansion of domestic demand as 'a long-term strategic principle' and 'a fundamental plan for realising a relatively rapid economic growth to further stimulate consumption and investment'.[3] In April 2003, the front pages of the national media reported that the first of the top twelve priorities set by the State Council was 'continuing the expansion of domestic demand'.[4] Henceforth the boosting of domestic demand in China, long the subject of foreign interest, was to be given priority in planning for a shift from investment-led to consumption-led growth. Henceforth much of the debate was to centre around the quality as well as pace of economic growth. In 2003 for instance, the authoritative and influential Beijing-based periodical, *Outlook Weekly*, urged that, at this current stage of China's development, expanding consumption was more important than increasing investment and that enhancing the ability and desire to consume rested not only on improving the consumption environment via improved marketing facilities and credit opportunities, but also on social and economic policies to increase incomes, reduce inequalities and secure China's all-round development'.[5] This article was interesting because it drew attention to a number of major constraints inhibiting the growth of a flourishing domestic market, chief of which, it suggested, was China's uneven development.

Simultaneously in late 2003, a new development strategy was outlined at the Communist Party's Third Plenum which rejected the monolineal or 'go-for-growth' policy of the past 20 years in favour of a more comprehensive, balanced and sustainable approach. The rapid rates of economic growth ranging between a reported 8 and 10 per cent, as welcome as they might be, were recognised to have had costs – to the environment, to health and to society. The new development policy was to be based on five principles: the promotion of harmony between city and countryside, between regions, between society and the economy, between man and nature and between domestic and external economies. The articulation of this new development strategy was also designed to distinguish and establish the credentials of the so-called 'fourth generation' of leaders headed by Hu Jintao and Wen Jiabao. In 2004 and 2005 both these leaders made a succession of important speeches stressing the importance of sustainability in supporting a new 'scientific development' concept for China which accorded a higher priority to the balanced and harmonious development of different regions, between city and countryside, to resource conservation and to stable and social development.[6] Indeed it may well be that the tempering of economic growth with social development will constitute a lasting legacy of these new leaders. As Martin Wolf of the *Financial Times* argued in 2003:

> Trying to achieve the better harmony between the development of the economy and of society may turn out to be the hallmark of the new government.[7]

In support of the social, the government has deployed two tenets: 'people first' (yiren weiben), which holds that development should be aimed at the equitable promotion of people's interests rather than enriching one segment at the expense of another. The second, 'building a moderately well-off society' (xiaokang shehui), is about translating economic growth into a better quality of life and is a term much used at all administrative levels to convince the population of official concern for their social well-being. The 'xiaokang' concept, which literally means 'small well-being' dates back to Confucian times and was revived by Deng Xiaoping and again used by Jiang Zemin in the late 1990s to denote the second goal of modernisation. The first goal in the 1980s was to double the size of GNP and feed and clothe China's population; the second goal was to further double GNP and simultaneously offer the Chinese people a 'xiaokang' or better quality of life which, after several decades and during the third phase of modernisation, should become the equivalent of the middle-class levels of prosperity characteristic of developed societies.[8] The new development strategy not only attached a new importance to increasing individual well-being and promoting social development alongside maintaining economic growth but also placed domestic demand at the heart of China's political agenda to counter its undue dependence on the vagaries of global demand.

Global demand

Within China, the new emphasis on domestic demand and the creation of a country-wide internal market was designed to counter the country's heavy dependence on exports and overseas markets or consumers. Given the explosion in the assembling and processing of manufactured goods and the boom in

China's exports, it is not surprising to find China described in the international media as 'the workshop of the world'. It is now commonplace to refer to China's 'daunting export machine' as goods labelled 'Made in China' increasingly dominate global markets and high-streets. China's phenomenal growth rates of around 8 to 9 per cent, if not 11 to 12 per cent according to some unofficial estimates, have been fuelled by exports. Taking advantage of cheap and plentiful labour, a co-operative government and foreign opportunities for investment, exports grew eight-fold between 1999 and 2003 and have continued to grow. In 10 months in 2003 alone, industrial production jumped by 17 per cent with the output of home appliances increasing by more than 50 per cent.[9] It is well known that China has become one of the world's main source of both labour-intensive products such as textiles, toys and shoes and technologically-intensive products such as widescreen televisions, computer software, video-games machines, home computers, DVDs, personal shredders and kitchen appliances. In 2003, China replaced Britain as the world's fifth largest exporter as China's exports to Europe grew by 50 per cent, to Asia by 30 per cent and to America by 25 per cent. Then it was also estimated that around 50 per cent of cameras, 42 per cent of computer monitors, 29 per cent of televisions and 24 per cent of washing machines sold world-wide were made in China.[10] On Christmas eve of the same year, an editorial leader in the London *Financial Times* wished its readers Merry Christmas – 'with thanks to China' where most of the festive presents, decorations and other accoutrements had originated.

> At this festive season, let us raise a glass to the people who make Christmas what it is – the Chinese. Although Santa Claus still sets off from Lapland later today, the elves who make the presents he delivers are mostly Chinese as are those who produce most of the paraphernalia associated with Christmas.[11]

The editorial went on to remind readers that China is 'of course, the new workshop of the world all the year round' and that 'like Britain in the nineteenth century, its manufactured goods increasingly dominate world markets because they can be produced more cheaply and on a greater scale than in other countries'.[12]

At latest count, in 2004, China was already the sixth largest economy in the world in dollar terms and the fourth largest exporter in the world, accounting for about half of the growth in world trade. If it is expected that China will overtake America as the world's top exporter by the end of the decade,[13] it is China's surging trade surplus with America which, exceeding US$200 billion at the end of 2005,[14] gives rise to current concern. In the meantime, new estimates of China's output which have been adjusted for previous under-counting have fuelled the realisation that 'China's exports are going to grow and grow'![15] It is estimated that by 2025, if recent growth in export value is sustained, China will supply a third of the world's merchandise exports, edging out many other countries which too are dependent on such exports.[16] If this reads as a singular success story – and it is – within China, there is also growing concern that this singular dependence on exports and external or world markets and above all on consumers in far-away America and other places has made China's continuing economic growth increasingly subject to the vagaries of the world market. This concern at China's vulnerability multiplied in the late 1990s as events in first one and then another of the world's major demand regions threatened China's export markets. Although China had showed itself to be somewhat immune to the domestic crises of other East and Southeast Asian economies in the late 1990s, there was considerable evidence of a knock-on effect and mounting problems in the export sector as neighbouring Asian economies went into recession. As Zhu Rongji acknowledged in 1999, it was the vagaries of the external market that might well threaten the growth of China's exports.[17] In August 2001, it was reported that problems deriving from the Asian crises had led to a drop in the growth rate of China's exports from a high 28 per cent to a mere 5.8 per cent in that year – and this was but a month before the collapse of the World Trade Towers in New York.

The second conspicuous threat to the buoyancy of global demand and therefore to China's export-market took place in the immediate aftermath of the terrorist attack in New York in 2001. The 9/11 events primarily about towers and the tragic loss of lives also spotlighted the role of the American consumer as the mainstay of both the USA, the Chinese and the global economy. Indeed in the immediate and stunned aftermath of these dramatic events in New York, it was shopping and spending which were cast as the new patriotism as former and current presidents encouraged their fellow countrymen 'to go out and shop for your country'. The mayor of New York also exhorted all citizens of America 'to shop for New York as the best possible way to help the city'.[19] Special days were set aside as 'shop for America days' and, to set an example, ex-President Clinton and a succession of well-known congressmen were to be seen in the shopping malls.[20] Shopping was newly defined as an essential public service or even duty in order to save the economy or at least avoid a national or indeed a world-wide recession. At the end of that year, newspaper headlines proclaimed the all-important role of the American consumer in the months following 11 September. A notable article in Britain's *Sunday Times* at Christmas of that year had the eye-catching headline: 'Hail consumers, we salute you for saving 2001'.[21] The article went on to note that if consumers had not continued to buy houses, cars and all manner of other consumer goods in the aftermath of 11 September, then the global economy would have been in dire shape in the face of declining demand, excess capacity and cuts in investment. If congratulations were in order in 2001, these soon gave way to persistent reports of an imminent global economic downturn brought about by recession in America and the ensuing global loss of that all-important being – the American consumer.

The American consumer

In the past few years both business analysts and newspaper headlines have highlighted the central role of the American consumer, and to a lesser extent the British consumer, in generating and maintaining world-wide demand. At the end of 2002, national newspapers on both sides of the Atlantic noted that not for more than a century had the global economy been so dependent on consumers to keep it healthy and buoyant. In March 2003, it was reported that the spending of the American consumer played a vital part in the world economy, accounting for some 70 per cent of America's GDP and 20 per cent of world GDP.[22] A combination of favourable tax cuts, rising property values and full employment had encouraged American consumers to spend even if they already had debts and there was much borrowing to fund further consumer purchases. In Britain too, rising property prices and the 'spend now, pay later' culture had encouraged an upswing in and dependence on maintaining levels of consumption. In turn, the acknowledged global dependence on consumers in America, and to a lesser extent in Britain, meant that any downturn in their consumer confidence was deemed to have world-wide repercussions. In recent years there has been much 'doom about the consumer boom' with many doubts expressed in the business sections of the national and global media that the rate of spending by both American and British consumers could continue at present levels and was at increasing risk from rising unemployment, a falling stock market and lower salaries and interest rates alongside the spectre of declining property and pensions values.

The question most often debated was not so much 'whether' but 'when' the consumer boom would end and would it end with a bang or a softer and slower slide into recession? One British commentator in October 2002 noted a growing worry: if US consumers who have fuelled global growth since the mid-1990s 'really are running out of puff' then 'the slack will be felt worldwide'.[23] In 2003, fears that American consumers were reining in their spending intensified as figures for consumer spending showed the sharpest falls since 9/11 amid signs of increasing 'consumer jitters'.[24] Indeed *The Economist* forecast that in America, Britain and Australia there would be a sharp drop in consumer spending even if house price bubbles did not burst and interest rates did not rise as, in all these countries, 'consumers have been living on borrowed time' and 'sooner or later consumers will have to face up to reality'.[25] Since 2003 there has been continuing debate about whether this gloom is justified or if healthier stock and labour markets will brighten consumer spirits. Whether it is boom or gloom, there is an increasing awareness both within and outside China that it is the indefatigable spending of the American consumer, followed by British and Australian consumers, which has been instrumental in providing markets for China's exports. In 2003, Britain's *Sunday Times* went as far as to note that the authority of the China's new leaders and perhaps even their physical survival depended on the economy and that the economy depended on American consumers.[26] In 2004 and 2005, the debate about the continuing health and resilience of the American and European consumer despite falling prices, rising costs of fuel and other resources and the mountain of domestic debt, has continued to feature in the business pages and commentaries of the world's media.[27] There is an increasing awareness within China too that its continuing economic growth if not political stability is dependent on American consumers and that this continuing dependence cannot be presumed and has to take account of a variety of economic and political factors. In addition to economic perturbations, there was also a growing recognition that China's rapid export growth and dominance of the world's merchandise market may not be uniformly welcomed by all countries and that such dominance might invite protectionist retaliation. It is not only alternative suppliers around the world and particularly China's Asian neighbours who fear competition and substitution but in the United States itself, now China's second-largest trading partner, the size of the soaring trade surplus has sparked widespread fears that China's manufacturing capacity threatens manufacturing jobs in America, especially in textiles and appliances as they are 'lost to China'. Such were the fears of China's dominance of world markets and manufacturing capacity that the US government, in the lead up to the last Presidential election, sought to show that it was sympathetic to US interests by imposing quotas on China-made apparel including bras, bathrobes and knitted fabrics and electronics such as televisions. Although many argued that the surge of such products on the market self-evidently invites a protectionist response, some like the American Dean of London's Business School, advised against such protectionism on the grounds that the American consumer has also been the beneficiary of lower-priced goods, that around 50 per cent of the manufacturing companies producing China's exports are in fact American or foreign-owned and that China has also become the second-largest buyer of US Treasury bonds – a contribution which tautologically has helped keep American interest rates low and consumer demand robust.[28]

Counter-arguments such as these have done little to mollify the political and popular image of China as a world-wide manufacturing threat resting on wage rates less than a tenth of those in the USA and a deliberately undervalued currency which unfairly forces US factories to close and deprive millions of workers of their jobs. In Britain too, similar closures and loss of manufacturing jobs to China alongside loss of service jobs to India, has caused growing official and popular recognition that these are countries to be reckoned with and indeed feared in the future. Again, the more recent world-wide rises in the price of oil and other raw materials exacerbated by China's demand has also generated new concerns about the dominance of this impending manufacturing and export giant. Although the US government's protectionist quotas affected only a small proportion of China's trade with America, the timing of the first of these measures on the eve of a visit by Premier Wen Jiabao to the USA fuelled fears in China that worse could come as governments might be tempted to cut China's exports in order to pacify those with manufacturing interests and jobs at risk. China's government is well aware that the growing spectre of a country buying up raw materials and flooding world markets with cheap goods or exporting deflation and destroying Western jobs may well generate new attempts to contain China's exports not only in America but also in the European Union and other existing markets. However this spectre has been countered to some extent by the potential and promise of China's own markets to ameliorate a world-wide shortage of demand. As large swathes of industrial capability come on stream in Asia and particularly in China, world-wide demand has not been able to keep pace with the increase in supply. If much of the increase in supply has been generated in Asia and particularly in China, much of the demand remains located in America and Europe.[29] Both the world-wide shortage in demand and the imbalance between supply and demand in the Asian region has directed attention to alternative sources of demand and particularly to Asia's consumers.

Asia's consumers

In the years following the Asian crises and subsequent downturn, the rising and respectable growth rates across much of East and Southeast Asia have been largely due to export-led recoveries. Indeed much of that continent's economic about-turn has been attributed to 'Uncle Sam's apparently insatiable consumption habits',[30] in that it is the USA which constitutes the critical market for Asian electronics, computers and cars and low-tech goods such as textiles, clothing and toys. In Asia, future growth rates have been premised less on the development of their own markets than on a prolonged North American boom which will continue to keep the export industries of Asia humming. However, as the *International Herald Tribune* noted in 2002, if the Asian region can feel happy that it is US consumer demand that has propelled it out of recession, it should also realise that US consumer demand 'may not' or rather 'will not' last.

> No one can tell when all this will end, but end it must whether through a long period of slow US growth or a sharp decline in the dollar or both.[31]

The article went on to warn Asia's governments that if American consumer demand and confidence continue to stagnate or decline, then the Asian region generally will have to look less to foreign demand and more than ever before to its own consumers and instead focus on stimulating and sustaining its own domestic demand. The *International Herald Tribune* bluntly stated the dilemma: 'Asia must consume or stagnate'.[32] Whether Asia's consumers outside China will step into any impending gap in demand by developing their own domestic markets remains to be seen.

At present the signals are mixed and the forecasts differ. In 2003 there were those who argued that, as memories of previous crises fade, the signs are that Asia's consumers, particularly in Korea, Thailand and India, are fuelling strong revivals of their economies. It has been observed that after decades of export-led development based on high rates of saving and investment with consumption suppressed, Asia's consumers are abandoning their thrifty habits and, with the encouragement of consumer credit by Asia's banks, are starting to spend at levels amounting to what some are calling 'a seismic shift' in consumer patterns. For instance, in October 2003, an article in *The Economist* noted that across all of Asia there were more than a billion baby boomers aged between 30 and 59 years who, with increasing spending power and richer than their frugal parents, are waking up and reaching for their wallets to spend on houses, consumer durables, luxury goods, tourism and financial products. Described as 'well-educated and sophisticated singles or couples enjoying a confidence in their own rising standards of living', they were likened to the Eisenhower generation in 1950s America.[33] In the belief that 'the engine of growth is the consumer market', Asia's banks began to openly encourage the use of finance and credit to foster domestic demand.[34] If optimists argue that new borrowing and spending patterns are transforming Asia's hitherto export-led economies, others are less sanguine and point to the example of South Korea which perhaps more than any other country in Asia had some degree of success in stimulating domestic demand. For a time, consumer spending appeared to be robust so that the world-wide indices in consumer confidence among emerging economies compiled in 2002 suggested that the rise in domestic consumption in South Korea was the fastest in the Asian region.[35] However this rise appears to have largely rested on a credit-card boom that later resulted in a record number of defaulters as easy credit fuelled record numbers of personal bankruptcies which came to threaten the very stability of Korea's entire financial system.

In 2003 the authoritative *Far Eastern Economic Review* argued that 'if Asian governments think expanded domestic consumption is a recipe for sustained economic growth then they should think again'. In support of this argument, it cited the observations of the chief economist at the Asian Development Bank who had concluded that the economic impact and importance of Asian consumers has been exaggerated and that domestic consumption is not a substitute for exports in Asia, largely because consumer demand is adversely affected by low growth rates, saturated financial systems and low incomes leading to weakened spending power. It went on to argue that the relative size of Asia's domestic demand outside Japan remains small in terms of the global context at roughly 24 per cent of the USA and 26 per cent of the EU.[36] These factors, plus the fact that most of Asia's population typically earn only a fraction of employee earnings in the USA, Europe or Japan, suggested to many analysts that manufacturing for domestic consumption in Asia is unlikely to deliver the economic growth rates returned by manufacturing for export and that any recent rises in consumption are short-term. They argued that in the near future Asia's consumers are unlikely to prove powerful enough to substitute for any slowdown in American or European demand for the region's exports. Again in October 2005, headlines continued to characterise Southeast Asia economies as those 'in search of elusive domestic demand'.[37] In these circumstances all eyes within and outside Asia have looked to China, as the world's largest untapped domestic market, to fill the demand shortfall. In the context of a world 'fundamentally short of demand' not only for Asian manufactured goods but also for American and European exports and services, it is not surprising to find that the potential of the hitherto closed China market has been represented as 'the last market' or the 'last great frontier'. This is not the first time that this market has been the subject of foreign interest. Indeed recent interest continues and revives an age-old image of China as a unique market of magical or mythical proportions. China, perhaps more than any other country, has been and continues to constitute 'a dream market' sustaining long-held foreign hopes for unlimited sales and riches.

An old dream market

The image of China as a land of opportunity or as a dream market dates back to the legendary Venetian traveller Marco Polo, who in his writings, whether or not he actually visited China, depicted a land of richness and prosperity with flourishing commerce and inter-regional trade. Marco Polo's vision of Cathay, his name for north China, as 'a fabulous land of wealth on the far side of the world',[38] was further and more seriously fostered by Adam Smith's work, *The Wealth of Nations*, which had enormous influence among academic, commercial and popular audiences in the eighteenth century. Adam Smith noted that China had for a long time been 'one of the richest, that is, one of the most fertile, best cultivated, most industrious and most populous countries in the world' and was ripe for the development of foreign trade. He thought that China's size together with her wealth of products meant that the country was 'not much inferior to the market of all the different countries of Europe put together'.[39] The embassy of Lord McCartney sent to China by King George III of England in 1793 also sparked a new wave of interest in a country reputedly offering tantalising opportunities for trade. McCartney himself concluded that though 'everything is covered by a veil, through which a glimpse of who is within may occasionally be caught', it was 'a glimpse just sufficient to set the impatient to work'.[40] Since the early nineteenth century, Napoleon's aphorism, 'Let China sleep; when she awakes she will shake the world', has irresistibly challenged each generation of foreign merchants as they looked to China's market potential. Indeed Napoleon's quote has launched a thousand articles with headlines such as 'When China Wakes', 'When the Dragon Awakes' or 'When the Giant Awakes'.[41] Like many before and after, Karl Marx too was impressed by the potential import of the China market for commerce, navigation and industry which he forecast would be on a scale 'never known before'.[42] Such influential texts and popular images nurtured the notion of a supposedly limitless domestic market in China based on the country's uniquely large and increasing population.

China's vast size and large population recurs time and again in Western images of China and has convinced Western governments, merchants and entrepreneurs that there is a giant market waiting to be tapped. In terms of numbers, the market based on some 150 million customers in the sixteenth century doubled to 300 million in 1800; it numbered 400 million before 1949 before it unabashedly swelled to more than a billion persons in the 1970s. By the 1990s the refrain '1.2 billion customers' with future growth rates projected to reach a total of 1.4 billion by 2010 and 1.6 billion by the middle of the twenty-first century became, in Joe Studwell's words, 'the commercial poetry of the decade'.[43] The statistical extravagance afforded by the potential of the largest single market in the world has given rise to more imaginative sets of calculations all resting on the idea of sales to a billion prospective customers. Nineteenth-century Manchester textile manufacturers imagined a market in which each Chinese added two inches to their shirt tails. Imaginations in the early decades of the twentieth century were captured by the numbers of apples, pills or cigarettes that might be sold to each of China's citizens or the amount of oil required for 'all the lamps of China'. Nobody summed up these statistical extravagances better than Carl Crow, an agent for foreign businesses, whose book entitled *400 Million Customers* was first published in March 1937 to be followed by four impressions within the year. He jocularly but exactly captured the prevailing mood:

> Any time an export manager wants to enjoy a pleasant day-dream of the future, in which fame and prosperity will unite to banish daily cares, all he has to do is to take a pencil and pad of paper and start figuring out what sales he could make if he could only find an advertising agent clever enough to induce a reasonable proportion of China's 400 million customers to buy his goods. Merchants wore out quill pens on the same pleasant speculations long before graphite pencils, calculating machines and advertising agents began to play an important part in the affairs of the business world. So long as people of one country make goods to sell to others, so long as ships cross oceans and international trade exists, the golden illusion of the sales which may be made to China's industrious millions will always be an intriguing one. No matter what you may be selling, your business in China should be enormous, if the Chinese who should buy your goods would only do so.[44]

His book, a vivid and lasting account which is now often quoted, concluded that all but a small proportion of China's population were no more than theoretical customers. Indeed very few could afford to purchase even an apple a day.

'I don't suppose there is a proprietary medicine manufacturer of importance in any part of the world, who has not, at one time or another, encouraged his imagination to play with the idea of the prosperous business he might build up, and the wealth he might accumulate, if he could, by some means, convince a reasonable number of Chinese of the efficiency of his remedies. The less the manufacturer knows about China, apart from the population figures, the less restricted are his day-dreams, and as he usually knows nothing about the country, his fancy is in most cases free to wander into distant and prosperous fields ... When he computes the number of China's millions who must, according to the laws of average, be suffering from some kind of ache at any given moment and reflects on the efficiency with which his pills would cure them or give them relief, it is easy for him to conjure up rosy day-dreams in which a private yacht occupies the foreground and a country estate can be seen in the middle distance.'[45]

He surmised that these dreams occupying the foreground and the middle-distance remained just these – both for himself and for many a foreign merchant.

> Now we have in China regular schedules of steam sailings, merchandising managers, sales conferences and advertising agents. A very large proportion of foreigners living in China are, like myself, primarily interested in selling goods to as many as possible of China's 400 million customers. We make market surveys, speculate what articles they will buy, how the article shall be packed, how advertised and what merchandising methods should be followed

... None of us ever prosper to the extent we think our work justifies, but we have compensations. The work is always interesting, and in spite of our years of disillusionment, all of us secretly cherish the thought that a reasonable number of the 400 million may buy our goods next year.[46]

The cherishing of these old dreams stopped abruptly in the mid-twentieth century with the war against Japan and then China's revolution. For thirty years, the China market was all but closed to foreign merchants and it was not until the post-revolutionary reforms of the late-1970s and the accompanying Open-Door policy that China re-opened its doors to trade with the West as a major part of its blueprint for new economic reform and development. Not only had China's population increased, but the world's largest and growing market of close on a billion persons promised to be much more accessible – so reviving anew old China dreams.

A new dream market

As market analyst and author Joe Studwell, a latter-day but more analytical Carl Crow, noted in his recent book entitled *The China Dream*, the oldest dream of all – the China market – has once again captured world attention.[47] Not only was 'the China Game' on again, but the greater potential of this new and larger market, now reaching 1.3 billion customers, seemed more enticing than ever.[48] Once more out came the calculators and computers as businessmen fell under China's statistical spell. Added to the dreams of pills for a billion ills and deodorants for twice as many armpits, now Coca-Cola, computers, automobiles and mobile phones were the subject of new calculations as company executives compiled endless charts confirming the scale and scope of the China market. Many a multinational business strategy was built around such calculations with marketing objectives based on the selling of products to the same proportions of China's population as elsewhere in the world. If Americans ate on average 20 chickens, Thais ate six chickens and Chinese ate only one chicken per year; if China's population drank an average of 15 cokes per year compared with the American's 800; if 40 per cent of American homes had computers compared with 4 per cent of those in China – then the potential for growth seemed endless. The products might change but the dreams remained. Now it was the potential for automobiles or for mobile phones with the prospect of a billion engines running or a billion voices calling that encouraged and excited the largest multinational enterprises, foreign manufactures and governments.

From the mid-1980s, notable presidents, chairmen and chief executive officers of the world's largest multinational firms, including such well-known businessmen as Jack Welch and Richard Branson, have rushed to endorse the dream. In 1984, the Chair of IBM noted that 'With their labour force, their resources and their markets, anything could happen. If we could just sell one IBM/PC for every hundred people in China, or every 1000 or even 10,000...' he left the sentence unfinished.[49] The General Manager of Asia General Motors similarly anticipated that 'before the year 2000, China will have become one of the world's biggest markets for automobiles.

This is not a dream, it is going to happen'.[50] Many chief executives and entrepreneurs felt that they had no choice but to be in China. The Chairman of Ford once said that he 'could not go down in history as the Ford Chairman who missed China'.[51] Richard Branson concurred: 'If you're in business, you've got to be there'.[52] In the mid-1990s many of his corporate British peers were publicly chastised by Michael Taylor of Morgan Stanley for 'a failure in imagination' in not taking sufficient advantage of and 'missing out on the twentieth century's greatest opportunity'.[53] News magazines with world-wide coverage featured maps of 'China Inc.' divided into spheres of commercial influence dominated by the multinationals including IBM, GMC, Wal-Mart, Starbucks, McDonalds and Nike.[54] Many European and North American governments sponsored trade delegations led by prime ministers or senior politicians. Germany, France, Canada, the USA and the UK among others all made mandatory official pilgrimages in the hope of signing deals offering access to the world's largest untapped market. Finally China's elongated negotiations anticipating entry into the World Trade Organisation (WTO) seemed to guarantee a new phase in the opening of and access to this market which would finally eliminate physical and political barriers.

Around the turn of the century, China's negotiated entry into the WTO revived expectations at the imminent opening of the long-imagined and now the world's second largest and fastest-growing economy. What distinguished this anticipated breakthrough from previous occasions was the immediacy of China's entry into the WTO which would oblige China to lower import tariffs and provide foreign firms and manufacturers greater access to China's domestic market. In 2000 Lawrence Klein, winner of Nobel Prize for Economics, was quoted as forecasting that China would 'as an economic giant participate in world economic development, and it will enter a new period of development following its accession into the WTO'.[55] Around the turn of the century too, in anticipation of WTO accession, foreign investors, entrepreneurs and manufacturers alike designated the new era as 'The Chinese Century'. As *Newsweek* noted, no one was more interested in making the WTO deal a reality than the USA.

> Under the terms of the trade deal, American companies in every sector will have a better chance of achieving breakthroughs in the China market than ever before. From Midwestern agribusiness to Detroit's big three automakers to Silicon Valley high-tech firms, American corporations in a few years will be able to sell goods to 1.2 billion people throughout China at relatively low tariffs.[56]

With headlines such as 'Enter the Dragon', even the hard-headed *Economist* noted in 2001 that in the aftermath of China's entry into the WTO, it is still the potential scale of China's domestic market that most appeals to foreign multinationals.

> After decades, or rather centuries, of foreigners' dashed dreams about the money to be made from adding an inch to every Chinaman's shirt-tail,

the promise that China had long held out may be about to be matched by reality.[57]

This time too, such dreams were aided and abetted by spokespersons within China who were more than hopeful that the lure of China's massive market potential would help in the negotiation of favourable terms for WTO entry. The astute and chief negotiator of China's entry into the WTO, Charlene Brockevsky, noted that at every opportunity and 'despite the vast vague market promise that had been there since Marco Polo' and some success and some scant returns, China itself based its claims for favourable terms on the fact that a market of 1.2 billion people put China in a different category from all other nations.[58] Several articles in the Chinese press highlighted China's 'untapped market potential' and the rich returns to be had for foreigners once China entered the WTO.[59] China's Minister of Foreign Trade also emphasised the large market potential for imported goods: 'Just imagine, the market potential is huge'.[60] Perhaps the most eloquent expression of the potential was that reported in *Business Beijing* which told its foreign readers to 'expect a boom' as a result of the breath of 'fresh air blown in by the WTO'. The same article quoted one Beijing official as saying 'the future's so bright we've got to wear shades!'[61] This time, and perhaps uniquely, it seemed as if the China market, long imagined, was about to materialise. Imagination apart, much serious analysis and column space in the international media and national newspapers has also generated some debate about the scale of China as a market – both in the past and in the future.

The debated market

In considering how best to tap and understand this market, the questions regarding size, segment and strategy were many and there was much analysis of China's potential in the short- and longer-term and of the constraints that seemed to inhibit the development of this market. In the pattern of the past, the optimists continued to outnumber the pessimists. In 2003, the *Sunday Times* noted that China's large consumer market continued to be eyed greedily by foreign firms who hoped to benefit from the emergence of a moneyed middle class.[62] Similarly *The Times* noted that China, like the rest of Asia, was only at the start of 'what looks increasingly like a long-term consumer boom'.[63] *The Economist* too suggested that no one in business needs reminding of the scale of the opportunities that lie in China's fast-growing economy or of the lure of China's billion-strong consumer market to foreign business and bankers who continue to flock to do deals or attend countless seminars on how to do business in China.[64] Headlines consistently speak of entering 'the dragon market' as the panacea for foreign firms facing shortages in demand at home. An excerpt from a very recent article in the Western press represents such a trend.

You have read the headlines and heard the spiel – so is 2005 the year for your business to head for China?

The country already has a reputation for being able to mass produce goods at short notice and low cost. Witness the likes of B&Q, Wal-Mart and Tesco which now source most of their homewares from the region …

But now there is another reason to consider China: the country is emerging as one of the fastest-growing and biggest consumer markets in the world.

The sixth-largest economy is expected to reach second spot in the next 10 years, and with the move to a more liberalized society and a burgeoning middle-class, analysts believe China will be fertile ground for foreign firms.[65]

The article went on to suggest that now it is an option, with the appropriate advice, to 'envisage moving your entire business to take advantage of China's low costs and enormous market potential'.

There are also those who are less sanguine, more critical or even pessimistic and who argue that realising the potential of China's market is a long-held dream that has been perpetually postponed and is likely to remain so in the foreseeable future. Analysts supporting this view note the recurring pattern of hope or dream followed by disappointment or disillusionment and suggest that 'a pendulum metaphor' best represents the rise and fall of foreign expectations of and experiences in the China market over past decades or even centuries. Just a couple of years ago, Joe Studwell reminded those entering the China market of this persistent pattern.

For centuries, businessmen have gambled their capital on buying camel trains, chartering ships, building railways and financing highways in their efforts to open up the China market only to face disappointment. Perplexed by a nation that has imported only a fraction of what would be expected from such a large populous country, entrepreneurs have tried to sell every service or type of goods imaginable in the hope of unlocking the collective China wallet.[66]

His study astutely documents 'the chase' of the China dream arguing that, with the rise of globalisation, the belief in China's unprecedented potential in the face of perpetual disappointment has taken on the order of an obsession. After a detailed study of the market at the turn of this century, Studwell himself doubted that the dream would ever be realised. Indeed he came to question the very dimensions of the China market, believing it to be something of a mirage or myth confined to the realms of the imagination. In support of this view, he quoted Paul Varg, an economic historian who had studied the China market around the turn of the previous century and had similarly concluded that 'the rhetoric concerning the China market was so wild' and the gap between the rhetoric and experience so great as to suggest that the China market itself was in 'the nature of a myth'.[67] Studwell concludes that the only reason that this most potent of dreams had not unravelled by the turn of the twenty-first century, is because of the sustained belief that it will materialise once better access is granted. If this is so, then the promise of better access via the WTO is likely to test this argument once and for all.

In the meantime many business analysts and commentators continue to describe China's domestic demand as 'slackening', 'sluggish' or even 'stagnant' and suggest that China seems more likely to remain a cheap manufacturing base focused more on foreign export than a flourishing domestic market for foreign products. It is true that a number of foreign entrepreneurs and joint-venturers in China who hoped to enter China's domestic market have been burned by experience and have turned instead to production in China for export. In 2003, the *Sunday Times* reported on a new breed of commuter on board the gleaming trains heading north from Hong Kong to the expanding cities of China's Pearl River Delta.

> They are the advance guard in a dramatic shift in the terms of engagement between China and the global economy. A decade ago, they might have been heading to Shenzhen or Guangzhou in the hope, frequently forlorn, of selling foreign products to that ever-elusive Chinese market of a billion consumers. Today they are more likely to be watching quality control at a factory, churning out products for their own domestic markets, made by China's workers at a fraction of the cost at home.[68]

In 2003, the *International Herald Tribune* also emphasised that no matter what people say, or might be said to dream, China does not have domestic-demand growth and is likely to remain dependent on the US consumer.[69]

A year later, a survey of business in China by *The Economist* in 2004 suggested that, despite the world's gaze, the world's hopes and the speed and scale of China's growth which 'are described in messianic terms' and have 'set off a tidal wave of foreign enthusiasm for China', the true size of the China market should not be over-estimated.[70] It surmised that the disparities in development and the levels of income mean that 'for most foreigners, the market will turn out to be smaller than expected and take longer to develop'. In examining the mismatch between excitable perception and sober reality, *The Economist* reminded its readers that it was well to remember that, in terms of GDP per capita, China still ranked below places such as Namibia, Guatemala and Morocco. It concluded that, although there are undoubtedly rich people in China who can afford villas, limousines and foreign holidays, they constitute a tiny minority of China's population. In contrast, the majority simply do not have spare money to spend and are unlikely to spend on goods for many years if only because they are so worried about the future that they are saving a large proportion of their meagre incomes. The article argued that the prospects of the 1.3 billion market, which has lured countless companies to China, is much more likely to be a 0.3 billion market of potential consumers who are dispersed, often inaccessible and very different from each other. In 2005, there continues to be much talk in the international press of both China's booming domestic market and of slowing or 'fading' domestic demand. A historical study suggests that much of the international gloom about China's domestic demand has its roots in an oft-repeated demand–supply cycle initiated by new demand, brisk sales, high prices and substantial profits only to be followed by exaggerated expectations, excess supply, falling prices and diminishing profits. Perhaps the pivot in this cycle rests on the exaggerated expectations of China's domestic market. While the dimensions and accessibility of China's domestic market continue to be much debated outside of that country, within China there is much talk of increasing domestic demand, consumption-led growth and a new consumer-oriented economy. For those of us who have been studying China for several decades, these are novel descriptions of China's political economy and mark the astounding transition of its peoples from comrades to consumers.

Comrades and consumers

During the 30-year revolution, the emphasis was on production, worker and comrade rather than on consumption and the consumer, with production lines and designs decided and regulated by officials or producers anxious to boost production and meet output quotas according to which they were remunerated – whether or not the goods were sold! This was because production, price and distribution were all decided centrally or by administrative fiat with little reference to consumption and therefore markets and retailing. Standardised goods at set prices appeared in the few shops regardless of customer demand and preference. In a reversal of the norm demand begets supply, supply was centrally planned without demand in mind or at the most generated a demand that was as limited as it was inadvertent. Indeed there was little knowledge or understanding of the concept of demand. The near omission of demand in the marketing mix was one of the legacies of the revolution which continued into the reform years. As one official noted in 2000 'in the planned period, production and sales were all regulated' so that 'people didn't know what demand was'.[71] If there was little understanding of demand there was also little attention given to consumption, customer preference or consumer taste by state, producer or retailer. During the revolution, it could be said that consumption centred around food either cultivated, rationed or purchased. Most family rice bowls were made up of staple grains to which were added vegetables, eggs and, less commonly, fish or meat produced on the farm or purchased in city stores. For years, one of my yardsticks for measuring wealth in villages was whether households consumed or sold the eggs of their few chickens, while in the towns it was the number of times per month households consumed eggs, meat or fish. For many, food supplies were sparse or insufficient while, for others, they were grain-centred and somewhat monotonous.

One of the first questions I asked myself when visiting China more than thirty years ago in the early 1970s was – need it be so difficult for city women to shop for and feed their families? Why did the planned economies of China and the Soviet Union make this everyday task so difficult that it frequently involved long queues for scarce supplies of a narrow range of staple and non-staple foods? It was this question that was responsible for one of my early studies entitled, 'The Family Rice Bowl: Food and the Domestic Economy in China' which was based on field research undertaken in urban and rural neighbourhoods around Beijing and Shanghai in the early 1980s.[72] This research focused on the contents of family rice bowls or the types and amounts of staple and non-staple foods consumed in urban and rural homes and their sources of supply be it state-rationing, shops, markets or private-plot production. This study of food and the domestic economy attempted to identify the political and socio-economic determinants of food intake, the dominant patterns of food production, purchase and processing prior to consumption and the sources and amounts of food consumed within households. It was intended to shift scholarly attention from production to consumption and from the production units of commune, brigade or team to family households which were still the primary units of consumption. While most economists focused on the size of the grain harvest, this study documented the contents and costs of the family rice bowl and investigated the sources of supply be it the farm, the government stores or the new private markets. In terms of consumption, it focused on the contents of the rice bowl not just because of the importance of food supply and nutrition, but because shopping for anything but food was a rare occurrence. There were few consumer goods available for family purchase and those such as a bicycle, watch or sewing machine had to be scrimped and saved for – sometimes over months or years. Shoppers in the few department or specialist shops could be said to be comrades on a rare purchasing expedition and only after several years of reform did some comrades become consumers.

Perhaps the most visible of the many rapid and radical changes in China over the past thirty years and one that has symbolised the reform, the development and the modernisation of China, has been the emergence of new patterns of, trends in and sites for consumption. The speed and scale of their emergence has taken even the most imaginative of long-term observers by surprise. Gone is the prevalent image of uniform blue, the monotonous rice bowl of subsistence portions, the grey concrete or sparsely-furnished home and quiet city high-street with the odd drab department store and spartan customer. It is very different now with the new and pervasive interest in consumption and lifestyle, new everyday shopping habits and the emergence of consumer desire and demand. Part I of this book narrates the changes during the first two decades of reform up to 2000 and argues that China experienced a consumer revolution during these years. One of the first and most visible changes was in clothes as new fashion items excited attention and demand. After years of absence or near-minimal supplies of goods other than foodstuffs, consumer durables of every shape and size appeared in the shops and markets. The sequential interest in style, colour, material and brand seemed insatiable as televisions, cassette recorders, refrigerators and washing machines first topped shopping lists followed by a second list comprising mobile phones, personal computers, DVDs, VCRs and other electronic goods. In yet a third phase, urban consumer attention turned to apartments and houses, automobiles and new leisure activities including travel and sport. For all these items, purchase might be limited but the interest was widespread. Away from the largest cities in small towns, suburban villages and even in far-off villages and markets, there was frequent evidence of a new interest in consumption, with goods observed on television or acquired via migration. In these early years, new and colourful clothes, sofas and televisions began to be much in evidence in richer regions of rural China, and even in poorer villages without electricity I saw the odd television or cassette recorder sitting in splendour on a family altar or powered by yards of battery awaiting the day of electrification.

Shopping itself fast became both a favourite form of recreation and a serious exercise in research as those who have attempted to shop or even move on the pavements of main shopping streets of the metropolitan or smaller cities and busy rural market streets will know. Visits to shops and markets became a new leisure and sociable activity with much noisy consultation between groups of peers or family members crowding around the shop counter or market stall. Each new item attracted crowds, queues and, with much talk and curiosity, frequently started a new fashion or craze. On frequent trips to China in the 1980s and 1990s, it was always very interesting to identify the latest 'must have' item be it a new durable or lifestyle attribute. Even among those with low incomes, items of consumption were of abiding interest, much discussed, and many were saving for some clearly identified item. In city and village fieldwork, nothing excited as much interest among assistants and informants as novel consumer items which were all but turned upside down and inside out as they were examined in great detail. This new interest in style, brand and price was fostered by new retail outlets including large shopping malls, sky-high advertisements on streets, on television and in new general and specialised glossy magazines. Eyes, and not just those on the billboards, became firmly fixed on consumer objects all of which generated new aspirations and the evolution of new lifestyles and new identities which, increasingly evident during the first fifteen years of reform, are charted in Chapter 2.

By the mid-1990s however, much of the novelty and initial excitement of such interests had faded as customers disappeared, shopping malls closed and spending gave way to greater saving. Chapter 3 charts this downturn and explores the reasons for the decline in interest and sales. It examines changes in consumption and lifestyle patterns, new threats to livelihoods and incomes and the many new demands on household incomes. Everyday demands on domestic incomes are as important as the level of income itself for an assessment of household spending and the feasibility of consumption-led growth. Did the downturn in household spending on durables mean that demand itself was declining or was it that, once again, a rise in China's domestic demand had been followed by a period of higher expectations, expanded production and excess supply? Probably a bit of both for the average propensity of households to consume remained limited but excess supply was also an important factor. Certainly China's government revised its own timetable and moved the achievement of the second of its three phases of modernisation further into the future. Originally it had planned to complete this second phase aimed at further doubling GNP and achieving a better-off quality of life for all by 2000. As this date approached, this phase was extended and merged into a third more ambitious phase to establish a modern society with the middle-class living standards of developed countries by the middle of this next century. Whether or not the downturn of the late 1990s was but a swing of the pendulum or more permanent, twenty years of reform had effected a consumer revolution in many parts of the country and had placed consumption and China's consumers at the centre of both national and international agendas. A consumer revolution is not just about the arrival of new goods but about the relations of persons to goods and the new attitudes and behaviours surrounding aspirations for and the purchase or possession of goods. What the downturn at the end of the twentieth century did was to shift attention from goods to consumers and pose new questions about the motivation and behaviour of the country's consumers and direct attention to the necessity of acquiring further knowledge and understanding of China's present and potential consumers. This new interest in China's consumers, which is outlined in Chapter 3, also coincided with a general new interest in measuring and understanding consumer behaviour in America, Europe and Asia.

Researching consumers

In the context of a world-wide shortage of demand deriving from the near saturation of older mature economies and the slow or limited success in the new or emerging economies, there have been concerted and world-wide attempts to investigate consumer behaviour and consumer confidence. As *The Economist* noted in 2002, 'the shift of attention to consumers is the single most powerful theme of our times'.[73] At the end of the same year, both *The Economist* and the *International Herald Tribune* noted how politicians and the mass media, as well as business analysts and retailers, now anxiously await the daily, weekly or seasonal reports on consumer spending, behaviour and confidence which have become the mainstay of economic forecasting.[74] Although 'knowing your customer' has customarily constituted an important mantra within marketing strategies, in practice marketing theory had tended to focus primarily on product characteristics, product development or the creation of brands and less so or only indirectly on the customer. A recent study of marketing by Elliott Ettenberg concluded that although 'everything else has been reinvented' including distribution, new product development and the supply chain, marketing remained 'a shockingly old-fashioned business' in which rules focused on the product and where to sell it rather than on the customer.[75] However once products became brands and brands became both representative of a lifestyle and tools with which companies sought to build and retain customer loyalty, global and national companies became more interested in customers and switched their interest from merely validating the qualities of products to marketing aspirations, images and lifestyles. If marketing is now less about products and more about styles of life or a search for a seductive brandscape then marketing, as *The Economist* has emphasised, necessitates new social knowledge.

> The new marketing approach is to build a brand and not a product – to sell a lifestyle – which requires far greater knowledge of the consumer. This is far harder than describing the virtues of a product.[76]

According to *The Times* in 2001 no subject is as closely studied at the turn of the twenty-first century than the consumer.[77] To research the lifestyle, images and aspirations of twenty-first-century consumers, companies have turned to new methodologies borrowed from social sciences and in particular from my own discipline of anthropology.

Anthropologists and sociologists are long used to studying the relations between persons and things, to recognising the significance of goods as a means of social communication and to analysing their semiotics or the language, signs and symbols of goods.[78] In recent years, anthropologists have also turned their attention to shopping as an under-researched mass activity or everyday practice in which the consumer engages in an on-going process of self-creation. In this process, goods become agents of change in the design and appropriation of new lifestyles by individuals, families and communities who take consumption as opportunities to rethink themselves and acquire new identities. If anthropologists have applied their usual tools of trade, first-hand field research or ethnography, to study these subjects, it is equally interesting to note that, in turn market researchers, in addition to the usual customer interviews, questionnaires and focus groups, have also embarked on a new practice also known in the trade as market ethnography. Now on behalf of the largest companies, specialist market researchers are sent into shops and homes to observe and collect details on individual and family consumer behaviour. As Professor Richard Elliott of the Centre of Consumer Research at Exeter University has noted, this current fashion constitutes a new business approach to studying consumers.

> Ethnography is derived from anthropology and is based on the idea that you get richer information by immersing yourself with a consumer.[79]

Although the new practice is both time-consuming and expensive, it is an increasingly popular practice as companies find that this new methodology provides new and immediate information on the motivation, behaviour and environment of consumers beyond the reach of the unidimensional questionnaire, video or focus group.

Despite the time and expense involved, international companies including Orange, Capital Radio, Unilever and the BBC have availed themselves of this anthropological tool. One such study, sponsored by BT, Unilever, Cadbury, Centrica and Vodafone, investigated consumer behaviour in the home and in particular preferences for certain brands, products and services as well as responses to differing types of advertising. In locations varying from Paisley in Scotland to Oxford Street in London, Tesco, Arcadia, Virgin and Abbey National have all recently collaborated on national studies to help brand managers understand how consumers behave in shops.[80] Researchers, posing as shoppers in supermarkets and toy shops, wait in the aisles to observe parents, children and others, and to record their conversations and choices which are then used to develop marketing-management strategies. Pioneers in this initiative have been inundated with requests from companies as diverse as Microsoft, Proctor and Gamble and News International for ethnographic studies and even training in the technique as they acknowledge the need to understand their customers better so as to continuously invent new products or brands and stay ahead in the retail game. One self-styled 'consumer anthropologist' at the forefront of this new field, has a background in behavioural science and theatrical performance skills which she deploys to make 'consumers the stars'.[81] With her handheld camera, Emma Gilding describes how she takes 'field trips to the medicine cabinet, the daily living room or shop counter following consumers in their natural habitat' and looking for clues to 'homo shopimus'. She became a founder and director of Ogilvy and Matthew Discovery Group which now sends camera-toting researchers to study consumers for clients such as American Express, AT&T Wireless and Huggies 'as if they were part of some undiscovered civilisation'.[82] They move in and sometimes spend several months with consumers where they observe body language and activities, talk to and participate in purchasing decisions. Our goal, as Emma Gilding emphasises is to 'put the consumer back into the equation'.[83] This is also the objective of a recent book entitled *The Future of Consumption* published in December 2003 in which the authors argue that today's consumer, overwhelmed with products, services and information, is not the passive participant of yesteryear's business-to-consumer equation. Instead, in the emerging paradigm, the consumer plays an active role which requires companies to create value 'with' and 'not for the customer' in a new 'consumer-to-business-to-consumer model'.[84]

This world-wide focus on the consumer as a necessary participant in the marketing chain has also influenced investigations of consumer behaviour, consumer preference and consumer confidence in China. Much of the research on China's consumers has been undertaken by a number of foreign market research companies eager to service those seduced by the potential of China's billion-strong consumer market. There is also a burgeoning China-owned and operated market research sector which services both foreign or joint-venture and Chinese-owned companies. Market companies in China deploy both conventional methodologies and those veering towards the ethnographic end of the continuum although the samples investigated cannot but be a drop in the billion-wide ocean. Chapter 3 concludes that most macro-marketing analyses at the turn of the century showed a China divided according to large geographic, provincial or economic regions which can be helpful in formulating large-scale marketing strategies. Additionally there are a number of micro-level investigations which, based on small-scale individual shopping surveys, are very localised in time and place. There have also been a number of attempts to identify the cultural precepts which might influence or differentiate the Chinese consumer from others, but so far there has been less attempt to understand the social context or the livelihoods and lifestyles of the different segments of China's population and the attitudes and practices which underlie both the everyday and the extra-ordinary purchases of China's consumers.

China's consumers

If there is a single distinguishing feature of an anthropological approach to the study of consumption, it is probably the inseparability of the material and the social processes involved in that just as persons choose goods so goods also play a part in the construction of personhood or identity. As persons become consumers, the meanings and messages attached to goods play a large part in defining who they are or wish to be and signal affiliation to a single or range of social categories and cultural values. As consumption comes to play a greater role in everyday practice so it may generate more diverse personhoods, social categories and social relations. This approach differs from those which detach the consumer from everyday persons, consumption behaviour from everyday practice and the consumer from other everyday identities to do with life-cycle, family, community and nationality. Undue emphasis on the act of purchase reduces the concept of consumer to purchaser or buying power which anthropologists would argue is just one element in the pursuit of well-being or generating a lifestyle. Many sociological and anthropological theories identify the consumer as a purveyor of meanings and messages to do with crafting his or her identity and constructing a lifestyle which involves or denotes individual expression in taste and preference, the exercise of self-conscious choices and the communication of aspiration and affiliation. In China over the past two decades, consumption has become one of the main arenas of choice which with the promotion of xiaokang, primarily a lifestyle concept, has led to increasing differentiation and more diverse personhoods, lifestyles, social categories and reference groups. Hence persons or consumers can be divided into lifestyle categories based on location, occupation, income, education, age and gender which are substantiated via the possession of goods and styles of life. Thus the chapters in Parts II and III explore the old, new or evolving socio-economic and socio-demographic categories of China's urban and rural population in ways that highlight the attributes of their livelihoods and lifestyles directly relevant to their everyday purchases, preferences and longer-term expectations.

Parts II and III segment demand into two pyramids: first according to income and lifestyle and secondly by age-category. Chapter 4 in Part II discusses the purchases and aspirations of China's millionaires and elite and owes much to a six-year annual survey undertaken for the *Far Eastern Economic Review* between 1998 and 2003. The lifestyles of the affluent have attracted much attention in the national and international media, but this chapter argues that, instead of a diamond-shaped society with a large or burgeoning middle class, Chinese society is more accurately represented by an income or wealth pyramid showing a very small minority at the top, the majority at the base and a small and burgeoning middle class sandwiched between. Not only are those between fewer than commonly imagined but many are more likely to be downwardly than upwardly mobile. Chapters 5 and 6 examine the livelihoods and lifestyles of the major population categories in China's large and small cities and in the countryside across China. In metropolitan and other cities, both middle-income professional groups and factory workers have been affected by state-sector reforms which have reduced security of livelihood and led to rising urban unemployment, protest and some poverty which all mirror a current urban conundrum in which there is a stark choice between stalled economic reforms or rising urban impoverishment and bitterness. For the majority in the countryside away from the suburbs and richer coastal regions, livelihoods are commonly fragile due to a depleted earth and under- or unemployment both on and off the farm. In much of the countryside too, rural reforms have arrived at an impasse in which the only way up for many of the poor is migration out or urbanisation. These two chapters seek to give as much analytical attention to poorer consumers and their everyday dreams, practices and purchases to supplement that normally directed to the affluent, the yuppies or nouveaux riche and the middle classes.

The three chapters making up Part III of this study divide the population according to age-category. Chapter 7 examines the most privileged category in terms of consumption or children who, in one- or two-child families, were among the first to benefit from new post-reform opportunities for consumption. This chapter outlines parental dreams for, expectations of and expenditure on children, child consumers and the influence of children on familial spending. It argues that because of the scarcity of children and the reversal of generational hierarchies, children in China may play a greater role in consumption decision-making than elsewhere. Chapter 8 turns to the youthful desires and dreams of both the urban young and single living at home with a substantial disposable income and the large numbers of rural youth who support their penurious siblings and parents. Although in China, as in most societies, it is the former with time, money and an interest in self-expression and trend-setting who are courted by marketing personnel, there is also an uneasy mix of youthful aspiration and alienation which both influences and is influenced by popular and counter cultures. In many societies too, including our own, it is the elderly who are increasingly disposed to allocate their incomes and leisure to retired and consumer-oriented lifestyles. Chapter 9 discusses the reasons why, despite the ageing profile, it is unlikely that China's elderly will have the leisure, the income or the wish to spend on themselves and thus constitute a growing and greying market. Instead they devote time, income and energy to investing in individual and familial sources of support and security for old age. These chapters in Parts II and III are intended to identify current consumer categories and their everyday purchases, preferences and aspirations between 2000 and 2005. They are also intended to provide a broader understanding of the current range of livelihoods and lifestyles in contemporary China which should underlie any assessment of China's social development and domestic demand in the future.

Demand and development

The final section of the book, Part IV, mainly based on current observation, data and debates during 2004 and 2005, also assesses the likely trajectories in domestic demand in the future. Demand is not only rooted in present circumstance and aspiration but also in senses of security and confidence that life will get better in the future. Indeed one of the most closely monitored of economic indicators the world over has become the consumer confidence index which measures the link between current spending power and future prospects and willingness to spend, borrow, risk or save. There is some debate about the degree to which hopes and fears can have economic meaning, but whether it is used as a measure or an explanatory tool, consumer confidence is about perceptions of short- and long-term livelihood security and lifestyle-aspirations for 'the future'. After surveying current consumer confidence indices for China, Chapter 10 examines a number of very contemporary issues that contribute to and detract from consumer confidence among China's populace. In this context, it examines the socio-economic problems which most concern China's citizens including unemployment, social security, the costs of public services, corruption, the environment and inequality. It is such concerns and fears that have determined the degree to which households spend and save and secure different forms of security including insurance and religious or other beliefs to help them to weather 'uncertain times'. The final chapter outlines the ways in which China's government recognises these concerns and has attempted to reduce insecurity, create employment, end corruption and stop or make-good environmental degradation. The present leadership is well aware that further family and individual spending requires the resolution of these problems; indeed the rationale for many present reforms is to effect an increase in domestic demand. Given the importance attached to domestic demand by China's government in maintaining economic growth, social stability and balanced development in the future, this study concludes by returning to the relationship between demand and development.

The introduction to this chapter linked China's current interest in expanding demand to broadening the notion of development to include social well-being and lifestyle aspirations. In this, China's government is following a well-worn global path that has long recognised that development begets demand, but what has emerged in China as a result of the reforms is a mosaic with uneven development and thus uneven demand. The pattern of inequality between coast and interior, metropolis and rural village and rich and poor is one of the most observable characteristics of present-day China and is sometimes labelled 'development with Chinese characteristics'. In pyramid-shaped China there is still much more concern for livelihood than lifestyle and little likelihood that a new and rising middle-income group will emerge in the large numbers expected in the near future. The demand pyramid that is China very much suggests that supply will continue to exceed demand at the top, bottom and middle levels of the pyramid. There is increasing recognition that the few high-income earners at the top tend to have met their lifestyle needs and subsequently do not make the major purchases that might make additions to or upgrade their existing durables, cars and homes; that the small band of middle-income earners have either acquired goods or are saving for services and security and are not expanding as fast in numbers as expected; and that the many low-income earners at the bottom do not have the means to acquire these items and upgrade their lifestyles in the foreseeable future. Simultaneously, the demand–supply cycle perpetually repeats itself as exaggerated expectations of China's market for so many goods leads to excess supply. Overall and certainly within China there is some impatience at the pace of development as the country proceeds – too slowly – to achieve the development goals it set for itself – that is to attain a xiaokang lifestyle or well-being by 2000 and internationally comparable middle-class living standards for all by the middle of the century. If the pace of development is not proceeding fast enough to generate sufficient demand then the question arises: how can the cycle leading to excess supply be broken and how can demand at the bottom of the pyramid be generated? It is a new and interesting question now much debated in international business and retail circles. There are several demand-led changes in a few developing countries that are beginning to challenge the conventional route based on conspicuous consumption at the top of the pyramid and the trickle-down effect. These experiences suggest that current concepts of demand may have to be redefined. Some analysts now argue that such a redefinition has the potential to turn the poor into consumers, create demand and generate mass consumption and – along the way – achieve development goals. The concluding pages of this study examine these arguments and recent moves to encourage micro-mass consumption in China, elsewhere in Asia and in some Latin American and African countries. They cite the influential economist C.K. Prahalad and others who, in favour of this approach, argue that demand- or consumption-led development may be the best means to simultaneously make good the world-wide shortage of demand *and* generate development. The realisation of this grand ambition awaits future experimentation and further study. In the meantime, the outline of China's experience presented in this book is intended to contribute to the continuing debates on increasing demand, generating development and the evolving relationship between domestic demand and development in the twenty-first century.

Part I
Narrating demand
A consumer revolution

2 Increasing demand

Spending and shopping

One of the most visible features distinguishing the early years of reform in the 1980s from the previous 30 years of revolution was the rise in incomes and shift in emphasis from production, work and worker-comrade to consumption, lifestyle and the consumer. Indeed it became common over the next thirty years of reform to talk of China's 'consumer revolution' to denote the new policies and practices encouraging consumption, the shift in supply to embrace food and non-food items, the change in spending habits and the increasing importance of demand – real or anticipated – in determining supply. Many date this consumer revolution some time around the early 1990s and, although this study will also argue that these years marked a watershed in terms of consumption behaviour, it also suggests that it was from the early 1980s that the rapid arrival of goods, the increase in demand, the sway of fashion and the new retail sites all encouraged shoppers to purchase new possessions, pursue new lifestyles and adopt new identities and thus become consumers both in attitude and practice. It can be argued that all these earlier city and suburban changes did themselves amount to a consumer revolution with all the qualities customarily attributed to that concept. Historians have argued that the profundity of the consumer revolution in Western Europe and America has only been recognised recently for it was often ignored or at least under-emphasised compared with the attention given to the industrial revolution. According to one such analyst, Colin Campbell, consumer revolution constituted a process comprising: new categories of goods, new times, places and patterns of purchase, new marketing techniques, new ideas about possessions and materialism, changes in reference groups and lifestyles, diffusion patterns, product symbolism, patterns of decision-making and the creation of demand. Campbell goes on to argue that the sum of these phenomena long passed unnoticed largely because of their gradual seeping nature over four centuries which contrasted with the speed of the industrial revolution.[1] In China in the 1980s and continuing into the 1990s, it can be argued that the onset of the consumer revolution was so fast and so highly visible that it could not escape unnoticed and indeed it might be hypothesised that here the industrial and consumer revolutions were so collapsed into little more than one decade that it is a moot point which came first.

In the first few years of Reform, city observers spoke of a 'consumer rush', 'a headlong rush into consumerism', 'a consumer fever', 'consumer madness' – the scale and scope of which, in terms of numbers, could be seen to give new meaning to the term 'mass consumption'. Indeed the flow of new goods, consumer choice, higher material standards of living, new lifestyles, new retail outlets and the development of new arenas for consumption, modes of communication and the onset of consumer desire were some of the most conspicuous of urban and suburban changes in the first decade of reform. This new interest in everyday purchases, alongside new worlds of goods and new physical, social and mental landscapes, rapidly spiralled into what can be described as the first phase of China's consumer revolution. Although most scholars refer to these phases as consumption upgrades or waves of consumption, they are significant. In China itself, it is common to talk of three separate consumer revolutions each with distinctive characteristics: the first in the 1980s, the second up to the mid- to late-1990s and the third bridging the century and continuing today.[2] Certainly each phase is marked by income and retail trends, categories of available or desirable goods and demand cycles. At the outset, consumption was designated a central role in the new blueprint for economic reform with economic growth centred on market supply and demand rather than state-led planned production and distribution.

In the early years of reform, Deng Xiaoping repeatedly referred to consumption as the 'motor of production' and his oft-reported mantra 'to get rich is glorious' not only sanctioned riches but the exchange of goods or services and the development of a retail culture. Indeed it was on the basis of rising expectations and living standards that the new leadership based its bid for legitimacy and for popular support in the pursuit of reform and 'socialist modernisation'. The pace and scale of the ensuing popular demand for new goods and services took all, including the government, by surprise. It was not long before consumption came to symbolise a novel and immediate freedom after years of controlled scarcity so that the defining features and categorisations of the revolution – of work, occupation, blue-trousered comrades and class origins or class labels – soon gave way to new lifestyle practices, perceptions and self-perceptions substantiated by consumption goods and services. It was almost too fast for a government still ambivalent about consumerism which it simultaneously encouraged and equated with hedonistic or bourgeois habits. Thus the first decade of reform was characterised both by policies to increase consumption and movements to contain the new trends. The first attempt to control consumption in 1983–4 was an 'anti-spiritual pollution' campaign in support of the 'habits of simplicity' and again in 1986–7 another campaign similarly supported an 'anti-bourgeois' movement. Neither succeeded in the face of popular clamour by both rural and urban populations to spend and acquire the new goods.

In any event by the end of the decade, the government itself was to turn to consumption in a new bid to retain legitimacy after the events of Tiananmen Square in 1989. The new policies encouraging spending and new forms of recreation confirmed one of my early contentions that the government deployed consumption either as an instrument of government or for compensatory popularity to soften the effects of unpopular policies such as that implementing the one-child family or of unpopular events such as that of Tiananmen. In the 1980s, it was apparent in my own fieldwork that one of the reasons the single-child family policy was introduced and implemented in the cities with less opposition than might have been expected was due to the simultaneous and spiralling opportunities for consumption. Subsequently it was observable that the government strategically and instantaneously encouraged consumption to deflect attention from the body politic after Tiananmen when a sudden flurry of retail and recreational opportunities and facilities were directed towards distracting the attention of the young. I can remember the exact occasion in summer 1990 just a year after the events of the previous June and in a dance-hall not far from the university quarter of Beijing, when I first noted the contrasting extremes between the dissent and dissidence of the previous year and the apparent hedonism of many of the student fraternity and their peers who now and in their fashionable attire were enjoying new pleasures and appropriating new goods. What a contrast this trend in Beijing posed with the disapproval and dissidence so evident outside the country. Similarly the anthropologist Yunxiang Yan has suggested that, of all the factors that contributed to post-1989 stability, it was consumption which received too little scholarly attention. He too observed the myriad of ways in which wage rises, business and the distribution of retail goods and money were deployed to alleviate discontent and ease social tensions.[3] Officially, much of the previous ambivalence towards consumer behaviour disappeared in 1992 when Deng Xiaoping toured southern China and appealed to the nation to embark on a period of faster economic development and expand the marketplace. In October 1992, shortly after this milestone-event, the Fourteenth Party Congress avowed that the party and government would build a Chinese-style market economy by the end of the century[4] thus ending fears of official ambivalence and popular constraint based on the threat of a second cultural revolution. In the 1990s, spending, entry into business and the rise of incomes provided a powerful impetus both for the production and the consumption of new goods and services.

In many ways, it is the shift in preferred and desired categories of goods which have demarcated and come to symbolise each phase of the consumer revolution. At the centre of the first, beginning in the early 1980s, lay the introduction and profusion of new consumer goods, the novel and exaggerated arrival of which, after years of absence or minimal presence assumed a status akin to that of the cargo cults of the South Pacific. The spread of and all-pervasive interest in goods, style, colour, material, and above all, brand, together generated 'a new world of goods'[5] increasingly evident in city and village, on the coast and in central provinces and in public and domestic spaces. In conditions in which all consumption was newly conspicuous, some goods were more conspicuous than others. Indeed one measure of change commonly used in China to signal shifts in consumer fashion are the identification of the 'san da jian' or 'three big items' most commonly desired and purchased. During the socialist revolution in the 1960s and 1970s, the three most popular items could be said to have comprised bicycles, sewing machines and wristwatches, the purchase of which might require coupons or could take many months or years of individual or pooled-household savings. In the 1980s, bicycles remained an important item supplemented with new foods and clothing, but the new 'three big items' were colour television sets, refrigerators and washing machines. In a second phase in the early 1990s, these were supplemented by three sets of electronic goods including telephones or mobile phones, air conditioners and video recorders (VCRs) and, increasingly, hi-fi units and microwaves. For the third phase in the consumer revolution around the turn of the century, it was a computer, a car and private housing alongside home furnishings, travel and recreation which attracted the attention of consumers. Because the third phase is quite different in characteristic and content from the first two, this chapter discusses in tandem the incremental levels and sequential patterns of spending characteristic of the first two phases of the consumer revolution between 1980 and the mid-1990s.

The first phase

Urban and rural household patterns and levels of spending began to change in the early 1980s as per capita incomes rose together with new opportunities for consumption. Then the first and most conspicuous of consumers were the farmers and their families and in particular those in the rural suburbs on the edge of the main cities and in coastal southern and eastern provinces who cultivated vegetables or produced other farm products for sale in local and city markets. By the mid-1980s, rural per capita incomes had tripled from Y133.6 in 1978 to Y397.6 in 1985 while per capita consumption almost doubled from Y138 to Y347 over the same period. Although in 1985 their incomes and consumption still amounted to only half of the average per capita income of Y685.3, farmers did produce most of their own food and thus had fewer cash expenses.[6] Indeed in the early 1980s, one of the first visible signs of the success of rural reforms and in particular of the household responsibility system whereby peasants leased and farmed lands allocated to them for their sole use, was the number of farmer shoppers who came to the city or town to purchase the first generation of new consumer goods. I can still remember such farmer shoppers who, distinguished by their rough dress and ruddy demeanour, walked the pavements of the main city shopping streets with high piles of shoe boxes strung together in sufficient numbers to fit the feet of extended family members or village neighbours. Farm households earning higher incomes purchased agricultural inputs such as tractors, fertiliser, light trucks and farm machinery as well as light goods. It was widely observed in the southern and coastal regions that the purchase of farm inputs from fertiliser to agricultural machinery increased after 1978 and that everybody was in the market for basic consumer goods from new clothes to washing powder. More visibly, farmers showed off their new prosperity by extending or rebuilding their houses. Rural per capita incomes and consumption continued to rise and almost doubled between 1985 and 1992 to reach Y784 and Y718 respectively but the rate of growth then slowed so that, between 1992 and 1995, per capita rural incomes rose by only 14 per cent.[7]

In contrast the per capita incomes and consumption of city residents which too had almost doubled between 1978 and 1985 continued to rise substantially over the next ten years with a surge in growth between 1992 and 1995 when urban per capita incomes rose from Y1,826 to Y3,830 making this the highest three-year growth period since 1978. Between 1990 and 1995, urban per capita consumption rose by 51 per cent with a 21 per cent rise in the same three-year surge between 1992 and 1995.[8] In addition, disposable income was higher in China at this time than in many other societies for only a small proportion or around 10 per cent of income had to be set aside to pay the rent and the costs of utilities such as electricity and gas. This was one of the reasons that Nobel Prize economist Larry Summers proposed that, for China, purchasing power was a more accurate indicator of likely consumption than income levels which were low by any comparable standard.[9] There was not just an increase in per capita consumption, albeit widely-ranging across much of rural and urban China, but also new patterns of spending emerged, the most important of which was the shift from food to non-food items.

Food consumption

One of the first and most conspicuous of changes in the early 1980s was the welcome array of new foods for everyday consumption. The reforms in the countryside which assigned production responsibility to households rather than to the production team, brigade and commune of revolutionary years generated new amounts and ranges of food for urban shops, rural markets and domestic consumption. New open-air markets, stores and supermarkets in the cities began to display plentiful stocks of vegetables, meats, fish and eggs in amounts and varieties not seen for decades. In the cities, there were significant changes in diet as the proportion of non-staple to staple foods increased, fine grains replaced the coarser varieties and to these were added larger quantities of meat, poultry, fish and eggs, fruit and vegetables. In the cities, the consumption of pork increased by 55 per cent between 1985 and 1991 alongside comparable rises in the consumption of vegetables and eggs.[10] Richer coastal and suburban villagers increasingly followed urban patterns in food consumption although, more generally in rural areas, there was not the same increase in the consumption of fine grains or non-staple foods. Although the proportion of eggs and poultry produced for self-consumption increased, meat, fish and fruit remained luxury items for the majority. In the cities, it was the expansion of the free market, relaxed price controls and proliferation of retail outlets from street-corner to market-street and supermarket that enhanced the amounts and range of high-quality foods available. In the cities too, and to a lesser extent in central, southern and eastern provinces, there was an increase in the consumption of packaged, processed and convenience foods such as biscuits, noodles and snack products, some of which were imported from Hong Kong or other parts of Asia. The supermarket became a common if not expensive outlet for food in the main cities and, with their wide range of fresh and packaged products, they began to replicate their counterparts elsewhere. The new supermarkets displaying a wider variety of modern foods and goods from canned fruits and instant noodles to cold tablets and laundry detergents also exposed the customer to a range of new stimuli, acquainting consumers with and encouraging them to purchase new goods. Eating at food stalls or in restaurants had a long tradition in China and, even during the revolution, eating in the work-unit cafeteria was an important part of the weekday routine in urban factories and families. Once private-enterprise stalls selling prepared food proliferated in the streets and markets, then both kiosks and restaurants began to mushroom and enjoy the daily patronage of city dwellers and rural visitors.

A novel and particularly visible change occurred in the largest cities when international companies such as McDonalds and Kentucky Fried Chicken (KFC) introduced Western fast foods. In 1987 the first KFC restaurant in China opened in Beijing, and heralded as the world's largest fast-food restaurant seating 500 customers, it subsequently set numerous records as it attracted thousands of customers per day.[11] By the mid-1990s, KFC, sometimes known as 'old-man chicken' in line with the ubiquitous portrait of its founding Colonel, had opened six more restaurants in high-value tourist and shopping areas in Beijing and in 21 other cities, to become a major source of profit for the international KFC company.[12] In the early 1990s, KFC had been joined by McDonalds which, opening in Shenzhen near the Hong Kong border in 1990, soon and with much fanfare opened a large restaurant in Beijing with 700 seats and 29 cash registers.[13] By the mid-1990s, there were 35 sets of 'golden arches' in Beijing alone, a further 200 restaurants in 17 other cities and at least one new franchise opened each week.[14] The food, decor, promotions and employee-welcome all took the familiar format recognisable the world over and this, together with a few adjustments to local taste, made McDonalds a very popular venue for eating and socialising in the largest of China's cities. Indeed McDonalds became increasingly popular among children, young persons, parents and grandparents who munched on their Macs and stirred their shakes at lunchtimes and weekends. In the early years, for some of my elderly Beijing friends, 'eating something interesting' became synonymous with eating McDonalds' hamburgers and Kentucky chicken.

Although the proud boast of McDonalds and announced on their billboards in Beijing, was 'to serve a billion customers', this was and still is something of an exaggeration, however new fast food habits and chains have certainly accelerated the growth of a number of similar venues opened by European, American, Asian and Chinese vendors. Dining in fast-food restaurants became a new form of recreation and an early landmark in the evolution of such venues was the Hard Rock Cafe in Beijing. This new temple of rock in Beijing, its stained glass windows etched with an overarching 'Hail Solid Rock and Roll' featured Elvis in the middle, a crown poised high above his head with 'the king' inscribed above and 'Love me Tender' below. The signature on the menu read 'Love All Serve All' and, shrine-like, the cafe displayed 314 rock and roll relics with a vault-like central dome painted in the style of the Sistine Chapel so that Beatles and Rolling Stones looked benignly down upon the customers surrounded by brass rails, dark-stained wood and an electric organ. Opened in 1993, it was sign-posted outside by tall scrolled pillars reaching upwards to an eye-catching red Cadillac suspended far above street-level.

This truly conspicuous temple of rock or of the 'modern other' was popular among the affluent city young, often dressed in modern Western attire. It was also symbolic of the surprising role which new forms of eating and leisure played in attracting he custom of increasing proportions of city individuals and families.

There was an important shift in the allocation of family budgets from food to non-food items. According to the National Bureau of Statistics, the proportion of urban household income allocated to food dropped from 58.6 to 49.9 per cent between 1982 and 1995.[15] In 1978 it was estimated that rural households spent 67 per cent of their total living expenditure on food and by 1990 this amount had fallen to 58.7 per cent, a figure which changed little over the next five years.[16] Another study showed further small decreases for both rural and urban households between 1993 and 1997. For urban households, the proportion of expenditure on food declined from around 50 to 46 per cent and for rural households it dropped from 58 to 55 per cent.[17] What all available studies have shown is that the proportion of income spent on food has declined as incomes rose with the average hovering between 50 and 55 per cent. In 1995 one study of urban households showed that the per capita total living expenditure allocated to food was around 60 per cent for the lowest income group earning an annual income of around Y2,000 compared with 40 per cent for those earning around Y6,000.[18] A year later, another study of urban households showed a similar divergence with the poorest urban households spending around 18 per cent more of their total expenditure on food than the richest urban households.[19] Although corresponding data on rural household groups is not available, similar trends were discernible although the picture was somewhat complicated by the fact that farms produced and consumed much of their own food. What trends over time and the study of middle- and higher-income groups in both rural and urban locations do show is that the decline in proportions spent on food overall permitted greater spending on clothes, durables, recreation and new forms of communication.

The sway of fashion

In the initial years of reform, the change from blue garb to a variety of dress colour and style was one of the most visible of changes first observable in city streets and later in suburban and the rural villages of coastal and central China. On one of my first field trips to Guangdong province in 1977, I used to wonder at the juxtaposition of young smartly-dressed men and women from Hong Kong linking arms with their blue-garbed kin; soon the differences were less discernible. The sway of fashion or the perpetual quest for each new wave of apparel was encouraged by a new interest in the novel or the different which, long suppressed during the revolution now seemed unleashed and unlimited. Some of the first crazes to follow in quick succession on city streets that I observed were for jeans, flared or bell-bottomed trousers, platform-heeled shoes and trench raincoats for the men and jeans, Western-style dresses of every description from tightly-tailored through to the frilly or diaphanous and maxi- or mini-skirts and even short pants for women. Such was the talk around this new and fast-growing interest in smart and fashionable clothes among men and women both young and old and the associated status of dress with the modern and the different, that I myself felt compelled to discard the jeans and unobtrusive blue garb I had long used for my own field work. All the surveys of household consumption between 1982 and 1995 suggest that the percentage of total expenditure spent on clothes was around 13 to 14 per cent for all but the poorest in the cities and the countryside for whom it was more likely to hover around 7 to 10 per cent.[20]

Although there was little change in levels of expenditure over time, the constant shifts in fashion were often so fast that, in the early years of reform, neither the fashion conscious nor production lines could keep pace. Foreign observers competed to be the first to discover the fast-changing shifts in fashion be it the length and cut of a skirt, the style of hat, the donning of gloves, sun glasses, hair dyes and cosmetics which were all seen to sweep the city shops, the market stalls and the streets. The advent of each new wave of fashion, product or style required constant updating or replacement as the penchant for change and experiment seemed endless. It is likely that younger women spent greater amounts on clothes, although male interest in clothes especially in the early years of reform was much in evidence. At the luxury end of the market, new fashion magazines and posters advertised expensive leather attire, suits, dresses and shirts, many of which were imported or replicated and manufactured in China. Leading foreign fashion houses and designers set up shop in Beijing and Shanghai and included Pierre Cardin, Elizabeth Arden, Louis Vuitton, Christian Dior and Gucci and less-exclusive companies such as Giordano, Benetton and Gap which all set new trends – at least in the largest cities. Once aesthetic considerations competed with utility and function, there was an emerging interest in or even preoccupation with fashion among the young and the old in pursuit of style with taste and preference expressed as desirable attributes in the pursuit of individuality. For many, it was white and brown durables for the home which also captured the imagination and aspirations.

Desirable durables

A third category of purchases to become newly popular and widely acquired across the cities, suburbs and coast comprised a broad range of new consumer durables which in the first instance were mainly domestic and labour-saving or for entertainment in the home. During the socialist revolution, there had been virtually no durables or appliances available for purchase apart from the 'three big items', a bicycle, sewing machine and wristwatch, each of which was proudly owned and displayed. Ownership of any other such goods was rare, highly privileged and largely confined to the private quarters of the top leadership echelons. With reform, the first set of 'new big three things' to appear in the shops and attract the attention of consumers were black and white and later colour televisions, refrigerators and washing machines, followed by electric fans and cassette players. I can still remember the first washing machines and refrigerators which were the source of much pride as they were prominently displayed in the only living room and the object of much curiosity among visitors. In the mid-1980s, it was the first televisions and tape recorders which were admired and played by my fellow field-workers and friends who on one occasion all but climbed inside a refrigerator so keen were they to view and admire it from every conceivable angle. However it also has to be said that, in these early years, householders sometimes told me that they were somewhat wary of showing off their acquisitions to their neighbours so unsure were they that government policy might not change and they would become the object of political criticism rather than admiration. However this was only a transitional phase for soon such goods became symbols of status, wealth and modernity, differentiating the colour of reform and the foreign from the drabness of an introverted revolution.

In a study of children's perceptions of their families in the 1980s and 1990s, I asked children in city and suburban kindergartens and schools to draw 'their families'. Many not only included life-size televisions and fashionably bright-green refrigerators prominently placed alongside family members but also, life-like, these goods were given their own faces and legs, suggesting that, perhaps in the absence of siblings, significant things vied with significant persons in defining the single-child's sense of self or family. Again I can still remember the first television set sitting-in-waiting for an electrical supply on a family altar and another powered by yards of batteries intricately tied together and stretching across a whole tabletop. The curiosity, pleasure and satisfaction in newly-won items were measured by the number of 'legs' owned by a household in that objects were commonly given numbers of legs so that one's household possessions or wedding dowries could be so reckoned or tabulated. It became common to talk of a '30-legged household' or a '20-legged dowry'. On Chinese television, goods such as washing machines featured in numerous advertisements and, life-like, were sometimes given tongues or even telephones to talk to one other and present their distinguishing features to potential customers. What surprised observers and analysts in the first years of reform was the speedy expansion of demand and the all-pervasive interest in goods in both the city and much of the countryside – perhaps not surprising after years of scarcity.

Some of the earliest figures on consumer expenditure suggested that as the proportion of income spent on food decreased so that on durables increased. By 1986 urban surveys in two provinces, Liaoning and Sichuan, suggested that as constraints on the supply of consumer goods and spending were relaxed, 12 to 13 per cent of household annual income was allocated to the purchase of durables each year.[21] One nation-wide survey conducted in 1985 in China's cities showed that the average ownership per 100 urban households for refrigerators was 6.58, 67 for black and white televisions, 17 for colour televisions, 41 for cassette recorders, 9 for cameras, 74 for electric fans and 48 for washing machines.[22] In rural areas refrigerators and colour televisions were owned by less than one out of every 100 households, black and white televisions were owned by 11, cassette recorders by 4, electric fans by 10 while washing machines were owned by 2 out of every 100 households.[23] As might be expected such items were most common in China's 10 largest cities and in Shenzhen where by 1986, 65 out of every 100 households owned a washing machine, 18 out of every 100 owned a refrigerator and 29 out of 100 owned a colour television set.[24] At first ownership of these goods was highest in Beijing and Shenzhen where more than 80 per cent owned a colour television, 70 per cent a washing machine and 60 per cent a refrigerator.[25] By 1990, more than 80 out of 100 households in all but one of China's largest cities and Shenzhen owned a washing machine while more than 70 per cent of households surveyed in all but three cities owned a refrigerator and colour television.[26] In addition to these labour-saving and recreational goods, households purchased electric fans, cooking appliances and cassette recorders. However by 1990, these popular durables had been supplemented by a wide range of new goods, the availability of which spurred a sharp rise in spending in the first half of the 1990s which could be said to amount to a second phase in the consumer revolution.

The second phase

The second phase in China's consumer revolution centred on electronic goods with air conditioners, hi-fi sets, video recorders, video cameras, fixed and mobile telephones, fax machines, microwave ovens, CD players and personal computers appearing on city shopping lists. Although this is a wide-ranging list, it was telephones, air conditioners and VCRs which constituted the 'three big ticket items' in the early 1990s, although these were soon supplemented by a second set of items comprising pagers, cell phones and computers. The purchase and ownership of these items spread rapidly in the largest cities so that it was the shift in interest to electronic goods that characterised the early 1990s. Teresa Poole, the socially astute correspondent for the *Independent* in the mid-1990s, visited Supreme Hi-Fi Garden one of the largest electronics stores which had opened in Beijing early in 1995. Previously it had been the site of a primary school, but with few pupils, the local education bureau had 'changed it into a shop to make money'. Built around a courtyard where school-children used to play, the showrooms offered state-of-the-art hi-fi and video, professional karaoke units, car stereos and computers, many of which were imported and some so up-to-date that they were still scarce in Europe. At the time of her visit in December 1995, Video Compact Discs (VCD) players were the preferred purchase. According to the manager of the ground floor, they were 'selling 100 to 200 VCDs per month at between Y3,000 and Y8,000 (£240–£640)'. According to a lively sales assistant, another popular line was the audio-visual tower-amplifier with five channels of sound producing 'the atmosphere of a movie theatre'.[27] By 1995 in all but two of China's ten largest cities plus Shenzhen, colour televisions were owned by 95 of every 100 households, more than 90 owned washing machines and more than 80 out of 100 had a refrigerator.[28]

In Shanghai, a random-sample survey in the same year found that the majority of households owned a colour television (94%), a stereo (68%), a camera (58%) or a video (54%) with fewer owning an air conditioner (26%), a stereo set (15%), a personal computer (4.3%) and a video camera (2.3%).[29] A year later, in 1996, even higher numbers of urban households owned such goods with 91 out of every 100 owning electric cooking appliances, 70 owning refrigerators, 32 cameras, 73 cassette recorders, 93 colour televisions, 20 game machines, 12 hi-fi systems, 20 video recorders and 90 washing machines. In rural locations, ownership of these goods was less wide-ranging with 65 of every 100 households owning black and white television sets, 65 owning sewing machines, 31 cassette recorders, 23 colour televisions, 20 washing machines and 7 refrigerators.[30] A study of the ownership of household consumer durables in Shanghai between 1981 and 1996 by Lu Hanlong also shows the change in ownership patterns of consumer durables characterising the first two phases of the consumer revolution. Lu documents the shifts in types of consumer durables purchased. Almost all had acquired bicycles, sewing machines and watches in the 1970s and 1980s while upwards of 70 out of 100 acquired colour televisions, refrigerators and washing machines and to a lesser extent video-recorders in the mid- to late-1980s with ownership of stereo sets, air conditioners and microwaves reaching between 14 and 40 out of 100 households by the mid-1990s. The survey also signalled the onset of the new trend-setting consumer items of the mid-1990s with personal computers owned by a mere 3.4 out of 100 households in 1996.[31] All these studies suggested that a variety of durables had become widely and increasingly available in city shops.

Shopping

Not only was there a profusion of new goods, but also they could be viewed and purchased in new spaces entirely given over to the display and retail of goods. In short, in large and small cities the world of retailing was transformed. During the socialist revolution, general trading and department stores were few and specialised shops rare. Even the main shopping street in Beijing, Wangfujing, boasted little more than a large book shop, a several-storeyed department store, a covered market and a tourist arts and handicraft store. The one department store, in which I too shopped in these early days, was dark with bare concrete walls and had heavy brown plastic padded blinds flapping at the door. Below and behind dusty glass counters was a narrow range of tired or faded goods, mostly small and made up of limited ranges of utility shoes, clothes, stationery, toys, plastic and other hardware daily necessities including the ubiquitous thermos flasks and old-fashioned alarm clocks. Alongside was displayed the odd luxury item such as a watch, sewing machine or bicycle. Cramped and crowded, blue-clad shoppers hustled around the counters waiting to make the small purchases from rather bored assistants. Recently a *Times* correspondent reminisced about his early visits to the No. 1 department store in Shanghai describing it 'as a monument to state-sponsored lethargy' with 'seven storeys of mind-blowing inertia', 'yawning staff' and the stashed look of a 'salvage clearance sale' with 'prize goods hidden away in glass cases that no one had the key for.' He was contrasting this scene with the rapid and radical changes in staff and customer behaviour wrought by the introduction of new retail sites which included an array of shopping malls, re-furbished department stores, small boutiques and speciality shops awash with colourful products and selling all the major luxury and utility items for persons and homes.[32] To long-time observers of China's cities, one of the most noticeable features of reform has been the introduction of the large plate-glass shopping malls purveying all manner of items and services.

Many of the newly-built or refurbished department stores and malls in China's largest cities were joint-ventures and modelled on their counterparts in North America and Europe or in other parts of Asia where there were already signs of a 'shopping-mall craze'. Beijing's Wangfujing was one of the first of the country's main shopping streets to be opened up to joint-venture retailers and by the mid-1990s, Shanghai too attracted a good number of foreign retailers. From Japan came Yaohan, Sogo and Isohan and from Europe and America, B&Q, Carrefour, Metro and Wal-Mart. Yaohan, a Japanese firm which had established a joint-venture store in Beijing in 1992, set out to build Asia's largest department store in Shanghai. Comprising more than 100,000 square metres of retail space, it was said to be only exceeded in size by Macy's in New York. Printemps, a French retail firm, opened a large department store and a designer-shopping centre in Shanghai which aimed to reproduce the chic ambience of the Champs Elysées in Paris. Many of the older department stores, both Chinese and foreign-owned, were refurbished with new and up-market product displays to encourage greater consumer interest. For instance the long-established Youyi Shopping Centre at the Beijing Lufthansa Centre, which was an early Sino-foreign joint-venture, was remodelled to create open and spacious floors given over to fashion, clothes, home furnishings, cosmetics and jewellery alongside an array of consumer services.

Many of the new malls and large refurbished department stores were designed to encourage customers to wander at leisure through new 'worlds of goods', seduced and lulled by such comfortable and cool new-style shopping environments. They offered new and modern spaces not only to observe and purchase the latest goods and gadgets but also to experience allied forms of entertainment and recreation. Frequently malls incorporated coffee bars or restaurants, ice-cream bars and open meeting or play spaces all designed to entertain or prolong customer stay. Many promoted their goods by celebrating new and exotic Western festivals alongside Chinese traditions. For example at Christmas, urban shops were inundated with coloured lights, trees and cards, the most flamboyant of which reached new decorative and musical heights while, at Easter, live rabbits jostled with chickens to inhabit large chocolate hutches or Easter eggs. In addition to creating a variety of shopping, leisure and entertainment venues offering an unrivalled array of fashion, culinary and recreational facilities, retailers competed to improve the quality of service for customers to help them choose and acquire new goods. Up-market departmental stores taught their young staff to be welcoming and to subscribe to a startling new maxim 'guke shi shangdi' which translated means 'the consumer is god'. One observer concluded that this new approach was working as the new retail sites with a 'pleasant shopping environment and better services really did enable shoppers to feel like gods'.[33] Many reports from the 1980s suggested that urban and suburban residents took full advantage of and delighted in the new range of retail sites and consumer goods so that shopping itself became not just an act of purchase or possession but also a popular and common form of recreation 'opening up dreams to which shoppers could aspire'. New worlds of goods encouraged new practices, the chief of which was the transformation of shopping from a small corner or utilitarian feature of domestic life into one of the most compelling of leisure occupations. Indeed in post-reform urban China, shopping for consumer goods was not only an immediate source of material gratification but the very visits to the new shops and malls became the most popular of pastimes whether or not a purchase was made.

As a form of recreation on evenings and days off, 'shopping' or visits to up-market department stores with their displays of colourful goods, lifestyle tableaux and dream-worlds offered a favourite and all-inclusive pastime even if only to look, to aspire and to be seen. Outings to the malls or department stores contributed to a new 'feel good' factor of the early reform years by permitting China's urban residents to embrace and be seen to embrace the colourful, the modern and the global. Indeed it was clear in the early years of reform that shopping malls or large department stores gave visitors a chance to browse, compare and learn about new and modern lifestyles even if, for most, these were the museums of the future rather than of the past or present. Many had to be content with the curiosity and dreams of window shopping as they consumed vicariously. As one young woman said:

> I like to go window shopping and always go to several stores – luxury department stores or small shops that sell particular products … I prefer to go alone to enjoy the pleasure of leisurely strolling around the store.[34]

Like many other such strollers, they did sometimes make a purchase.

> I buy wholly on impulse. I believe my first instinct and follow this judgement in value and style as a mode of purchasing … I'm proud that all my relatives and friends think that I am a shrewd buyer and the things I buy are in good taste.[35]

In contrast, others researched their choices extensively before making a purchase. In the late 1980s, my usual Beijing hotel was located close to a new shopping mall and I can remember how I was a popular call-in for friends who often took the opportunity to also visit the mall to ponder and plan for future purchases. Shopping alone or in groups was both a serious and light-hearted affair with much spirited discussion among accompanying family members or peers as to functional detail, aesthetics or monetary value. Indeed the strategic resolve and research involved in individual, familial or peer group purchases soon gave consumers in China a reputation as 'informed and sophisticated'[36] or 'canny and discriminatory'.[37] In the Chinese language, a new term was coined, which literally means 'shopping-study' to reflect the serious dimension which could also slide into a form of retail therapy cheering to the self and image.

> I seldom go shopping with a particular need to buy something and purchasing something depends on my mood. If I am melancholy or distressed, I tend

to go shopping. Walking slowly before a beautiful collection of goods, I gradually calm down. Therefore, for me, shopping is often good medicine to treat emotional calamities.[38]

Surveys of shopping habits and marketing images of the time suggested that young single women who lived at home and frequently spent at least half and often all of their monthly income on clothes, accessories, cosmetics and hair styling were the most avid of shoppers.[39] Coopers and Lybrand, which regularly conducted small focus groups sessions with consumers in Shanghai in the mid-1990s, distinguished several categories of shoppers: men aged 30 to 45 years who were 'utility shoppers' in that they bought whatever they needed or their wives and children asked them to buy; women aged 30 to 45 years who appreciated 'value and convenience'; and consumers up to 30 years of age who are 'highly aspirational and interested in ownership and leisure'.[40] The latter was also the age-group for whom shopping was primarily an enabling exercise, encouraging them to keep up with the latest fashion or newest style to appear on the market. Perhaps this new and acceptable opportunity to exercise individual choice and agency contributed to an early preoccupation with the novel and the fast changes in taste and preference which was characteristic of the times. Such was the fondness for perpetual novelty that product lines had to be constantly updated or replaced as the pace of change increased. To both keep pace with and encourage change, advertisements featuring the new must-have fashion brand and fast-evolving lifestyle appeared on billboards and the commercial magazine and media industry flourished as never before.

Advertising and branding

Another of the most visible changes observable in the street, on buildings, in publications and on television from the mid-1980s was the arrival of advertising. During the revolution, any promotion on billboards was limited to political slogans, perhaps a Mao Zedong thought or government propaganda for family planning, productivity and political education. It was only during the reform years that advertisement hoardings replaced political slogans and posters. At first, advertisements for goods were largely static though informative with stilted language conveying any utilitarian or technical advantages of the product and stating in great detail the source and address of the supplier. However in subsequent years the advertising industry burgeoned so that by the end of the first decade of reform it was estimated that the industry had grown from just 10 people in 1979 to 11,100 agencies with a total of 128,000 employees in 1989.[41] Many of those involved in the design and production of advertising were employed either by state-run media agencies or private domestic agencies, international firms and joint-venture advertising offices. As a result of their labours, consumers were newly bombarded with advertisements for goods and logos alongside colourful contexts and beautiful girls so that soon, above the streets and providing a new focus for millions of cyclist-eyes, were large and colourful hoardings featuring watches, computers, furniture, toiletries, cars and other goods. Many large companies hired the roof spaces of main-highway buildings to advertise their wares, often to the benefit of cash-starved government offices which benefited from the constant sale and resale of such spaces. Colleagues at China's Academy of Social Sciences, which had a building on the main Changnan avenue stretching East from Tiananmen Square, used to joke that they never knew if their building's roof would sport advertisements for sneakers or disposable diapers, such was the turnover in leases profiting this Cinderella government unit. As television rapidly became the most widespread form of popular entertainment, it constituted the most important vehicle for product advertisements. As well as the national China Central Television (CCTV) station, provinces and the largest cities soon had their own commercial channels via which advertisements reached most urban households and a good portion of the rural population. Not only was advertising space surrounding the most popular programmes sought after and the subject of competitive bidding, but television stations also introduced feature programmes on fashion, make-up and home-furnishing to introduce or guide readers in the use of new products.

New popular and glossy magazines, produced for both everyday and a more sophisticated readership also played an important role with advertising pages and feature articles publicising design, cosmetics and fashion products, their use and efficacy. For instance, via both Western- and Chinese-sponsored publications such as *Elle, Cosmopolitan* and other fashion names, a young female readership in China became familiar with the names of Estee Lauder and Christian Dior. Magazines and television programmes produced guides or tips on how to be stylish, up-to-date and above all fashionable. National and local newspapers joined the club as they played an increasing role in advertising products while in department stores and malls there were frequently first-hand demonstrations and promotions to attract customers for new wares. A few companies, such as Avon and Mary Kay cosmetics, had some success in introducing new health and beauty lines by using direct or private-party opportunities for personal demonstrations within the homes of potential customers. As the internet came on stream, a segment of potential consumers spent as much time in front of their monitor as in front of their television screens. The response of advertising agencies was swift and trend-setters such as Ogilvy and Mather began to conduct as much business via internet advertising as they did through conventional media. Over the decade 1985 to 1995, marketing techniques became increasingly sophisticated and studies in the mid-1990s showed that urban populations studied and were influenced by advertising messages prior to the purchase of a 'da jian' or big ticket item. In a Gallup survey of 1994, 60 per cent of city consumers said that they studied advertisements in order to make knowledgeable decisions about different brands prior to purchasing goods such as a refrigerator, air conditioner or rice cooker.[42] Indeed brand had become an increasingly important concept in urban and southern China as many international and domestic companies rushed to associate their products with a new or well-known Western or Chinese name in a bid to build both brand awareness and loyalty.

In the first few years of reform, new products were often associated with and known by their Western labels. Levis were associated with jeans, Rolex with watches, Coca-Cola with carbonated drinks, McDonalds with fast food, Mary Kay and Revlon with cosmetics, de Beer with diamonds, and Vuitton with bags, while Armani, Dior, Gucci, Gap and Benetton became synonymous with fashioned clothing. Large multinational firms either retained their Western trade names or employed local companies to translate their brand names into appropriate Chinese equivalents. Specialist consultants with the by-line, 'Want to sell to 1.2 million customers?', set themselves up to translate Western brand names and advise how such names, promotions and packaging would sound and be understood in all the major Chinese dialects. For new labels a range of auspicious or lucky colours and numbers or literal sounds with fortuitous meanings were deployed. For example Terry's Orange became Gu Zhen or 'fruit leisure' and Gillette used the Chinese name Jili which means 'lucky'. Some foreign-language brands became well known despite the expense of their items; others belonged to the popular and everyday including Coca-Cola for drinks, Proctor and Gamble for soap, shampoo and detergents, Levis for jeans and Kodak for films.

Companies placed much emphasis on promoting brands in China largely because brand-recognition and sales in Hong Kong, Japan, Singapore and Taiwan had already made Asia the fastest-growing market for most of the top international brands. Those in the luxury good and fashion business such as Gucci and Armani reckoned that roughly a third of their sales were in Asia and that Asian customers continued to display high levels of brand loyalty.[43] In the face of predictions that Asia, in the very near future, would make up half of the world's luxury branded-goods market, most retailers had come to think that they could work brands harder in Asia than elsewhere. China was expected to follow suit. Certainly brand curiosity there quickly became brand fascination with high levels of recognition. Such was the adherence that brand labels were often overtly displayed or even transferred to the outside of garments and gadgets where they could be easily seen and admired. In the very early days of reform, overseas-Chinese relatives complained that their folks back home did not just want a pen, a watch or a suit but a Parker pen, a Rolex watch or a Dior/Armani article of clothing and many said they avoided a visit rather than bring a nondescript or the 'wrong' gift. In 1994, a survey conducted by Gallup showed that 41 per cent of urban and 30 per cent of all respondents stated that they would buy a leading brand regardless of price and that recognition of foreign brands was highest in the largest cities with Coca-Cola and Pepsi-Cola leading with 94 per cent and 85 per cent recognition in selected cities and 62 and 42 per cent for the rural sample.[44] However in a survey of urban quality of life conducted in Shanghai in 1995 most goods owned by the sample of 1,042 households were in fact made in China. The major exceptions in which a goodly percentage were foreign brands included colour televisions (48%), refrigerators (22%), cameras (25%), stereos (17%), watches (28%) and videos (44%). For other items including air conditioners, washing machines and stereo-sets, less than 10 per cent were imported and for black and white televisions, electric fans, bicycles, pianos and video cameras less than 3.5 per cent were imported.[45]

A survey of shopping habits of 1,000 families in eight districts in Beijing conducted by a market research company in 1996 suggested that shoppers looked for new styles (37.5%) and high-quality goods (33.4%) despite high prices, although about 50 per cent also expressed an interest in brands. One reason for the popularity of international brand names were that they were thought to signify quality and reliability generating trust between consumer and company.[46] The association with quality and a guarantee was no mean attribute in a society where there were common complaints that so many goods produced locally were of poor quality and there was little in the way of product guarantee or consumer protection. However by the mid-1990s, a number of Chinese brand names such as Qingdao (beer), Forever (bicycles) and Legend (computers) had taken their place alongside international brands and offered similar guarantees of quality but at a price that was significantly lower than their international counterparts. Foreign brands were also counterfeited with near-replica versions and labels widely available at standards that were 'good enough' in quality and again at much lower prices. Counterfeited replicas found ready sales among city shoppers who could never have afforded the original and, indeed, it is as likely as not that the handbags featuring on this book's cover are counterfeited brands. It could be said that, in some respects, the popularity of the counterfeit reflected and confirmed the status of the original brand in signifying the association of name with quality, luxury and lifestyle. Indeed it has become a world-wide marketing truism that brand names are not only about product, choice and quality but also about the appropriation of new identities and lifestyles.

Selling identities

Anthropologists have long recognised that the acquisition of goods is significant in acquiring new individual and collective identities and that shopping is an opportunity for definition and redefinition of the self, signifying new affiliations. Rising incomes and the availability and accumulation of goods rapidly encouraged the expression of individuality and the adoption of new lifestyles or life-affirming identities that combined privilege, the modern and the Western or global. Certainly the acquisition of new possessions became a source of immediate status so that those who first purchased the novel and more expensive brands became the trend-setters as these goods or brands became fashionable and assumed a new status. Conspicuous consumption, and most consumption was still conspicuous, suggested higher income and spending power so that many individuals and households proudly showed off their new attire, jewellery, wide-screen televisions, hi-fi and karaoke systems to a foreign field-worker. Such items became de rigeur as new reference groups set the pace and became trend-setters for lifestyles to which others might aspire. In the 1980s the most desirable lifestyle attributes were those that were perceived to be both modern and western. Indeed it was via goods that young individuals, the female gender and whole families or communities attempted to discard the uniformity and drabness of the revolution and 'catch up' with the modern and Western or global. Take for example, the adoption of the ubiquitous blue jeans which for many became a highly symbolic act signifying difference and defiance. As one young student explained to his teacher:

Jeans are the symbol of the new fashion, and are still novel for some in China. But it's more than that. The older garment, the … Mao suit was well-balanced, right-thinking and stable, someone who conforms. But jeans would make you feel independent, just like cowboys from America – wearing them would make you feel like a real individual. Its an utterly different feeling from the sense of dependence we used to have … all in those Mao suits … real conformists. So you see what jeans can mean to us.[47]

Others emphasised the daring shaping and contouring of the body outline that the jeans afforded.

Similarly the appropriation of fashion, jewellery and cosmetics was another very visible use of goods to re-craft an identity, this time gendered. The new emphasis on the feminine or women 'who know how to be women' was in stark contrast to the revolutionary years when the image of Iron Girls, the language of comrades and the unisex blue garb inscribed androgyny and the loss of a female-specific identity. In interviews conducted during the reform years, women acknowledged that their 'coming out into society' was an important legacy of the revolution, but that it had come at the cost of losing 'something of their female selves' or 'the difference between themselves and men'.[48] The widespread use of fashions and accessories to 'become women' constituted an explicit and conscious rejection of the past, just as the assumption of new feminine identities incorporated changing notions of beauty influenced by global images. As a spokesperson for Mary Kay Cosmetics noted, the lifestyles of women, especially in Shanghai, have changed dramatically as they 'actively want to make themselves look more beautiful'.[49]

For male or female and young or old, the acquisition of new identities and images not only signified difference from or rejection of a revolutionary past and the appropriation of the modern and progressive but also made exciting new claims to be cosmopolitan, global or Western. In this respect one of the most important points about the rapid profusion of new things or goods in the early years of reform was their association with 'the outside', 'the global' or the cosmopolitan' and particularly 'the West' – a generic term inclusive of North America and Europe. In other words what was new was perceived as an import whether or not it had been produced or reproduced within China. The profusion of goods and lifestyles originating in the West not only brought with them new images and new reference groups that were 'of the West' but during the initial years of reform, it was via its goods that the 'West' first came to be known or imagined. Of course the presence of persons and things Western in China was not a new phenomenon given the previous century of contact prior to 1949 but that presence, significant though it had been, was very much limited or bounded by treaty port and mediated by missionary and merchant. Without fast media communication and a mass market, contact had been largely conducted via persons rather than goods and not much beyond the largest cities and communication routes. Now it was television screens and shop counters which constituted the main points of encounter and reduced the distance between China and the Western other. In post-reform China, there was a sequence of representations of the West which variously influenced individual and collective quests to acquire new and modern identities. First, and almost overnight, the previously negative image of the West as capitalist and exploitative was transformed into an image of a desired destination fostered by the new reform government's bid to modernise and 'catch up with the West'. Interviews with young persons during the first 10 years of Reform show there had been a shattering 'loss of confidence', 'loss of faith', or 'despair beyond words' as 'the door swung open' and they became aware of a West different to that previously portrayed. As one young man said 'when we became open and turned to the world outside, we found we had got the wrong image of ourselves and of the world. We felt cheated'.[50] The immediate ideological disillusionment and depression that followed had the appearance of a visible gap into which images and things 'Western' might conveniently step with a seduction enhanced by new notions of and acquaintance with 'the West'.

It was interesting to observe the early ways in which everyday knowledge of the West was first constituted via a collage of foreign objects featured on billboards or in advertisements or via foreign lifestyles featured in imported Western magazines, television series or soap operas. In the late 1980s I can remember the silence of the Beijing streets during the first showing of the 'Starsky and Hutch' series and thereafter the influence of its images, style and, it was reported, the adoption of blue sirens that subsequently had to be banned. Initially 'the West' as the new desired destination, was imagined as a seductive repository of all good things so that part of the attraction of international brands was their association with and assumed popularity in the West. In a teacher's interviews and conversations with young students, 'the West' was represented as 'a land of plenty, of profusion, of the good things, of the good life, high earnings, where there are no taxes, no poor, a freedom to do anything, earn anything, spend everything and own anything.'[51] With a millenarian or utopian flavour, this image of the West served as a foil illustrating all that China was not. This criticism of China's revolutionary past reached its apogee in what became known as the Heshang phenomenon which referred to the debates surrounding a six-part television series shown twice in 1988. The very title of the series, 'Heshang', gives a clue to the content. 'He' refers to the Yellow River, cradle of Chinese civilisation, and 'shang' means dying before coming of age. The television programme juxtaposed the shadowed Yellow River culture of China and the bright ocean culture of the West, negated the achievements of Chinese culture and catalogued a history of previously lost opportunities to learn from a superior West.[52] Making up for lost opportunities, the rapid appropriation of Western items continued apace not only in the pursuit of new and modern lifestyles but also fostered by the ubiquitous practice of gift-giving or exchanges.

Gifts and guanxi

In the first years of reform, new goods were not just enjoyed for their novelty and acquired to signal status and prestige but their exchange was also used to establish and maintain social networks in the interests of enhancing social relations and facilitating access to resources, services and favours with kin, friend or official. Horizontal ties of friendship and kinship and vertical patron–client relations with government cadres were collectively referred to as 'guanxi' and, based on personal connexion and reciprocity of favour, were pervasive throughout all forms of political and social life in revolutionary China. In post-reform years, the importance of inter-personal networks or 'guanxi' connections soon spiralled and became essential to all aspects of social, political and commercial life. Economically, the advent of the new market economy demanded new forms of entrepreneurial individual and institutional responsibility for procuring raw materials, credit, expertise and markets and widened the need for such networks. In the absence or under-development of formal mechanisms to facilitate individual and institutional linkages or business and organisational transactions, many sociological studies showed that access to any resources, services or job and protection from predation became dependent upon negotiated personalised connexions and networked mutual obligations now cemented by the passage of goods.[53] Previously, during the thirty years of revolution, guanxi relations had largely been limited to relations with the bureaucracy for political favours but now 'guanxi' extended to include all other socio-economic relations in an expanding edifice of elongated patron–client relations paved and eased by simultaneous and deferred gift-giving obligations.

Even the simplest service could be dependent not just on 'who you know', but 'who you know knows who'. Eventually the mobile phone with its by-line 'connecting people' or a 'one-to-one connexion' proved tailor-made for negotiating guanxi relations, the number and type of which have become the most valuable of operational assets and important sources of status and security. Indeed these networks became such an important part of everyday life for all but the poorest or 'bare sticks' of society that they have generated their own vocabulary. For example 'guanxixue', translated as the art or study of personal connexions, is not the specialised study of social scientists but the everyday study of everyday relations by the population at large who soon required their own resources for such a purpose. Now listed alongside other expenses in all households and public units of government from one end of the country to another, is a new budget item for guanxi gift-giving. The passage of goods as gifts became such a conspicuous adjunct facilitating inter-personal relations that it has been argued that there were three economies in China: the State redistributive, the commodity and the gift economies with the latter relying on the passage of goods as well as money to procure favours, deals and ordinary everyday public services. If sociological studies showed that gift and monetary relations had acquired an unprecedented importance in everyday life, they also revealed that they had become a central feature of all transactions in the new market and political economy. They also became the basis for widespread bribery and corruption. The boundaries between gift and bribe might be blurred in the Chinese context but certainly the passage of gifts facilitated connections and transactions in both the city and countryside, reflected the greater interest in goods and the spread of a new consumer culture which more than any other feature distinguished the first decades of post-reform China. Indeed it seemed in the decade between 1985 and 1995 that new everyday purchases and consumer policies were spreading beyond the cities to the countryside and were here to stay.

The spread of consumption

How extensive were the first two phases of the consumer revolution across the length and breadth of China? By the mid-1990s, the demand for major durables such as colour televisions, washing machines and refrigerators had expanded rapidly over the previous 10 years. In 1997, it was reported that around 25 per cent or 45 million of the 220 million or so households were 'taking part in the economic boom'.[54] According to the National Bureau of Statistics, retail sales grew by an extraordinary 22 per cent per year in the decade 1985 to 1995 as those with surplus income developed a taste for shopping and spending.[55] However, shopping and spending were constrained by income levels which in the early decades of reform very much coincided with location and was limited to the cities, suburbs and richer rural regions. Wu Yanrui, in his excellent study of consumption, concluded that the most important factor influencing the demand for durables, as elsewhere, was discretionary income or that over and above the expenses of basic needs such as food and shelter. His research suggested that there was a high income elasticity of demand for consumer durables in that a rise in household income would produce a more than proportionate rise in expenditure on household durable goods[56] and that, as consumer income increased between 1985 and 1996, ownership of the major household durables also grew with much of the increase taking place in the early 1990s.[57] The effect of income on demand was also shown in regional variations in household ownership of consumer durables. The largest disparity was that between rural and urban households and ten-year data from the State Statistical Bureau suggested that rural households were at least ten years behind their urban counterparts in terms of possession of consumer durables such as refrigerators, washing machines and colour televisions. In 1996 urban households owned an average of 93.5 colour televisions, 90 washing machines and 70 refrigerators per 100 households, in contrast to rural households which owned an average of 23 colour televisions, 20.5 washing machines and 7 refrigerators per 100 households.[58]

It is not surprising to note that by the mid-1990s it was the metropolitan cities of Beijing, Shanghai, Guangzhou and Tianjin which led the way in both income-growth and the consumption of new goods. They constituted the new trend-setters along with the export-processing zones such as Shenzhen in close proximity to Hong Kong which attracted much foreign and particularly overseas Chinese investment. Subsequently other coastal cities caught up and residents of the richer eastern and southern provinces began to enjoy higher per capita incomes and greater opportunities to acquire new consumer goods and a 'modern' lifestyle. By 1996 colour television sets were the most popular consumer items with a mean for all urban households ranging between 80 and more than 100 and a national average mean of 93.5 per 100 households. The national urban average mean for washing machines was also a high 90.6 with the mean per 100 households ranging between 78 in urban Jiangxi to 101.4 in Beijing. With the exception of Beijing, Shanghai, Tianjin and the coastal cities, there was a lower rate of ownership of refrigerators although the average mean per 100 urban households was still a high 69.6.[59] These high rates suggested to Wu that urban demand for these goods was 'already satiated' by the mid-1990s.[60] It was a different story in the rural areas of China where the rates of ownership were considerably lower and it was only the suburban households in the vicinity of the largest cities which had rates of ownership ranging between 50 and 70 per 100 households of the same three durables which was much higher than those for the less-developed northern, western and central regions. For colour televisions, the national average mean per 100 households in 1996 was 23, which ranged from the suburbs of Beijing (76), Tianjin (60), Shanghai (53), Liaoning (44) and Guangdong (39) to between 10 and 20 in rural Anhui, Jiangxi, Henan and Hubei and to less than 10 in rural Hunan, Guangxi, Guizhou and Sichuan. Similarly for both washing machines and refrigerators the national mean was 20.5 and 7.27 per 100 households with the highest rates of ownership in the suburbs of the largest cities leaving the rest of the countryside with a mean of around 15 washing machines and less than 5 refrigerators per 100 households.[61] These figures suggested to Wu that, outside of the suburbs, only a minority of rural households were familiar with the consumer durables already considered essential items in urban households. He concluded that in the cities with few new buyers and only replacement purchases, future urban demand was dependent on the introduction of new products and good-quality items and that it was the rural market which presented the most opportunities for new sales of household goods. These findings were confirmed by other studies which showed that, in cities further inland and in the northwest, retail sales lagged behind so that their residents had experienced less dramatic gains in their standards of living.[62]

Thus during the first two phases, the country's emerging class of newly rich of small but growing numbers began to splash out on high price-tag and imported first-generation items such as colour televisions, washing machines, telephones, hi-fi systems, video recorders, cameras and then mobile telephones, pagers and home computers. Although such conspicuous consumption was confined to the high-earning and spending trend-setters, the appropriation of new goods had become of wider interest and a mass activity although the items purchased might be fewer, cheaper and home-produced or even counterfeit rather than expensive and imported. For an increasing number of China's urban population, for whom the costs of rent and utilities were low, disposable incomes and purchasing power had increased and many were eager to sample new goods to signal that they too belonged to new affluent groups and to 'modern' times. Consumption had become a new and relatively inclusive urban experience as ownership of small goods and as widespread aspirations for new lifestyles opened up broader opportunity structures beyond those associated with political position and prestige. The most conspicuous changes in city landscapes and mindscapes might be confined to urban, suburban and coastal regions, but even if elsewhere all that could be afforded were the smaller and cheaper goods, there were widespread hopes of emulating the new reference groups and dreams of catching up with richer persons and locations. By the early to mid-1990s, there may be fewer goods available or purchased in the countryside but my own field experience did suggest that even small county and township settlements had developed or changed compared with 10 or 15 years earlier. Travelling widely by car in China in the 1980s, I used to miss such cross-road centres on passing through if I blinked or was slow to register their presence. In contrast by the mid-1990s, many had burgeoned into large and small bustling towns or cities adorned with markets and shops selling wide varieties of small goods. By this time too, migrant populations totalling tens of millions of persons had moved goods as they travelled between city and countryside so that in all but the poorest and more remote villages of the north and west, clothes had brightened, food was more plentiful and markets revived. Here new goods were saved for and treasured – especially the coveted television set, which now permitted around 80 per cent of the population to consume vicariously. A popular film of the times, 'Ermou' featured a young woman village entrepreneur who sold noodles and her blood to save for a television set larger than that of her neighbours. Finally the splendid object is acquired and moved to the village home where its size is such that it has to displace the family from their bed and, still with its price tag visible, is watched by the whole family and admiring village neighbours. As I have already noted, in the most remote of villages without electricity, the odd television set can sit in waiting or be powered by yards of batteries intricately tied together and stretching across whole tabletops.

In the mid-1990s, China had witnessed two major phases amounting to its own consumer revolution and many of the characteristics associated with any consumer revolution were spreading to the remote corners of China. Hopes were high within and outside China that the present consumer boom would continue and lead to further waves of consumption. Indeed the promise and potential of China's domestic market seemed limitless and it was widely forecast that consumer goods would continue to sell well in China where plans were afoot to expand the retail sector and refurbish department stores, build new shopping malls and establish giant chain stores. In 1996, *The Economist*, in a 'Business in Asia' survey, forecast that consumer-goods companies operating in China had a chance to repeat what they had accomplished in America at the turn of the last century. If they established national brands by out-marketing local producers and demonstrated that their products had clear advantages then surely it could be forecast with some confidence that the China market had a 'lot more room for growth'. Indeed it forecast that by 2006, more of China's consumers would be familiar with international brands.

> The better-off Chinese consumer will get up, wash her hair with Proctor and Gamble shampoo, brush her teeth with Colgate toothpaste and apply a little Revlon lipstick. As her Toyota grinds to a halt in yet another traffic jam, she will light up a Marlboro, glance at a copy of the Chinese edition of *Elle* magazine on the passenger seat and try to find her Motorola phone to call

her secretary. At work she will put down her can of Pepsi by her Compaq computer and load Windows 06.[63]

It seemed to many as if the new culture of consumption was here to stay. Perhaps nobody could have foreseen that the boom of the mid-1990s would be followed by the closing of shopping malls one after another and that the average propensity to consume or ratio of consumption spending to household income would decline with more saving than spending.

3 Weakening demand

Saving and segmenting

By the late 1990s, it was clear that the earlier explosion in and profusion of goods had not heralded a prolonged or sustained consumer boom so much as another cycle in which an increase in demand was followed by exaggerated expectations and excess supply. Domestic demand for existing consumer durables and electronic goods fell short of supply. Meanwhile two of the 'super three new big things' demarcating the onset of the third phase in China's consumer revolution, were so new and 'big' that only a small minority could acquire or even aspire to their ownership. If shopping can be taken as one barometer of domestic demand, then, from the mid-1990s, all the signs suggested that the average propensity to consume was diminishing as fewer customers frequented the malls and the department stores. There was more interest in window shopping than purchasing, more interest in bargains than brands and fewer customers for most foreign-branded goods. The fast-expanding retail sector was thrown into disarray as shopping malls closed, some very soon after their grand openings. Above all the growing interest in spending was inhibited by further economic reforms which threatened urban jobs in the state sector, by declining income-growth, uncertain pensions and by rising costs of services and utilities. These all dealt a substantial blow to up-market spending and made it more common to save rather than shop despite the government's best efforts to encourage consumption. For many intellectuals in the cities, the material habits of the West no longer constituted such a desirable model especially if, as it seemed, the rush to emulate foreign lifestyles, ambience and architecture was causing China to lose a sense of its own cultural identity borne of a long history and tradition. Foreign manufacturers hoping to sell China-made products in the domestic market were forced to turn to the export market to sell their goods. As for the outside view of China's market: either demand had weakened or perhaps it had never been as deep or as wide as it had promised. Certainly, around the turn of the century, there was greater recognition that the still-opaque China market had once again proved difficult to penetrate and that, after 15 years of reform, it had become increasingly differentiated, requiring new levels of market research to identify the new and multifarious segments. In the meantime, the first sign of a downturn in the average propensity to consume in the mid-1990s was a levelling off in retail sales in most goods, pushing the acquisition of two of the 'super three new big things' and thus the onset of the third phase in China's consumer revolution further into the future.

The third phase

In the late 1990s, sales of the 'super three big things' (chaoji san da jian), comprising houses, cars and computers were expected to herald a third phase in China's consumer revolution. Analysts in China, who based their expectations on previous experience in Japan and South Korea which had suggested that the onset of this third consumption upgrade would require around 7 to 10 years of capital accumulation, forecast that China would follow suit in the late 1990s or to be exact 1997.[1] Despite these optimistic forecasts, the sales of all three items started slowly and were largely limited to the rich and super-rich. The government, hoping that the escalation of a housing market would spur domestic demand, set about in 1991 to both privatise existing housing stock and build and expand the number of new houses and apartments for the private market. Home ownership was a new concept and, as elsewhere, the purchase of a new house constituted the highest-cost and longest-term purchase a household was ever likely to make. It was estimated that, by the mid-1990s, a third of all urban households had some form of ownership rights, although most had purchased the housing already allocated by the state or work-unit at highly subsidised prices.[2] Only a very few had bought the newly-built apartments or suburban villas built and sold by commercial developers in the largest cities. In 1995, 7 years after work-units began selling houses to their occupants, it was estimated that 29 per cent of city residents lived in apartments they had purchased from their work-units and another 11 per cent owned housing they had either bought themselves or had inherited.[3] This left some 60 per cent still renting from work-units, municipal governments or private landlords. By the end of 1998, the government had hoped to build some 300 million square metres of new urban housing and facilitate purchase by permitting mortgage loans of up to 70 per cent of the value of a new home over a 20-year period. However the cost of new houses in relation to income remained exorbitant, with a newly-built small two-roomed flat on the outskirts of Beijing reported to be on sale in 1995 for 1.2 million renminbi (£100,000).[4] Much of the newly-built housing remained unsold and at the end of 1997, *Newsweek* noted that 'rows of cavernous villas stood empty'.[5] The housing reforms certainly stimulated an interest in 'a home of one's own' but, in these early years, demand for newly-constructed housing remained slow as households saved to make a deposit, borrow and refurbish and furnish their own homes.

Cars too remained beyond the reach of most households given that even a Chinese-manufactured 1.8-litre basic sedan sold for eight times the average family income. A survey undertaken in 1995 by the Diamond Marketing Group found that a mere 1.7 per cent of Beijing's homes had a private vehicle although China's most ambitious urban consumers were saving for a private automobile.[6] By the mid-1990s, private car sales amounted to a mere 10 per cent of all car sales which in total were still small in number with the remainder sold to government departments and to other state or public organisations, although even here demand was weakening as reforms dented institutional and individual budgets.[7] Many of the rich already had the use of an official car and, even for the super-rich, the high prices, the large size of cars and the fees, taxes and costs of fuel in relation to income and savings, remained a deterrent limiting private car sales. In 1996, car sales were reported to have slumped across China with 'fields outside many cities being used as car parks for unsold vehicles'.[8] In 1997, passenger car production was reckoned to reach just 482,105 units with sales of 474,950 although only a small percentage were private purchases.[9] In 1998, despite increasing production of passenger cars and availability of finance, the disincentives for ownership were deemed to be considerable in that in addition to US$12,000 for the minimum purchase price of the car, a further US$4,000 or so was required for registration, insurance, fuel, maintenance, parking and assorted taxes.[10] An analyst for Western Securities in Shanghai wondered why people would purchase a car given that the prices were so high and that taxis were plentiful.[11]

In the late 1990s, the small proportions of car sales that were private was a subject of some concern. The President of Fiat International and the company's chief representative in Beijing reckoned that less than 1 per cent of China's population could afford to buy a car.[12] The Vice-President of Shanghai GM estimated that, at best, there was less than 5 per cent and, at worst, virtually no private buyers, although it is also true that some estimates did reckon that private buyers made up 15 per cent of the total.[13] Despite such small percentages, the potential for private car sales and especially for small passenger cars was still deemed to be 'huge' but dependent on lower prices, rising incomes, easier credit and lower government taxes. Optimists took their cue from per capita GDP in the main three cities which was fast reaching the range of US$4,500 to US$5,000 or levels at which car sales typically start to take off. As one optimist noted:

> As you see increases in these cities you see more of the true bona fide private buyer emerge – the guy who drives to work each morning.[14]

The chief executive of Ford Motor (China) calculated that with only one vehicle for every 100 people in China compared with 75 for every 100 in the USA and 12 to 15 per 100 in Brazil and Thailand, the potential was still obvious and that 'the challenge is reaching the potential with a business equation that is viable'.[15] On the basis of such optimism, car production in China increased year by year despite the slow-down in 'demand' which was deemed 'quite significant'. In 1999, *China Daily* observed that China's car market could be characterised by 'weak demand and zero growth'.[16]

The cost of the third 'super' consumer item, a personal computer, was more affordable for a larger number of households but, even here, the number of private purchases remained small for some time. In 1996, 3.4 per 100 households owned a computer in Shanghai,[17] and in 1997 personal computers were reported to have penetrated only 0.6 per cent of China's market.[18] Again, although owning a computer was more a matter of aspiration than possession, in China's main cities in the mid-1990s the potential for future sales was still deemed to be considerable. The Ministry of Electronic Industry forecast a 40 per cent growth in the home computer market in the late-1990s.[19] Local manufacturers and in particular Legend, the publicly-traded China computer maker which had the largest share of the domestic PC market, positioned themselves in readiness for rising domestic demand. Legend's Vice President for sales estimated that home-PC sales would rise from 30 to 40 per cent of Legend's total sales in 1999.[20] It is true that more and more urban families aspired to own a computer for their children's education, email and for financial information or the international news, but most analysts thought that the short- and medium-term potential lay with the corporate and small- or medium-sized private sector. Sales were projected to rise but, as an electronics analyst at Deutsch Morgan Grenfell cautioned, there were no signs of an immediate take-off:

> You will see most of the growth coming from corporate rather than retail sales over the next few years. GDP per capita still needs to reach a certain level before you'll see a big take-off in retail sales.[21]

It was not only retail sales of the 'three super big things' that were slow, for retail sales in general also slowed down in the latter half of the 1990s. Indeed the growth in retail sales was reported to have fallen from an average of 25 per cent per year between 1985 and 1995 to less than 11 per cent in 1998 and around 7 per cent in 1999.[22] This was largely because of a slow-down in sales of items which, previously popular, had already been purchased by most city households that could afford to do so. One reason given for the slow-down was that consumers in major cities had already purchased the essential 'big ticket items' of the 1980s such as refrigerators, washing machines and television sets and were not inclined to upgrade these items. A mid-1990s survey of 1600 households in Beijing by the Diamond Information Industry Market research agency found high rates of ownership for colour televisions (98.5%), refrigerators (96.7%) and washing machines (93.2%).[23] Once these items had been purchased, Beijing households turned to smaller household and electronic appliances characteristic of the second phase in China's consumer revolution. However even for these smaller items the China Base 98 Survey, conducted by Grey Advertising in Hong Kong via door-to-door interviews in Beijing, Shanghai, Guangzhou and Chengdu in early 1998, found that very few households had made such purchases in the previous two years.[24] Although household electrical appliances had started to enter some rural households in the suburbs of large cities and in coastal regions, many farmers were still struggling to get sufficient food on to the table the whole year round. One report showed that rural incomes were spent on food (47%), clothes (14%), daily necessities (19%), housing (17%) and cooking materials (3%).[25] In these circumstances there was little left over for the purchase of durables so that supply began to exceed demand. Each year in the late 1990s, China was reported to be awash with cheap goods, with several commentators writing about the over-supply of white goods in the face of over-production and sluggish demand. Even in

1996 it had been reported that consumers were not buying all that factories were producing and that stocks of unwanted goods were piling up.[26] In the late 1990s, it was reported that supply had outstripped demand since the early 1990s and that the market for refrigerators, washing machines and VCD players had reached saturation point. Excess Chinese capacity in video recorders was reported to be 74 per cent, while demand for air conditioners amounted to just 50 per cent of the units produced.[27] Over-supply was part of a general and continuing tendency to over-estimate potential demand in that, for almost all items, there were a plethora of manufacturers who had little experience in matching supply to demand and continued to churn out goods that 'nobody wants', leading to stockpiles that 'jumped to record levels'.[28] However over-supply was also due to sluggish demand in that the households which had the means and the will to purchase such items had already made such purchases and there were few successors with either the means or confidence to follow in their footsteps.

Ready means or access to disposable income and savings were important for there were few sources of credit to compensate for making purchases whether large or small. Although credit cards had been introduced into China in the mid-1980s, their use was limited. In 1985 the Zhuhai branch of the Bank of China issued the first credit card in China and shortly afterwards other branches and banks including the People's Construction Bank, the Industrial and Commercial Bank and Agricultural Bank of China had issued a total of about 800,000 cards, mostly in the large cities and coastal regions.[29] In 1992, the practice had been reported to be spreading in the more economically-developed coastal regions and cities but, in the early years, a predominant proportion of all transactions were between businesses for big-ticket items such as tractors and train-loads of raw materials for which alternative means of purchase were complicated and slow.[30] Although stories circulated of farmers in Zhongshan city in Guangdong province using credit cards to obtain cash from automatic-teller machines, the numbers using credit cards remained small. Those authorised to use credit cards were limited in number and potential card holders were required to pay a deposit of several thousand yuan in order to obtain a card.[31] In practice, the cards were more debit than credit cards as all cardholders had to deposit funds into their card accounts prior to purchasing items. Such was their continuing rarity that individual credit card holders were often referred to as 'dakuan' or 'big-money earners'.[32] Indeed most card holders comprised self-employed workers, government employees with high incomes and entrepreneurs and managers who frequently travelled on business trips.[33] In 1999 it could be said that few ordinary citizens had a credit card, that the majority still paid cash for any consumer goods purchased and that there was a shortage of ready cash for such purchases.[34] Given the fact that the super-rich had purchased almost all the new 'big-ticket' items, that the rich were saving for such items and that the market for durables was all but saturated or slowing, it is not surprising to find a decline in retail sales. What was more surprising was that the speed and scale of the downturn was such that the fast-expanding retail sector of the early 1990s experienced some considerable down-sizing and some dramatic closures.

Malls and markets

Only by observing closely did there appear to be a linkage between the numbers of 'shoppers' to be seen in the malls and markets and the downward trends in retail sales. It was not that shopping did not continue to be a favourite activity with crowds much as before, but that it was more a form of recreation as much about observing and acquiring product and lifestyle information as about purchase and possession. The habit had been identified as early as 1993 from a number of reports. As one young woman noted at that time, 'I like to go window shopping and always go to several stores' but 'seldom go shopping with a particular need to buy something'.[35] However the frequency of such observations by foreign reporters increased in the late 1990s as they noted that, despite falling prices which should have been good news for consumers, those frequenting the shops 'continued to look but not always to buy' or were 'only window shopping'.[36] The 'shopping experience' of one very active 68-year-old Beijing woman was not atypical. On her day off from her job as head of a neighbourhood committee, she rose early to embark on her weekly venture into the shops:

> Every Sunday I go window shopping to get some information about the market … I don't buy anything; I just go for fun. I walk around floor by floor just to get information about the prices. When I get back I tell others, family and friends.[37]

Although she had been a shopper in her time and loved to indulge her new interest in clothes, she had not continued the habit.

> I am not particular about food, but I am particular about my clothes. I love rings, earrings and necklaces. But I already have all of these. So I don't need to buy anything.[38]

In 1997, *The Economist*, in an article entitled 'Window Shopping in Shanghai', reported that most of the visitors trooping through the bright new Yaohan shopping stores 'were only window shopping'. The article quotes Bernd Schmitt, an expert in consumer behaviour from Columbia Business School in New York and China's first professor of marketing, who observed that visitors to the swanky department stores 'look in order to learn, but often buy nothing'.[39] A year later in 1998, at the opening of a new shopping plaza with a five-floor emporium in Beijing, it was reported that few had come to purchase, although many came to window shop.[40] Further south, in the large city of Guangzhou, typical Sunday crowds in the main shopping streets were reported to 'be looking and not buying'.[41] Again, in another large department store in Beijing, when the *Independent* correspondent asked the assistants how business was going, they shook their heads and said 'too few customers'.[42] Even in the popular IKEA store to which crowds in Beijing and Shanghai thronged, few were reported to be making purchases.[43] In these circumstances many of the largest malls and department stores quickly ran into difficulties as their number proliferated and the luxury end of the market for expensive foreign and Chinese brands declined. According to official figures published for the first ten months of 1997, showing an overall fall of 11 per cent in retail spending, it was luxury sales that showed the steepest decline. For China's largest department stores, it was reported that sales fell by 46 per cent, profits collapsed by 59 per cent and that 15 per cent were showing substantial losses.[44] As China suffered a glut of new shopping centres, many of which were often empty, retailers turned to cut-throat discounts and knock-down bargains to entice customers. In the newly-opened Sea Sky department store in Beijing, the furniture section displayed a sign that read: 'Buy this furniture and you get a 25-inch colour TV thrown in'. At the Guiyou department store, a shopper could secure a VIP card for less than £10 which then gave a 15 per cent discount on all purchases.[45] Shortly after the opening of the largest and newest shopping mall in China, the Dongan Plaza, clothes shops were already observed to display a 50 per cent discount sign on the door. When incentives and bargain-offers failed, malls and stores either shut down or redefined their objectives.

Many shopping malls and department stores closed, with some shutting their doors very shortly after much-fanfared openings. In Beijing alone, 10 shopping centres built in anticipation of a continuing consumer boom were reported to have closed down between the middle of 1996 and the end of 1997.[46] One of the largest shopping malls in Beijing, the Venture New World Shopping Centre which had opened in 1996 both as a novel attraction as well as a shopping destination closed in 1999 after running a 2-year loss of Y31 million (US$3.7m).[47] A branch of the Hong Kong chain, Sincere, also closed within 2 years of opening.[48] When Shanghai Yaohan (Next Age store), the largest retail operation in China and the whole of Asia and second only to Macy's in New York, opened in 1996, several hundred people trampled its floors every weekend. However so few actually spent any money that, even as it opened, some observers wondered if the store would ever provide a return on its investments. Shortly afterwards, in 1997, faced with mounting debts, it was forced out of business.[49] Some struggled on despite disappointing sales. For example France's Printemps which had aimed to create the ambience of the Champs Elysées in Shanghai, sold out to a local company at a heavy loss in 2000 after 6 years of struggling to turn a profit.[50] These sobering experiences caused some large international retailers such as UK's Marks & Spencer to hesitate before entering China's market. Marks & Spencer had considered setting up shop in Shanghai but did not do so after recognising the limited spending power of China's consumers and remaining unconvinced that 'the losses were containable'.[51] Small specialist shops also suffered a decline in sales, causing some to close down. According to one retailer in Guangzhou, who had returned from America to make his fortune in boom times, business in his two optical shops had soured after the mid-1990s when both shops lost money as the Y1,080 Ray-Bans gathered dust.[52]

By the end of 1998, nearly half of Shanghai's 3 million square metres of retail space lay vacant and sales were slow in those malls that remained open. In the same year, a foreign correspondent visiting the mezzanine and second-floor shops in Shanghai's Hong Kong Plaza on up-market Huai Hai Road on a Friday at 11.30am observed them to be bereft of customers. In one, the most recent sale had been two days earlier and made up of two shirts. Fashion and clothing retail were said to have been 'hit pretty hard' by slow sales, while authorities were 'cracking down' on the illegal imports of foreign luxury goods. It was estimated that up to 80 per cent of luxury goods on display in Shanghai's up-market stores were smuggled goods which would have been too expensive if they were subject to normal taxes.[53] According to the China National Commercial Information Centre, consumer demand plummeted from 11 to 6.8 per cent in the first half of 1998 even though the State Statistical Bureau's retail price index slipped over roughly the same period from –0.4 to –2.1 per cent. It also reported that 57.7 per cent of the country's leading department stores suffered declining profits in the first half of 1998 with an even higher number showing negative growth.[54] Certainly the lot of the international brand marketeer became much more difficult after the mid-1990s when prevailing trends in consumer behaviour reflected a turn away from luxury high-price foreign-branded goods and towards greater price sensitivity and a keen eye for bargains.

Shoppers were proving to be inveterate bargain hunters and bargains were predominantly made up of goods produced locally, while counterfeited foreign brands also had price advantages. By the mid to late 1990s, Chinese-made versions of new durables had improved and even for counterfeits there was little difference in quality and style between the original and the copied versions. Indeed many foreign manufacturers had under-estimated domestic competition when assessing the Chinese market. For example when Whirlpool established its own factories in China in 1994 to make refrigerators, air-conditioners, washing machines and microwave ovens, it assumed that its main competitors would be other foreign firms. Instead its chief competitors turned out to be Chinese appliance-makers such as Haier and Guangdong's Kelon which both had technology that nearly matched their own, lower prices and a styling and distribution that reflected a greater knowledge of the local China environment. By 1997, having lost more than US$100 million, Whirlpool shut its refrigerator and air conditioner plant while their microwave factory survived mainly by turning to exports. Their washing-machine factory began to make appliances under contract to Kelon which sold them under its own Chinese brand name.[55] In 1995 almost all urban working families owned a washing machine, but only a small minority of wealthy individuals owned an imported Siemens model which was five times as expensive as the basic model produced by Jiangsu province's White Swan group.

In other industries too, foreign brands were losing out to cheaper Chinese brands. Motorola was losing market share to Eastcom, a distribution partner than now made and sold its own mobile phones at a lower retail price than the American equivalent. Ericsson, Lucant and other equipment makers also lost ground to domestic telecom firms such as Huawei whose manufactured goods were almost as good and much cheaper. American Compaq, which once dominated China's PC market lost out to Beijing's Legend brand which proceeded to expand and dominate the China market. While global brands for goods such as PCs could still outpace the locals in terms of billboard space in the cosmopolitan cities, domestic vendors tended to have networks that reached the smaller cities and towns. Likewise markets for video compact disc players and television sets overflowed with domestic products so that international brands for the most part were crowded out by local and cheaper equivalents. To add to their woes, many of the successful foreign-branded products were pirated, forcing some foreign companies to fight for shelf space with what appeared to be close copies of their own wares. Copying became so pervasive that market research usually reported sales far in excess of actual production! Certainly visitors like myself to the largest cities could not fail to notice the 'Prada' and 'Vuitton' bags piled high on market stalls and the near-replica white and brown durables on shop floors and shelves.

Many retailers redefined their venues and restocked to service the new bargain shopper. For example Beijing's up-market Venture New World Shopping Centre turned itself into a comprehensive wholesaler offering inexpensive, varied and abundant goods in order to pitch their business at the mass market.[56] Numbers of shopping centres became comprehensive wholesalers and most small commodity wholesalers performed well because their goods were abundant, varied and inexpensive, thus supplying the bargain buys that most shoppers preferred. One set of stores that could be seen to prosper were the cheaper-range chain and discount stores. New chain-store businesses with low price and high volume strategies grew rapidly and were widely welcomed by low- and middle-income families. China's chain-store businesses could be said to fall into seven broad categories: supermarkets, convenience stores, brand-name specialist shops, department stores, snack counters, service centres and building-material shops. In Beijing in 1994 there were 150 chain stores or companies with 2,500 outlets but, by the end of June 1997, the number had jumped to 1,000 stores with 14,000 outlets.[57] Two other retail forms also did well during this period. One very visible and popular retail outlet open to the smallest of traders was the ubiquitous market stall. As any traveller in urban China can testify, the expansion of market stalls selling clothing, shoes, hardware, toiletries and other small and cheap goods proliferated to the degree that it was difficult to see how the myriad of small and competing vendors made a living. In the early years of reform, I used to joke that any urban resident with a downstairs window looking on to the street had been tempted to turn it into a small shop, either for their own benefit or for the benefit of members of their extended family who often brought goods from the countryside. Small mobile wagons also permitted retailers to take goods and services into residential districts and even to people's doors. Reminiscent of age-old peddling, distributors went directly to customers, bringing with them daily necessities for immediate purchase. Eager to attract custom, department stores launched neighbourhood consumer exhibitions to introduce and demonstrate new products. According to a business report in 1998, one store sold as many as ten microwave ovens during one such promotional session, a new service which was responsible for adding Y80,000 (nearly US$10,000) to its turnover.[58] Another equally successful small-scale initiative was direct home-selling of goods at reduced prices. For example in Shanghai in 1996, the American firm Mary Kay set up an operation using agents to organise house parties with the aim of selling cosmetics directly to invited customers. Within 6 months it was reported to be selling more than all the department stores in town.[59] It was a similar story for pioneering Avon which also set up a successful direct-sales network of house parties in China's cities, at least until such ventures were banned in the wake of several pyramid-selling scandals.

There were a few exceptions in this period of slow-down, lower prices and excess supply of durables. Some foreign companies which produced and marketed small and cheaper goods were less affected than others by the decline in up-market retailing and stayed the course. Many small firms producing paint or fibres, special plastics or industrial bearings quietly continued to hum. The demand for mobile phones seemed unquenchable. In 1990, 20,000 phones were sold and by 1994, 1.57 million were sold, with mobile phone users numbering nearly 3 million.[60] In 1995 this number had increased to 3.4 million and 2 years later, in 1997, to 13.2 million, a figure which still added up to less than 1.1 per cent of the potential of China's domestic market.[61] In this same period, Ericsson, Nokia and Motorola each derived a tenth of their world-wide revenues from China[62] and the number of pagers soared into the millions, beating even the much flaunted high-status mobile phones into second place. Fast-food chains such as McDonalds and Kentucky Fried Chicken continued to be popular as they opened new outlets in China's major cities and spawned a number of domestic equivalents. Proctor and Gamble continued to corner a substantial portion of the domestic market in shampoos, soaps and detergents for washing clothes and Kodak too continued to do well. Indeed China, a nation where photographs are keenly treasured, had become Kodak's third largest market by 1998. Based on the usual calculations, Kodak still hoped that China would become the largest film market in the world:

> Each year the average Chinese household shoots a little less than half a roll of film. If only it could be persuaded to snap a full roll, that would be the equivalent of adding an entire American market to the world film business.[63]

In addition to continuing to eat out, play bowls and perform karaoke, China's rich began to sightsee, both within China and abroad. Most of the trips were short and within China, with the majority taking place at Spring Festival or National Day holidays although, for the first time, travel overseas was made easier for both business and pleasure. Passports and foreign visas, originally only issued to high-ranking officials and their well-connected kin or students studying abroad, gradually became more available although it has to be said that any travel abroad was still confined to high-income and other privileged groups. However these items and activities were but small drops of comfort within a declining retail sector which was marked by exaggerated expectations and excessive supply. That demand did not meet expectations was due not only to a slowing of income growth but also to a new frugality encouraged by rising public service and utility costs and a new insecurity.

A new frugality

In the late 1990s the slump in spending was attributed either to the higher costs of the newest goods or to the rising costs of services for health and education against a background of the growing spectre of unemployment, lower income-growth rates and fears for old-age insecurity. It was also mooted that, if households were saving for high-cost long-term purchases such as an apartment or an automobile, they were not buying the increasingly available array of smaller cheaper domestic or electronic goods. There was an element of irony in this observation for this was not what the government had intended when it began to rely on the private housing market to stimulate consumption and expand domestic demand. More importantly however, there was a substantial downturn in the growth of urban and rural incomes while new and further reforms generated job insecurity and raised the costs of housing, health care and education. Interestingly the same door-to-door interviews conducted by the ChinaBase 98 Survey in Beijing, Shanghai, Chengdu and Guangzhou showed that upwards of three-quarters of 800 respondents were concerned about higher health costs (83%) or the climbing costs of renting or buying a home (78%). More than half said that they experienced a 'real sense of uncertainty' about the future, mainly due to worries about job insecurity and unemployment as a result of the restructuring and down-sizing of state-owned enterprises and government departments. Again more than half (58%) said that they were saving more than they did a year ago.[64] In 1998 there was said to be a certain 'tightening of belts' as incomes rose less readily than before and, for some, the incomes themselves and the 'iron rice bowl' seemed a lot less secure than before, leading to 'new fears about spending'.[65] A year later another commentator also noted that 'consumers, fearing redundancy and the withdrawal of cradle to grave social services, are refusing to spend'.[66]

By the mid-decade the sharp rises in urban incomes evident in the early 1990s had levelled off and there was a reduction in expectation that such increases would continue in the future. As early as 1996, a year in which average urban per capita income increased by a mere 8 per cent to around Y3,800,[67] it was observed that 'people were not buying all that factories were producing because wages were not growing as fast as they had'.[68] In 1997, the Asian financial crisis had adverse repercussions for China's growth rate and consumer confidence. Furthermore urban incomes, once the bedrock of security, became less secure as Zhu Rongji's reforms of state-owned enterprises increased unemployment and threatened pensions. Many workers were laid off or reduced to part-time hours and, by 1997, the number of registered unemployed sharply increased to some 5.3 million with surplus urban labour estimated to be around twenty million. In the first half of 1998, a further three million lost their jobs at state enterprises when the government announced plans to slash the number of ministries from forty to twenty-four.[69] These trends caused one Beijing economist to forecast that there would be 18 million fully-unemployed in China's cities by the end of 1999.[70] As previously secure urban workers joined lengthy job queues or looked to make their own pensions arrangements, those in work feared reduction in hours or wages or being laid off. Even retirees, many of whom had previously enjoyed secure pensions and benefits from a lifetime in state employment, suffered reductions in the amounts paid or delays so that they might not be paid for months at a time. In the civil service too, unemployment became an explosive issue as the reforming Premier Zhu Rongji imposed cuts of up to four million government jobs.[71] Although urban jobs felt less secure than during revolutionary years and urban per capita incomes showed little sign of the same growth as in the earlier reform years, urban residents were still privileged compared with their rural counterparts.

In the countryside, the dramatic increase in rural incomes of the mid-1980s was followed by a period of stagnation or fall in real terms as returns from agriculture declined and the costs of agricultural inputs, infrastructure and other resources increased. This imbalance particularly affected the incomes of the 60 per cent or so of rural farmers who were almost entirely dependent on field agriculture, although incomes from combined on- and off-farm production were not high. Although much attention had been given to the country's richest farming enterprises, which earned tens or even hundreds of thousands of yuan each year, the average annual income of the 900 million rural residents in the mid-1990s was still around Y1,200 plus income in kind and at least 70 million villagers still earned an annual cash income of less than Y300.[72] If the gap between rural and urban incomes was wide, the gap between the rural rich and rural poor was even wider. Although China had effected a significant reduction in poverty, much of this took place in the early 1980s when agricultural production was first privatised and became the responsibility of individual peasant households. Despite high rates of economic growth nationally, 300 million or so of China's residents still lived below the World Bank poverty line of US$1 a day,[73] while many more hovered just above this line and struggled to make ends or had little in the way of surplus cash for other than living expenses.[74] It could be observed that large proportions of poor peasants had never seen or bought a Coke or a consumer durable. It seemed to poor and middle-income villagers that their incomes were dropping further and further behind those of urban workers and that there were fewer opportunities for employment in the countryside than in the cities. With shrinking amounts of farmland, increasing costs and rising surplus labour, tens of millions of rural migrants were leaving the countryside for the cities each year in the hope of finding work and making badly-needed cash contributions to family incomes in order to meet the rising costs of agricultural production, schooling and healthcare.

What concerned both urban and rural residents was not only the levelling off or decline in incomes but also the rising costs of housing, utilities and educational and health services. By the mid-1990s it had become apparent to all income groups that individual households would increasingly have to assume the full burden of these costs which hitherto had been subsidised by the state, urban work-units or, to a lesser extent, rural village administrations. Now the gradual withdrawal of public 'cradle-to-grave' services meant that the greater proportion of service costs had to be met from family incomes. By the mid-1990s too, housing reform had gained momentum as the reforms raised the average rent of public housing and as public housing units were sold to employees at preferential prices and new housing units were built for the private housing market. Whether urban housing was owned or rented, the costs were much higher in the mid-1990s than in previous decades. Gone were the days when nearly all urban residents paid a nominal rent for public housing amounting to less than 1 per cent of their wages. By 1996–7 it was reported that urban rents had risen eight-fold while those who had purchased their work-unit home or bought on the private market paid at least the equivalent or higher in mortgage payments.[75] In the countryside, long dominated by private housing stock, almost all households owned their own homes which were passed from generation to generation. What was distinctive about the first decade of reform was the explosion in rural house-building in suburban and coastal China as richer peasant households invested their gains in improving old and building new houses. This trend, which rapidly improved the standards of village housing, continued but at a slower pace as rural residents felt the pinch between declining incomes and rising costs of production inputs and services. Alongside the rising costs of both rented, purchased and owned housing, there were simultaneous rises in the prices of electricity, gas and other essential utilities. Although these rises all generated new anxieties about the cost of living, the most talked-about costs in both urban streets and rural villages were those to do with health and education.

The costs of health care had risen dramatically in both city and countryside, coinciding with the steady erosion of most previous benefit or insurance schemes. Before the reforms the health care expenses of urban residents were mostly covered by work or other units while low-level rural co-operative schemes subsidised health clinics run by the much-celebrated 'bare-foot doctors'. It has to be said that bare-foot doctors were more feted outside China than within, where their rudimentary knowledge and skills often had villagers preferring to trek to a commune clinic or hospital for all but the most common of ailments. During the first decades of reform, the health care of urban residents had continued to be covered by work-units, at least to some degree but, during the 1990s, reforms to relieve state-owned enterprises of their social burdens had reduced the level and coverage of such benefits. Similarly any rural co-operative schemes run by communes had dwindled or disappeared as farmers took household responsibility for production, procuring inputs and processing services. In China, health care had never been delivered without levying a charge but, with state-regulated fees and work-unit or commune help, the costs were manageable for all but the seriously and chronically ill. Although the government intended to institute new schemes facilitating health insurance for both urban and rural populations, these were not yet in place and in the meantime health care had been privatised with escalating patient costs. Those employed in small enterprises and the self-employed had to pay in full for any service while state-subsidised facilities run by local work-unit or village clinics and hospitals had declined or disappeared. Although there were higher standards of care at county level and in city hospitals, it was not always affordable without the accumulated savings or loans from immediate family, kin or friends. In all the hundreds of household interviews I conducted in China's city and countryside communities in the early 1990s, the poorest households and those most indebted were normally those where there had been chronic illness or accident-related injuries which had required expensive or long-term treatment.

In the same household interviews, the other most talked about cash expense had to do with education including the school fees for each semester, levies for textbooks, buildings or teacher-support, the costs of school dinners or transportation costs and the extra fees for boarding where distances were too great for the daily commute. The sum of these various education fees could be very high in relation to urban and rural cash incomes especially at secondary levels of education and where there was more than one child of school age. In a high proportion of China's rural villages, there was much scrimping and saving to meet the costs of the fees for educating children in primary schools, never mind secondary and higher education. These were the subject of much complaint in families of school-age children and the result was that many in the poor regions of the countryside could not afford to have their children in school long enough to acquire and maintain literacy and numeracy. In the cities almost all children did proceed to junior-middle school which, along with senior-middle school, was an expensive item taking major portions of family budgets. Schools with the best reputations and standards were fiercely competitive and their fees often required parents to work overtime, moonlight or take several jobs. Certainly after meeting the rising costs of education and health, households had less in the way of disposable incomes for other goods and services. According to one official survey, even the top 10 per cent of city dwellers had an average disposable income of just US$1,240 per annum.[76] Those with less, constituting the majority of urban and rural populations, were even more hesitant to spend on other goods and services and more inclined to save rather than spend.

The increase in savings suggested that by the late 1990s many households had become afraid to spend what they might need for tomorrow or for a 'rainy day'. Chinese household savings during the early mid-1990s reached a high 35 per cent of disposable income.[77] While urban per capita incomes doubled between 1992 and 1995, urban savings expanded by about three times from Y8,678 hundred million to Y23,467 hundred million. Likewise for rural households, per capita incomes slightly more than doubled during the same period while savings rose about three times to reach Y6,196 hundred million.[78] One estimate suggested that the inflows of household savings billowed from 18 per cent of all bank deposits in 1980 to around 60 per cent in the late 1990s so that in 1998 banks were sitting on nearly US$600 million of household deposits.[79] In the first 9 months of 1998, urban and rural savings increased 16.8 per cent over the year-earlier period so that deposits totalled Y5.1 trillion or about US$615.2 billion.[80] By the late 1990s it was clear to many observers that saving took precedence over spending.

> Increasing housing, medical insurance and educational expenses have all forced people to tighten their purse strings, as well. And the Asian financial turmoil hasn't helped. At the end of the day, Chinese prefer to save rather than to spend.[81]

Headlines proclaiming the new frugality or thriftiness or the general propensity to save rather than spend were the subject of much debate both within and outside of China. Within China, the government immediately introduced measures to drum up demand while at the same time advocating socialism or modernisation with 'Chinese characteristics'.

Chinese characteristics

Saving and the new frugality was not what China's government intended in its continuing attempt to increase spending and consumption. Swiftly the government acted to extend credit facilities and to cut taxes for house and car purchasers and, in an attempt to reduce the savings rate, introduced a series of interest cuts from May 1996 which reduced deposit rates and introduced a new tax on interest income.[82] To encourage the flow of idle cash into the economy rather than letting it sit in savings accounts, the government also introduced what it called 'economic holidays'. In a radical departure from past practice, China adopted a 5-day working week with week-long holidays around Spring Festival and National Day introduced to encourage shopping and spending as well as family festivities. Commercially, western festivals such as Christmas and Valentine's Day were deployed to tempt customers to spend in the shops, although it has to be said that the appropriation of Western goods and practices was also subject to a more discerning eye as many increasingly looked to China's own cultural roots. There was something of a reaction against the mindless adoption of Western goods and practices which had become synonymous with the global and the modern. Although the interest in and even passion for things cosmopolitan continued unabated among some and particularly the young, it was matched by an element of official and unofficial concern that the wholesale embrace of or opening the door to the 'modern', the 'Western' or 'the global' would erode or undermine China's distinctive culture and identity. The initial rush by the urban and the young to reject or even abandon their own culture to become Western, global and cosmopolitan lasted in its most extreme form for only a decade or so. By the mid-1990s, there were new fears expressed that China was destined for cultural oblivion as what was culturally specific or distinctively Chinese would be consigned to history, the museum or the tourist attraction. Residents of large cities, such as Beijing, needed to look no further than their own cityscape as, section by section, it was razed to the ground. The pace and style of reconstruction was such that jostling for space and emphasis were tall Greek and Roman columns, half-timbered dormer windows, medieval knights on armoured horses, Rodin's thinker in male and female forms, a Chinese Wall Street, Las Vegas-lit night palaces, Greek gods and James Bond or Playboy equivalents. In this post-modernist landscape, the older Chinese style was relegated to the odd roof, a wall, a left-over hutong or alley and a few famed temples, places and gardens or theme parks packaging China's history for tourists. Several years ago, the flashing of three neon signs prominent one above the other at an interchange in Beijing seemed to me to symbolise this juxtaposition: 'Californian Beef King Noodle USA', 'Karaoke and Seafood from around the

World' and 'Oriental Civilisation Garden'. Shanghai too was commonly described as 'a window on China from the West and a window on the West for China'. To many, Westernisation seemed to have spread at breathtaking speed with shopping malls, bowling alleys, coffee houses, cyber cafes and American fast-food outlets the new landmarks. The pace of change seemed staggering particularly to the older generation. One elderly woman scholar told me that after returning from a sojourn abroad she felt like Rip Van Winkle. Many city residents said that they felt like foreigners in their own country and thought the borrowing and appropriation of 'things' from the West represented a threat to China's culture.

These perceived threats to 'Chineseness' coincided with a crisis of confidence in what constituted the 'Chinese characteristics' that should be preserved for future generations. What lent urgency to the 'rescue of China's body and soul' was that it took place against a background of thirty years of socialism and the Cultural Revolution which had particularly trampled on China's own culture and ancient civilisation. In the aftermath of the Cultural Revolution, it had become customary in China to talk of being left with 'a big mess', 'a wound', 'a scar', 'a lost generation' or 'a loss of who we were' and it was the anticipation of another level of loss due to the onslaught of cosmopolitan consumer goods and ways that spurred the search for culturally-specific Chinese characteristics. By the mid-1990s, it was not so much the definitions of socialism or capitalism in Deng Xiaoping's memorable phrases about black and white cats and 'socialism with Chinese characteristics' that were the focus of attention, but definitions of 'Chinese characteristics' – and this was so both in the discourse of the official media and in everyday conversation. I can still remember the urgency in the voice of a young civil servant who on a long car journey and in our ordinary conversation asserted with some vehemence that 'what we want is an identity but first we need to find out what our identity is!'. At the centre of this search for an identity or Chinese characteristics in the late 1990s there was an unapologetic revival of China's cultural roots or Confucianism. There is a popular saying in China that 'a fallen leaf returns to its roots' and now it was the uprooting of Confucian precepts that was to be blamed for China's current loss of distinctiveness and continuity. In the late 1990s, it became common to talk of China's past as a broken narrative: that Confucianism had a history of 2,000 years, socialism a history of 30 years and recent contact with the West a mere 15 or so years. Therefore in terms of sheer longevity, the Confucian inheritance appeared to have served China well in the past and to this end Confucius himself was rehabilitated in service of the future. A symbolic moment for me in the mid-1990s was a visit to an old school in a poor Anhui village habitually flooded on the banks of a Yangtze tributary, where for the first time I saw that Confucius and Sun Yat-sen had taken their place alongside the old Gang of Four (Marx, Lenin, Stalin and Mao). There have been many such moments since.

It is probably helpful to think of Confucianism as a repository of myths, symbols, heroes, art forms, customs, values, symbols, rites, artefacts, festivals and institutions which can act as markers defining Chinese culture. In the reassertion of Confucian and neo-Confucian influences in the late 1990s, state leaders made offerings to Confucius on the occasion of his birthday, while people flocked to the newly renovated Confucian temples and to his birthplace. Countless books on the life and sayings of Confucius were published in textual and cartoon form and national 'civilising' campaigns were launched in support of his precepts. Many of these campaigns advocated the Confucian way which, in contrast to the West, accorded a lower priority and less status to the material or commerce, money and profit. Exactly 100 years ago and in the last decade of the nineteenth century, when the wealth and power of the West had similarly attracted attention, a succinct new formula had been deployed: Western learning and knowledge for practical application, for technology, the material or 'the outside' and Chinese knowledge for the base, the social, 'the inside' or the spiritual. What underlay this 'tiyong' division at the end of last century was the observation that Western societies were beset by 'money worship', 'the pursuit of profit' or 'social confusion' which were all qualities deemed inappropriate to China's own development. In an equivalent moment now, the image of the West was similarly seen by policy makers, intellectuals and the older generation to incorporate selfishness, egoism, permissiveness, materialism, decadence and money worship. The West represented 'a place' where people are primarily motivated by money and possessions and 'look out for themselves' or have a 'cold face'[83] and thus as much a source of spiritual pollution as of good things. In an equivalent response at the end of the 1990s, the 'tiyong' formula was revived to encapsulate a similar mood strengthened by a greater acquaintance with Western values and societies via television, other media and direct observation. Indeed many of those who came to know the West better or at first hand complained that those who appropriated the goods and ways of the West made no effort to understand the ethics, intellectual ideas and social processes that characterised those societies. Even so it was argued that now more was known about the West, it was most important that China retain its own 'ti' or 'spirit' in the face of a threatened invasion of Western materialism and individualism.

For many intellectuals it was the fears for both the distinctiveness of China's culture and for a distinctive future that ended their indiscriminate love affair with Western goods and ideas in the mid-1990s. It was not so much that the interest in things Western waned but that there was a more self-conscious and selective approach to the appropriation of global and cosmopolitan lifestyles and products rather than the wholesale or promiscuous cultural borrowings of the previous decade. In a much-remembered conversation discussing attitudes towards and utilisation of 'things Western', an elderly professional woman in Beijing quickly retorted that much had been adopted 'without discrimination'. This new plea for discrimination was echoed in another interview with a different young man on the theme of the blue jeans. He said:

> We allowed jeans in ... and they didn't do any harm. I think we should allow in religion and the God, and other Western things, and see how they fit too. Generally in China we've been told the God is a bad thing, but most people don't know much about it, so how can we judge? I think these things should be imported, and examined carefully, and then accepted or rejected. As we did with jeans.[84]

Not all would equate the import of jeans and God, but the principle of selectivity is well expressed. However although this new selectivity in choosing Western goods was widely discussed in some circles, it is unlikely that such discussions in themselves would have led to a downturn in consumption of foreign goods if there had not been a simultaneous slowing down of income growth and some job insecurity alongside the rising costs of housing, health care and other public services. Outside of China, the downturn in the average propensity to consume, described in headlines as 'slow', 'sluggish' or 'stagnant', was also as unwelcome as it was unexpected and led to renewed debate about the size of potential of China's market and the 'inscrutability' or not of China's consumers.

From the mid-1990s, reports began to accumulate that perhaps demand had not just weakened or that, once again, the present and potential of the domestic market in China had been over-estimated. As early as 1995, a report on consumption in *The Economist* had the headline, 'China's Consumers Inscrutable or Just Hard to Find?' Its survey suggested that perhaps only 100 million had an income of more than US$1,000 and that by international standards, the rest hardly had any money to spend on everyday consumer goods let alone at the luxury and imported end of the market.[85] In 1996 the same journal estimated that the number of urban residents who could be relied upon to shop and spend was around 200 million.[86] A year later in 1997, the number with an average income of more than US$1,000 and rich enough to afford even the most modest of items such as detergent or packaged food was down-sized to 120 million.[87] A survey of multinationals in 1999 showed that around half had found the market for their foreign brands in China to be small or certainly much smaller than they had expected.

> There are, for a start, fewer potential consumers of foreign-branded goods than it might appear. Out of China's 1.3 billion people, only a few tens of millions, mostly in coastal regions and cities, are yet rich enough to become consumers of foreign brands.[88]

Again in 1999, reports noted that the number of those keen to spend or splash out was very small, perhaps representing no more than thirty million people, that they were confined to cities such as Beijing, Shanghai, Guangzhou and Shenzhen and that, even for this group who for the most part were not rich by world standards, it was easy to over-estimate their purchasing power.[89] Whatever the numbers, and the estimates were wide-ranging, they were far from the sum total of China's 1.3 billion population.

In these circumstances many foreign businesses which had targeted China's domestic market, either via a local agency, in joint-ventures or entirely on their own, found it more difficult than they had expected to break into the market to sell consumer goods and services locally, let alone make a profit. Some took a long-term view, but many faced with small returns and on-going difficulties in negotiating better entry into the domestic market turned to export-processing where there were more successful precedents. Indeed it could be argued that development of China's base for global manufacturing in toys, textiles, electronic items and other consumer goods was accelerated by disappointments in the domestic market as many turned to manufacturing for export following bureaucratic difficulties and disappointing sales. Most had set out to tap what they thought of as 'unlimited domestic demand' and only subsequently switched to exports where they might bide their time and await new developments in domestic demand. One commentator in 1999 succinctly summed up the prevailing mood with the headline, 'Infatuation's End':

> They still come, but China's numerology has lost its power to enthral. Too many companies have lost millions and wasted years of management time dealing with Chinese bureaucracy and the Chinese partners which had been imposed upon them. What had seemed to many investors like a market of infinite possibility now looks instead more like a black hole of infinite dimensions.[90]

By the mid- to late 1990s then, it seemed to many analysts, company directors and multinational companies that not only was this market much more difficult to penetrate than they had expected but also they were still years away from realising China's potential as a consumer market. It was not only proving a much smaller market than anticipated but also more complex and differentiated than they had imagined. At this time it seemed a daunting task to try to understand this vast emerging market and fathom who wanted what and where. In the short space of fifteen years, it was easily observed that China had moved from a society with a high degree of egalitarianism and with few or minor differences in consumption patterns and lifestyles to a society with greater wealth but also greater differentials in incomes, living standards and lifestyles. It was the increasing differentials between rich and poor which had stretched the disparities and inhibited upward mobility, the participation of the majority of the population in the third phase of China's consumer revolution and the spread of the first two phases to new population categories. Although the capacity for family consumption had greatly increased during the years of reform, this capacity varied widely across locations and income groups, leading to variations in consumer purchases and behaviour and differentiated or segmented consumer markets. In these circumstances, market interest in the varieties of China's consumers heightened and with the first rule of marketing in mind, 'know your customer', analysts turned their attention to researching and segmenting the market.

Market research

As consumption proved to be less vibrant than expected and as demand seemed sluggish, there was increasing interest in researching China's domestic market to assess and analyse the numbers, the location and product preferences of present and potential customers in order to better stimulate and sustain existing demand. Both foreign- and Chinese-owned firms aimed at a better understanding of consumer–product or consumer–brand relations to ensure successful outcomes for their product or brand promotions. For this they turned to a small number of market research companies which had been established in China from the mid-1980s. The first major external agency to establish offices in China was the Survey Research Group (SRG). Established in 1984, its main clients were large firms from the United States to whom it offered an in-house customised service on attitude towards and usage of consumer products based on the findings of focus groups, individual interviews, retail audits and media monitoring. Like other agencies which followed, the SRG saw itself as an interpreter of customer preference and behaviour for foreign businesses.[91] Gallup Research opened for business in Beijing in January 1994 in what it claimed was the country's first nationally-licensed market research joint-venture. It worked closely with local university researchers and its early customers also reflected strong links with US-based multinationals and trade agencies funded by the US government.[92] The first Chinese-owned and operated market research company opened in 1988 in the southern city of Guangdong where it employed interviewers to question large-city consumers about product choice and preference.[93] One of the largest and most successful of China's market research companies, Horizon, was founded by the sociologist Yuan Yue in 1992. From small beginnings in Beijing, Horizon's client base expanded in the mid-1990s to include more than 600 domestic and international companies so that, with earnings multiplying ten-fold between 1993 and 1997, it became the leading local privately-registered agency by 1998.[94]

Most foreign investors, manufacturers and retailers recognised the importance of market research in preparing to enter the largest mass market in the world. Many of the most successful companies took the advice of market research analysts in offering new products and establishing new retail operations. In 1985, Proctor and Gamble was one of the first foreign companies to use market research prior to establishing itself as the leading purveyor of shampoos, washing powders and soaps.[95] Unilever's confidence in the sales of its products was also based on market research showing rising incomes among China's urban population, new and rising exposure to television advertising and evidence of a new interest in hygiene, image and fashion. From its beginnings in 1987, Unilever planned to consistently expand the company's operations and invest at least £64 million every year for 5 years in order to boost sales of Omo, Lifebuoy and Lux seven-fold to the value of £1 billion by 2000.[96] In the 1990s the research findings of Horizon were used by many famous names including Microsoft, Ericsson, Mitsubishi and Coca-Cola.[97] Marks & Spencer opened its own office for market research in 1996 and after a year spent analysing customer demand and the shop sales of other retailers, it decided not to open a store in China until there were more middle-class customers.[98] In the late 1990s there was a revival of interest in market research and development as foreign investors and joint-ventures in the retail sector and in product development questioned why their retail operations were languishing or failing and why products which sold world-wide had not had the same success in China. Companies new in China and fearful of following the trajectory of their predecessors also took a greater interest in market research before choosing their place and mode of entry. In addition to exploring product characteristic and preference, some considerable attention was directed towards China's consumers, their geographical location and cultural characteristics.

Most of the first exercises in market research had to do with matching product appeal and promotional messages to customer preference. In the early 1990s, it would be true to say that most foreign producers had assumed that winning over the China market would not be too difficult and they just had to get the product 'right' and distribute it widely. However most soon found themselves facing a Chinese puzzle: the products they thought were good and sold easily elsewhere were not selling in China. Suppliers asked themselves whether this might be because the price was too high or because the name, packaging or advertising of their products was inappropriate and lacked customer appeal. Hence market research tended to be product-oriented, based on questioning customers as to their attitudes and preferences towards pricing, retail services and advertisement style or content and shopping environments. In terms of the conventional marketing mix, three of the classic four Ps, 'product' (including brands and packaging), 'pricing' and 'promotion', took precedence and it was only in the mid-1990s that product characteristics and preferences gave way to greater interest in the fourth P, 'place', largely because of the size, dispersal and geographic differences within China's potential customer base and/or the beliefs that China's unique cultural characteristics might make it one of the world's most inscrutable and impenetrable of markets. The increased demand for market information spurred a number of analyses of China's consumers, most of which focused either on geographic location or cultural 'Chinese characteristics'.

A question much debated was whether or not China's consumers displayed characteristics that were culturally-specific or uniquely Chinese. Some argued that China's consumers differed little from their counterparts elsewhere and that international market strategies and global products were just as applicable to China's markets; others emphasised China's distinctiveness or unique cultural precepts and practices which they thought distinguished this market from all others. Oliver Yeo, in his comprehensive 1994 study of Chinese consumption, argued that understanding Chinese cultural values contributed to a better understanding of the behaviour of China's population as consumers.[99] In examining the relationship between Chinese culture and consumer behaviour, he profiled a number of cultural values which he thought were particularly relevant to consumption. These included the importance of the family, the necessary exchange of favours or gifts and a number of traditional beliefs such as those in 'fate' or 'face'. Similarly, Ambler and Witzel in their authoritative guide to *Doing Business in China* also explored some of the differences between Chinese tradition and Western decision-making theory and argued that differences in motivation, assessment of consequence and perceptions of harmony, certainty and self-interest might well affect consumer preference, motivation and decisions in China.[100] Others argued that it was less the differences between Chinese and other cultures that shaped China's domestic market and consumer behaviour than the large size and variations in geography and development.

An important factor identified as characterising China's domestic market was the geographic diversity of the different regions each with their own very different levels and rates of economic development. Such was the local variation that most analysts and market research agencies represented China's consumer market as 'a mosaic' and segmented the market along geographic lines, distinguishing coastal from inland regions, eastern and southern from northern and western regions and rural from urban, suburban or metropolitan locations. In making these sub-divisions, information about consumers was usually relayed in the most general of terms. Ambler and Witzel in their guide to doing business in China divided the country into twelve physical regions according to significant differences in topography, climate, culture and economy. In addition, and as a simpler entry point, they also offered a more manageable and 'quick' segmentation into seven regions.[101] Within China, market analysts tended to take less account of geography and divide China by province and administrative subdivisions. To do so they turned to published sources of quantitative data including that collected and analysed by the State Statistical Bureau which provided general information about population numbers, city, town or rural residence, incomes and assets. For all analysts, whether foreign or Chinese, one of the frustrations of conducting market research in China was the sheer geographic scale of the market place which made the logistics of conducting investigation into the potential market outside of the main cities where seven out of ten of China's population resided, very difficult. Within cities, most market research was based on bespoke qualitative data obtained via surveys, structured interviews and focus groups which, alongside retail audits and media monitoring, were the most common sources of information. Many firms were also heavily reliant on the feedback from their own sales-persons, product tests and retail-reports which reflected the preferences of their existing customers. The sheer geographic size might make it more difficult to conduct market research than elsewhere but, according to the director of business development in North Asia for AC Nielsen, 'Once you reach them, Chinese consumers are eager to share information about themselves and fascinated by a wide range of consumer goods'.[102]

To extend the number of informants and obtain speedy or direct feedback, some firms also began to make use of the internet. In seeking to define 'exactly what the Chinese want to buy', one Beijing-based marketing company called MadeforChina.com organised its own email-based market research. Hoping to adjust their brand-marketing campaigns to a geographically dispersed market, the company began to send information about products directly to clients' computers. In this way it hoped not only to ensure direct feedback but also to build on-going relationships with consumers:

> Email marketing will appeal to multinational clients selling into China since the technique encourages customer feedback, reaches a tightly targeted but geographically disperse audience, allows nation-wide real-time introduction of products and creates a direct relationship between the company and the consumer, an important way of encouraging repeat business.[103]

Many potential informants were enticed to cooperate in the research by companies offering free internet usage for a period of time. The advantage of this offer was 'the positive way in which consumers got to know our company' and their gratitude for 'helping them get online for free'.[104] According to the Vice-President for Business Strategy at Ericsson in China which also participated in such email marketing research, the 'most important thing we can get from this email promotion is feedback from the audience about both our advertising and, even more importantly, our products'.[105] However although internet users seemed eager to share their responses and preferences and provided an important source of information for companies, it only captured a very small self-selected market segment of 'netizens' mainly made up of well-educated and metropolitan male computer-users less than 30 years old.[106] One of the disadvantages of most market research conducted in the mid to late 1990s was that it was mainly based on China's thin layer of existing customers which were far from representative of China's populous or potential market.

By 1998, the number of registered companies conducting market research in China, both local start-ups and foreign-joint-ventures, had risen from virtually zero to close on 850.[107] Nevertheless conducting market research using techniques developed elsewhere has proved more difficult than in most places. In 2000, the *Far Eastern Economic Review* concluded that market research in China 'is easier said than done' and that it took hard work to find the kind of basic market data that is available elsewhere due to the size and diversity of China's population, under-trained researchers and potential sensitivities:

> The major obstacle to teasing out good market information is the sheer size of China. Undeveloped communications means a regionalised and fragmented market, with wide discrepancies in consumer behaviour. A population of 1.2 billion means acquiring even the simplest data on a national scale – the number of consumers of a certain age earning a certain salary, for example – becomes a monumental task.[108]

One attempt to search out and directly question country consumers was conducted by Saatchi and Saatchi's regional strategic planning director for Asia, Sandy Thompson. She travelled for 6 weeks across 12,000 kilometres of China's roads and, along the route, her team conducted numerous interviews in groups ranging from schoolgirls and teens to professional women and farmers. It was from these grass-root interviews that she felt she gained invaluable insights into the emotions, humour and aspirations of her informants.[109] Using methods reminiscent of ethnography, China's Emma Gilding thought that the information she collected added up to more than focus groups or interviews could ever provide and had helped the advertising agency's creative team come up with concepts that would work in one of 'the world's most inscrutable markets'.[110] That this is still the case was confirmed by Oliver and Crowther in 2004 when that company observed that China's markets remained difficult to reach not only because of size, fragmentation and diversity but also because of the rate of market change, the questionable quality of much of the secondary data and the difficulties in the way of conducting direct enquiry.[111] A representative of AC Nielsen, perhaps the most assiduous and authoritative of the foreign market research teams in China, has long argued for a more nuanced approach:

> The more complex individualistic environment means companies must be extremely confident of their target market, and must 'stratify' the market accordingly, tailoring their operations to clearly understand categories of Chinese consumers.[112]

Perhaps it is a clear understanding of categories of China's customer base that is still missing. The preoccupation with products, population numbers and place or location in researching customer preference meant that for a long time it was population categories and their socio-economic characteristics which remained under-researched. A letter to *The Economist* in August 1997 written in response to a previous article on the subject aptly summed up this omission:

> Sir, I agree with your basic premise that doing business in China has proved to be something of a challenge. [The China Syndrome, 21 June 1997] But in identifying the factors that have created this situation, you have overlooked one of the more obvious: understanding Chinese consumers.
>
> Many businesses have rushed into this potentially massive market without fully appreciating what lies ahead of them. It may well be impossible to second-guess ad hoc government legislation, but to miscalculate the size of a market (especially for high-ticket items like cars) suggests that some blue-chip companies simply have not done their homework.

Two years later, *The Economist* suggested that foreign companies that were still struggling in the China market, still had stars in their eyes and still had not done their homework:

> The story of foreign business in China can best be told as a series of fallacies unravelled, often through painful experience. Few companies are stupid, but many have behaved stupidly in China. In a market that is both complex and fast-changing, firms have launched schemes based on market research so scant that it would never have satisfied them elsewhere.[114]

As this study has suggested several times, one of the main problems in navigating the China market was basing it on a more realistic assessment rather than consistently exaggerating demand.

Ambler and Witzel in their exploration of and guide to the China market also noted that the largest gap in marketing knowledge was information about consumers, exploration 'beyond' or 'behind the numbers' of potential consumers or 'real information' about 'real people'.[115] This was because those who attempted to segment the market still mainly based their analysis on quantitative data utilising national and sub-national statistics to investigate income levels, income distribution and consumption expenditure and correlated these across geographic and administrative regions. Conversely the qualitative data utilised by market analysts working with focus groups and individual informants rarely contextualised these in relation to larger socio-economic categories. In this context, questions such as who are the rich, who are the poor, who has disposable income and what are their life's expectations and lifestyle aspirations all remained under-researched. In recent years, anthropologists have found identifying social categories and investigating perceptions around livelihoods, lifestyle differentiation, status and hierarchy to be fruitful areas of enquiry in studying everyday consumer practices and purchases. As this study has begun to suggest, consumer goods and practices were also used to define and redefine identity and differentiate social categories in the early years of reform. While it is commonplace to conclude that consumption is directly related to level of personal income, it is also clear that consumer choices and lifestyles are as much about location, generation and gender as socio-economic position, as well as about a sense of future and the degree of confidence in the economy and public policy. Hence the next two parts of this book bring the study up to date and explore new and evolving socio-economic and socio-demographic categories of the population in an attempt to assess their security of livelihood, lifestyle choices and aspirations for and confidence in the future. Although this exploration does include some discussion of consumer preferences and priorities, it is not a substitute for market research. Rather, based on documentary and field research, it is intended to act as a background or supplement to more targeted or segmented investigations of potential customers, as a more accurate guide to estimating rather than exaggerating the growth of domestic demand in the future and as an informative and up-to-date read for those more generally interested in livelihoods and lifestyles in this fast-growing and changing country.

Part II

Segmenting demand

The wealth pyramid

4 Elite lifestyles

The good life and upward mobility

At the outset of the economic reform, Deng Xiaoping had famously declared that 'to get rich is glorious'. Since then, and especially following the reaffirmation of this message on his milestone trip to the southern provinces in the early 1990s, millions of China's citizens took him at his word and grasped the opportunity to 'become rich quick' or at least to become more prosperous. Now, to be a millionaire overnight is quite a common dream and millions are working very hard in the hope of new riches. Within and outside China much media and market attention has been given to the 'swelling numbers' of the 'newly affluent', 'high-income' or 'moneyed strata' who are frequently labelled China's 'new elite' or 'nouveau riche'. In a sense, given the previous absence of material wealth and disposable income and the disdain for monetary accumulation or exchanges during the revolution, all affluence could be said to be novel and riches 'nouveau'. Such was the novelty of high incomes, the individual accumulation of assets and conspicuous lifestyle consumption that all these features have been seized upon as evidence of the rapid economic growth, the success of market reform and China's new wealth. Indeed it is the elite lifestyles and growing accumulation of goods and assets that have constituted the most important yardstick measuring China's economic success and emerging market. The newly affluent seem to be living out the expectations inherent within Deng Xiaoping's dictum of 'letting some grow rich first for others to follow'. The lifestyles of the super-rich or elite fill the pages of the many new glossy magazines and are on nation-wide display on television. Although it can be argued that China's elite have an importance beyond their numbers, such is the attention given to the conspicuous lifestyles of the rich that any bystander could be forgiven for thinking that much of urban and suburban China already belongs, or could soon belong, to this category of high or at least middle-income consumers. In fact an analysis of this category suggests not only that it is a much smaller proportion of the population than presumed but also that it is not necessarily paving the way or even becoming the model for an upwardly mobile or expanding middle class.

A closer examination of China's 'elite' suggests that this category can be defined by both income-level and lifestyle and that the newly affluent make up a minority, concentrated in location and comprise a number of overt occupational categories. The majority of the 2.2 per cent of China's population who are estimated to have reached a 'high-economy' income, as defined by the World Bank's GNI standard, live in the southern cities of Shenzhen and Guangzhou which are both in close proximity to Hong Kong, the capital Beijing or the coastal cities of Shanghai and Tianjin and the richer suburbs of all these major cities.[1] In these locations there are three major social categories which can be said to make up the elite in terms of assets, income, occupation and education.[2] The first, the 'official' category, is that made up of high and middle-ranking officials, functionaries and staff members who are leading cadres in government institutions, Party and mass organisations or managers in successful state-owned and operated enterprises, all of whom are likely to have access to state assets or status and thus to be in a position to barter administrative power and prestige for money and material items. Individuals and well-connected families with ties to the government and Party have long constituted China's most privileged class. Although their official take-home pay may not be high in monetary terms, they are frequently in a position to receive extra payments or bribes in cash and kind, to control large sums of public funds and assets which can be sold on, or to do business in or with the private sector.

A second high-income category is made up of those who participate in the vibrant private sector which has emerged as one of the most dynamic components of the Chinese economy responsible for much of the post-reform job and wealth creation. This category includes those who set up, run or manage private enterprises, those who are self-employed, have employees, investors or shareholders and those who take advantage of new opportunities in marketing property and credit or other professional services. As well as the emergence of a private-enterprise category of owners, managers and agents, there has been a significant expansion of high-salary professional and technical personnel including lawyers, doctors and accountants employed in state, joint and foreign ventures or agencies or who offer their services and skills on a self-employed basis in the private sector. This third category, often referred to as the 'new high-income white-collar strata', has grown rapidly due to the expansion of opportunities for higher education within China and abroad and the competitive demand for personnel with professional and technical qualifications in the new market and expanded state sectors. Many in this third category are graduates of the top Chinese universities or returnees from abroad who have become leaders, managers or office workers in foreign government, donor or commercial organisations or in joint wholly-owned foreign research, business and professional service ventures.

In terms of age, many of the newly affluent are of the younger and middle generations, between 30 and 45 years old, who have taken advantage of new opportunities to acquire marketable skills and qualifications and to establish private business, retailing or software companies. In terms of numbers, there has been a range of estimates of the newly affluent with most suggesting that they rose from one million or so in 1995 to around 2.5 or 3 million at the turn of the century and since.[3] In 2001, China's own economists reckoned that there were 3 million 'yuan millionaires' (US$121,000) and over 1,000 'yuan billionaires'.[4] This is certainly only a small proportion of the 1.3 billion anticipated by the business world outside of China. The income level defining the newly affluent is usually set at Y2,000 (US$240–250) cash per capita income per month, much less than US$1,000 (Y8,000) which is estimated to be the minimum level of income necessary for consumer spending to take off.[5] For so many of the newly affluent however a tally of monthly income may represent but a small proportion of their income and source of accumulated wealth. They may well receive the equivalent of many tens of thousands of US dollars per year in bonuses, profits or illicit gains. In 2003, the top 20 per cent of urban dwellers, numbering around 100 million people, were estimated to have average disposable incomes of Y15,380 or around US$2,000 which was almost double the average urban per capita income of Y8,250.[6] In Beijing it was estimated that the average annual salary of bosses of private companies in 2002 was around US$8,000 (Y65,000) or Y5,000–6,000 per month which was at least four times the average earnings of a civil servant each month.[7] However what differentiates elite earners from others is not only their levels of income but also their patterns of consumption and lavish lifestyles.

In the mid-1990s such was the visibility of the newly affluent that Shanghai's popular *New People's Evening Daily* reported that 'yapashi' (yuppies) had emerged in Shanghai and were to be distinguished both by their high earnings and their 'independent' and 'stylish' lifestyles.[8] A number of early surveys of high-income groups suggested that the lifestyles of the elite could be identified by their novel, exclusive and stylish attributes and activities which were expensive to acquire. Dubbed 'the big spenders', the country's new prosperous households of cosmopolitan city and coastal regions were not put off by the high price tag of international brands for large- and small-ticket items which befitted a quality lifestyle. Moreover they tended to make purchases all the year round rather than at the peak times of Chinese New Year or Spring Festival. One of the first surveys of high-income shopping habits in Beijing was undertaken in 1995 by Yugong Market Research and Policy Analysis.[9] It showed that income and age were the most important factors affecting consumption choices and that those in the high-income bracket and at a younger age were more likely to buy 'famous brand products' and imported, high-quality and new-style goods even if the price was higher. The goods that the one thousand families surveyed had already purchased included a colour television set (97%), a video-cassette player (61%), a telephone (34.6%), a stereo (29%), a camera (12%) and air conditioners (8%), although only 3.2 per cent then had a private car. In terms of percentages of income, the amounts spent on various commodities were fairly evenly distributed between children's education (30%), PC and electrical appliances (29%) and housing, furniture and interior decoration (26%). Only a small percentage were willing to spend on travel (5%) or a car (5%). Over the next ten years the acquisition of a house or an apartment with designer interior decoration, a car, foreign or domestic travel and more expensive recreational activities came to characterise an identifiable elite lifestyle. In the new glossy magazines ranging from *Trends Gentlemen* to China's *Tatler*, it became not so much the single product that was marketed but an entire lifestyle that was at once independent, expensive and cosmopolitan. More recent surveys of China's millionaires suggest that the members of this privileged category enjoy just such a metropolitan lifestyle.

China's millionaires

The number of millionaires or super-rich in China is sometimes taken as a measure of the remarkable speed of social change in contemporary China. As *China International Business* noted in 2003:

> If there are indicators that testify to the huge changes taking place in China, the birth and mushrooming of millionaires is surely one of them.[10]

The numbers have grown. In 1993 the State Administration of Industry and Commerce identified 488 millionaires within the country's private enterprises.[11] The following year the Development and Research Centre of the State Council concluded that altogether in China there were 5,000 millionaires.[12] In 1995 the *People's Daily* reported that more than one million people possessed one million yuan (US$120,817) worth of assets and more.[13] In 2003 it was reported by the official China News Agency that there were three million who had made their wealth in sales and service industries, security investment and hi-tech sector.[14] In Zhongguancun, known as China's silicon valley or a 'millionaire-producing machine', more than 1,000 millionaires were reportedly created in 2002.[15] One survey reported in 2003 found that 20 to 30 per cent of senior managers in large and medium-sized IT enterprises had annual salaries of more than Y1 million.[16] Many had started their own very successful companies, had become property developers or were top managers in state-owned enterprises who had been encouraged to purchase stakes in the companies. In 2004, an analysis of the super-rich compiled by the American *Forbes* magazine over the previous five years showed that China's rich are on average in their mid-forties and worth US$230 million. Some are technological whizzkids, although three-quarters of the top 100 had made their fortunes in property or at the head of sprawling conglomerates. Government connexions remain important and one-quarter were also members of the Communist Party which provided both useful political connexions as well as protection.[17] A number of the high-profile rags-to-riches stories of China's millionaires have been featured in the media and show that while some have taken advantage of connexions, protective bribes and unpaid taxes, most also splash out on villas, limousines or expensive entertainment.

There have been a number of surveys of the spending patterns of China's 'big spenders'. One of the first investigations was undertaken by the Beijing-based Horizon Research Company in 1995 which found that reinvestment, socialising and children's education were the key spending areas.[18] The report suggested that 'their daily consumption is still quite conservative'. Personal spending and family expenditure accounted for 24.1 per cent of their income, savings took up 3 per cent, while a high 70.4 per cent stated that re-investment in their enterprise took up the major portion of their income. However around half of those surveyed wanted to provide the best possible education for their children. The report also suggested that many of the key decisions to do with family or personal daily consumption were made by wives who claimed to be more influenced by price and quality than any promotional materials and were as likely to purchase domestic as foreign brands. Several years later, in 2002, the China Private Economy Research Society found that most of the two million owners of private enterprises surveyed spent their income on food (30%), education (20%), clothes (14%), entertainment (7%) and health care (7%). Again a common finding in analysis of expenditure of the rich was the high proportions of income spent on education either for themselves or for their children.[19] Perhaps the most significant finding of the surveys of China's millionaires was that, like low-income and mid-income earners, the rich had increasingly shown some reluctance to shop and spend. This reluctance was said to be due both to a lack of goods that were attractive to wealthy consumers and to government policies which did not sufficiently spur consumption.[20] It is also true that many of the super-rich were reluctant to indulge in conspicuous displays of wealth and attract undue attention, either from the government whose support for entrepreneurial endeavour could not necessarily be assumed or because they had something to hide. For many years the government continued to show some ambivalence towards the super-rich as it debated whether or not to extend Party membership to private entrepreneurs. There have also been a sufficient number of high-profile court cases in which ostentatious displays of wealth were followed by questions and charges of corruption and tax avoidance to warn the super-rich against drawing attention to their wealth.

In a recent case, Shanghai's flamboyant property developer Zhou Zhengyi, who was eleventh on the *Forbes* rich list in 2002 earning him the media-bestowed sobriquet of 'the richest man in Shanghai', was accused of illegally acquiring state land and bank loans and flaunting his wealth. In reporting his precipitate downfall, the media made much of his very public lifestyle which was said to include 'a collection of sporting cars' and 'a number of sexual affairs'.[21] So many on the *Forbes* super-rich list have been arrested on charges ranging from fraud to tax evasion, that the list itself is sometimes dubbed a 'death list'. Certainly the large number of high-profile cases have encouraged fellow tycoons to keep a low profile. Huang Jianping, the founder of JP International Group of Companies which operates in several market segments including agriculture, education, the environment, railroad construction and telecommunications and has key domestic and foreign competitive connections, is reported to have said that the elite must avoid ostentatious behaviour and maintain a certain degree of social anonymity: 'If you claim you're wealthy, your lifetime is short'.[22] In support of his beliefs he drove a Shanghai-made Volkswagen rather than a flashier import and has set up a foundation to fund scholarships for study at a college in Sichuan province. Given that millionaires in China get a bad press because it is assumed that they must have engaged in dubious dealings or evaded tax and the government's clampdown on corruption, which is discussed in more detail in later chapters, it is not surprising that few want their lifestyles to attract attention. When the young 31-year-old chairman of Shanda Electronics which manufactures computer games in Shanghai's Pudong district was interviewed in the *Guardian* on the day that he appeared second on China's own rich list, he proved to be no exception. Sensitive to the image problem of the super-rich, he spoke of his membership of the Communist Party and his contribution to society rather than his fortune of around US$1.05 billion – which apparently was a source of shame rather than pride to his parents.[23] Again in 2005, most of China's ten known billionaires who had made their fortunes by developing real estate declined to be interviewed for an article on their rags-to-riches stories. It was not the rags they minded so much as the riches as some admitted that they did not want any publicity or scrutiny in a country still officially communist and uneasy about the creation of individual wealth.[24] However for most, the very existence of China's millionaires provided a new yardstick by which to measure the success of the country's reform and individual achievement. To become a millionaire became the stuff of many a common entrepreneurial dream.[25] As one young 29-year-old man who started a small plastics factory with his mother mused:

> I have to become a millionaire. I don't want a fancy house, I just want to be a regular person. But if you aren't a millionaire, your life is very restricted. In this world, in China, money is everything.[26]

Few lived such dreams and achieved millionaire or super-rich status, but more became wealthy and entered China's rich or elite band characterised by high income levels and matching lifestyles.

China's elite

In comparison to the very small numbers of China's millionaires or super-rich, the next tier of rich might have fewer assets and less wealth but they were still within the 2.2 per cent earning high-economy incomes and, compared with the rest of China's population, could also be labelled China's rich or elite. Made up of the three major social categories detailed earlier in this chapter, most of 'China's elite', like the millionaires, live in the half-dozen or so main cities and their surrounding suburbs. According to an official government survey in 1998, it was estimated that China's elite consumers represented no more than 30 million people who mainly lived in cities such as Beijing, Shanghai, Guangzhou and Shenzhen and that, for the most part, the top 10 per cent of city dwellers had an average annual disposable income of just US$1,240 per person – which did not make them rich by world standards. However if GDP per head was adjusted for purchasing power then the incomes of the top 10 per cent of city dwellers was probably closer to US$10,000 per year, which was more in keeping with the presence of wide-screen televisions, luxury stereos and home-karaoke machines in their apartments.[27] One of the most regular surveys of China's elite was that published in the *Far Eastern Economic Review* which was updated each year from October 1998 to December 2003. It was based on interviews with some 1,000 to 1,500 top corporate managers, senior-level cadres, entrepreneurs and educators living in Beijing, Shanghai and Guangzhou. Around three-quarters of the respondents were male, aged between 30 and 45 years and married with one child. Mostly earning between Y2,000 and Y6,000 per month in 1998 and Y4,000 and Y8,000 in 2002, they did not see themselves as super-rich but as members of China's upper middle class – more affluent than most – and enjoying a comfortable lifestyle. As for the future, they expected to have increasing opportunities to improve their standard of living. On the eve of the new century, they were asked to list the essential components of 'the good life'. First on the list for 75 to 80 per cent of the respondents were a happy marriage or relationship, good health, children and job security. These were followed by a number of middle category items which, ranked high by around 50 per cent, included leisure, a high-paying job, owning a car, travelling abroad and a college education. Less than 10 per cent cited good-quality clothes or accessories, club membership and expensive jewellery as essential components of 'the good life'. A slightly lower percentage had already acquired each of these attributes although higher numbers expected to have more leisure, a high-paying job, a car and to travel abroad in the next few years.[28]

The annual survey showed that individual and household monthly incomes for this group had increased steadily over the 6-year period. In 1998, just over one-third earned less than Y2,000 (US$242); the same proportion earned between Y2,000 and Y4,000; and a slightly smaller number, mostly entrepreneurs and joint-venture managers, earned more than Y4,000 per month; in addition a small but significant 7 per cent of entrepreneurs earned more than Y15,000 per month.[29] In the following year incomes increased so that only a fifth earned less than Y2,000 per month,[30] and in 2002 almost all respondents earned between Y4,000 and Y8,000.[31] In 2003 the average personal income was Y5,800 per month with household monthly incomes ranging between Y8,000 and Y9,000 with an average of Y8,300.[32] Since there was little inflation, disposable income had also risen although so too had the cost of housing, utilities and services. In 1999 any surplus income had been spent on home improvements (48%), savings (47%), education (34%), stocks and shares (31%), entertainment and social activities (27%), new clothes (18%), property (15%), new cars (15%) and vacations (14%).[33] In 2000 most respondents wanted to spend their surplus income on housing or property (30%), a car (20%) and slightly less on children's education (11%).[33] Over the next few years of the survey, savings and education dominated the list of outgoings followed by a home, a car, computing hardware and travel or leisure activities, all of which became the most popular items to be saved for and purchased. Items such as domestic appliances and fashionable clothes or adornment were no longer high priorities, partly because they had been acquired and, now commonplace, were no longer regarded as luxuries. As significant items were acquired over the six-year survey, new priorities emerged with travel, leisure, hobbies and recreational entertainment becoming increasingly popular activities. However from the late-1990s, the most prominent goal of China's high-income categories was home ownership together with refurbishing or making home improvements.

A home of one's own

In the cities of China and among high-income groups, 'owning your own home' has become the most important material pre-requisite for a good life or successful lifestyle and one of the most observable of changes in cityscapes has been the growing numbers of apartment blocks and villa estates. While those employed and housed in the public sector have been permitted to purchase public or work-unit housing in which they already resided, private entrepreneurs and young professionals have been encouraged to purchase housing in new apartment blocks or segregated residential estates. By 1998, work-units in Shanghai controlled only 30 per cent of cheap housing, the remainder were privately owned (40%) or rented (30%).[35] Much of the luxury housing being constructed on the private market then was well beyond the pockets of most local households and precluded ownership by all but the high-income entrepreneurs, professionals and officials. In 1997 it was estimated that half the residential properties purchased in the commercial market went to individual private buyers,[36] but after deposits were reduced and mortgages became more obtainable, the market for private housing developed apace. Although much that was opulent and far too expensive for most city residents remained empty, sales of residential housing increased by 40 per cent after 1999 so that private buyers bought 88 per cent of the new houses.[37] By 2000, in China's sophisticated city of Shanghai, 25 per cent of urban residents owned their own home compared with 10 per cent in 1997.[38]

For China's elite, owning your own home, apartment or villa is part of the new affluent lifestyle and aspired to by all members of higher-income groups and, as the *Far Eastern Economic Review* surveys show, 'an essential component of the good life'. By 1998, around three-quarters of the elite surveyed owned their own homes and the remainder expected to do so within the coming year.[39] This is a high proportion for even in Beijing and Shanghai it was estimated that only around a fifth (18.20%) had purchased a city-centre flat by 2003.[40] Certainly the young entrepreneurs and joint-venture employees were among the first to buy houses on the private market and take advantage of the new mortgage-lending opportunities offered by the big-four banks. The government not only promoted a private housing market permitting developers to construct new varieties of housing, but also newspapers, television and magazines all advertised down-town apartments, town houses or suburban villas set in estate compounds that offered amenities such as man-made lakes, bowling alleys, golf courses as well as fountains and gardens. Among the newly-rich and aspiring, property purchase is one of the main dinner-table subjects of conversation and certainly sales figures confirm that both home ownership and home furnishing are indeed 'hot topics' among this relatively privileged younger generation – perhaps the first to have an opportunity to both live separately from their parents and express their independence and individuality in their own separate 'life-spaces'.

By the turn of the century, there was a burgeoning home-improvement and furnishing industry in metropolitan China. In 1999, the *Far Eastern Economic Review* survey of the elite suggested that around half of the respondents had spent their extra income on home improvements and appliances.[41] Domestic interiors, previously cramped, plain, utilitarian and make-shift, have been given a make-over with new wall- and floor-coverings, furniture and soft-furnishings. Moreover the bulk of new housing coming on to the market is sold as a bare concrete shell devoid of any fittings or decorations so that new homes have required flooring, plumbing, bathroom and kitchen fittings, lighting and other fixtures and furnishings. Hence interior decorating and refurbishment or furnishing has become the source of much media and retail interest and, since the late 1990s, one of the largest boosts to consumer spending. Numerous general and specialist magazines have 'home sections' on how to transform life-spaces via the use of domestic furnishings, television shows choose spaces to make-over, while many manufacturers and retailers of household goods and furnishings have taken advantage of a growing and buoyant market for their goods. A number of small and specialist shops began to provide furnishing and decorating services. There were many home boutiques such as one of my favourites in Beijing named 'Lifeshop' which had soft candles and embroidered cushions and other stylish home objects to add to the fine fabrics on offer at the very expensive up-market home-decor shop next door. Shanghai's classiest shopping street, Huaihai Lu, incorporated a new furnishings mini-mall offering gilt tapestry, framed art and traditional Chinese-style armchairs upholstered with Victorian floral fabric while, across the street, imported furniture stores offered competition. One of the most interesting development has been the introduction and popularity of many Western do-it-yourself chains such as Sweden's IKEA, Britain's B&Q, Germany's Obi and America's Wal-Mart which were soon followed by the development of Chinese-owned equivalents such as Homemart and Orient Homes.

Sweden's IKEA opened its first stores as joint-ventures in Shanghai in 1998 and in Beijing in 1999 as a 'window on the furniture styles of the world'. At first its simple household styles were too expensive for its target customers and, although IKEA counted around 70,000 visitors a week and profits rose 45 per cent within a year of opening, many of these first visitors came to window-shop. One shopper observed that, although he appreciated the fact that 'the furniture is designed for people to live comfortably', we are here 'to look at foreign style, a new style to broaden our horizons'.[42] Once IKEA realised that the store was considered too expensive by its target customers – young privileged professional couples – the company lowered prices by nearly 10 per cent, causing sales to rise by 35 per cent in 2003 and by 50 per cent in the first three months of 2004.[43] The marketing manager of IKEA China described the store's mission as providing well-designed and 'smart solutions' for China's homes at low prices. As a result the store's prices were considered mid-range in Shanghai with most customers earning around Y3,300 per month compared with an average of Y1,000 per month. Most of IKEA's customers are in the age range of 20 to 35 years although the store is beginning to attract a number of customers in their mid-fifties. Many customers are double-income well-educated couples with or without children who spent roughly Y300 a visit.[44] The lay-out, products and services normally offered by IKEA have been adjusted to take account of China's housing size, styles and customer priority and preference. For instance there is a balcony section, less emphasis on 'do-it-yourself assembly' and more on the 'living room' than on smaller less-visible kitchens and bedrooms. To acquire familiarity with people's lifestyles and their home aspirations, IKEA has conducted home visits, surveys and focus groups to help Chinese customers understand the IKEA concept; the company also posts in-store instructions and design advice, publishes brochures and catalogues and operates a detailed website. IKEA has expanded fast, opening a giant new store in Shanghai and a second store in Beijing and it has plans to have ten large stores up and running in China by 2010.[45] In the meantime, three of the most immediate challenges facing IKEA have been the difficulty of setting prices that attract customers and benefit the company, the plethora of counterfeited IKEA products and the direct competition of other retail stores such as UK-based B&Q, the largest DIY retailer in Europe and the third-largest in the world which also has several stores in China.

Britain's B&Q opened its first store in China in 1999 and within five years it had opened 18 stores which earned a profit of £400,000 on sales worth £131 million. The giant Beijing store was reportedly one of the largest of its kind in the world: each day it expected around 5,000 customers, the average purchase amounted to more than Y650 and it did not seem to be unusual for young professional persons to spend a total of some Y80,000 on furnishings.[46] Such a sum frequently represented not only a portion of their own earnings but also contributions from their families who helped them with both a deposit on the house and its decoration. Although China's B&Q stores follow the usual B&Q patterns of lay-out or display and look very much like their counterparts elsewhere, there is a much greater emphasis on services or installations. Indeed many sales included some form of service and each of China's B&Q stores have a 'home solutions' section consisting of a floor of designers at computer terminals ready to create the ideal kitchen or living room or fit out an entire home according to the needs of any potential customer. This is because, as for IKEA, these stores are not so much DIY (Do it Yourself) as BIY (Buy it Yourself) or CIY (Choose it Yourself). Labour is cheap and there are few precedents for the professional classes involving themselves in or having the requisite skills for domestic installation and decorating. Some do take advantage to learn at the DIY classes arranged by these chains as well as from television programmes and magazine articles featuring 'how to' undertake home-fitting and decorating. B&Q was one of a number of such chains which expected to take advantage of the new interest in home-furnishings. In 2000, the *National Home Centre News*, a US home-improvement trade magazine, called China the next 'hot spot'.[47] In 2001, B&Q estimated that China's home improvement market could be worth about Y200 billion (US$24 billion), given that 'Chinese people have the money, intention and desire to improve their homes'.[48] However such forecasts depend on sequential house purchases but the experience of early home-owners among China's elite suggest that home purchases, improvements and furnishings tend to be a one-off event which once more or less complete did not invite successive moves or make-overs. It was certainly the case that, for the generation of China's elite surveyed by the *Far Eastern Economic Review* in 1999, almost 100 per cent already owned a wide range of domestic appliances including refrigerators, washing machines, air conditioners and colour televisions. More than 85 per cent had microwaves and VCD players with growing numbers acquiring video cassette recorders (75%), CD players (59%), digital cameras (24%) and

DVD players (12%).[49] What is interesting about the 6-year survey is that it showed that, for this executive class, once home ownership or refurbishment, domestic appliances and electronic goods were acquired, they no longer featured on the lists of wanted or desired items. In their place, car ownership and foreign or domestic travel and recreation began to feature high on elite 'wish lists'.

A car of one's own

In many consumer surveys in the late twentieth century including those of China's elite, it was ownership of or access to a car which constituted the most potent symbol of 'the good life' and by 2000 it was estimated that 40 per cent of car sales were to private owners.[50] The main obstacles to greater private car sales continued to be their high price with the most popular brands selling in the price range Y100,000 to Y120,000 which was a substantial sum even for China's elite. Although more bank loans had become available for car purchase and increased credit was available, most preferred to save and to pay in cash. The first generation of private car-owners had tended to be the super-rich earning high incomes, those in official, managerial and private entrepreneurial positions and the princeling sons of officials who could often be seen driving around Beijing in imported luxury limousines. Once fewer had access to official cars and small higher-quality cars became available in larger numbers and at lower prices, a growing number of high-salary office workers and young entrepreneurs began to own or aspired to own a car of their own in the near future both for status and convenience of travel. In China's capital city, a proverb circulated to the effect that if you go by foot you can cover 15 km, by bicycle 30 km and by car 100 km – so that visiting more distant kin, a restaurant in Tianjin or even the seaside at Beidaihe and other resorts became feasible journeys. In large sprawling cities such as Beijing, residents were more likely to appreciate the convenience of car travel than in cities with crowded narrow streets. For older age-groups, it was reported that it was the convenience and increase in mobility in all weathers which spurred purchase. However most city buyers were reported to be in their twenties and thirties and were more motivated by the desire for a lifestyle change than by a need to get to work more easily.

For the young, an automobile perhaps more than any other object signified a fast-moving lifestyle and a new-found sense of freedom. Toyota attempted to appeal to this age-group by using an advertising slogan, 'even further, even freer'.[51] Ownership of four wheels was marketed both as a potent and very visible symbol of independence and as an attribute of a successful and luxurious lifestyle. Mobility could be flaunted and envied. As early as 1997, the correspondent of the *Independent* reported there to be plenty of style-conscious hip young Chinese people who could not wait to drive down Chang-An Avenue, in light blue metallic BMWs, with the mega-bass sound system blasting out Coco or the Backstreet Boys. In numerous glossy car magazines such as *Trends Gentlemen*, a lifestyle magazine targeted at young professional men or middle-ranking Chinese male employees in foreign companies with high disposable incomes of between Y3,000 and Y10,000 (US$400–1000), car ownership along with sport and after-shave was associated with sportsmanship, celebrity, success and speed.[52] In 2001, the State Statistical Bureau reported that 4.6 per cent of China's households owned a car and that, of Beijing's 15 million population, 400,000 owned cars.[53] In the same year, a survey by the Association of Chinese Consumers found that three out of ten urban residents hoped to buy a car in the next 5 years and so replicate 'the good life' of the elite.[54]

In 1998, at the outset of the *Far Eastern Economic Review*'s six-year survey of China's elite in the three main cities, 14 per cent owned a car although about 50 per cent of the respondents intended to purchase a car within the next 3 years despite the high costs of automobiles and motoring in relation to income.[55] By 2000, 25 per cent of the informants owned a car while 20 per cent or so hoped to purchase a car in the next year. Then the most popular brands were a BMW, Mercedes Benz, Honda, Berwick (GM) and Volkswagen, in that order.[56] Two years later, in 2002, 58 per cent of respondents in Beijing and 41 per cent in Shanghai had a car, most of which were company-supplied, and 37 per cent in Guangzhou had a car, around half of which were company supplied.[57] By 2003, 70 per cent in Beijing, 31 per cent in Shanghai and 35 per cent in Guangzhou had a car and, interestingly, the proportion of company cars had declined in all three cities – to 36, 27 and 19 per cent respectively. More Beijing respondents preferred to travel by car to avoid the over-crowded buses than in Shanghai where a well-organised system of taxis and buses remained convenient modes of travel. In Guangzhou a high proportion (61%) owned a motor cycle compared with 12 and 19 per cent in Beijing and Shanghai. This survey also suggested that there would be an increase in car ownership following entry into the WTO when it was anticipated that there would be a wider choice of models at cheaper prices.[58] In the meantime, in 2002, one in two of Beijing's rich owned a car, which was considerably more than the overall average of only 4 vehicles per 100 of the capital's households.[59] If in the main cities increasing traffic jams suggest that car ownership and usage has constituted one of the most visible features of the new metropolitan high-income lifestyles so, more recently, has travel abroad for tourism alongside a host of new leisure or recreational activities.

Travel and leisure

In 1999 around 48 per cent of China's elite surveyed by the *Far Eastern Economic Review* placed 'travel abroad' as an essential component of 'the good life', although only 10 per cent said that they had already travelled abroad with 36 per cent expecting to travel abroad within the next 3 years.[60] The figures were not high but the very idea of travelling abroad for either business or as a tourist was relatively new. Only in the past few years have passports and foreign visas, which were previously and exclusively issued to high-ranking officials or their well-connected kin and students, become available to business entrepreneurs and high-income tourists. In 1999 travelling abroad for business was still more common than for pleasure but, even so, only 13 per cent of those surveyed said that they had taken an international business trip in the previous 12 months. Joint-venture employees, respondents more than 45 years of age and those with incomes of more than Y4,000 per month were more likely than others to have travelled abroad. The list of international business destinations visited in the previous 12 months included nearby Hong Kong (42%), Japan (18%), the USA (20%), continental Europe (19%), Thailand (15%), Singapore (13%), Malaysia (8%), South Korea (7%), Australia/New Zealand (8%), the UK (4%) and Canada (4%). As for travelling for pleasure, some 9 per cent of those surveyed in 1999 said that they had taken a pleasure trip abroad in the past 12 months, with 2 per cent reporting that they had taken two trips. Again joint-venture employees, those aged 45 to 54 years and those earning more than Y4,000 per month were more likely to have taken a pleasure trip. The destinations visited for pleasure over the previous 12 months included Thailand (44%), Hong Kong (40%), Singapore (15%), Malaysia (12%), South Korea (10%), continental Europe (8%) and Japan, the USA and Australasia all at 6%. However when respondents were asked which countries they would most like to visit in the next 12 months, they expressed a strong interest in travelling to continental Europe (30%), the US (27%), and Australia/New Zealand (24%), followed by Asian destinations such as Singapore (16%), Hong Kong (16%), Thailand (13%), Japan (12%) and South Korea (8%) with the UK trailing at 7 per cent.[61] In 2000 those surveyed travelled regularly for business and tourism, making on average two international trips a year – mostly to Hong Kong.[62] Three years later in 2003, over 30 per cent had a passport and between one-fifth and one-quarter of the respondents had travelled internationally with the USA (34%), continental Europe (30%) and Australasia[30] the most sought after destinations for business and pleasure. Hong Kong (37%), Singapore (21%), continental Europe (19%), Japan (16%) and Thailand (15%) were the most common business destinations, followed by the USA (11%), South Korea (10%), Australasia (8%), Canada (7%) and Malaysia (8%). Hong Kong was also the most visited tourist destination (36%) followed by Thailand (28%), Singapore (18%), Malaysia (14%), South Korea (11%) and continental Europe, Japan and Australasia all at 9 per cent. Most travellers surveyed used Chinese airlines and a remarkable 12 and 17 per cent of Guangzhou respondents purchased first class tickets on business and holiday flights.[63]

The travel experiences and preferences of those surveyed reflected an increase in the wider interest in and frequency of travel. Between 1992 and 2004, the number of outward-bound tourists jumped from 2.93 to 28.8 million.[64] Much of that increase took place from 2003 for even in October 2002, it was estimated that only four million Chinese had travelled abroad.[65] Such is the recent interest and enthusiasm for overseas tourism that the World Tourist Organisation forecast that the numbers would reach 100 million by 2020 with the Chinese replacing the Americans, Japanese and Germans as the world's top travellers.[66] In nearby Singapore and Hong Kong, their rate of spending has made the Chinese welcome tourists. Again, in 2002, it was reported that tourists from China spent twice as much as the Japanese in Singapore and already accounted for some 47 per cent of all tourist spending and 8 per cent of all retail sales in Hong Kong.[67] Two years later spending by mainlanders was reckoned to be worth HK$4,810 per visit, which was some 52 per cent higher than in a similar survey in August 2003.[68] In the battle for tourism in the Southeast Asian region, shopping festivals such as the Great Singapore Sale, the Hong Kong Shopping Festival and the Thailand Grand Sale play a major role in the attraction of Chinese and other Asian tourists who love to go abroad to shop and eat.[69] In Britain, where 22,000 Chinese tourists spent a total of £17 million in 2004,[70] shoppers at the Bicester Village outlet for fashion items at mark-down prices are often joined by 'an even more furiously focused group of shoppers or tourists from China who produce brown-paper patterns of the feet of family and friends to stock up on dozens of pairs of shoes from K shop'.[71] Domestic tourism too, and in particular short-distance two-day sightseeing trips, have become very popular during the past few years among relatively wealthy urban entrepreneurs, young professionals with disposable income and well-off elderly retirees. The introduction of the so-called 'golden week' holidays around Labour Day and National Day and the shortening of the working week to five and a half and then five days led to a surge in weekend and week-long trips. In 1999 more than 40 million Chinese spent Y14.1 billion (US$1.7 billion) on domestic sightseeing during the National Day holidays in October[72] and, since this time, record numbers have taken advantage of higher disposable incomes, more public holidays and a greater interest in and better facilities for short-distance tourism.[73] Even at the turn of the century, more than 40 per cent of the elite surveyed by the *Far Eastern Economic Review* travelled within China and 50 per cent thought that such travel would become a regular part of 'the good life'.[74] In preparation, many locations in China market themselves as tourist destinations. For example Hainan Island has rebranded itself as a playground for China's new rich, complete with beach resorts, golf-course, 5-star hotels, multi-storey condominiums, villas and shopping malls. With its own emerald beaches, this southern resort hopes to provide serious competition for Phuket and Bali.[75] That it has already found some long-sought-after success is indicative of the growing interest in travel not just for sightseeing and pleasure but also for sport and cultural activities.

The six-year survey also reflects the growing interest in cultural, sporting and other recreational activities. In the first year, 1998, more than three-quarters of the respondents said that they attended cultural events and more than 80 per cent said that they played a sport although not always on a regular basis. Many went to fast-food restaurants (70%) while more than 60 per cent enjoyed karaoke sessions – a favourite form of entertainment.[76] Wining and dining for lunch or dinner at a restaurant or at a night club or karaoke bar for both entertainment and business was common among the young and high-income entrepreneurs, with more than a third enjoying such entertainment ten or more times during the previous month. These elite high-income earners also spent a goodly portion of their income on entertainment and gift-giving to establish guanxi connections which comprise one of the most important means of doing business. On one of my recent trips to Beijing I was amused to note the name of a down-town restaurant in large neon-lit letters: 'The Social Court for Business'! When asked what alcoholic beverages they had consumed in the past 4 weeks, the favourites were local beer (84%), foreign beer (60%), red wine (52%), followed by white wine (19%), champagne (13%),

XO brandy (13%), 12-year whisky (7%) and VSOP brandy (7%). Not surprisingly, given the costs of some of these bottles, those in the high-income brackets were much more likely to have consumed alcoholic beverages than other categories of respondents.[77] In more recent years, investors have been looking for ways to encourage wine enthusiasts either by importing foreign wines or by improving domestic quality and varieties as well as broadening the mass market for cheaper Dynasty and China Great Wall wines. Wine has become a popular beverage among higher-income groups with an increase in the number of up-market outlets in the metropolitan cities. Again in 1998, just more than half of the respondents (56%) preferred to spend their leisure time and particularly Sundays relaxing with family and friends or to pursue personal interest hobbies (9%), watch television (8%), exercise (7%), read (6%) and shop (4%).[78] However, it was quite evident from the survey in later years that, although China's elite continued to work very hard, they would prefer to use their new-found freedoms and opportunities to seek a better work–life balance with more time for personal leisure activities such as reading newspapers or magazines and playing sport including swimming, badminton and table tennis or golf. In 2003, it was estimated that only 15 per cent of young persons between 15 and 35 years actively played sport, although it was expected that this may change with the prospect of the Olympics in 2008.[79] There are signs that in addition to golf, new recreational activities in gyms, health clubs or on dry ski-slopes may become increasingly popular. Within the home, as soon as new forms of domestic entertainment such as cable and satellite television, Hollywood and Hong Kong movies, the internet and CD-ROMs became available, these products and facilities were rapidly acquired by many members of China's elite.

Communications and computers

By the late 1990s, the 6-year survey of China's elite suggested that the previous interest in new consumer items to adorn the person and equip the home had been supplanted by a greater interest in computers, telephones and other means of communication. Ownership of a mobile phone, a fixed phone line, a desk-top or lap-top computer was more generally and increasingly common among those with high- and middle-incomes in the cities. Of those surveyed by the *Far Eastern Economic Review*, almost half had direct telecommunication access to the outside world with around 40 per cent using International Direct Dialing (IDD) lines installed at home. Those in Shanghai had the highest proportion (50%) followed by Beijing (36%) and Guangzhou (30%). Not surprisingly, respondents earning more than Y4,000 were more likely to have IDD lines (50%) compared with those earning less than Y2,000 per month (23%).[80] More than fixed lines however, it was the use of mobile phones which showed the fastest rates of expansion. Throughout urban China, the total number of mobile phones had risen more than ten-fold from 5 million in 1995 to 57 million in 2000, rapidly turning China into the world's second largest cellular phone market.[81] In 2000, Motorola was the most popular make closely followed by Nokia and Ericsson.[82] Indeed by the turn of the century, mobile phones were no longer considered to be a 'luxury product' in China's major cities and, by 1999, a high proportion of the elite surveyed had mobile phones (85%) and pagers (87%) with around a third owning electronic diaries. Again the proportion of those owning mobile phones was higher among those earning more than Y4,000 per month (94%) and dropped to 66 per cent for those earning less than Y2,000 per month.[83] By the end of 2002, almost all of the elite surveyed (98%) owned a mobile phone[84] and two years later a staggering 334 million or so mobile users had spawned a 'thumb culture', which in addition to phoning included a whole host of other activities such as complete communication and entertainment centres for playing games and for downloading news, music and cartoons.[85]

Following on from the mobile phone, it was desk-top and lap-top computers with new opportunities for email communication and access to the internet that captured the interest of increasing numbers of China's high-income earners. In 1999, about two-thirds of those surveyed owned a desk-top computer, 10 per cent owned a lap-top computer and 29 per cent had a printer with ownership of each directly related to income and type of employment, with those in either joint-venture or educational units more likely to own a computer. Twenty-three per cent of the respondents used a computer at home daily, but a higher proportion had access to a computer at work (76%) either on a daily basis (43%) or two or three times a week (23%). According to this same survey some 34 per cent of the respondents had access to the internet, with a higher proportion among those residing in Beijing and Shanghai (40%), among younger respondents under age 35 years (43%) and among those working in joint-ventures (53%). Around half of the users had access to the internet at home (53%) and 23 per cent said that they used the internet on a daily basis. A higher proportion (76%) had access to the internet at work, where 43 per cent said that they used the internet on a daily basis with another 23 per cent saying that they were on-line some two or three times a week. The majority of those who used the internet at the office did so to find information about companies (75%), to send and receive email (69%), to obtain news (47%) and to access either financial (39%) or educational information (22%). A few pursued on-line studies (14%). A small proportion (less than 6 per cent) used the internet to plan travel, bank or shop on-line, largely because these were all quite difficult operations due to restrictions on credit-card use and other methods of payment. This could change in the future as the government and central banks intend to make it easier for consumers to shop on-line and there are increasing numbers of small e-businesses in travel, retail and office-supplies or software and high-tech equipment.

Most of the respondents thought that the demand for and use of the internet would increase substantially in the near future and a further 17 per cent planned to purchase a desk-top or a lap-top computer (9%) in the coming year.[86] By 2000, 62 per cent had access to the internet at home, where it was mainly used for email communication and to access news and current affairs.[87] By 2003 about 85 per cent of respondents owned a computer, 20 per cent owned a hand-held computer and 50 per cent said that they used their computers 'a lot'. The majority were experienced web-surfers and nine out of ten of under-35s used the internet with almost equal numbers having access at home or at work, while a few made use of the expanding number of internet cafes. Among older respondents, 35 per cent of those over the age of 55 and 35 per cent between the ages of 35 to 55 years used the internet to search for information, send and receive emails and read news and current affairs.[88] The increase in computer ownership and usage among the elite surveyed was reflected in China's urban population at large. For instance by 2000 it was reported that a total of 13 million urban residents had access to the internet with a high proportion having access at home (45%), in the office (30%), in internet cafes (30%) or at school (13%). However for China's population as a whole, the numbers accessing the internet were still infinitesimal, growing from 0.8 million (0.12%) in 1997, 2.2 million (0.2%) in 1998 and 3.2 million (0.3%) in 1999 with an estimated 4.7 million (0.4%) in 2000.[89]

The shift in consumer interest to computers and communication alongside home improvements and travel did not completely cancel out the previous interest in personal adornment including designer clothes, accessories and jewellery. Even though such items no longer featured on the wish-lists of high-income earners or high on their lists of 'essentials' for 'the good life', a high 81 per cent of the elite surveyed in 1999 agreed with the statement that 'looking their best was important' to them, while 30 per cent reported that they wore designer clothes regularly or most of the time. Women (42%) were more likely than men (26%) to wear designer clothes, as were those under 35 years of age (40%) and those with incomes of more than Y4,000 (40%). The proportions wearing designer clothes dropped to 19 per cent among respondents earning less than Y2,000 and to 13 per cent among those older than 55 years of age.[90] It is commonplace in Beijing and Shanghai to see outlets for Pierre Cardin, Maxims, Prada and other well-known fashion houses, which along with many international brands had looked to the fashion-conscious elites of China as of Asia to maintain their labels and sales. The taste for diamond jewellery and especially diamond wedding rings also developed rapidly so that by 1999 China was reported to be the fifth largest market in diamonds[91] and, according to a spokesperson for de Beers, this 'boom market for diamond jewellery' was expected to become the world's largest market for diamonds.[92] Although many of the world's leading jewellery and watchmakers expected China to become Asia's premium market for such luxury goods, there is some evidence that the taste for designed fashion and diamond jewellery did not rise as much as expected, as other items began to take precedence in consumer preferences and budgets once individuals and families acquired new opportunities to purchase computers, cars and homes. By 2002–3, around a third of China's elite respondents said that they owned designer-labelled clothes or accessories including shoes, handbags, expensive watches and jewellery, which was a much lower proportion than those acquiring and accessing new forms of communication.[93]

In purchasing all items, questions of great interest among China's elite purchasers were quality, price and the association of these with brand labels. In 1999, some 59 per cent of respondents indicated that brand names were important to them; this importance was especially marked among males, the young and the higher-income groups. Indeed a goodly portion of consumer items already purchased were well-known foreign or joint-venture brand names, including entertainment equipment (92%), household appliances (84%), PCs/peripherals (48%), luxury clothing or accessories (29%) and motor vehicles (28%). However it appears that the group of elite consumers surveyed were becoming less inclined to buy foreign or joint-venture products as a significantly smaller percentage of respondents said that they planned to purchase foreign products in the near future. In this same survey, the foreign- or joint-venture branded items featuring on wish lists included PCs/peripherals (23%), motor vehicles (19%), entertainment equipment (19%), luxury clothes and accessories (7%) and household appliances (5%). Those that still favoured foreign or joint-venture products did so because they were still seen to be clearly superior to locally-produced goods. Just more than half of the respondents (58%) thought that foreign-made goods were generally of better quality than local goods which, indicative of rapid improvement in the quality of domestic products, suggests that these were increasingly in direct competition with foreign-made goods. Rather than name and price, it is quality and efficiency that attracted China's elite; indeed a high 84 per cent said that they were willing to pay more for better-quality products and services.[94]

By 2002 and 2003 however, a high proportion of the respondents surveyed reported a definite preference for Chinese brands, and this was particularly marked among those over 55 years of age (66%) and those resident in Beijing (70%). Just over half of those under the age of 35 (54%) report such a preference while men 'in a hurry' thought that they might well make quick decisions based on brand recognition.[95] Fashion and designer clothes were something of an exception, although even here more of China's elite were familiar with designer names than owned such a label. In 2000, only a third owned a garment or accessory bearing the name Alfred Dunhill (37%), Cartier (15%), Gianni Versace (12%), Gucci (11%), Louis Vuitton (11%), Christian Dior (9%), Hugo Boss (6%) or Burberry (6%), with a total of 37 per cent owning no goods or accessories with such a label.[96] Again in 2001, only a small percentage owned a watch bearing the name Seiko (16%), Omega (11%), Longines (8%) or Rolex (8%) although the latter constituted the 'most wanted' label.[97] As later chapters will also show, price and quality are increasingly seen to be combined in China-made equivalents, especially in the computer market where in 2003 the most ubiquitous were the home-based names of Legend and Lenovo with Intel, Dell, Founder, Epson, Microsoft and Compaq each having between 9 and 11 per cent of the market share.[98] Many and certainly greater numbers of the younger respondents were satisfied by items that had 'an international image' and it mattered less whether or not they had been imported. If the lower price of high-quality China-made goods increasingly influences the purchasing decisions of elite consumers, so too they are showing a propensity to save and a greater interest in purchasing financial products.

Money matters

Although the *Far Eastern Economic Review* surveys of the elite suggested that familial relationships, children and health are more important to the respondents than material riches, it is well to remember that they constituted a privileged cohort in terms of wealth and that they gave a great deal of attention to money matters as a pre-requisite for living well and achieving 'the good life'. Money has become important not only to the mega-rich but also to members of the next tier of China's rich who also aspire to a good life: 'It is good to make money, better than joining the Party – if you can make money you can live better'.[99] However the six-year survey also suggests that, even among China's elite, there is a growing trend for 'less' or 'more cautious' spending and for greater saving to ensure 'a better future for themselves and their families'. In 1998 savings were the number two destination for any extra cash[100] while, a year later, in 1999, those earning less than Y2,000 were more likely to save their extra income (58%) compared with those earning between Y2,000 and Y4,000 (53%), and even those earning over Y4,000 saved 40% of their income. Of those receiving the lowest increases in salary the previous year, respondents in Guangzhou reported saving 67 per cent of their extra money compared with those in Beijing (46%) and in Shanghai (37%). In terms of age, those above 55 were the most likely to save their extra income (62%) compared with the 35–44 age-group (47%).[101] Most said that they were saving because they observed that unemployment was increasing, they foresaw increases in the costs of rents, services and school fees or because they expected to purchase 'big ticket items' such as a house or car in the near future.

Although credit cards do not have a long history in China and cash is the preferred medium of exchange, 68 per cent of China's elite surveyed in 1999 said that they had a charge or credit card. Those most likely to possess a card included joint-venture employees (80%), employees of local firms (66%), entrepreneurs (61%) and educators (56%). Younger respondents under the age of 35 were more likely to have credit cards (77%) than those over 55 (51%), as were those earning more than Y4,000 (77%) compared with those earning less than Y2,000 (54%). Surprisingly some 43 per cent of the respondents reported owning an international credit card including Visa Classic (16%), Visa Gold (9%), Mastercard Classic (10%) and Mastercard (6%) with the remainder having an American Green or Gold card.[102] It is also a sign of the times that, by the turn of the century, 69 per cent of the respondents had life insurance, slightly more than 50 per cent said that they owned local stocks and securities and nearly 40 per cent had household insurance. Around a third of those surveyed in 1999 had foreign-currency accounts, although only a very few had unit trusts and mutual funds (2%) or foreign stocks and securities (2%). When respondents were asked what financial products they expected to own in the next twelve months, there was a wide variety of responses: local stocks and securities (14%), foreign stocks and securities (4%), foreign-currency accounts (7%), unit trusts/mutual funds (3%), life insurance (16%) and household insurance (19%).[103] These percentages were still small, but around the turn of the century such financial products were high on the list of anticipated expenditure in the coming years, although they remained secondary compared with spending on housing, car and travel.

Two years later, in 2002, and despite the continuing limits on the use of credit cards which is detailed in later chapters, a greater number of respondents had credit cards with 84 per cent under the age of 35 and 64 per cent over this age using plastic money.[104] In 2003, the majority of respondents also reported that they had accounts with or had performed transactions at a variety of banks, with around two-thirds using the ICBC (Industrial and Commercial Bank of China) followed by the Bank of China (50%) and China Construction Bank (48%). Few used foreign banks which remained well below their domestic counterparts with HSBC leading the way at 6 per cent followed by Bank of East Asia, Citibank and Standard Chartered at 2 per cent each and American Express, Bank of America, ING and UBS all at 1 per cent. More than 90 per cent had savings accounts and a growing range of financial products had been acquired including medical insurance (81%), life insurance (70%), real estate investments (50%), Chinese stocks (47%), household insurance (40%), car insurance (40%) and bonds (20%). Less than 5 per cent had foreign stocks, commodities, overseas bank accounts, unit trusts and futures options. The high-earners in Shanghai were much more likely to have purchased shares in domestic companies (60%) than their counterparts in Guangzhou (44%) and Beijing (35%), while 27 per cent of the respondents in Shanghai owned bonds compared with 15 and 17 per cent in Beijing and Guangzhou. A high 60 per cent of the respondents in Guangzhou and Shanghai had invested in real estate, while those in Beijing were more likely to have car insurance (51%).[105] Stocks and shares and real estate did not have the same reputation as savings for reliability and security and, given that profits and salaries fell by 12 per cent or remained static for the majority of respondents (48%) and that the costs of services had risen incrementally, it is perhaps not surprising that a high proportion (62%) banked as much of their monthly income as possible.[106] This emphasis on saving can also be linked to the degree of confidence which respondents had in their own and in their country's future.

There was a strong correlation between confidence in the future and income level, with around 50 per cent of those earning more than Y5,000 in 2002 'quite confident' that 'the future was bright'; of those earning between Y3,000 and Y5,000, 35 per cent were 'highly' and 52 per cent 'quite' confident that they had a bright future while around 20 and 50 per cent of those earning less than Y3,000 were either 'highly' or 'quite' confident that they had a bright future. More than 60 per cent of the respondents thought that China's population generally was quite optimistic about the future although the rest were not quite so sure; most thought that the economy would perform about the same or even a little better in the future although a small minority said that they were much more pessimistic about the future of the economy. As to WTO membership, the majority thought the outcome would be positive although a small minority thought that China would neither gain nor lose from its membership of the WTO.[107] Altogether the executive classes were continuing to enjoy increasing incomes and more prosperous lifestyles than ever before, with increasing ownership of well-furnished homes, cars, a variety of financial products and new opportunities to travel abroad. Although most expressed a confidence about the future and expected to maintain these incomes and lifestyles, they were not immune to the effects of rising costs and shared some of the general uncertainty deriving from rising unemployment and lesser social security. They too, along with the general population at large, increased their savings to 'bank for the future'. Indeed it was estimated in April 2004 that more than a half of the country's cash deposits were owned by the richest 5 per cent of China's population.[108] This did not mean that the elite stopped spending but that, in their own words, they did so 'more cautiously and wisely'. Nevertheless throughout the reform years, they have practically and symbolically been perceived as already living the good life to which all might aspire – very much in line with Deng Xiaoping's dictum of encouraging some to get rich first – to be followed by others. However if some have got rich first, it is not at all clear that their lifestyles and consumer habits will be emulated by rising numbers of middle-income earners who for many years have been expected to follow suit and swell the numbers of middle-class consumers in contemporary China.

The middle classes

There is a widespread assumption that rapid economic growth and booming private enterprise have led to a new and burgeoning middle class with spending habits to match their expanding aspirations. Outside of China, business analysts look to a rising and aspiring middle class to expand China's market beyond the small but conspicuous elite. Over the years Western media reports have spoken seductively of 'the stunning growth of a flourishing Chinese middle class',[109] the 'swelling ranks of China's affluent',[110] 'one of the fastest growing middle classes in the world',[111] and 'an increasingly populous upper and middle class in China'.[112] Within China, there are similar perceptions about the rise of the 'middle-income' or 'middle' strata. In November 2001, China's own chief negotiator at the WTO accession talks boasted that within 2 years 'some 400 to 500 millions or a third of China's population would enjoy middle incomes making China's market much bigger than that of the United States'.[113] Such estimates may have been used to stretch China's bargaining power at the WTO table for most calculations within China are more conservative. For example an official at the State Information Centre estimated that, by 2005, China would have 200 million middle-income consumers who could afford to buy cars and housing and spend money on leisure travel.[114] As with many other sets of statistics in China, there is little consensus when it comes to estimating the numbers of present and potential middle-income groups. A study of China's social classes published by the Chinese Academy of Social Science in 2002 was even more tentative.[115] It suggested that the country's middle class was still small in number amounting to only 15 per cent of the population compared with 60 per cent in America, and forecast that, even in five year's time, the numbers of China's middle class would be no more than 100 million people. The conclusion of the authors was that these numbers did not warrant the journalistic hype which surrounded the size, income and expectations of China's middle classes.

The same study suggested that there is a large gap between the very rich and those with middling incomes and that there is but a thin wafer of a middle class between a few super-rich and the large swathe of lower income groups that make up the majority of China's population.[116] The findings of these sociologists were supported by studies of the Gini coefficient, an international index used to measure income inequality, which have showed that income disparities in China had increased gradually from 0.28 in the early 1980s to 0.38 in 1995 to 0.458 in the late 1990s and to 0.5 in subsequent years.[117] There is a widespread consensus that these increasing disparities have direct bearing on patterns and directions of social mobility, leading to a polarisation between rich and poor and the squeezing of the middle classes already sandwiched between the few and the many. As early as 1994, a study undertaken by the Social Investigation Centre of People's (Renmin) University in Beijing showed that, in both the cities and the countryside, the richest fifth of households received 45 and 49 per cent respectively of total household income. In contrast the share received by the next or second fifth of rural and urban households was around 15 per cent.[118] In 2001 China's rich, accounting for less than 20 per cent of the population, still owned more than 80 per cent of the country's bank deposits.[119] The study of China's social classes published by the Academy of Social Sciences suggested that China's social structure is best characterised by a pyramid rather than the diamond-shape typical of Japan, Hong Kong, Korea and Taiwan where rising numbers of middle-income groups have left small proportions at the top and bottom of this diamond-shaped social structure. Some of China's sociologists writing in this study concluded that, instead of the diamond shape that might have been expected given the market reforms, the development of a private sector and the expansion of white-collar strata, China remains pyramid shaped with small numbers of people in high-income groups, very large numbers of people in the lower strata and fewer numbers with intermediate incomes than might have been expected. They also argued that with increasing income disparities and polarisation between rich and poor, the share of wealth received by China's high-income strata is excessive and makes inroads into the legitimate share of both intermediate and low-income strata. The resulting wealth pyramid showing the distribution and movement of income between various social strata suggested to them that it is not at all clear that a middle class will emerge in the future.[120] A similar study, based on the distribution of wealth in Shanghai, also suggested that a large middle class may not emerge there in the near future, for it too confirmed that there had been increasing polarisation between the haves and have-nots during the 1990s, leading to a widening gap between the few rich and large numbers of poor with 'not much of an intermediate group'.[121] Indeed there is widespread government, academic and retail concern about the lack of social mobility and the inability of low-income groups to better their position and acquire middle-class lifestyles.

Although skilled and technically qualified employees in the state-owned enterprises, civil servants and other white-collar employees may earn middle-incomes, very few experience upward mobility into elite income levels of Y2,000 or more per month which is around three times the average urban annual income of around Y8,000 per year, or expect to appropriate a lifestyle to match. On the contrary, most feel themselves to be struggling to maintain their previous standard of living or to be increasingly impoverished and downwardly mobile. Incomes for much of the middle strata are not rising fast enough to keep pace with costs and aspirations even though civil servants and others have received small rises in income. For example between 1999 and 2002, civil servants received three pay rises ranging between Y80 and Y100 per month, amounting to typical salaries of around Y1,200 per month out of which increasing subsistence and service costs have to be met although they also receive a range of supplementary benefits.[122] In addition the tax system relies heavily on middle-income salaried workers. Although a systematic and regular taxation system was introduced in 1994, it was estimated in 2001 that most of the tax-paying population was made up of salaried categories and foreign expatriates with China's own rich paying personal income taxes that amounted to less than 10 per cent of the total. This calculation led an article in *China Daily* to conclude that China's richest personnel including private enterprise employers and managers 'have the smallest tax burden in the world' and that those earning the lower incomes have a much heavier tax burden than those who make more money.[123] The spectre of graduate unemployment and further lay-offs in the state-owned enterprises and the civil service outlined in later chapters have led to some degree of uncertainty and insecurity among certain of the existing middle strata who not only have less in the way of disposable income but also feel themselves to be insecure and impoverished rather than upwardly mobile. They are very aware of the growing disparities between the few rich and themselves. In one survey in Wuhan, reported in 2002, three-quarters of the respondents thought that they lived in an unequal society with increasing differentials in which income or wealth, power or influence and higher education were beyond the reach of the majority of the population. They, like the majority earning low incomes, have continued to experience high costs and also feel threatened by the spectre of unemployment and old-age insecurity.[124] In 2002 too, Mastercard calculated that those earning more than US$5,000 per year, which might allow for the purchase of a car and saving for a flat, amounted to 64 million or 5 per cent of the population and might rise to 155 million by 2010.[125] So it has continued. In 2005, *The Economist* reported that people with money for discretionary spending were still in the minority, perhaps amounting to 300 million.[126] In the same year, *China Daily* estimated that the country's middle class comprised a mere 'sliver of the population' amounting to 100 million.[127]

The argument that it is the anticipated numbers of middle-class consumers that has led to exaggerated expectations and excess supply is supported by the slowing of retail sales from the turn of the century not only for houses and cars but also for durables including popular gadgets and phones. The market for small household appliances and white goods has continued to be overcrowded as local and foreign firms jostle for a share of a dwindling market. Despite over-production and lower prices, goods sit in workshops and on shop shelves. There is still little upgrading as those who have already made such purchases continue to be unable or are unlikely to do so. In 2003, The *Financial Times* drew attention to 'growing over-capacity' as a major problem in China. For example in the first ten months of 2002, China had made 24 million air conditioners and only sold 14 million. Others, including manufacturers of microwaves and television sets, expanded their capacity and as a result prices fell between 60 and 75 per cent so that firms increasingly turned to export to soak up excess stock.[128] The *Financial Times* reported in June 2004 that China's over-optimistic television manufacturers now have four times more capacity than they need.[129] By 2004, even the growth in mobile phones was levelling off, suggesting to business analysts that, though market penetration was still only 20 per cent, most people who could afford a mobile phone already had one.[130] Updated analyses of the sales of 'three new big things' including luxury-end houses and cars also followed a consistent pattern. There had been an upswing in the construction and sale of luxury apartments and suburban-estate villas in the early years of 2000 but it too was followed by an inflated housing bubble, a slowing of the market at the end of 2003 and a vacancy rate of 26 per cent for residential units despite falling prices and rents and the abandonment of many half-completed projects.[131] An expert on Beijing's development is quoted as saying that what the city needs is not the high-end residential, office and shopping complexes that it is getting but low-cost homes that could be afforded by most urban residents.[132] His advice has not been heeded, because still most of the flats built in the largest cities at the luxury-end of the continuum and floor after floor of empty skyscraper flats lie in darkness as they have been bought not to live in but for investment. In Shanghai it is estimated that four out of five luxury flats are purchased by non-residents.[133]

Similarly, the market for cars, often dubbed 'the hottest consumer product' and the ultimate measure of an accelerating middle class, suggested that the numbers acquiring a 'middle class' lifestyle were not rising. Here too there were fears that an early boom would be followed by a slow-down. In 2002, the data released by the State Economic and Trade Commission indicated that production and sales of cars had increased by 36 per cent with sales of more than 1.06 million units furnishing profits for the auto industry of 55 per cent to total Y38.5 billion.[134] A year later, in 2003, sales of locally-made passenger cars rose by 75 per cent to 1.97 million as more private buyers took advantage of a wider range of models at lower prices and the availability of loans for car purchase.[135] The sudden increase in demand, making China the third largest car market after Japan and the USA, took even the professionals by surprise. In the words of the Chairman of General Motors China: 'there wasn't anyone anywhere in the world in 2001 who forecast even close to what we've seen'.[136] Such rapid and recent increase in sales fed the numbers game and the ambitions of car-production companies. Optimists forecast that demand would keep rising, perhaps by as much as 20 to 25 per cent each year, and that China would overtake Japan as the second largest national market to the USA.[137] With forecasts like these, the world's top automobile makers who were beset by price wars elsewhere saw China as 'the new promised land'[138] and set about increasing their production capacity and lines. Volkswagen, GM, Toyota, Honda, Nissan, Peugeot Citroen, Daimler Chrysler and Ford announced new investment totalling more than US$20 billion.[139] Manufacturers of luxury vehicles including Aston Martin, Jaguar, Cadillac and Mercedes Benz all increased their production and/or retail centres in China. The rapid growth of the sport utility vehicle (SUV) market encouraged Beijing Jeep, Mitsubishi, GM, Honda and Nissan to introduce new models and increase production.[140] For saloon cars, limousines and SUVs, local makers also began to introduce and expand production lines so that competition for market share increased, leading to falling prices but also to reports of over-production, over-supply and declining sales.

In 2003, Goldman Sachs estimated that eroding market share and prices had halved the margins of the market leader, Volkswagen, to 5.8 per cent. Business analysts began to suspect that the spectre of over-capacity already stalked the industry.[141] In that same year KPMG forecast that in 2004 over-capacity would reach 90 per cent with China producing 4.9 million cars although demand was only for 2.6 million cars.[142] Interestingly a survey by General Motors indicated that in 2003 only 7 million of China's households could afford to buy a car.[143] Sales above this figure were largely fuelled by the government's encouragement of credit for the purchase of cars. A government crackdown on car loans has been responsible for the downturn in car sales since 2003. The growth in car sales slowed abruptly to 12 per cent in 2004 and fell by nearly 8 per cent in the first quarter of 2005 despite a price war among foreign firms which led to a fall in price of Volkswagen's popular Jetta model by one-third.[144] Just as the world's carmakers are increasingly relying on China with its 1.3 billion customers to make good shortfalls elsewhere, over-capacity problems are exacerbated by the expanding production of domestic car firms which are buying foreign-car technology and employing cheaper labour. Cheaper and smaller cars seemed to be attracting more customers at the bottom end of a market and here local manufacturers were more competitive than foreign-led ventures. By late 2004, domestic manufacturers had cornered the crucial market for small cheap cars such as Cherry's QQ and FAW's TJ 7101U which now appeal to middle-class buyers no longer able to borrow heavily to pay for larger vehicles produced by foreign firms.[145] Two of the top-selling models are now Chinese brands, largely because foreign cars remain expensive in relation to income and there was a growing consensus among analysts that demand could well tail off once the demands of the wealthy and middle-income minority were satisfied. Even present-day car ownership at 7 to 8 per 1000 is still miniscule in per capita terms,[146] and far from the numbers anticipated even three or four years ago. The founder of the consulting firm Automotive Researches Asia concluded in June 2004 that 'we are going for overkill just as we have in other industries'.[147] In 2004 too it was reported that the market for luxury goods in China probably amounted to only 10 to 13 million, mostly made up of entrepreneurs and young professionals working for multinational firms.[148] For all these goods and especially for cars it was admitted that 'the fact is that ordinary Chinese are not getting rich enough to snap up all the consumer goods flooding the market'.[149] Analysts concluded that 'to keep the Chinese Express rolling, the emerging middle class need to get on board'.[150]

In 2004 too, the founder of Automotive Researches Asia noted that 'China's rich are not a limitless pool. There is talk of an emerging middle class but I can't see it'.[151] They certainly could not be seen in the up-market shopping malls. As in the mid-1990s, regular observers like myself and media correspondents continued to comment on the numbers of 'depressingly empty' department stores and boutiques selling luxury and other items. Although it does also have to be said that many high-end retail outlets found it difficult to make a profit because of the high taxes and duties which can make goods 30 per cent more expensive than say in Hong Kong and the plethora of good-quality cheaper or counterfeited goods. Nevertheless there is a consistent pattern from the turn of the century showing excess supply and early saturation of a limited market confirming the conclusion of China's premier national newspaper, Renmin Ribao (*People's Daily*) that 'most people have yet to join the middle classes'.[152] The next two chapters illustrate why, despite the appearance of the super-rich and high-income earners in the metropolitan cities, the majority of China's population in both city and countryside have yet to acquire middle-incomes or, if they have middle-incomes, have to yet to acquire middle-class lifestyles.

5   An urban conundrum

Impoverished workers

In the cities, where now approximately 500 million or two-fifths of China's population reside,[1] much has been made of the rise of the affluent and the super-rich elite who have benefited from the reforms and are now to be seen in visible numbers in modern commercial offices, smart shops or restaurants, flash cars and new high-rise apartment blocks or suburban villas of large and sprawling metropolitan cities. However the majority of China's urban population are not members of China's elite and it is as important to assess how they have fared as a result of rapid economic growth and urban reform. Since the onset of reform, there is no question that for almost all of China's city residents, incomes and standards of living have risen and there are greater working opportunities and life choices than before. That said, these income rises, choices and opportunities have been offset for the majority of urban workers by loss of status, rising costs and less security in employment and livelihood than in previous decades. As earlier chapters have shown, there was a steady increase in urban per capita incomes in the initial years of reforms and these have continued to rise at the steady rate of 14 per cent per year from Y5,425 in 1998 to Y6,280 in 2000, Y7,703 in 2002, Y8,472 in 2003 and Y9,422 in 2004.[2] However steady rises and average incomes provide less than the full picture which at the turn of the century was as much about inequality and insecurity as about rising standards of living. Within the cities, the Gini coefficient showed that inequality had risen sharply over the years: 0.16 in 1978 to 0.29 in 1999.[3] Although in this standard international measure of income inequality, zero represents perfect equality, 0.29 may represent an under-estimation in that it does not take into account any undisclosed income of the affluent which may take it well above official estimates. In 2001 it was estimated that the richest 20 per cent of city households received 42 per cent of total urban income whereas the poorest 20 per cent received only 6.5 per cent of the total urban income.[4] While the Gini coefficients reflect growing inequality in the cities, there is also evidence as outlined in the last chapter that most of China's urban population are located at or near the base of the urban-wealth pyramid. In 2002, when the *Far Eastern Economic Review* noted the growing wealth gap within and between cities, it suggested that the number of poor was growing faster than the middle classes and super-rich.[5] These reports and similar field observations of my own and others suggest that, despite rising incomes and standards of living, many city workers were caught in a downward spiral of social and economic impoverishment.

One of the reasons for the decline in the social or political status of workers has been the general down-grading of the privileged status of the large numbers of factory workers in post-reform China. Twenty years ago, accounts such as this would have drawn attention to the privileged political and economic status of the urban proletariat, many of whom worked in the state-owned enterprise sector earning stable wages, higher than average incomes and many benefits including housing, health care and pensions. It might have been expected that this group which made up the majority of the urban populations in most large cities, would become the new middle classes continuing to enjoy privileged lifestyles which would gradually be matched by the growing numbers of self-employed in the private sector. Instead a high proportion of urban workers have lost their once-secure employment and conditions of work have changed in ways that have reduced full-employment, guaranteed rates of pay and social security. Certainly the workers themselves, after the initial flurry of opportunity and spending in the early years of reform, have felt themselves to be disadvantaged and impoverished as the state sector itself has been increasingly the subject of reform and down-sizing. Only a minority of the laid-off had the capital, skills and connections to make a purposive and successful transition to the private sector. Indeed many have been reduced to trading in the petty informal sector as their once-secure factory livelihoods were threatened or lost. As a result there has been a rise in the numbers of 'urban poor' made up of the unemployed, the low-waged and migrant labourers. Outside this official category, large numbers now work in the informal sector to earn low incomes and even those on middle-level wages, who also have to meet the rising costs of urban living, fear impoverishment or unemployment and now tend to save more than they spend. It would be true to say that for the majority of China's urban population there is an overriding concern for maintaining livelihoods rather than pursuing the lifestyles of the aspirant middle classes. That there has not been an equivalent upward mobility or the embourgeoisment of major sections of the urban population after the example of China's immediate East Asian neighbours is very much due to the transitional reform process. In China the marketisation of the urban economy has required the reform of the state sector resulting in unemployment or lay-offs in state enterprises, the under-development of a substitute private sector and the rising costs of urban living. In short, the privileged livelihoods of the majority of China's urban workers have been threatened over the past 10 to 15 years by the very process of reform itself and in particular by the restructuring and shrinking of state-owned enterprises.

State-sector reform

On the eve of reform, the significance of the state sector cannot be over-estimated. State-owned enterprises were the site of China's heavy and a considerable number of light industries, they produced around three-quarters of China's goods and they employed most of China's urban work force. Given that their production was planned centrally, they were less companies than arms of government-bureaucracies in that production and price were determined by state plans with the state both meeting the costs and accruing the income. For their employees, state-owned enterprises were dubbed 'iron rice bowls' because of the cast-iron guarantees of a job for life followed by a pension plus cradle-to-grave services and subsidies which frequently included low-rent factory housing, schools, hospitals or clinics and recreational facilities. The largest state-owned enterprises were like single-industry factory-cities providing employment, housing and services for all age-groups and over a wide range of activities. For thirty revolutionary years, state-sector employees not only enjoyed social security and socio-economic privileges unprecedented in China but also high political status as 'the vanguard of socialism'. If this all added up to a ranking and lifestyle that was the envy of the minority outside the state sector, the shadow side of this privileged political and social status was that, in market terms, many of the state-owned enterprises were unprofitable, produced unwanted goods and cost the government in both resources and revenues. Thus in the shift to a market economy, the dismantling of the large state sector constituted an important priority in the urban reform process. In the 1980s, the government began to free prices of inputs and outputs, assign responsibility to state-owned enterprises for their own profits and losses and introduce new codes for book-keeping, independent management and for determining bankruptcy. It was one of the legacies of central planning that enterprise managers had little sense of the relationship between supply and demand or as one enterprise manager put it 'any habit of linking factory output to the consumer'.[6] Not only did many state-owned enterprise products have little or no market, but many state-owned enterprises themselves were handicapped by out-of-date machinery, poor-quality management, corruption and the siphoning away of resources which together with the costs of supporting surplus workers and providing cradle-to-grave social welfare resulted in substantial and increasing losses.

By the mid-1990s, it was estimated that the number of loss-making enterprises had increased from one in ten in the mid-1980s to one in two a decade later,[7] and it was no secret that many of these loss-making enterprises became increasingly reliant on successive loans from China's state banks to stay in operation. In turn, the continuous draw on state banks and the accumulation of loans by state-owned enterprises led to expanding mountains of bad debt within the banking system – probably amounting to as much as 70 per cent of all bank loans.[8] By 1997 it was estimated that state-owned enterprises had accumulated Y70 billion (US$8.48 million) in losses, leaving the banks staggering under the weight of non-performing loans of around US$500 billion.[9] As the reforms proceeded, it became clear that the inefficiency of the loss-making state sector and its threat to the stability of the banking system could restrict or even undermine further economic growth. Indeed in 1997, the World Bank warned that the failure to address enterprise reform could 'corrode the very foundations and credibility of China's entire economic regime'.[10] At the Fifteenth Party Congress in the same year, China's leadership declared that drastic action was necessary to speed up the reform programme and push the majority of state-owned enterprises into profit on the grounds that 'If we fail to push the reform forward, there will be no future for our state-owned enterprises' and 'the reform of the state-owned enterprises is the key link in our overall restructuring'.[11] Thus this Party Congress gave the green light to a major reform programme for state-owned enterprises which included a number of stark alternatives: the establishment of shareholding or limited liability companies, mergers or closures. Speech after speech made clear that bankrupt or loss-making state-owned enterprises could no longer be bailed out by either banks or the government as in the past.

In March 1998 the new Prime Minister, Zhu Rongji, embarked on a second stage of state-sector reform as part of bold and wide-ranging programme affecting not only state-owned enterprises but also the civil service and the banks. The guiding principle underlying the restructuring of the state sector was 'grasping the big and letting go of the small' (zhuada fangxiao). In practice, this principle allowed larger enterprises to reform and prosper and become key pillars of China's national economy while smaller enterprises were to be sold or, if bankrupt, closed down. The majority of the state-owned enterprises that survived this process were to be cut loose from the state and those that remained within the state sector could no longer expect to be subsidised by bank loans. Simultaneously, steps were taken to reduce the burdens on enterprises due to supporting surplus workers and subsidising social services or welfare. This ambitious three-year plan aimed to transform China's ailing state-owned enterprises by either revitalising, selling off or shutting down some 100,000 state-owned enterprises, more than half of which operated at a loss.[12] The radical nature, the unprecedented scale and the social consequences of these reforms were such that collectively they were sometimes dubbed 'China's new industrial revolution'. Certainly such a programme posed an enormous economic and social challenge, at the heart of which lay a conundrum: how to modernise the state-owned enterprise sector essential to economic reform and further growth without creating urban unemployment and social insecurity on a scale likely to threaten the very stability of the party-state. It is this conundrum which has perplexed if not plagued China's leaders in their continuing attempt to reduce and reform the state sector in China. The social costs of allowing state enterprises to downsize or go bankrupt on the scale envisaged by Zhu Rongji were almost inconceivable. For a start, the reforms meant laying-off millions of workers and dismantling the system that guaranteed workers life-long employment, pensions and social benefits, thus radically redefining the previous socialist contract between urban citizen and state. The most immediate effect of these reforms was a rise in urban unemployment.

The unemployed

Both within and outside China, unemployment has been identified as 'the most explosive issue' with potential consequences for economic growth, social stability and political legitimacy. However because of the ambiguities associated with the term 'unemployment', it is difficult to define and count the unemployed of

China's cities with any accuracy. While numerous workers are 'unemployed' in the conventional sense of the term, those 'laid off' but retained on a 'semi-employed' or on a 'benefits only' basis and those 'awaiting' employment or 'not yet in their first jobs' are not always added into official estimates of unemployment. The term most often used in China to refer to those laid off is 'xiagang' which literally means 'denuded of a post'. Those laid off have been let go in terms of employment but they still have links with their work-unit which may continue to provide a living allowance, housing, subsidised health care or other benefits. Young persons entering the urban work force for the first time are often referred to as 'waiting for employment' and thus not counted in official estimates of the unemployed while under- or un-employed workers and rural migrants either trying for or between urban jobs are frequently counted separately. In these circumstances it is very difficult to obtain accurate figures on unemployment and in the on-going debate about numbers there is a general consensus that the actual numbers not working are much higher than those calculated for official purposes. According to government figures, it is estimated that between 1998 and 2002, a staggering total of between 24 and 26 million state-owned enterprise workers, amounting to 10 per cent of the work force, were laid off,[13] which is much lower than the estimates of some of China's own economists who calculate that as many as 46 million or around one-third of existing jobs were eliminated between 1995 and 2000.[14] A media report in 2001 estimated that since the early 1990s, more than 80 million or so former state-owned enterprise workers had been 'let go'.[15] Other unofficial reports at the turn of this century suggest that those officially-termed unemployed who numbered less than 10 million did not include the 20 to 30 million workers laid off or the 12 to 13 million or so new entrants to the labour force each year.[16] If all the categories are added into the unemployment statistics then, according to one recent report, the real number of unemployed could be as high as 100 million.[17] On the eve of the new century, the *International Herald Tribune* reported that China was fast becoming 'a land of lost jobs'.[18]

Some cities of China suffered greater losses than others. For a conspicuous microcosm displaying all the stark dimensions and challenges of China's urban conundrum there is no need to look further than the northeast provinces of China. Home to 107 million people and once the showcase of China's industrial development, it has more state-owned enterprises than in the rest of the country put together. It is now frequently referred to as a 'rustbelt' to describe the desolate landscape of an array of elephantine empty or idle factories. In the three northeastern provinces of Heilongjiang, Jilin and Liaoning, the bulk of China's heavy industry had been developed in the early and mid-1950s with Soviet help. Heilongjiang alone produced half of China's petroleum, 40 per cent of its timber, one-third of its heavy industrial machinery and most of its coal, chemicals, steel, trucks, ships and machine tools. The large factory-cities with their housing, schools and hospitals employed around three-quarters of the region's workforce who earned high salaries and received numerous benefits. However these cities, once dubbed the cradle of China's planned economy, have experienced a long downward slide as the northeast has fallen further behind the southern and eastern coastal provinces. Their share of production has declined to around 9 per cent of China's total, resulting in empty or idle factories and millions of unemployed or laid-off workers.[19] It is estimated that one-quarter of the 27 million workers laid off between 1997 and 2002 resided in the northeast. Officially urban unemployment in Liaoning province is 6.8 per cent, a figure well above the national average of 4 per cent and the internationally recognised danger-line of 5 per cent. However if the broader and conventional definitions of unemployment are used then the figures are much higher – hence other reports speak of 28 million laid off in the past five years with 'real' unemployment of more than 20 per cent.[20] In Daqing alone the work force is estimated to have shrunk by 15 per cent in the past five years and it is estimated that half the labour force in Liaoning's mining cities are jobless.[21] The unemployment figures for Liaoning province illustrate the rapid rise of unemployment in the mid to late 1990s from 329,000 in 1995 to 830,000 at the end of 1996, 1.8 million by the end of 1997 and 2.2 million or 18 per cent of the work force in 1998 as many factories either closed down or were in their death throes.[22] In Shenyang, the capital city of Liaoning province, it was estimated that as early as 1997 the proportion of unemployed was nearing 20 per cent.[23] For those remaining in employment or retaining an attachment to the factory, previous benefits including help with medical, educational and heating bills disappeared as factories shed their servicing and welfare roles and the state did not have the funds or mechanisms to assume the same responsibilities. In the cities of the northeast, unemployed workers felt increasingly disadvantaged by the reform process and have expressed considerable resentment about the contrasting riches of the coastal provinces. However, such high numbers of unemployed were by no means confined to the northeast. For example, in the city of Tianjin, Beijing's near neighbour, it was estimated in 1997 that around one-third of the city's 2 million workers had been laid off and that, as factories lay in ruins, 'being laid off' had become a daily threat to millions of workers.[24]

In theory, unemployed and laid-off workers were supposed to have access to incomes and allowances which were designed to cushion any stopping of or reduction in wages. There was a system of unemployment insurance in place which, established in 1986, was largely aimed at urban workers in state firms, although in 1998 a State Council regulation had deemed that insurance should be extended to cover those employed in private and non-state sector firms.[25] In 1997 it was estimated that 54 per cent of those in full-time employment, excluding self- and casually-employed workers, were covered and that 55 per cent of the unemployed received some benefit, the levels of which showed considerable variation.[26] For those who had been employed for more than 5 years, the benefits were supposed to amount to between 60 and 70 per cent of previous wage levels for the first twelve months followed by 50 per cent for the second year of unemployment.[27] However a survey by the State Planning Commission's Macroeconomic Research Institute at the end of 1999 disclosed that only 18 per cent of employed households were participating in any unemployment insurance programme and that the sums received were small and well below the minimum state-set levels necessary for subsistence. In four major cities, just 11 per cent of the employed were participating in just such a programme while among the unemployed less than 3 per cent were receiving any benefits.[28] One of the main problems is that the scheme is enterprise-based and very few firms could afford or chose to make the necessary contributions. Secondly, only a very few who lost their jobs were categorised as 'unemployed' and therefore eligible for pay-outs.

Similarly, although laid-off employees were entitled to a living allowance, the conditions were such that only a very small percentage of their number received any payments, despite further attempts by the government since 1997 to extend coverage. In Beijing, laid-off workers were supposed to receive a monthly allowance for two years of between Y145 and Y172 but, here and elsewhere, living allowances for laid-off workers were unlikely to be paid on a regular basis.[29] The large central city of Wuhan promised a standard payment of Y280 per month, but after conducting interviews with some 50 laid-off workers in autumn 2000, the scholar Dorothy Solinger concluded from this and other sources that 'hardly anybody' was receiving the full amount due.[30] In a survey of nearly 2,500 workers in ten cities of Hubei province, the provincial branch of the official trade union found that just more than a third were receiving an allowance.[31] Nationally it was estimated that only 3.5 million drew payments with most getting no allowances at all despite the fact that it was reported that Y84.7 billion had been paid out for this purpose.[32] Again, for a combination of reasons it was estimated that tens of millions of the laid-off either did not qualify for inclusion within eligible categories or that indebted and bankrupt firms could not afford their contribution to the funds out of which allowances were supposed to be paid. Income compensation was an important lifeline for those unemployed or laid off but even more important for their future well-being was an opportunity for re-employment offered by the creation of new jobs for those pushed out of work by state-sector reform.

Job creation

Of course not all those suffering job losses remained out of work and re-employment and job creation have been major policy priorities over the past few years. To this end the government introduced tax-breaks and other incentives to companies that hired the unemployed and laid-off and set up re-employment centres to provide job-introductions and occupational training. In 1994, an experimental 'Re-employment Programme' was piloted in 30 cities and then extended nation-wide. By 1997 it was reported that nearly 30,000 job introduction centres had been set up nationally.[33] The Beijing Municipal Bureau of Labour set up 214 employment service organisations which registered and held regular meetings of unemployed, offered occupational match-making services, conducted computer searches and set up training courses in hairdressing, cooking and dress-making.[34] In Shanghai, the municipal government pioneered a 'model' re-employment service centre which undertook to 'caretake' laid-off workers for three years by disbursing benefits and allowances, providing retraining and assisting in the search for new employment. This example was followed by others, but generally it seems that such re-employment services did not have the results anticipated. Many of the unemployed did find new jobs but it was estimated that fewer than 20 per cent of re-employed workers found such work through job introduction centres and many did not avail themselves of the services because of the paucity of jobs, funding and the cumbersome mechanisms available to help the unemployed and laid-off.[35] It is very telling that increasingly the government has encouraged the unemployed and laid-off to move directly on to the open labour market where experience suggested that they had more likelihood of finding jobs. The media variously reported that between 30 and 60 per cent of workers laid off or unemployed found new jobs via a range of alternative channels.[36] Many of those without work were to be seen in parks, on street corners or at other designated locations where in informal labour markets and for a few cents, job seekers advertised their skills via hand-lettered signs identifying them as would-be cooks, maids, clerks or labourers. However as more and more workers suffered job losses, it became increasingly difficult to create sufficient numbers of jobs to meet demand. One of the reasons the government has had to maintain high rates of economic growth is that it aimed to create a minimum of around 8 million new jobs each year. It estimated that an extra 1 per cent of GDP growth created between 700,000 and 800,000 jobs and on this basis a 7 per cent growth rate could be expected to create 5 to 5.6 million jobs and a 9 per cent growth rate a total of 6.3 to 7.2 million jobs.[37] Nevertheless the rate of re-employment has declined year on year from 50 per cent in 1998 to 42 per cent in 1999, 35 per cent in 2000, 30 per cent in 2001 and 9 per cent in the first half of 2002.[38] There was considerable variation in local rates of re-employment and much was dependent on surrounding resources, levels of investment and range of occupations. It stands to reason that unemployed workers in large cities such as Shanghai stood a much better chance of finding another job than did workers residing in regions or towns dependent on a single industry or mine which itself may be in a state of decline. In mid-2002, the Ministry of Labour and Social Security reported that about 60 per cent or 17.26 million of the 26.11 million workers laid off from state-owned enterprises since 1998 had been re-employed but mostly in the private and service sectors of the economy.[39]

The development of a vibrant private sector has been deemed one of China's greatest commercial achievements since 1978 when it numbered a bare 130,000 individual businesses.[40] Both the formal and informal sectors have expanded during the reform years, although again it is difficult to estimate the exact size of the private sector, largely due to definition and difficulties in counting. Some state businesses are, in effect, run on private lines by their management and conversely many firms labelled 'private' in official reports are in fact controlled by local governments. In early 2004, a Beijing-based think-tank reckoned that the private sector contributed just over 60 per cent of GDP inclusive of TVEs (Township and Village Enterprises) and businesses financed by foreign investors worth about 15 per cent.[41] Only a year earlier, the World Bank's Country Assistance Strategy report of January 2003 concluded that although the private sector had emerged as the 'most dynamic component of the Chinese economy', its contribution was nearer 30 per cent.[42] Whatever the precise definition, size and contribution, it seems that the private sector has grown around 20 per cent per year or more than twice as fast as the economy as whole and that it has been responsible for most of the jobs created in recent years.[43] It was estimated in 2000 that 75 per cent of urban jobs created were in the private sector[44] and that, between 1995 and 2001, private-sector companies created around 17.5 million jobs in some of the largest of China's private enterprises and export zones.[45] For example, large private enterprises such as Galanz produced one in every three microwaves sold the world over, Pearl River Pianos became the world's second-largest piano maker, Legend (renamed Lenovo) became the nation's number one PC manufacturer and collectively-owned Haier bcame the leading white-good producer in China. Firms such as these all built reputable domestic brands and extended their export markets into Asia, Europe and North America.

Although such large private enterprises are now referred to as an important part of the 'socialist market economy', in comparison to the state-owned enterprises they remained at a disadvantage in terms of access to capital, ownership rights and in their relations to the government. In 2001 it was estimated that the private sector still amounted to less than 30 per cent of GDP but private companies created 17.5 million jobs in the 6 years prior to 2001.[46] However, the World Bank's strategy report quoted above noted that, though the growth of the private sector continued, further expansion could not be taken for granted without further market reform and improvements in the business environment.[47] During the past few years some municipal governments have taken the necessary steps to encourage private enterprise in sectors that were customarily the prerogative of state-owned enterprises. In northeastern Changchun city, local authorities purposively set out to build a more favourable environment for the budding individual entrepreneur and put the growth of the private economy 'on the fast track'. As a result, detailed plans were drawn up, restrictions on access to private investment were eased and training programmes were instituted so that by the end of 2004 the value of the private economy had increased to 52 per cent.[48] Despite the establishment of large private enterprises to do with autos, food and health, most of the new jobs created in the private sector in China's cities have been in the wholesale, retail, dining, entertainment and other service sectors. Many are in what is usually termed the informal sector and it was estimated that between 1995 and 2001, an additional 75 million 'quasi-private' new jobs lay outside the official statistics or in the 'shadow economy' which included street vending, casual construction work and domestic service.[49] Indeed it was the myriad of small family-run firms, 90 per cent of which employed fewer than eight persons, that continued to make up the bulk of the private sector.[50] Perhaps the best-known family-controlled businesses are located in and around Wenzhou city in Zhejiang province where 91 per cent of its 240,000 enterprises are privately-owned companies making pens or low-voltage equipment and vast quantities of shoes, toys, ties, watch movements and Christmas decorations. One small town is a base for kitchen-equipment makers while another turns out 8 billion pairs of socks per year, amounting to one-third of all socks sold world-wide. In Wenzhou itself, 3,000 small firms have clubbed together to contribute parts to and assemble 750 million cigarette lighters or the equivalent of 70 per cent of the world's production. These businesses, busy taking global markets by storm, have created real wealth for their owners and employees, giving Zhejiang an annual urban per capita income in 2002 of Y12,700 which makes it the third highest in China, ranking just behind Shanghai and Beijing.[51] However although 'the Wenzhou model' has received much attention nationally and internationally, it has to be said that outside of such locations only a small minority of the jobs created have had such successful outcomes.

Most of the jobs created are small-scale, scattered and self-employed or in the service sector where casual employment, long hours of work and low wages are the norm. Many of the newly unemployed and laid-off have no option but to turn to the informal sector, which many do with a great deal of energy and creativity. Middle-aged, their education was probably disrupted by the Cultural Revolution and, without transferable skills, it has been much more difficult to re-employ them in skilled occupations in the state or private sector where information, insurance and financial skills are in great demand. Hence many of these former state-sector workers turned to casual work in household cleaning, street trading, catering, security services and property management or in community or small commercial services. Factories may have been in decline or sites derelict but, in the same large or small city, streets bustled with market stalls and sidewalk food stalls while pedlar vendors lined the pavements and sold their services or every conceivable item, often at heavy discounts. Despite evidence of much creative ingenuity, it has always been something of a mystery to observers such as myself as to how those in the same proximity and selling much the same objects – be they lighters, socks, soap, matches or any other goods procured for re-selling – could earn enough to make ends meet. Some, like one laid-off worker who had not been paid on a regular basis for the past 3 years and was still officially registered as a worker in an electrical machinery factory, had turned to moonlighting and earned more than his previous factory wage. He had purchased a ramshackle Lada for use as a taxi and, cruising the city for several hours each day, had picked up enough passengers to take home around Y3,000 per month, which was far in excess of his previous factory wage of Y300 per month. In co-operation with his father who was a low-ranking city bureaucrat, he eventually managed to share-purchase a house and set about saving to pay the education fees of his 11-year-old daughter. Now that the factory would not be responsible for his daughter's fees, he worried constantly about financing her education which already cost him Y300 per month. He feared that he would need Y40,000 to pay for high school and accountancy training but he was determined to find this sum so that she 'never ever has anything to do with factories'.[52]

Although stories about new jobs and high incomes for the laid-off abound in the national and international press, there have been as many reports of such workers who found it much more difficult to make ends meet. One young man on the streets of Beijing had been jobless for 18 months in the northeastern city of Harbin after being laid off from his job in the state grain department. With no prospect of work in the city, he finally left his family and journeyed to Beijing where he joined the ranks of the unemployed trying to make a living by illegally hawking goods on the pavements. He sold scarves and needed to sell 10 a day to live at the barest of subsistence levels.[53] More typical still is the story reported in *The Economist* which featured a couple of workers in their early forties who lived in the back streets of Shanghai and had both lost their jobs. Mr Zhang lost his job pressing caps when the hat factory in which he was employed was taken over and 150 workers were laid off; his wife lost her job when the food shop in which she served was merged with another. For a while, Mrs Zhang sold bedding on commission for one of China's new fly-by-night private companies but that too soon came to an end. At first they were more fortunate than most of the people in a similar position in their street for Mr Zhang received Y260 and his wife received Y140 from their former firms. However these payments were not expected to last much longer, so Mr Zhang peddled rice bowls and chopsticks in the street while his wife got up at 3am to cook rice balls to sell to those queuing at the bus stop. Because they were either 'not qualified' or 'too old' for any likely jobs, they did not expect to be re-employed in a factory or indeed in the formal sector. They lived in constant fear that as the pace of lay-offs rose in their city, there would be increasing competition in the street which would depress the market for chopsticks, rice bowls and rice balls in their neighbourhood.[54]

Dorothy Solinger's observations and research in the large mid-China city of Wuhan confirmed that the fears of the laid-off were more than justified. Again she thought it was difficult to see how competing vendors could earn sufficiently to make a living.

> Along the streets ... you can get your shoes shined for two yuan by three different pedlars in just one block; buy the same pair of nylons for the same 10 yuan or the same ballpoint pen for two or three yuan in the same lane or you can choose any one of ten pedicabs to deliver you as far as a couple of miles away for as little as three to five yuan.[55]

Many of the laid-off workers she interviewed told similar stories illustrating a common and downward trajectory. One of her many Wuhan informants was a female worker who, first let go by her own firm and later dismissed from a private enterprise when its business deteriorated, was currently dishwashing at a restaurant for 12 hours per day for Y300 per month or about US$1 per hour. Another, in her third post-enterprise position, was charged with simply standing at the gates of the idle plant where she had once been gainfully and purposefully employed. A third woman did housework when contracted by the local Women's Federation which could amount to as little as once a month at an hourly rate of Y3.2 earning her a mere Y30 per month. Dorothy Solinger found that these sobering vignettes and those that graced the pages of Wuhan city papers typified the lot of the unemployed or laid-off who went on to find work in this most crowded of informal sectors.[56] In addition to the practical difficulties, what also irked this first generation of informal-sector workers was that they had been forced to leave steady jobs in which they had felt themselves to be privileged and valued. In this process, they had to abandon an 'iron rice bowl' and instead 'create their own rice bowl' which rarely gained anywhere near 'iron' status or security. As a trade-union official journal noted, it was like an American dream in reverse – they woke up poor!

> For a long time, they've been drifting outside the enterprise in a socially marginal situation, especially those in small-scale, scattered, mobile informal departments … They meet up with many problems and annoyance, but lack any organisation's loving care, are without any opportunity to get education or to participate in society.[57]

In a similar vein, the very fine and experienced scholar of labour market reform, Dorothy Solinger, concluded: 'Regardless of the ambiguities, it is certain that quite precipitously millions of past renowned, now former workers are comprising a sorry – and terribly sizeable – mass of new-born marginals'.[58]

Worker resentment

The conundrum at the centre of urban reform positing enterprise reform against unemployment has generated a large amount of bitterness which periodically and increasingly spills over into unrest. Forced to find alternative work outside the state sector, this trajectory was so different from the life-long factory employment that the once-privileged workers had anticipated.

> I was stupid, I wanted to go into the factory because they told us this was the heart of China, the way forward. It would set me up for life. My parents said I'd share the iron-rice bowl. Huh![59]

Many had lived their working and family lives cosseted within factory compounds so that they were unprepared for the new challenges and opportunities set in motion by the reform process. Disoriented by the demands of a market and competitive economy, many began to wish themselves back in time and looked with undisguised longing for the days of the iron rice bowl. At their old workplaces, some of the idle gathered for much of the day drinking tea, reading the papers and 'grousing' until the shift whistle still blew. 'We call it the non-working day', they noted as they recounted, with all-too-apparent resentment, the way they had been left behind in the reform process. 'During Mao's time', one worker said, 'we would work hard because the factory would take care of us. Now if they do not pay us, we have nothing at all. Before social welfare came first, now as long as you make money that is all that counts'.[60] Rather than grapple with the complexities of today's reforms, many expressed a wish to return to the golden days of the 1950s before the Great Leap Forward and the Cultural Revolution. As one said, 'we respect Mao not Deng. Deng forgot about us'.[61] It was not uncommon for older workers to feel that they had given their lives to the revolution only to have received little in return during the reform years.

Many workers felt that they had not only been let down by the state but also abandoned by the state as officials, bosses and managers were seen to pocket wealth, profits and assets. It was this sense of betrayal that caused even more resentment than their own lay-offs or reduced salaries. Some experienced a sense of hopelessness and could see no sign of alternative or improvement while others took a much more active stance as resentment gave way to labour-related demonstrations and unrest. For several years now there have been waves of small-scale demonstrations or strikes by Chinese workers expressing anger when factories stopped paying wages, ended both meagre unemployment and other benefits or closed enterprises altogether. As early as 1993 there were reports of up to 35 labour disputes in Beijing provoked by enterprises deducting or failing to pay wages and within a few months it was estimated that the number had risen to 137 such incidents.[62] Others who were owed wages demonstrated in the hope of forcing payment. In one case in Guangdong in 1997, women workers collectively demanded back pay owed over three months by a Taiwan-owned shoe factory. Yet others took to the streets in open protest about the severance or redundancy terms offered by bankrupt enterprises. In 1997 in Chengdu, the capital of Sichuan province, 500 furious workers blocked a road to protest over the announcement of bankruptcy by a shoe factory in which the workers had been offered redundancy payments equivalent to £3.83 for each year of service.[63] In 1997, the government, fearing a winter of discontent, tried to keep secret a wave of worker protests, unrest and violence by the unemployed and laid-off. Most of the public incidents or unrest were fuelled by the rampant profiteering and asset-stripping of venal officials. In Shenyang, workers complained that it was the way that predatory bosses pocketed undue wealth through bribery, kickbacks and payoffs that bothered them even more than their low salaries.[64] In Sichuan there was a series of cases in which workers blocked main roads as a result of the allegedly corrupt behaviour of silk factory bosses who were said to have misappropriated cash funds for their own use.[65] The events of 1997 caused one trade-unionist exiled in Hong Kong to forecast that 'the labour situation in China is a time-bomb waiting to explode'.[66] This turned out to be something of an exaggeration but thereafter there were several waves of protests and increasing reports of labour-related violence as a result of enterprise mergers and closures that laid off workers but benefited bosses. In some cases, violence erupted and bosses were murdered because severance sums were too low to tide workers over to new jobs or to start a business. In 2000, miners within 400 kilometres of Beijing were outraged not just by the derisory severance pay offered but also by the murky process of partition in which parts of the mine were transferred to friends and relatives of local power brokers.[67]

Over the years the numbers of workers' demonstrations grew, with reports that they numbered around 60,000 in 1998, 100,000 in 1999 and 120,000 in both 2000 and 2001.[68] In 2001, occupations of bankrupt factories and street gatherings were said to be daily occurrences in some northeastern cities with some gatherings also observed outside the City Hall or Provincial and Party Headquarters in Henan, Hunan, Hebei, Hubei, Shaanxi and Sichuan.[69] In 2001, a national report commissioned by the Communist Party again identified unemployment and unrest by laid-off workers as one of the most potent of threats to reform, social stability and Party rule. It acknowledged rising urban anger over unemployment and corruption which led to local and even large-scale conflict in the cities and forecast that the number of labour-related incidents would rise as tens of millions became and remained unemployed.[70] In 2003, it was reported that 10 million people had taken part in 700 protests and 600,000 complaint petitions against lay-offs, buy-outs and corruption.[71] Western-press observers periodically forecast that labour-related protests could multiply and eventually bring down the government. However, despite the rising numbers of demonstrations, the protests have so far continued to be enterprise-specific and muffled largely because the laid-off tended to retain their housing, services and benefits which tie them to the very enterprises about which they were protesting. As one Western diplomat noted in 1997: 'They are not content but they are not going to get in the government's face. This is not Gdansk'.[72] Although there are reported to be signs that labour is getting better organised especially in the northeast,[73] incidents still tend to be brief, fragmented and contained. This is largely because the government has recognised that the workers' outbursts are often justified, especially where local corruption is involved so that limited street demonstrations against local bosses and officials have been permitted in the hope that they will not expand and result in the spread of pent-up labour-related protests and violence.

A second and more recent cause of disquiet and rising public anger in the cities has been the loss of homes to make way for new and commercial developments. Since 2000 such cases are reported to occur at the rate of 80,000 per year in Beijing and Shanghai and, because of the Olympic Games and other redevelopments, there are plans to relocate another 400,000 urban residents by 2007.[74] Some years ago I can remember having my attention drawn to the single little old house that stood valiantly for many years at the foot of a tower block in central Beijing because the occupants had stood firm and refused to move. Now there are many reports of the way in which the fast redevelopment of China's main cities such as Beijing and Shanghai have forced people to move from their city-centre homes with little consultation or compensation that is deemed fair. Although those resettled are often offered alternative accommodation, it is often at some distance on the edge of the city and certainly the real estate is likely to be worth much less than their existing sites. Those that stay put or challenge the developers often have their water and electricity supplies cut off or are intimidated until they consent to leave. To make matters worse, the developers' agents often act in collusion with local governments and such has been the series of high profile conflicts between evicted residents and property developers that the government has amended China's constitution to strengthen the rights of property-owners. Nevertheless there are cases where lawyers and other spokespersons who have tried to defend the rights of those evicted have themselves been subject to some harassment.[75]

Such protests and evidence of disgruntlement and unrest sent warning signals to the government which has taken the threat of worker violence so seriously that, rather than risk the spread of demonstrations and spiralling unrest, it has stalled the reform process. I have often contrasted the sequence of the reform processes in the former Soviet Union and China: in the former, reform began in the cities and almost immediately stalled, while in China, reform was initiated with some success in the countryside only to be stalled once it embraced state-enterprise reform in the cities. China's government, despite its determination to pursue radical urban reforms and close loss-making state enterprises, has moved cautiously by starting and stopping reforms, taking half-measures or even postponing reform by bailing out yet again a failing state-owned enterprise. Despite the restructuring, mergers and closures after 1997, 174,000 of the original 262,000 state-owned enterprises were still operating by 2001.[76] It should also be said that some state-owned enterprises have successfully made the transition to become modern and profitable. When more recently in 2005, Will Hutton of the *Guardian* visited the shipbuilding company Hudon-Zhonghua, he observed that it had experienced spectacular growth by combining all the Chinese advantages of scale and cheap labour with a commitment to high-quality engineering and ICT systems. He concluded that it built high-tech ships as well as anyone and for a fraction of the cost.[77] State-owned enterprises remained dominant in the heavy industries such as power, steel, chemicals and armaments and in banking, telecommunications, wholesale distribution and in certain transport activities. However by 2000, it was reported that the state-owned enterprise share of the economy had declined from 75 per cent in the late 1970s to about 28 per cent. Altogether state-owned enterprises still accounted for some 44 per cent of the country's urban employment and for as much as 70 per cent of government revenues.[78] According to a report in *China Economic Review*, at the turn of the century state-owned enterprises still employed about 83 million people, represented 12 per cent of total employment and 47 per cent of workers in the manufacturing sector and accounted for 38 per cent of GDP, for 45 per cent of China's imports and for 50 per cent of its exports.[79] In 2002, the state still controlled half of industrial output and employed 35 per cent of urban workers despite having halved its workforce in the previous 12 years.[80]

Despite several years of reform resulting in a small number of 'giant' pillars of the state sector in oil, electrical power, steel and coal production and the establishment of the supervisory State-owned Assets Supervision and Administration Commission (SASAC), many of the remaining state-enterprises continued to be characterised by excessive employment, high inventory levels, low productivity, low capacity utilisation, inefficient scales of production, outdated technology and social costs. According to a World Bank study published in 2003, the overall profitability of state-owned enterprises doubled between 1999 and 2001 although about half still continued to run losses and only kept operating with government bail-outs and cheap bank loans plus tariff protection.[81] Thus it was anticipated that many of their privileges would end with banking reforms and the strictures of WTO membership when the removal of subsidies, reduction of tariffs and other forms of preferential treatment were likely to exert further pressure on state-owned enterprises, inhibiting them from engaging in an increasingly competitive market, improve their efficiency, reduce losses and reduce the workforce.[82] The state-owned enterprises likely to be most affected by WTO accession are industries such as machinery, electrical equipment, smelting and processing of metals, textiles, chemicals and chemical fibres, transport equipment, non-metal mineral products and food processing, which together still accounted for 72.5 per cent of the workforce employed by state-owned enterprises in 2002.[83] Media reports emphasised that additional job losses were inevitable as a result of continuing enterprise reform, the reform of the banks and membership of the WTO. In 2002, JP Morgan estimated that because of these factors a further 35 million workers or 17 per cent of the workforce were surplus or redundant to future requirements.[84] In the same year the *China Economic Review* estimated that between 2001 and 2006, state enterprise reform could lead to 35 million redundancies while membership of the WTO could cause unemployment to rise by another 25 million.[85] In 2003, the Minister in charge of SASAC said that some 2,500 large and medium-sized state enterprises were effectively bankrupt but had yet to be closed down[86] and in 2003, it was estimated that 6 million state enterprise workers could lose their jobs in that year alone.[87] In the face of such forecasts, perhaps it is not surprising to find that the government slowed or halted further restructuring and reform of the state sector which it feared could only add to the rising numbers of unemployed and urban poor.

The urban poor

Until the mid-1990s, poverty was regarded as largely a rural phenomenon and there were few official or unofficial references to urban poverty or to the poor in China's cities and towns. The low incidence of urban poverty, slums or street dwellers in China, unusual in Asia, Africa or Latin America, was largely due to the iron rice bowl made up of wages, pensions and subsidies which not only privileged city populations but generally shielded them from the worst forms of poverty. For those who worked outside the state sector in collective or neighbourhood enterprises, wages might be lower and the benefits less generous but they still allowed their workers to live above subsistence levels. Urban residents without wages or family support were provided for by the five guarantees of shelter, food, clothing, health insurance and burial expenses. Although there were inequalities deriving from differences in work-unit type, wages and benefits, these rarely translated into major lifestyle differences. This may have led to a uniform drabness but not to the observable wealth extremes so common in cities elsewhere. However, although the standards of living have risen for most and urban lifestyles are more colourful, significant socio-economic differentiation became a marked characteristic of China's cities during the reform years, leading not only to the emergence of the city elite as described in the previous chapter but also to the emergence of the urban poor. Since the mid-1990s there have been many references to China's 'new' urban poor and widespread concern at the numbers of households which fall below the urban poverty line. The urban poverty line is usually set at Y1,700 but, depending on location, can rise to Y2,400 per year which at Y150 to Y200 per month is deemed to be a sufficient sum to purchase the minimum acceptable food basket for an adult plus a margin to cover other running expenses.[88] In terms of the present average income of Y8,000 per annum, the poverty line represents austerity and is only sufficient to avert severe hardship.

The variations in the poverty line obviously affect official headcounts of the urban poor: the most common estimates suggest that, by the mid-1990s, some 12 to 13 million or 9 to 10 per cent of urban residents were living below the poverty line. In some cities the proportion was estimated to be much higher, reaching 30 per cent in the Shanxi provincial capital of Xian and 60 per cent in the northeastern city of Shenyang.[89] In 2002, a report by the State Council's Research Centre and the Asian Development Bank estimated that on the basis of per capita income there were some 14.7 million 'poor' but, on the basis of per capita spending, the corresponding figure rose to 37 million urban poor or 12 per cent of the urban population.[90] However even this revised estimate excludes the poor among migrant workers who were estimated to number some 30 million in 1999.[91] On the basis of per capita income and exclusive of poor migrants, 'the number of urban poor' was estimated to have risen to 22.48 million in 2004.[92] Hitherto, the urban disadvantaged or 'old poor' consisted of the elderly or disabled who had no family or kin support and households with a high number of dependants; now the 'new urban poor' is an expanded category made up of unemployed or laid-off workers, urban migrant populations and the elderly on fixed or small pensions. If the category of urban poor is more broadly defined then it expands to include lower-paid workers, often earning a wage of around Y300 to Y400 per month which is much less than the average city wage of Y700 to Y800 per month or Y8,500 per year.[93] Most of the lower-paid describe themselves as just 'getting by' with some scrimping and saving as they struggle to meet the basic expenses of food, clothes and education fees. One full-time clerk in her late thirties who worked in the general office of one of Beijing's big knitting and weaving factories earned Y300 per month which enabled her to 'barely make ends meet'. In an interview reported in the mid-1990s, she said that her priorities had become the traditional 'four basic necessities' of 'choie, mi, you and yan' or fuel, rice, oil and salt and that there was little left over to pay for the rising costs of heating which meant that she was often cold.[94] Even those earning a higher Y400 per month still found it difficult to make ends meet. For example one young married 36-year-old woman worked in a state-owned noodle factory from 6am to 5.30pm six days a week to earn Y400 per month with no housing or other benefits. She lived in her aunt's house so that she and her railway-worker husband could earn enough in wages and allowances to pay the tuition fees for her son's middle school. In an interview reported in the international press, she described how they 'scrimp and save', buy the cheapest food and never waste water or electricity. 'We can still get by, we can still eat every day. I don't want much for myself. Most of my hopes are for my child. Nothing else really matters'.[95]

Many feel a sense of frustration that things will never get better. As one taxi-driver who had waited at the airport for five hours in the hope of a fare said, 'I don't know how anyone will improve things. Even when we work hard we live bitterly'.[96] They are also aware of the growing differentials between their lot and that of their bosses. The full-time clerk on Y300 per month had resigned herself to the growing wealth gap that has left workers like her behind: 'We are helpless. Rich people can be capable', she also added with some resentment, 'they also have lots of guanxi or influential connexions'.[97] When the 36-year-old woman worker earning Y400 per month was asked whether the state still took care of its workers, she retorted that 'you had to be kidding' and went on to say that, although there were now fewer differences between state and non-state workers, there was a much greater gap between bosses and all workers in both sectors. With thinly-veiled bitterness, she observed that the bosses took all the money and still got housing even though 'everyone knows how corrupt they are'.[98] In sum, several categories of city residents have emerged who feel themselves to 'just be getting by' and these do not include migrants who, while not always categorised as 'the urban poor', nevertheless remain the most disadvantaged of all urban social categories.

The migrant

In recent decades large populations of rural migrants have become a prominent feature of China's cities. During the revolution, one of the most stringent boundaries was that between city and countryside and there were few circumstances in which rural residents were permitted to cross the divide and move to the cities. During the reform years, movement was permitted and, since the late 1970s, it is estimated that some 300 million rural workers have spent some time labouring outside their home villages.[99] Male and female or younger and older rural migrants leave their families behind to work and to share dormitories, take lodgings or sleep on work sites, only returning to their families at periodic intervals. They either return temporarily during festival holidays such as New Year or in times of illness and hardship or on a permanent basis following a period in the cities. Some go to and fro for several years and, at any one time, urban migrants are estimated to be in excess of 100 million, although here again unofficial estimates suggest a much larger figure of around 120 to 130 million rural workers.[100] Some cities attract more migrant workers than others. For example, Beijing has an official resident population of some 11 million with up to 3 million migrants while China's largest city, Shanghai, although it has almost double Beijing's population can attract 3 million migrants within a single year.[101] In these and other large cities and the special economic zones of the south and eastern regions, migrant workers are concentrated in the lower-paid or temporary jobs in manufacturing, employed alongside other itinerant or unskilled labourers as cleaners, waiters, construction workers and rubbish collectors or work in sweat shops or make-shift factories. Other 'waidiren' or 'outside people' enter domestic service, offer their services as decorators or set up market stalls. For so many of the young and middle-aged, migration offers opportunities not just to find work but also to broaden their life horizons, to experience city life and perhaps to acquire new skills and savings.

Many of the younger migrants find their new lives in the city a welcome contrast to life back on the farm or in remote or derelict factory-towns. One young boy from Hunan province, eking out a living selling roses in the fashionable streets on the east side of Beijing, could be seen each night on his beaten-up old bicycle as he journeyed the 10 kilometres to a crude brick room over the west railway station which he shared with two other children and the adult couple who employ them.

Asked why he had come to Beijing, he said: 'Because my family has no money'. He earned a pittance but he thought it was more fun to be in Beijing than to work on his family's one-sixth of a hectare farm at home.[102] Another young man was sent from a far petrochemical town to Beijing by his parents who were worried that the unemployed 21-year-old with a humdrum school record had too much time on his hands. They feared that he was likely to end up in trouble as he did little but ride around on motorcycles with other youths. 'My parents thought it would be better if I came to Beijing', he said, 'there is more opportunity here'. The slim, quietly spoken young man had found a job waiting on tables at a Sichuan restaurant in the Palace Garden estate which is one of the sprawling middle-class resident developments rising out of farmland near the site of the main complex for the 2008 Olympic Games. His job, his meals in the restaurant and a warm bed in a nearby dormitory provided by his employer were enough of a pull. 'I love it here, I get a chance to meet so many people'.[103] My own interviews with thirty or so young migrant women who gathered together on Sundays in Beijing also suggested that it was the opportunity to escape from the village, to observe city life, to acquire a job and new skills and to earn and save for the future that had lured them all to the cities and was enough for them at this stage of their lives. Others, young and old, felt that they had no choice but to come to the cities, pushed as they were by the needs of their families and the lack of local employment. Choice or not, for most migrants their jobs were precarious and many struggled to earn enough to subsist and save.

One 41-year-old woman who had left the fields of Hunan to file metal badges and earn the equivalent of US$100 per month told a BBC reporter that she had never expected to feel that 'life is so good':

> I'm very happy. My life is much happier than my mother's. She had to stay at home and tend the field. I've seen the world, I've been out and now I'm earning money to build my own home.[104]

Another young man from the west of China earned £64 per month on a construction site in Shanghai and because he moved from job to job, so plentiful was the work, he was allowed to bring his wife. Although surrounded by luxury apartment blocks and living in one room with no running water or heating, they felt extremely fortunate. As the young woman noted: 'All my friends envy me. They want jobs here because wages are so much higher in Shanghai. Shanghai is the place to be'.[105] What happens to such migrant opportunities when 'history's biggest construction boom'[106] fades in the major cities is anyone's guess. Now many return home without having found pavements lined with gold or even the most menial of work. In extreme circumstances, unsuccessful migrants without alternative means of support turned to begging and became part of a growing army of beggars that has sprung up in China's cities in recent years. China's cities were beggar-free for many decades during the revolution and early years of reform, but in recent years the many beggars to be seen in the streets, around hotels and outside railway stations are often destitute peasants who have fled their poverty-stricken villages for the cities. Such numbers have impelled many municipal authorities to introduce regulations barring beggars from certain offices and areas of their cities.[107]

However if, for the majority, the opportunities and conditions of work and living were better than those they had left behind in the countryside, migrants also remained the most disadvantaged of social categories in the cities. At the end of 2002 it was reported that poverty was most severe among members of the 'floating population'[108] while a simultaneous report by the Development Research Council linked to the State Council and Asian Development Bank estimated that the poverty rate among migrants concentrated in lower-paid and temporary jobs was 50 per cent higher than for urban workers.[109] In work, migrants have been concentrated in the lower-paid or temporary jobs, sometimes having to sell their labour power on a daily or casual basis. Those employed in factories in city manufacturing or in economic zones may have the benefit of a steady wage but it comes with long hours, piece-work, rigid discipline and poor working conditions. Many are on short-term contracts or they themselves are only able to withstand the rigours of such employment for a short period due to strains on their eyesight or general physical health. Despite the promulgation of stringent safety and labour laws, the majority have no employment contracts which would protect their lawful rights at least in theory and work in hazardous and exploitative conditions where wages are withheld for months at a time and the costs of cramped lodgings are charged to the workers. The problem of unpaid wages, especially but not only in the construction industries, sometimes stretching to shortfalls of many months has become an issue that has received publicity in recent years. In 2004, the All-China Federation of Trade Unions estimated that the total unpaid wages bill owed to 100 million migrant workers amounted to around Y100 billion (US$12.2 billion) and there was talk of penalising employers who did not meet their back-wages bill.[110] According to a Beijing Youth Legal Aid and Research Centre poll of 8,000 migrant contract workers in eight provinces between December 2003 and May 2005, nearly half had not received the wages owed to them, with shortfalls varying between Y100 and Y5,000.[111]

There have been so many recent protests by migrant workers who, with wages owing to them, were unable to return to their families for the Spring Festival or had to return empty-handed, that the government has had to intervene. In December 2004, the State Council issued the Labour Guarantee and Supervision Regulation to give better protection to the rights of migrant workers. The problem is not so much the absence of legal rights as the complicated legal procedures necessary to claim against recalcitrant employers and the refusal of employers to issue formal employment contracts to migrant workers who make little fuss knowing that there are many others queuing for their jobs. Although some protest, most are reluctant to claim their due and embark on any legal process which is likely to be lengthy and have little chance of any favourable outcome. Most migrant workers say that they cannot afford to insist on the formal contract necessary to lodge an official complaint. Living conditions too are often in regimented dormitories or make-shift lodgings with a number bedding down at work sites. Those in large factory dormitories work from dawn to dusk and are so exhausted on their days off that they are virtually confined to their dormitories where they lived in spartan conditions and continue to be timetabled by a myriad of regulations. Indeed many migrants have rejected such regulated living and working conditions and the low wages that come with domestic service or work in the special economic zones of the south and voted with their feet. Already in Beijing and the coastal cities there is a shortage of nannies who earn lower wages, work long hours and have less freedom than say house cleaners who can earn twice the monthly income (Y1,000) of a nanny (Y500). In the special economic zones of Guangdong and especially in South China's Pearl River Delta there has been a shortage of labour, leaving many factories in dire need of workers since 2003 largely because of the working conditions.[112] Indeed there are signs that many migrants are becoming more discriminatory and may be able to claim better pay and conditions of work in the coming years. Many have moved on to Shanghai and to East China's Yangtze River Delta where wages are reckoned to be 5 per cent higher and working conditions better. But even in Shanghai, the government received 15,000 complaints and 3,300 protests in 2003–4 from migrant workers forced to work long hours or owed back pay.[113] As manufacturers move inwards looking for cheaper labour, migrants can also find work nearer their home villages, although it is probably the wage levels which will determine their final destination. The Ministry of Labour and Social Security thought that it was 'the matter of pay' that was all important:

> Statistics show that if a company pays a worker less than Y700 (US$84) per month, it will have trouble filling vacancies. If the offer is aboveY1,000 (US$120) per month, migrant labourers will flock.[114]

Outside the large economic and manufacturing zones, lodging conditions in the cities may be less regulatory and in some cities such as Chengdu in Sichuan province, penalties have been introduced for employers who do not safeguard the access of migrant labourers to the same rights as urban citizens including an insurance package contributed to by both employee and employer and consisting of personal allowances, reimbursement of medical costs and compensation for 'unexpected losses' such as industrial injury.[115] Few have such a contract and, even when they do, migrants remain 'second class' urban citizens seldom permitted to change their 'hukou' or registration from rural to urban residency.[116] This prohibition means that they are not eligible for urban services such as housing, health care and education or the subsidies, insurance and benefits normally available to urban residents. The incidence of anaemia, rickets and serious malnutrition has been found to be higher among children of migrant workers than urban residents[117] and, excluded from formal education, the plight of migrant children has attracted much attention in the national and international press. Most children of migrants have been educated in informal schools set up outside the state education system for they were both unable to pay the extra fees charged to migrants and to meet the stringent entry conditions into city schools. Where they do integrate, it is not an uncommon experience for migrant children, like their elders, to face discrimination because of their country backgrounds, ruddy demeanours and rustic ways. Migrants report that although they can be fortunate and find steady jobs, often working in the same employment for many years and earning good money, they are still treated as outcasts. In a recent interview with one migrant worker who had been drilling foundations in Shanghai for a multinational construction firm for nine years, earning twice as much as a new migrant labourer and working for 'a good boss' who provided free uniforms, washing powder and basic medical treatment, he said that he has never made a friend from Shanghai and still feels as much of an outsider as ever. Despite his many years in that city, he says that he is known as a 'mingong' (peasant labourer) which can easily become a term of abuse and no migrant he knows has made local friends.[118] Discrimination against these 'outsiders' has not ceased with time as they are often seen to be the cause of rising crime in the cities and a source of competition for employment in a tightening city job market. Although migrant and urban workers tend to occupy different segments of the labour market, migrants are regularly blamed for many social ills and indeed, to reduce tension and 'unseemly' migrant gatherings, the government has itself periodically cleared the streets and work-sites, sending many migrants back home. In recent years however, the government has been caught in a dilemma between migration as a cause of urban social pressure or rising crime and urbanisation as a useful means to reduce under-employment, poverty and potential unrest in the countryside. To reduce the latter, the government plans to move a further 200 to 300 million migrants to cities and towns in a step which, unless it is managed well, is likely to expand the numbers of 'urban poor'. Today it is not just the numbers hovering below the poverty line in the cities, be they resident or not, who continue to feel impoverished but so too do white-collar workers.

Urban impoverishment

Scrimping and saving has not been confined to the lower-paid manual workers, for those in white-collar offices and the professions have also found that their salaries have not been as steady or as high and certainly did not go as far as they had hoped. This had the effect of leaving them too with a feeling of impoverishment and insecurity. Although the wages of white-collar workers and those in the professions were much higher than for the lower-paid manual workers, the rising costs of health, education and other services and fears for both their jobs and their long-term security all contributed to their feelings of impoverishment and fears of downward mobility. Towards the end of the 1990s, the circles of risk had extended to include those in professional, office and skilled employment. In 1998, the Bank of China shed half of its staff and, in 1999, the four big commercial banks which nation-wide employed 1.3 to 1.4 million staff announced plans to cut between 10 and 30 per cent of their workforce. Mines and key industrial or machinery plants followed suit with China's two largest oil companies publishing plans in 1999 to cut one million jobs over the next few years.[119] However the most ambitious of government plans was to downsize China's large civil service in the interests of establishing a more efficient and competent public sector. Towards the end of the century, Premier Zhu Rongji launched a major programme to reform the administration and reduce the number of personnel employed by the state. In a three-fold programme aiming to separate government from enterprise management and to reduce the number of state and Party organs at central and local levels, the government planned to cut administrative staff by about 50 per cent.[120] In the government sector too, the over-arching slogan of reform was 'small government big society' which aimed to reverse the previous trend of 20 years when employees on the state payroll had more than doubled from 14.72 million in 1978 to 34.13 million in 2000. The government expressed concern that the ratio of government employees or those said to 'eat imperial grain' to those governed increased from 1 to 50 in 1978 to 1 to 38 in 2000. In the capital city of Beijing, it was reported that as many as 1 in 11 'ate imperial grain'.[121] Most of the reforms were directed towards reducing the 9.72 million bureaucrats who staffed the Communist party, government agencies and mass organisations at all administrative levels.

In 1998 the State Council was down-sized from 40 to 29 agencies and a quarter of its internal departments were closed and half of its workforce lost their jobs. In 2001, nine more state industrial administrations were abolished. The plan was to reduce the number of officials by some 50 per cent but, not surprisingly, this programme of restructuring, mergers and closures which resulted in lay-offs met with some considerable resistance. So great was this resistance that many displaced staff were kept on by other means or as a result of redefining job specifications, creating subsidiary organisations or granting temporary leave.[122] Nevertheless, in 2001, it was reported that the number of the country's administrative personnel had been cut by a total of 1.15 million, although this fell far short of the 50 per cent anticipated.[123] The Party too, proud of its size and protective of its influence, proved reluctant to reduce its numbers so that only about 20 per cent of its administrative staff suffered the cuts.[124] Despite the difficulties and resistance, at the Fourth Session of the National People's Congress in 2003 the government reiterated its commitment to administrative reforms.[126] Whether the government will be able to maintain the momentum of institutional reform is another matter for it has had a significant effect on morale. Although civil servants and public-sector professional employees are more likely to retain their jobs than not, their tenured positions, stable salaries and privileged benefits no longer feel so secure. For those employed in the professional private sector, wages might be higher but the provision of housing and medical insurance was no longer obligatory and largely left to the discretion of the enterprise. In fact the provision of benefits is variable and has very much depended on the size of the enterprise, the type of economic activity and the will of the directors. For example in high-tech enterprises, highly skilled professional staff were likely to be provided with housing and other benefits. Even within the same enterprise different categories of employees might receive disparate benefits dependent on the type of work, level of skill and experience or seniority. Nevertheless the benefits are not as widespread or as dependable as before, hence urban couples or families frequently try to keep one member within the state sector to take advantage of any benefits while the other(s) seek employment in the private sector where wages are generally higher. This arrangement is sometimes known by the popular expression, 'one family, two systems', which derives from the 'one country, two systems' framework applied to the relationship between China and Hong Kong. Such dual options are less available to today's younger generations for even new graduates are finding it much more difficult to obtain jobs than in the past.

In part the decline in graduate job prospects is due to the recent programmes of expansion in higher education which were intended to broaden access and improve the quality of the labour force and at the same time spur domestic consumption. In June 2003, the largest cohort of university students ever to graduate numbered around 2 million amounting to a 46 per cent rise over 2002.[126] Finding jobs for the expanding number of graduates in addition to finding jobs for the 10 to 12 million young people who enter the labour market each year is a daunting prospect for any government. Both the Prime Minister and Vice Premier have made several speeches about the critical importance of finding jobs for all new entrants to the labour force including graduates if they do not want to add to the 'huge', 'difficult' and 'long-term' task of reducing the nation's unemployment figures.[127] They might have added political instability to their list of fears due to disappointed unemployed graduates joining forces with resentful laid-off workers and disgruntled farmers. In 2003, in Shanghai alone, there were 83,000 new graduates and so dire were their prospects that 27,000 applied to take exams for the available 2,500 civil service jobs. In the same year, it was anticipated that about half or 50,000 of the 113,000 graduates in the southern province of Guangdong would fail to find work. In northeast Heilongjiang, where prospects for employment were even less promising, the number of new graduates rose by 25 per cent to 100,000.[128]

Although the government took steps to expand employment opportunities for new graduates by promising to create more government jobs and proposing tax breaks and bank loans for those starting up their own businesses, it also called on new graduates to lower their sights and consider taking jobs that are less well-paid and less prestigious – or even consider a move to the countryside to work in agriculture, health care and poverty relief. Not surprisingly perhaps, given the costs of higher education, students have shown some reluctance to abandon their hopes of a well-paid urban job. Many say that they would rather just 'await employment' in the cities than take a job in the countryside. As one student said 'people invest huge amounts of time and money to get an education on which they want every chance to make a good return'.[129] In conversation, most students say that they need not only a degree but also an element of luck in landing a job that is well paid and has prospects. The sudden rise in graduate unemployment not only affected the expectations and prospects of the younger generation, but many of their families too had hoped to recoup some of the expenses of a costly higher education and expected to rely on their prospering children for support as they aged without secure jobs or pensions. Thus few urban social categories thought themselves to be exempt from feelings of insecurity and impoverishment which in turn affected the balance between spending and saving in the cities.

Spending and saving

For most of the urban population, the later 1990s marked a sea change with the substitution of caution, retrenchment and saving for spending and consumer splurges. Many had already taken out a mortgage on the house in which they lived and most of those who could afford the basic appliances such as a colour television, refrigerator, washing machine and audio equipment had already purchased these items and were unlikely to upgrade from choice. Many aspired to further home improvements, computer ownership, a car and travel abroad but they only expected to do so 'sometime in the future'. By 1999 it was clear that the downturn in spending was not just a temporary blip as the rising numbers of jobless did not have surplus income to spend and those with jobs felt at risk and also did not spend. They were careful and 'nervous about spending money' as a result of concerns about economic growth, inflation, rising costs and their own insecure futures. In August 1999, *The Economist* correspondent too observed that China's citizens had reacted to the chill winds of state-sector reform, rising unemployment and higher education and medical costs by squirreling away their savings in the banks rather than spending their money: 'Consumers facing redundancies and the withdrawal of cradle-to-grave services are refusing to spend'.[130] In other words, they were unwilling to spend today what they might need tomorrow. Again in 2000 and 2001, although government leaders were talking about the need for a new and significant revival in domestic consumption, there was still no sign of consumer spending as urban residents, fearful of redundancy and rising costs, preferred not to shop and the money that might have been spent was saved instead.[131] Since the turn of the century, reports have continued to suggest that the majority of urban consumers remain cautious about making purchases – both large and small – because they are so worried about the future that they are saving large proportions of their income. Savings mushroomed and although some were set aside for a specific longer-term purpose, such as purchasing a computer, a home or a car, most of the savings were earmarked to meet the costs of education and other services or for a more vague 'rainy day' or 'the future'. At the end of 2003, household savings were reported to have risen 19.2 per cent to Y10.4 trillion, perhaps signifying that consumers felt a need to save for healthcare, education, housing, pensions and other services no longer provided by the government.[132] In 2004, a report also confirmed that, such was the search for security, increasing amounts of household income continued to be placed in savings.[133]

Although most express hopes that their situation will improve in the future, almost all, with perhaps the exception of the elite, found that they had either experienced or expected to experience some degree of impoverishment. The majority of urban residents, including former state-sector and other factory workers and those in managerial, professional or private enterprises, felt that there was a growing wealth gap with more downward than upward mobility. Rather than emulating the elite and acquiring their spending habits and lifestyles, those in the middle were busy affording public services in the short-term and securing their future in the long-term. Instead of advancing affluence and rising levels of education and employment, the embourgeoisment of a large section of the urban population has not taken place to the same degree as in other East Asian societies. Hence hopes of an expanding urban middle class in China with rising disposable incomes and domestic consumption are not backed by a closer examination of the incomes, expenditure and savings of the majority of urban residents as they go about their everyday consumption, meet the costs of services for themselves and their children and worry about their future security. Increasing the number of middle-income residents in the cities will require continuing or further economic growth and reform and both of these are placed at risk by the conundrum that remains at the centre of urban reform: how to pursue marketisation and at the same time maintain the livelihoods and not impoverish urban residents further. If urban reform is plagued by a conundrum, rural reforms too resulted, after some initial success, in an impasse which according to China's government may be best resolved by either increasing urbanisation and moving China's farmers to the cities or establishing anew 'a socialist countryside'.

6 A rural impasse

Fragile livelihoods

Achieving a 'well-off society' requires not only securing the livelihoods and improving the lifestyles of urban residents, but also those of China's 800 million or so who reside in the countryside who make up around 65 per cent of China's population. In January 2003 at a national conference on rural areas, Hu Jintao noted that rural areas 'face the most arduous tasks to realise the goal of building an overall well-off society'.

> Without the affluence of farmers, the country as a whole cannot become affluent; without the modernisation of the countryside, the country as a whole cannot modernise.[1]

Hu Jintao went on to add that, for this reason alone, the government should attach great importance to issues of rural development and focus on 'the task of building an overall well-off society in the countryside'.[2] Little over a year later, at the Opening Session of the National People's Congress in March 2004, China's Premier pledged to make improving the lot of China's hundreds of millions of rural poor 'a central task and basic goal for his government'.

> The works related to the countryside, agriculture and peasants are the most important among all the important works.[3]

Rural development, and in particular the improvement in farmers' incomes, is not only linked directly to improving the welfare and well-being of farmers and their families but also to maintaining China's long-term stability and economic growth, increasing productivity and expanding domestic demand. Successive leaders have stated quite explicitly that the rural sector with 65 per cent of the total population provides the greatest market potential and has a crucial role to play in reviving sapping consumer demand. Since 1998, much importance has been attached to developing the rural market.

> We shall tap the purchasing power dormant in the rural areas. One of the greatest assets underlining China's strong growth is its huge market potential among the farmers, driving up demand for both consumer and capital goods.[4]

Again in 2004, Wen Jiabao made the same point to top officials.

> We must always take increasing domestic demand as the starting point of our
> economic development. The key to boosting consumer demand lies in the
> vast and largely untapped markets of China's countryside.[5]

Accordingly, poverty alleviation and major rural development programmes in the
large and poor western and central provinces have been framed by the need to
boost consumption and increase domestic demand in the countryside.

Alongside the new emphasis on the importance of rural development and
demand is an explicit acknowledgement that farmers' living standards despite
initial rises remain far behind those of their urban counterparts, that productivity
is low, that under- and un-employment is common and that taxes, levies and fees
collectively known as the 'farmers' burden' generates both resentment and unrest.
After the early success of rural reforms raising farm family incomes and well-being
in richer regions, sustaining and spreading rural development and reducing the
wealth gap between town and countryside has proved to be a much more difficult
challenge. Both Hu Jintao and Wen Jiabao have lived for significant periods in the
less-developed western provinces and share what seems to be a firm commitment to
addressing the so-called 'three rural' or 'sannong' problems: nongyu (agriculture),
nongcun (village) and nongmin (farmers).[6] In recent years, the government has
initiated a major development effort in the large and poor western, northern and
central provinces and introduced a raft of reforms to reduce rural inequality and
resentment and to prevent a further and widened gap between China's villagers
and their urban counterparts.

Widening the gap

Given the long-standing and continuing inequalities between city and countryside,
it is ironic that farmers were the first to benefit from the economic reforms in the
late 1970s and there was a moment when they led the way in rising incomes
and in consumption. As a result of the market reforms introduced in 1978, rural
communes, production brigades and production teams were disbanded and
replaced by a production responsibility system in which land was distributed to
peasant households for their use in return for the sale to the state of fixed portions
of harvested crops and other products at prices set by the government. Over and
above such dues, farmers could grow crops of their own choice and sell their
products freely on the market. In addition, they were permitted to diversify their
activities to establish on- and off-farm sidelines or work part-time in many of
the new rural enterprises established in villages and nearby towns or even travel
to cities to find work. Agricultural production linking remuneration to output,
non-farm activities established by enterprising villages and towns, individual
commercial activities and migration-out in search for work all provided new sources
of employment and rural income. In the first years of reform, per capita rural
incomes more than doubled from Y133.6 in 1978 to Y397.6 in 1985; in the same

period per capita consumption also more than doubled, making rural households the chief beneficiaries of the new market reforms and narrowing the pre-existing urban–rural gap in which urban per capita incomes were more than twice those for rural households and urban household savings more than twice the level of rural households. Narrowing the gap was helped by the fact that urban incomes had risen by only 61 per cent, per capita urban consumption by only 47 per cent and urban savings had grown at a slower rate in the same period. However after 1985, when both rural as well as urban incomes rose slowly, rural per capita incomes, per capita consumption and household savings increasingly lagged behind those of the cities.[7] By 1992 and 1995, per capita rural incomes rose only 14 per cent while urban per capita incomes surged ahead, more than doubling in the same period. Similarly rural consumption slowed as urban spending per capita rose by 51 per cent between 1990 and 1995 and rural savings trailed off while urban savings deposits ballooned. Urban household incomes rose by 57 per cent between 1985 and 1995 so that, by 1995, average urban household income was approximately 2.5 times that of rural households.[8] Since the mid-1990s, this gap between urban and rural incomes, consumption and savings has continued to increase. Rural per capita incomes have consistently grown at half the rate of urban incomes so that in 2002 the average rural per capita income was Y2,476 compared with Y7,703 in the cities.[9] In 2003 official estimates suggested that urban residents earned on average three times as much as those in the countryside although several analysts in China, including an official in the National Bureau of Statistics, estimated that in real terms, the urban–rural gap was as high as five or six to one.[10] This gap, which takes into account the subsidies and services exclusively available to urban residents and the fact that the rural population pays more in taxes than they receive in subsidies and have significant production, welfare and other costs, is very high by international standards. If the slow growth in farmers' incomes has contributed to a serious and widening rural–urban wealth gap, the gap between rural locations also suggests that there is widening inequality within rural China.

In 1978 the range in rural per capita income or the gap between the highest in the south and the lowest in the north was a mere Y221, but by 2000 this gap had risen eight-fold to Y1,774.[11] For 20 years, from 1980 to 2000, the Gini co-efficient for rural China showed a rise from 0.24 in 1980 to 0.28 in the early 1980s, 0.31 in 1990, 0.38 in 1993, 0.42 in 1995 and 0.458 by the late 1990s.[12] To deal in averages conceals the inequalities and the differences in per capita incomes which are mainly regional or topographical. Indeed the sharpest divergences lie between coastal or eastern provinces and especially the rich metropolitan suburbs with ready access to city markets and services and the interior or remote western regions where villages can still be without roads or water supplies. One very good map published in *The Economist* in 1998 showed the range of GDP in China as varying from Y250 to Y500 in the western provinces, Y500 to Y700 in the central regions and more than Y1,000 on the coast.[13] In 2000, per capita GDP in the western provinces fell to just 40 per cent of the east.[14] In 2001, coastal regions with 536 million people had a GDP per capita of Y164,377 compared with central provinces with 439 million people and a GDP per capita of Y54,407 and western provinces with 286 million people and a GDP per capita of Y47,582.[15] Added together, the central and western provinces with more than 50 per cent of the population, had less than a third of the total GDP per capita of the coastal provinces. There is some debate about whether the poor remain concentrated in the 'officially-designated' poor counties, most of which are in the western and central provinces or are dispersed more widely across both lesser and more-developed regions. My own experience in the western and central regions suggests that the rural poor there have seen precious little of the wealth enjoyed elsewhere and, in 2004, one estimate suggested that only about 10 per cent of the poor live in coastal provinces while 50 per cent of the rural poor live in the west.[16] It is certainly the case that half the population of China lives in the interior, less hospitable and mountainous western and central provinces and that a goodly proportion of this population continues to hover below or around the poverty line despite the major efforts by the government to reduce poverty.

Poverty alleviation has been a major goal of China's government during the reform period and China has been widely applauded for its achievements in reducing absolute poverty in the countryside. The decline in absolute poverty, which began with the adoption of the household responsibility system and other economic reforms in 1978, has been the result of both broad reform-driven economic growth plus a much-advocated national poverty alleviation programme. Initiated in the mid-1980s, this programme was largely made up of the distribution of loans for agricultural inputs, education and services together with a variety of infrastructural projects including water-storage and road-building. Since the mid-1980s too, international aid agencies, bi-lateral and non-government donors have been urged to invest in poverty alleviation especially in the more remote western provinces where development programmes are largely located. Useful as these have been, my own experience is that the portfolio of specific poverty-related programmes initiated by the government and other international agencies has had mixed results and that China's much-admired reduction in poverty may owe as much if not more to general economic growth than to any direct poverty-related interventions. Whatever the impetus, there is every evidence that there has been a reduction in the population living below the poverty line although where this poverty line should be drawn has been the subject of some debate. Within China, official estimates are based on the government's austere poverty line of US$0.66 per day and show that rural poverty declined from roughly 250–260 million or a third of China's rural population in 1978 to 42 million or one-twentieth of China's rural population in 1998, to 29.3 million in 2001 and 28.2 million in 2002–3.[17] The World Bank, which deploys the less severe poverty line of US$1 per day, has calculated that the numbers living below this poverty line declined from 360 million in 1990 to 215 million in 1999, giving a drop in the poverty ratio from 28.2 to 17 per cent. It estimates that by 2015 the number of poor in China will have declined to 53 million.[18]

Whatever the precise numbers, the reduction in absolute poverty constitutes a major achievement during the reform years, although one of the most important features of China's rural society is the large numbers of farmers and their families who continue to hover around and just above the poverty line regardless of where it is drawn. If around 200 million are thought to live on US$1 a day, there may be as many as 400 million who subsist on less than US$2 a day.[19] That is, around half of China's rural population remain poor and vulnerable, earning wages that allow for little more than subsistence and which rise and fall with the vagaries of the seasons, employment, ill-health and fortune. This should not detract from the very real improvements in the living standards across much of China since 1978, but there have been fewer improvements than anticipated. At the outset of reform there were expectations that just as farming incomes in richer regions and households increased in the early years so others would gradually catch up, initial inequalities would close and a middle strata would emerge. Not only have these expectations not been realised, but rural society too can be represented by a wealth pyramid characterised by a small proportion at the top, a thin middle strata and the majority of the population at the base hovering around the US$2 a day mark with evidence of increasing disparities and polarisation in the countryside. In 2002, an article published in the *Hong Kong Economic Journal* warned against the real possibility of social unrest in the countryside as the result of the growing impoverishment of so many farmers as their incomes fell 'dramatically' between 1997 and 2000.[20] In 2003, it was estimated by the National Bureau of Statistics that of 807 million farmers, 22.8 per cent lived below the poverty line set by the government, 63.2 per cent had reached or exceeded this line, 3.7 per cent were relatively affluent and 0.3 per cent were wealthy.[21] A study by the Chinese Academy of Social Sciences suggested that not only did the richest one-fifth of rural households receive close to 50 per cent of total rural household income but that the incomes of the next-richer one-fifth of rural households, sharing less than 20 per cent of total rural household income, had sunk to match the incomes of larger numbers of poorer rural social strata.[22] In 2003 too, China's *Business Weekly* noted that despite the reduction in poverty, there was no room for complacency as 'the number of impoverished rural people remains alarming'.[23] In many ways the easy gains had been made so that continuing to increase the incomes of China's farmers has proved to be a much more difficult task in recent years. It has been especially difficult for farmers who rely solely on the land to make a living or to expand their range of agricultural and on-farm activities and thus sustain and improve a livelihood made all the more fragile by a depleted earth.

The depleted earth

One of the major changes in the countryside during the reform years has been the decline in agriculture as a proportion of GDP, of rural incomes and of rural occupations. By 2004, agriculture produced only 14 per cent of China's GDP which represented a decline of 19 per cent since 1982, while just 60 per cent of farmers' incomes still derived from agricultural field work.[24] Agriculture may still engage more than half of China's population but more and more villagers depend on alternative on- and off-farm activities to augment their incomes from the land. Indeed in the central and western provinces, poorer rural households almost entirely depend upon agricultural field income for here the range of on- and off-farm activities is much narrower than elsewhere. In these provinces, farmers often cultivate crops on less than hospitable terrain or in environmental conditions which require back-breaking effort for small and diminishing returns. However, for almost all farming households in the centre and the west, land comprises one of the most important farming assets and sources of income and security. Initially, during the early reform years, the distribution of commune lands to individual farming households equalised access to land and the periodic redistribution of farming land is meant to continue to maintain fair farm holdings. In practice however, the periodic distribution of land according to changing household size and composition has discouraged investment in land improvement or long-term planning and resourcing and is decidedly unpopular with farmers. Moreover not all land is of similar quality and, although much effort was made initially to equalise the distribution of land holdings according to type and quality, those who either benefited initially or have improved or invested in their lands have been reluctant to participate in any periodic pooling and redistribution. For the most part then, land holdings have not kept pace with changes in household size and composition and both land-short farmers and those with surplus land are known to enter into informal contractual arrangements with neighbours or employ additional workers to help farm their land. However even where household plots of land may be too small to develop or too steep to mechanise, the small plots of land are precious and carefully farmed as they are often the sole source of food supply and income generation. For centuries there has been a shortage of arable land which makes up less than 10 per cent of China's land surface and even in richer suburban fertile plains and valleys, productive lands are dwindling as a result of the expansion of metropolitan cities and small towns, the spread of economic zones and the use of land for non-agricultural purposes. The Department of Rural Development at the Chinese Academy of Social Sciences estimates that since the early 1980s as many as 30 to 40 million peasants have lost their land and, as Chapter 10 shows, it is the illegal encroachment on farm land for urbanisation and industrialisation often at the behest of or with the connivance of local governments which has become a subject of serious concern and the subject of many a protest[25] sometimes with violent outcomes.[26]

The scarcity of arable land is also due to environmental factors including water shortages and pollution, while many of China's upland areas suffer denuded vegetation cover and erosion due to long use, under-investment, flood and drought. In the central and western provinces where the dependence on agriculture is the greatest, both natural environmental factors and under-investment in the land have affected the quality of the land. Thus the majority of China's increasingly fragile lands are located in poor counties where the severity of environmental destruction is such that their population increasingly exceeds the carrying capacity of the land. Of all the environmental factors, it is China's water supplies, never plentiful or stable at the best of times, that have fallen to dangerously low levels due to drought, rising demand, pollution and pricing policies. By the late 1980s, it was estimated that China only had about a fifth of the world's average supply of water per person and in some regions the shortfall was even greater. For instance in the north and northeast regions of Inner Mongolia, Shanxi, Shaanxi and Gansu provinces, water supply per person is just 4 to 5 per cent of the world average. The larger area to the north of the Yangtze river possesses a mere 19.1 per cent of China's water supplies compared with regions south of the Yangtze which, covering 36.5 per cent of China's total surface area, contain 80.9 per cent of the total water supplies.[28] Even more alarming are the statistics that show that the combined area of the three valleys of the Huang (Yellow), Haihe and Huihe rivers account for 39 per cent of China's total arable area, 35 per cent of its population and 32 per cent of its GDP but a mere 7.7 per cent of natural water resources. In 2002, per capita water supplies in these three river valleys were estimated to be just 500 cubic metres.[29]

If the middle and upper reaches of some of China's largest rivers including the Yangtze and its tributaries suffer denuded slopes and soil erosion, large swathes of rural China and especially the loess plateau, an area the size of France that spans the northeast provinces, also suffer serious water shortages. On this plateau, the rainfall is around 20 to 55 cm or 8 to 22 inches per year and, when the rains do come, they tend to contribute to the erosion and soil-leaching common in the region. The government, aided by the World Bank, has made elaborate plans to rehabilitate the loess plateau via reforestation and these have had some success in encouraging higher precipitation and preventing loss of water and topsoil. However despite these efforts there has been increasing desertification. Few think of China as one of the world's leading deserts, but it has been estimated that centuries of continuous firewood collection, excessive grazing, over-cultivation and deforestation have turned a quarter of the country's lands into desert. In 2000, a Ministry of Science and Technology task force calculated that desertification directly affected 110 million people, cost the country around 2 to 3 billion dollars annually and that 800 kilometres of railways and thousands of kilometres of roads had been blocked by sedimentation. Indeed it thought a line could be drawn across China dividing the 'yellow' northwest from the 'green' southeast to show how the areas affected by 'useless sand' amount to 2.5 million square kilometres or 27 per cent of China's surface area.[30] A mere two hours drive north of Beijing in Hubei province there is clear evidence of encroaching sands due to a series of violent sandstorms dumping entire dunes into once fertile valleys. Moreover the sand is on the move, with dunes hovering only 70 kilometres north of Beijing and with a drift of around 20 to 25 kilometres per year, it may even threaten the capital city itself. Already it is possible to observe a surreal landscape with entire swathes of countryside stripped of grass, topsoil and mature trees with the ensuing loss of subsistence crops and livestock including horses, goats and pigs.[31] In this extreme case, farming has had to cease and animal grazing stopped in favour of massive spending on reclamation and replanting.

The increase in intensive farming and booming industrial development also make additional demands on the dwindling water supplies. Meeting the needs of Beijing alone has diverted precious water supplies from water-scarce Hebei province and there are reports that this diversion has affected the water available to farmers and led to some open feuding between local and national government bodies. Such an increase in demand is not confined to the northern and western provinces for the Ministry of Water Resources has estimated that, nationally, China consumed four times as much water for each Y10,000 (US$1,200) of GDP in 2003 than the world average.[32] As for the future, it is predicted that water shortages will peak around 2030 with per capita water resources falling to 1,760 cubic metres.[33] China's serious water shortage cannot just be attributed to natural causes, inadequate conservancy infrastructure and excess demand but also to waste and pollution. Many river and coastal regions have been badly affected by the pollution emanating from local industries which in some locations has reached such proportions that both water supplies, land, crops and animals have been badly affected. Indeed across the country, rapid industrial development has poisoned water supplies at an alarming rate, damaging animals, crops and drinking water. As *China Daily* noted in 2002:

> The shortage and contamination of water … have affected the sustainable growth of agriculture and menaced the quality of farm produce.[34]

An example that is often given is that of the Huaihe river which is said to 'badly pollute farmers' fields' along its banks[35] and it has been described as a 'foul smelling toxic soup'[36] or a 'foul-smelling oily black water full of dead fish' arguably responsible for the sudden death of 2000 ducks on the northern outskirts of Beijing.[37] In some villages it is reported that the waste from factories upstream has contaminated the water for irrigating the crops, while in others it is the villagers' own activities such as industrial-scale pig farming that are reported to spoil the water. In Shandong many of the 9 million farmers left short of grain due to a prolonged drought in 2003 argued that the water shortage had been exacerbated by factory waste which had made nearby rivers unusable either for irrigation or for drinking by farm animals.[38] In 2005, the water quality of the Haihe, Huaihe and Huang (Yellow) and other rivers was described as 'relatively poor'[39] and it was estimated that 300 million or one-third of rural residents drink unsafe water.[40] In many regions, it has been difficult to persuade local governments to forgo the temptation of rapid industrial development and quick profits in favour of avoiding damage or improving a damaged environment, although the increasing number of successful law cases claiming damages for pollution may persuade some to mend their ways. In the meantime, however, it is difficult not to conclude that a combination of natural and man-made factors have led to a serious depletion of the land and degradation of the water supplies so essential to agricultural livelihoods.

Agriculture is constrained not only by environmental limitations and degradation but also by economic factors such as the decline in returns from agricultural inputs and rising production costs. Initial improvements in the agricultural terms of trade were pivotal in explaining the high rates of agricultural growth in the early years of reform, but these came to a halt in the mid-1980s and it was only in 1994 that the terms of trade again improved, helping to end the agricultural stagnation that had lasted for nearly a decade. In the mid-1990s, prices paid to the farmers for the sale of grain and other agricultural products were increased and new arrangements made whereby state offices guaranteed to buy grain at these higher prices. In line with a continuing state monopoly, farmers were paid a 'quota' price for that part of their harvest they were obliged to sell to the state and a higher, fixed or 'contracted' price for the remainder. At the same time, the hitherto wasteful over-staffed grain offices were exhorted to reduce staff, improve storage quality and follow standard policies in grain resale. The result was a rise in productivity with a number of record harvests in the late 1990s. However the raising of guaranteed grain prices proved to be such an incentive that in the face of both local and national stockpiles, local grain offices were tempted to underpay the farmers or even resort to IOUs, while others with brimming silos simply refused to buy the grain. This practice became such a source of disquiet and unrest that some analysts argue that instead of insisting on production quotas, the government should withdraw from the grain market and substitute a free market without any state intervention. This would certainly be an unprecedented step given that central control of the supply and distribution of maize, wheat and rice has been a centuries-long hallmark of imperial rule continued by successive republican and revolutionary governments.

Most farmers still grow grains for their own subsistence as well as for sale to the state, but an additional constraint affecting all those growing grain and adding to the unpopularity of grain production among farmers has been the rising costs of production inputs and services which had to be offset against any rise in prices. It has been common over several years of field research to find that farmers are struggling to meet the costs of agricultural inputs such as seed, fertiliser and pesticide, never mind the costs of irrigation and maintaining or improving the land, and that returns from grain sales barely meet the expenses of production. Where arable land is limited and of poor quality, grain yields are often barely sufficient for family consumption, animal feed and seed and are unlikely to generate much of an income. It is then difficult for these farmers to meet production costs without an additional source of cash income which in fertile areas may derive from cash crops such as cotton, tobacco and oil crops or from the production of vegetables in locations close to city or export markets. However with the exception of vegetable growers who make a substantial profit, farmers including those in richer regions have to subsidise field cultivation with agricultural or non-agricultural activities either on or off the farm.

Non-agricultural occupations

One of the marked characteristics of the reform period has been the movement of farmers into non-agricultural occupations on either a part- or full-time basis. At the very least, farmers have attempted to supplement field production with on-farm sidelines such as raising pigs, poultry, goats or cattle or carpentry, bee-keeping and fishing, mushroom or silk farming. Throughout China, the most successful and richest of farming households are those which have diversified and/or developed a number of activities or income streams in addition to cropping. Indeed in much of coastal and eastern China, it is cropping which has become the sideline as these alternative on-farm activities take the most time and earn the bulk of the cash income. Many farmers are very successful and may move out of field production altogether to become specialised at raising livestock or undertaking handicraft or other business activities; in poorer regions many so venture but many also fail and many more dream of becoming successful entrepreneurs. Enterprising farmers I have worked with have shown much initiative, often reading about and then experimenting with new activities such as producing passion fruit, showing movies, developing a tourist attraction and other ideas which might be novel but highly risky and sadly sometimes quite unsuited to the venue. One very common pattern that I have observed time and again is the way in which one farmer who successfully produces mushrooms, eggs or some other product is then emulated by fellow villagers which then leads to mass production but no ready or large-enough market, resulting in stock-piles of unwanted products. Some of the most common constraints inhibiting the development of successful sidelines or specialisation include a lack of the start-up capital required by even the most minimal of sideline ventures and the shortage of micro-credit which would enable many farmers to purchase an animal or other asset. In addition to the shortage of credit, and as serious, is the absence of knowledge necessary to establish new activities or products and a realistic assessment of potential markets. Many times I have wished for colleagues in the field who had the requisite technical knowledge to consider the options for local farmers and help them choose what could grow or develop in a particular region or help farmers negotiate markets for both their agricultural and non-agricultural products. I have spent many years worrying about the most common solution recommended by both government and international donors alike, the ubiquitous orange tree, which struggles to thrive in the less hospitable central and western regions and offers a long-term and then not a sure market or secure profit to those who wait in hope. One of the reasons it is so difficult to raise rural incomes in western and central regions is not only the physical limitations on agriculture but also the less-successful development of alternative non-agricultural activities or local rural industries.

In the early years of reform, it had been anticipated that township and village enterprises would continue to be the key to rural development, providing new sources of employment, soaking up surplus labour, generating new and higher rural incomes and furnishing substantial local taxes for schools, hospitals and old-age support. As in the revolutionary years, rural industry was seen to be the major impetus for rural development, turning peasant into worker and bridging the rural–urban divide. By the mid-1990s, it was estimated that there were about 25 million township and village enterprises which managed as private or collective village businesses employed 125 million workers and accounted for 40 per cent of China's exports and 30 per cent of farm household income. Such was their importance that it was assumed by the government and analysts that township and village enterprises would lead the way in rural industrialisation and modernisation supporting both village employment, amenities and services and subsequently the development or expansion of small towns in which peasant-workers would both work and reside. Such was the vision, but hopes of realisation were dashed as many rural enterprises began to splutter in the 1990s due to competition from the cities, the substitution of capital and technology for labour in certain types of light manufacturing and over-production making it more difficult to market the most common of products. Only the most-established township and village enterprises on the east coast managed to survive, unlike many in the central provinces which could not compete with those in the cities and on the coast which had geographical, technical and marketing advantages.[42] In 1997, nation-wide figures showed that one-third of the township-run village enterprises had been sold off, turned into share-holding co-operatives or closed due to the vagaries of the market, local mismanagement or individual enrichment.[43] Indeed by the time township and village enterprises began or were about to be developed in the western regions, there had been a nation-wide slow down in the growth of rural industries as the market for low technology, low added value, low-quality and labour-intensive products became saturated.[44] Tougher lending rules and fiercer competition forced villages to close or privatise most of their existing collective industries.[45] The story of one rural hamlet in Hunan province which established a small chemical plant producing goods for export illustrates both the rise and fall of township and village enterprises. Initially it was so successful that the increasing profits both supported village services and added to the incomes of villagers, many of whom became part-time farmers with sufficient resources to purchase a refrigerator, television and modern furniture. Subsequently however, as a result of competition from elsewhere in Asia, the factory abruptly closed, leaving the village with debts and unemployed farmers who were forced to live on past savings.[46] This is only one example of many such factories which, producing chemical, dairy and other products, were forced to close down because of competition from more efficient distant plants. By the turn of the century, the scale of closures was such that *China Daily* observed that rural industries, 'once the nation's locomotive, continue to fade into oblivion'.[47]

Some of the township and village industries passed into private hands and many new small and large manufacturing and assembly plants have been established in accessible regions of southern and eastern China where, as a result of foreign or mostly overseas-Chinese investment, raw materials or component parts are imported and take advantage of cheap local labour. For example on the coast, in the Pearl River Delta or in other regions within and outside the special economic zones, manufacturing units are concentrated into highly-competitive clusters specialising in the production of goods such as clothes, sneakers, textiles, shoes, buttons or light-fittings. Here villages which previously had been almost entirely reliant on agriculture, often resorting to grain handouts in poor harvests or dependent on a handful of small sideline-factories to supplement meagre incomes, have been transformed. In many of these villages, turning the paddy fields into factories combining cheap foreign capital and labour has increased not only the world's supply of light manufactured goods but also the incomes of village peasants who draw salaries and pensions beyond the wildest dreams of their poorer ancestors, many of whom had long resorted to foreign migration to supplement family incomes. Now villages own factory sites and provide the electricity, water and workers, foreign manufacturers supply the raw materials and the machinery for assembly and village managers undertake to deliver the processed goods and pocket a processing fee in return. In the most lucrative of situations, it is the villagers themselves who have become enterprise managers, employing others to work in both factories and fields. One village, now more of a town, has become 'the light capital of the world' with more than 1,000 official and 600 or so unofficial lighting factories producing 46 per cent of China's total domestic lighting market and employing around 40,000 poor migrants, mostly young women from inland provinces, as workers. In the main streets of the village-town, hundreds of shop-fronts display untold variations in street lighting, chandeliers, halogen, central and bedside lights which on average change style once a fortnight. One resident in every 40 men, women and children is reported to be a factory owner while others have become wholesalers.[48] So successful has been the development of local industries that entire villages have given up farming in favour of local employment in lucrative village industries. Households may leave just one family member in agriculture or sometimes employ migrants to farm in their stead. Whether these villagers are re-categorised as 'town residents' or remain 'rural workers', it is confidently expected that they will constitute a hybrid urban–rural social category growing in numbers. In October 2002, data provided by the National Bureau of Statistics reported that between 1979 and 2001, the total number of people employed in agriculture fell by more than 20 per cent and as a result the agricultural share of total employment fell from around 70 to 50 per cent during that period.[49] Many of those moving out of agriculture also move away from their villages and migrate in search of a source of cash income to subsidise agriculture, invest in non-agricultural activities and improve standards of family living.

Movement and migration

Another of the major changes wrought by reform has been the movement of millions of rural residents to other villages, towns and cities to find work and the reliance on migrant remittances to augment the incomes of those back home. This migration was in stark contrast to the revolutionary years when very little movement was permitted, with grain and other allocations of essentials entirely dependent upon local household registration. On my first travels in rural China in 1973, I was struck time and again by the importance of location, location and location and the contrast in livelihoods between remote and mountainous villages with no topsoil and those nestled in fertile lands in valley, plain and suburb. As for those on the coast with the additional resources of the sea – they were in heaven! Mao Zedong's development policies were almost entirely based on the idea of self-reliance and self-sufficiency which meant that location very much determined subsistence foods as well as livelihoods, not to mention life-chances and life-choices. This all changed in the 1980s when villagers were permitted or even encouraged to migrate to other places to look for work. For most rural residents, the very idea of movement was a novel option or opportunity but it fast became a regular and normal practice for rural households in central and other provinces to have a member or members working elsewhere. In the 1980s, such was the novelty of movement still, that I used to joke that it was the suitcase which, more than any other single object, symbolised the changes wrought by reform. The total number of China's migrant population has risen with each year. In 2002, the National Bureau of Statistics revealed that China's floating population exceeded 120 million people of whom 42.4 million or 35 per cent had crossed provincial boundaries.[50] In 2005, *China Daily* reported that currently there are 150 million migrant workers and that four out of five rural families has a member who is a migrant worker.[51] Most migration in China is characterised by the movement of individuals rather than families and undertaken by men and women of all ages who, whether they work away from home for shorter or longer periods, make frequent visits to their families and friends at New Year or to help with busy agricultural seasons before eventually returning to their home villages. It was the temporary nature of their sojourn in the cities and the frequency of their travel between home village and destination that early earned rural migrants the label 'floating population'. The distances travelled might be short – to the smaller but expanding local towns – or comprise much longer journeys to major cities or to distant and richer coastal villages where they tilled the fields vacated by others. There are ambitious plans to build new towns to encourage movement and urbanisation which are discussed towards the end of this chapter.

At present, it is a fair guess that around three-quarters of rural migrants have moved to towns and cities with the remainder moving to other rural villages. It is the frequency of travel and the informality of much of the work which makes it difficult to arrive at a firm figure for the numbers of rural migrants in the cities at any one time. New China News Agency reported in 2003 that rural migrants constituted around 30 per cent of the urban industrial work force and that the provinces with the highest number of out-going migrants included Sichuan, Anhui, Hunan, Jiangxi, Henan and Hubei.[52] It is interesting to note that these are by no means the poorest provinces, which suggests that much of the migration across long distances is not necessarily undertaken by the poorest families from the poorest rural regions. Indeed, as elsewhere, the process of migration requires some initiative, knowledge and contacts so that in the poorest regions, the help of other villagers or local government bureaux and other agencies has been necessary to facilitate such movement. Much of the impetus for migration derives from family need and individual initiative but it has also been encouraged by local governments as a means of reducing food shortages or unemployment 'in their patch' and of making welcome cash contributions to augment local household incomes. Indeed the numbers of young female and male labourers absent from the village at any one time has left land cultivation and other agricultural activities in the hands of married and middle-aged women and the elderly, leading to widespread concern about the feminisation of agriculture. Given the customary role of women in China's agriculture, it is not at all clear that there are grounds for concern about the quality of their agricultural labour apart from the extra demands on female time. However, the scale of migration by both young men and women has led to a general shortage of agricultural labour in some villages which has to be of some concern. For village families, any reduction in labour supply is often outweighed by the transfer of cash remittances which have come to comprise an important component of household income in China's villages.

In 2003, national data suggested that it was the wages paid to rural migrants working in cities rather than any higher profits associated with farming that had contributed to recent rises in average rural per capita incomes. This report noted that between 1989 and 2001, the share of profits from agricultural work in farmers' per capita net income had fallen from 72.2 to 61.7 per cent, whereas the corresponding rise in the contribution made by migrant workers' earnings had increased by about 10 percentage points to 32.6 per cent.[53] A year later, an analyst from the Chinese Academy of Social Sciences estimated that 70 per cent of migrants sent a portion of their earnings back home with about half sending more than 40 per cent of their earnings. He concluded that remittances amounted to an average of 40 per cent of total rural income and that, throughout rural China and especially in poor villages, it is these remittances that have been responsible for improving rural incomes.[54] Certainly it is evident in village fieldwork that it is the rural households and communities that have migrant members which have a higher standard of living reflected in their new and larger houses and greater number of durables. The differences between migrant and non-migrant households are apparent but less so in the more remote western provinces as poorer migrants frequently find it more difficult to procure jobs that are secure, well-paid and not of the most menial type. Moreover as the previous chapter showed, migrants in the cities are often not paid regularly and owed back-pay. In the weeks before Spring Festival and other holidays, the media is filled with tales of migrant and especially construction workers who have not received the wages owing to them. In 2004 for example, it was estimated by researchers at the Chinese Academy of Social Sciences that migrant workers and particularly construction workers were owed a total of US$12 billion in back wages, which must have affected their return and reception back in their home villages.[55] For every story of a successful migrant remitting larger sums for house-building or smaller sums for sibling or children's education or consumer durables, there are stories of those who do not find work and return home empty-handed or with just sufficient to tide the family over for another year. Many leave their villages periodically to do just this as even small cash contributions can make a significant difference to a family's livelihood and help meet the rising demands that are continuously made on the cash incomes of rural households.

Cash demands

The major demands on the cash incomes of rural household across the country include cash for the purchase of production inputs, funds for education and health care and fees for local taxes and levies. High on the priorities of farming budgets are agricultural inputs such as seeds, fertiliser and pesticide and items necessary for sideline activities such as raising animals, handicraft tools or any raw materials for assembly. Even the poorest farmers scratching a living on less than fertile hillsides struggle each year to find the cash for seed, fertiliser and a pig or a few chickens. Without ready cash there are few alternative sources other than to borrow from family or friends, and one of the impediments to rising agricultural yields, mechanisation and animal stock or initiating other non-farm commercial sidelines has been the lack of access to small cash loans or micro-credit. Although there have been some poverty and micro-credit schemes whereby low-interest loans are made available for farmers by the government and international donor agencies, there is little in the way of small loans available for sustained agricultural or non-agricultural activities and even those available are declining. For instance, in 2001 it was reported that agricultural loans from rural credit co-operatives were only half of those obtained the previous year while a mere 1 per cent of loans for agricultural restructuring in Henan province had been 'firmed up' by 2001.[56] In 2002, Xinhua reported that 'difficulties in securing loans was a serious and increasing obstacle to raising farmer incomes'. It estimated that about 20 per cent of villages in major grain-growing regions were 'zero-loan villages' where farmers are reported to have said that banks 'support industry but not agriculture' and 'support the rich but not the poor'.[57] It is my own impression, gained during long periods of development experience in rural China, that it is not always so much a shortage of central government funds that is the problem, but that 60 to 70 per cent of the funds available have been diverted by local officials towards non-agricultural activities, leaving agricultural households almost entirely reliant on their own cash resources.

In addition to meeting the very necessary costs of production inputs, education constitutes one of the most expensive items on the household budget for all families in the countryside. For more than a decade, primary schooling has been compulsory in the countryside too, but it is also expensive as the fees can range from tens to hundreds of yuan per year to cover tuition, food and books, plus the costs of boarding for more advanced studies and in the more remote regions. As the next chapter emphasises, educating and enrolling their children in school is a high priority for most village parents who commonly dream of their children's success or mobility but, for all income-brackets, the costs of education are considerable and loom large in any household budget. Meeting the costs of schooling and finding the cash each semester to pay the fees is one of the most common topics in village conversation. Poor parents in the countryside save very hard to pay the primary school fees of their children even if just for a few years, but so difficult is the struggle that children enter school late and are frequently taken out of school when family funds are depleted or where their labour is necessary for the subsistence of the household. Stretched budgets are not confined to the poorer central and western regions for, even in villages near Tianjin and Beijing, I have observed and heard of cases where relatives go cold and hungry to help each other with fees to keep children in school. Parents in the richer rural regions too plan and save for the schooling of their children but in these locations their incomes are more likely to allow for extended schooling through to secondary middle schools and higher-level education.

Health care and medical costs too have escalated in the countryside and are increasingly prohibitive, especially in cases of serious and chronic illnesses. As for education, these costs may range from a few yuan for the village doctor and his medicine to many hundreds of yuan for hospital treatment. As in the cities, user fees and charges for medicines are increasingly the main means of financing the rural health care system and health care costs have risen across the country – although it has to be said that these rising costs are partly due to improved standards of medical care. However better care is often only available in county hospitals some distance from villages so that costs of travel, hospital admission and medical fees for a rural household can often drain family savings or put households into debt for many years. I have certainly come across many such cases. For thirty years I have observed that the poorest households were not those with the lowest incomes so much as those with illness and high medical costs. Those who have access to treatment are the fortunate ones, for fees are often demanded up front and there are many cases of patients having to leave before their treatment is complete while, for others, the absence of any surplus income or savings makes the very thought of treatment impossible. The effect of the rising costs of health care will be examined in Chapter 10; suffice it to say here that, in the countryside, there are sadly all too many reports of the return of many of the communicable diseases such as schistosomiosis (snail fever), tuberculosis and hepatitis B. Their reappearance has the potential to affect millions of rural residents, many of whom will find it difficult to pay for curative or alleviating treatment. Certainly any village household which is affected by illness or an untimely accident is unduly disadvantaged by the loss of the labour power and can be bankrupted by the serious or chronic health problem of a family member.

In addition to the costs of services, farmers also have to pay an array of taxes, levies and other fees. In the mid-1990s, it was estimated that as many as 360 taxes and fees had been imposed on peasants by all levels of government and that, over the previous decade, the rural tax burden had risen by 80 per cent so that taxes amounted to around one-third of farmers' cash incomes.[58] Apparently Premier Zhu Rongji once estimated that the sums charged to farmers amounted to more than Y120 billion including Y30 billion of agricultural tax, Y60 billion of fees collected by township governments and various other ad hoc fees.[59] It has been calculated that rural incomes may be only one-sixth those of urban dwellers but rural residents are expected to pay three times as much tax.[60] Indeed the collective total of taxes, levies and fees exacted in rural China is often referred to as the 'farmers' burden' and it is villagers who frequently have to compensate for the shortfalls in local government funds. Many local governments have been starved of central government funds and alternative resources since the mid-1990s when a series of tax reforms gave the central government a bigger share of the pie and left the lowest tiers of rural government continuously short of funds. Since that time, many local governments have come to rely on rent from lands used by the privately-owned industries or have fallen into debt and become increasingly extractive as they seek to maintain local services as well as support expanding local bureaucracies. In 2001, it was estimated that since the mid-1980s, the number of civil servants in township governments had increased ten times.[61] As grass-roots officials provide fewer services and become less protective of those they govern, it has become common for analysts to talk of a 'predatory local government' in rural China. Even in times of hardship and despite government orders to the contrary, fees are exacted by local officials so that, in some areas, it is estimated that the scale of peasant indebtedness is such that the number of loans taken out to meet local levies alone amounted to hundreds of millions of yuan or Y667 to Y1,000 per head of China's 900 million rural population. In many cases the creditors were most likely to be the county and village cadres or their kin who in effect are said to have become the 'new landlords'.[62] Cases of non-payment frequently resulted in repossession and loss of goods and, in one report in 2003, 80 per cent of the farmers in one village were reported to have suffered the confiscation of household goods because of the non-payment of taxes.[63] Local officials were also widely blamed for extracting fees and levies to line their own rather than village pockets. Although the state was supposed to take no more than 5 per cent out of rural incomes, there were reports of local officials imposing exorbitant levies and fees in cash and kind for their own enrichment as well as to support local government and business.

Villagers were not only forced into paying extra levies but to their fury, local taxes and levies were often siphoned off for the building of offices for the local government or for purchasing flash new cars and other luxuries for local officials. The actions of any local officials who abused their positions and extracted fees over and above accepted limits attracted the most local criticism. There were stories in the media of lone villagers or groups of village-representatives travelling long distances to petition provincial or even national leaders about the abuses of local officials. Over the past decade such resentment has also spilled over into sporadic demonstrations which, sometimes violent, constituted protests against local governments which imposed crippling taxes and levies, owed farmers for their grain or enriched themselves. In the mid-1990s, reports of violent clashes between police and villagers and some bloodshed in different villages and townships in Shaanxi, Hunan and Henan involving 100,000 peasants suggested that protests often start with a petition and balloon into demonstrations. These were sometimes led by village leaders themselves who often found themselves in the difficult and unenviable position of having to administer and collect taxes on behalf of an exploitative local government.[64] At the close of the century, there were so many reports of increasing numbers of such confrontations between villagers and officials that there were fears of a chain reaction and widespread disorder. For example in 1999, there were reports of rural unrest and violent clashes with the police in eastern Jiangsu and southern Hunan province because of arbitrary and excessive taxation.[65] Further west in northeast Shaanxi province, more than 12,000 farmers sued officials who had imposed levies which had amounted to a quarter of their incomes.[66]

In sum, the exaction of taxes, fees and levies plus the costs of services and production inputs were such that the majority of rural households had little surplus cash over and above these expenses. Many found themselves unable to meet these costs which rose faster than incomes which, as earlier sections in this chapter showed, had barely increased in the 1990s so that, although some did have savings, many found themselves with debts to the local government or to kin and neighbours. For the majority outside of richer coastal and suburban locations, it could be said that the demands on cash incomes were higher than the incomes themselves. In 2001, the deputy director of the National Bureau of Statistics noted that official estimates of average per capita peasant income, Y2,366, should be reduced by 40 per cent to account for income in kind resulting in a potential purchasing power of around Y150 per month. After a further reduction of 20 per cent to cover the cost of working capital for seeds, fertiliser, pesticide or diesel fuels, a mere Y120 was left for spending on consumption.[67] He could have added that, so long as much of this sum is taken up by taxes, education and other necessary services, there will be little surplus cash for spending on consumer durables or other items that might make for a comfortable lifestyle.

Consumption and lifestyles

If average per capita rural incomes have risen to between Y2,500 to Y3,000 in the past two to three years and the costs of services and production inputs take a major portion of that income, then much of the remainder of that income especially in the poorer central and western regions has been spent on food for the family table even though the costs of food consumption relative to income have been declining. In 1978 it was estimated that rural households an average spent 67 per cent of their total living expenditure on food; in 1995 the proportion had fallen to 58.6 per cent and in 2002 to 46 per cent.[68] The diet of farming households, which tends to include a narrower range of staple and non-staple items than in the cities, varies enormously according to income and location. In richer regions, well-off households now enjoy finer grains, more eggs, meat and fish and a variety of beverages; conversely those eking out a subsistence and living in remote and mountainous terrain eat coarser grains and less protein with hot water and home brews remaining the main beverages. Here families are still struggling to put sufficient grains on the table in all seasons and frequently have to resort to loans or hand-outs of grain to tide them over in hard times. On many visits to these regions I have had no choice but to eat coarse porridge supplemented by wild greens made palatable by my own sugar supplies often shared to repay hospitality. Similarly, given the distribution of wealth in the countryside, the cash sums available for goods and durables range from meeting very basic needs to small or large luxury and personal items. Again the most observable gap in addition to that between the rural and the urban is that between the coast and the interior where in the poorest and most remote regions, light is still provided by match flames and candles rather than single weak light bulbs, where most houses are barely furnished with basic wooden furniture, utensils and tools for daily use and there is no sign of a consumer durable. There local shops stock the most basic of items including matches, oil and paper. However in the eastern and southern provinces or coastal hinterlands and city suburbs, it is a very different story as more goods are purchased and owned including sewing machines, bicycles, wristwatches, radios and televisions in middle-income households plus electric fans, refrigerators, comfortable sofas, video recorders, large colour televisions and motor bikes, a car or truck in the most entrepreneurial of the richer households. Television sets, either black and white or colour, are now to be seen in much of rural central and northern China. In one rural north China village for example, virtually every household had a television set with a quarter owning a colour television by the end of the 1990s.[69] What is noticeable over much of central and western China is that even the smaller consumer durables ranging from a watch, bicycle, sewing machine and radio to a television, refrigerator and washing machine remain extraordinary rather than everyday purchases in that they are planned, saved for and usually purchased at set times of a life-cycle or year. Spring Festival is a time for the larger of the extraordinary purchases which are purchased from family savings or sometimes brought home by migrant workers. Indeed as earlier chapters have noted, migration has been as much about the movement of goods as persons and has constituted a major route for the acquisition of durables. In addition, in most of China's villages, there are two once-in-a-lifetime occasions when household consumption is most conspicuous: these are the building of a new house and the marriage of a son or daughter of the household.

One of the most discernible of changes in much of China's countryside during the reform years has been the widespread increase in house building or, at the very least, the remodelling and refurbishment of existing housing stock. In eastern, southern and parts of northern China, both new and made-over housing may be several storeys high or an enlarged single-storey courtyarded complex in brick and tile, very much replacing the old three-roomed arrangement of two living-cum-bedrooms leading off a central cooking and living area built of packed mud or concrete. In the early years of reform, one of the most conspicuous signs of rising incomes in rural areas was the new standards of housing with the most elaborate now incorporating separate bedrooms for family members, bathrooms and separate enclosed kitchens leading off private and tiled courtyards. I have never forgotten one of my first experiences of the new trend on the banks of the Yangtze River not far from Wuhan in the mid-1980s when I was led to the one new multi-storeyed house in the village, from a courtyard in which a large and elaborate fountain was turned on and off for my benefit, and up and down the stairs into the many rooms including a bathroom which was an admirable novelty in those days. New and refurbished housing, incorporating news-papered and postered walls, comfortable furniture and a range of durables which have been purchased from pooled family savings or migrant earnings, has contributed to the overall rise in standards of living in the richer regions of rural China. The poorer western provinces however are still characterised by clay-walled and straw-roofed housing with sparse wooden furniture including a table, bed and perhaps a number of low stools which it has to be said has made field work a back-breaking affair over the years. One of the occasions when house-building and refurbishing often occurs is around the time of a son's marriage or family division into separate households which may take place some time after the marriage of the younger generation. Building and refurbishing a house is often associated with the betrothal and marriage of a son, each phase of which incorporates a considerable number of transactions between the families of the bride and groom and constitutes a most important occasion for the bulk purchase of furnishings and durables.

Marriage has become the once-in-a-lifetime opportunity for the younger generation to acquire a range of consumer durables, the value of which is very much dependent upon the income and savings of the participating families. The cash sums and goods transferred from the bride and groom's family to the young couple normally include furniture, bedding items and major appliances. In richer regions, marriage transactions previously included a bicycle, wristwatch, radio and sewing machine; now they are likely to include a television set, tape recorder, washing machine or motor cycle to the value of tens of thousands of yuan. In poorer regions a bed, a set of bedding and a cupboard may be more likely. In terms of consumption, the important point is that both the families of the bride and groom and increasingly the bride and groom themselves, make use of this unique opportunity to provide and furnish their own rooms or house and acquire assets which will set them up for years to come. Whether the generations co-reside or are in households, wings or courtyards nearby, household visits almost always take in the newly-wed bedroom or quarters in order that the contents of the room can be admired; the value of each of the new(ish) possessions can be cited quite precisely and are the source of much pride. Increasingly my own field studies have suggested that it is the young bride and groom themselves who have increasingly taken charge of the negotiations whether or not they are co-residing with the parents of the groom or bride or setting up a separate household of their own. In a new trend, they identify their needs and assert a new sense of entitlement in order to take maximum advantage of this opportunity to set themselves up with an array of assets and material goods. Where newly-married couples do co-reside with the older generation, then family division and the establishment of separate households is likely to take place some time after marriage. However it is increasingly common for young couples to set up their own households on marriage and they are very well aware that the assets and goods acquired at the time of marriage are likely to be one-off and may have to last a very long time as in all likelihood there will be few opportunities to accumulate further possessions in the future.

Unless a family member has the opportunity to move away from the village and earn a higher income, it is much more likely that, apart from the odd purchase, the younger generation will need the bulk of their income plus on-going contributions from their parents to support their children's education as well as to meet the costs of taxes, health services and production inputs. Although the occasions for splashing out and for saving and purchasing durables may be few and far between in most rural villages, there is a good deal of interest now in living a more comfortable life, enormous satisfaction at acquiring new possessions and a new knowledge of material possibilities. New and rising aspirations have been fuelled over the past decades by an easy acquaintance with and the familiarity of modern life images or lifestyles via television and other mass media, local examples of conspicuous consumption and migrant stories from the cities or richer regions. For example, much is known about China's richest village, located 100 miles north of Shanghai and now a model for emulation in which residents have in effect become shareholders in the village-owned textile and steel industries with an average living space of more than 450 square metres and at least one family car. As one local official noted, 'People here have five main aims in life: money, a car, a house, a son and respect. We give them that. Every family here is rich'.[70] Indeed the main road is decorated with smiling pictures of every household in the village with each household's assets listed in detail for the many visitors and foreign journalists: size of the family, value of their property, average level of education, numbers of Party members as well as how many cars, mobile phones, televisions, washing machines, computers, air-conditioning units, motorbikes, cameras, fridges and stereo systems they own. Across much of rural China, the expansion of village horizons to embrace knowledge of consumer trends and the lifestyles of those in Shanghai, Hong Kong or other cities within China and abroad has redefined images of well-being and the 'good life', especially but not only among the younger generations. They now aspire to improved material standards of living including new housing and to acquiring a wide range of consumer durables in the foreseeable future. Of course peasant aspirations for 'a good life' are not new, but what is different are not only the numbers of new material objects deemed desirous but also a new sense of peasant entitlement with some disgruntlement at the delay in fulfilling such aspirations.

My own field work during the first decades of reform suggested that rural villagers then did not expect to acquire the same quality of life or levels of consumption as city residents. Indeed given the rural–urban divide, the two were perceived to reside in quite different worlds. However more recent field work conducted in villages in rural north and south China suggests that villagers are better acquainted with other places and other lifestyles. They are now more likely to feel that they deserve a better quality of life and even assert their rights to similar standards of living as their urban counterparts. How far this new sense of entitlement has spread is not clear, but what is clear is that such aspirations for new and improved lifestyles are not yet matched by livelihoods that can sustain such lifestyles. There is not only a gap between desired lifestyle and livelihood, but this gap has widened since the early consumer spree in better-off rural regions between 1978 and 1985. Although there has been a steady but small rise in standards of living since 1985, this has not yet translated into an increased demand for consumer goods that is widespread across much of rural China. However as urban sales of consumer durables are beginning to slow, many manufacturers and retailers are looking further afield to the untapped markets in the countryside and especially to the county seats and market centres where there is more of a small-town ambience. In 2003, it was estimated by market researchers AC Nielsen that more than half of the middle- to high-end washing machines sold each year were purchased in towns outside the 26 cities that make up the country's largest markets.[71] According to the same market researchers, it is the villages of China that remain 'the great unknown', not only because of the difficulties in gauging demand but also because of the obstacles to access and the costs of establishing the requisite distribution networks. This is one of the reasons for the importance attached to returning migrants in transporting goods and fuelling new consumer aspirations in the countryside. Boosting domestic demand in the countryside itself is also one of the reasons why the government has directed greater attention to raising rural incomes and, with these twin goals in mind, why the new leadership has recently embarked on a series of reforms to improve rural livelihoods and lifestyles.

Recent rural reform

At the 2004 National People's Congress, Premier Wen Jiabao pledged to make rural reforms a top priority in the coming years, largely because 'rural incomes had grown too slowly and development in different regions of the country was not balanced'.[72] There was much talk about the general problems besetting the three 'nongs' of agriculture, village and farmer, but more specifically, the government set out to increase investment in and restructure the agricultural sector, reduce taxes and fees and promote village democratic management. Although over past decades there had been much talk of 'consolidating the position of agriculture as the foundation of the national economy' and 'giving priority to solving the problems facing farmers', the resources allocated to the agricultural sector have not always matched the rhetoric and have not been sufficient to increase farming incomes. My own field work and that of others over the years suggested that much of the investment earmarked for rural development or poverty alleviation was too often directed and diverted towards the establishment or maintenance of township and village enterprises rather than improving agriculture and directly helping farmers. Time and again over the years, I observed how government funds in central and western provinces were used to bail out non-profitable local enterprises, perhaps with formal or informal links to officials, or to fund large-scale infrastructural projects. This was so especially in the western provinces which enjoyed a privileged status in terms of poverty alleviation, development investment and donor attention. This may end because of the decline of government-run township and village enterprises and a higher priority accorded to increasing and widening investment in agriculture. The government budgeted in 2004 for a large 20 per cent jump in spending on agriculture and rural investment and, in the first 5 months of that year, official support for the farm sector increased by 2.5 per cent to Y2.5 million (US$302 billion).[73] In addition to increasing investment, the government also aims to restructure agriculture, perhaps once and for all resolving the tension between the state-regulated production of low-price grains and the cultivation of more profitable cash crops. For decades much of the state's pricing and investment policies have been designed to protect grain production in sufficient quantities so that China can be largely self-sufficient in rice, wheat and maize. This may have been an important goal in terms of national grain security but it has not been so good for farmers.

Prolonged low prices for grain have prompted many farmers to turn to cash cropping and, just as there has been a move from agriculture to non-agricultural occupations in the countryside during the reform period, so also there has been a comparable shift away from grain production within agriculture. This is mixed news for China's government which has always remained wary of importing large amounts of grain and any substantial or long-term reliance on an international grain market dominated by the Western powers led by the EU and the USA. In addition, fears that domestic production of cereal and staple food crops such as wheat and rice would be affected by foreign competition were exacerbated by the terms of WTO entry whereby China's average tariff on agricultural imports will fall from 22 to 15 per cent in trade-weighted terms, quotas will disappear and state-run distribution monopolies will end. It is anticipated that these are likely to result in the opening of China to imports of cheap foreign food including EU and US grain surpluses, thus threatening the livelihoods of millions of China's farmers.[74] Abroad, China has led an ad hoc group of twelve developing nations which, accounting for two-thirds of the world's farmers and more than half of its cereal production, are working to end US and EU farm subsidies and to maintain national tariffs to protect their countries' farmers from cheap American rice and wheat imports. Internally, China's government is sending ambiguous message to grain farmers. On the one hand it is intervening in the grain market to offer incentives to grain farmers via direct subsidies, floor prices and higher returns; on the other hand, it is moving towards greater acceptance of the role of the market in regulating grain supplies and prices by announcing measures aimed at introducing more competition in the procurement and marketing system hitherto dominated by state-owned enterprises. In 2004, the Agricultural Ministry announced plans to liberalise distribution, to phase out the state-trading companies that dominate many sectors like grain and to build sufficient transport, storage and marketing facilities to make for greater market efficiency. It also showed greater flexibility in defining national self-sufficiency by allowing grain imports to rise to 10 per cent of consumption.[75] Although, thanks to the weather and higher prices, the 2004 harvest was expected to reverse the recent decline in grain production and bounce back to around 455 million tonnes, it was predicted that China would still need another 37.5 million tonnes to meet that year's demands. Part of this deficit was to be made up by reserves, but in 2004 it was expected that imports would also rise to 8 to 10 million tonnes compared with 1 million tonnes in 2003.[76]

It can be argued that maintaining self-sufficiency in such land-intensive commodities as grain makes questionable economic sense in a country that has relatively little arable land and little water to spare in the northern wheat-growing regions. Those within and outside China who favour WTO entry argued that the challenges and opportunities of WTO entry would be good for China's agriculture because it would lead to a more rational policy which uses the country's foreign exchange resources to purchase imported grain and allows farmers to switch to more profitable cash crops. Although China may be particularly vulnerable to competition in cereal and staple crops as a result of WTO membership, greater access to foreign markets is expected to bring significant new opportunities for fruit, vegetables and meat products. Already exports of sweetcorn, peppers, mushrooms and leeks to countries such as Japan and South Korea are large enough to have prompted a backlash from farmers in those countries. Foreign investors have argued that China's agricultural sector, with cheap labour, good available soils and proximity to large regional markets, is ripe for development. Some farmers have agreed to deals in which they lease out their land and link up with hi-tech food-processing businesses, markets and distributive networks. Although foreign investment in Chinese agribusiness is still very small compared with manufacturing, in the eyes of a growing band of investors, China could become 'Asia's farm and kitchen' as well as 'the world's workshop'. According to Greenfields, a regional investment group in China, 'countries like Japan and South Korea can no longer afford produce which has been air-freighted from the USA and Australia or that produced by their own farmers and will turn to China'.[77] The sweetcorn market in Japan alone is said to be worth US$400 million and Syngenta, a Swiss agribusiness and seeds giant, has teamed up with Greenfields to encourage farmers in China to grow sweetcorn and iceberg lettuce, which are both relatively new crops there.[78] Big chains such as McDonalds, Wal-Mart and Carrefour are sourcing food more locally to the benefit of farmers within a 100-kilometre ring of the main cities.[78] The production of quality and soft foods and new convenient forms of packaging are all helping China's fast-growing fresh-food industries and thus contributing to a rise in rural incomes for those involved in the new ventures which remain promising but still limited to very particular regions. Generally, the expansion of new ventures within and outside agriculture requires that there be new investment in rural development and greater access to rural credit for China's farmers.

Much of the investment in recent years has been directed towards the western regions which are made up of the six provinces of Gansu, Guizhou, Qinghai, Shaanxi, Sichuan and Yunnan plus the three autonomous regions of Ningxia, Tibet and Xinjiang and encompass 5.4 million square kilometres or more than half of China's land mass on which live 300 million people or a quarter of China's population. It is estimated that more than half of China's 80 million poorest, many of whom belong to the Hui, Zhao, Yi, Dai or other minority nationalities, live in these western regions. Originally these provinces attracted a mere 5 per cent of foreign investment in China but, in recent years, the well-publicised government programme dubbed the 'Go West Campaign' or the 'Great Western Development Project' has been developed. Its purpose was to embrace ecological protection, infrastructural construction and investment in railways, roads, water supplies and a gas pipeline with the aim of accessing natural resources, improving education and developing enterprises. In this way President Jiang Zemin hoped to build a new silk road linking and reviving trade routes between the east and the west of the country, thus acquiring a legacy that would replicate Deng Xiaoping's development success in the eastern coastal provinces. Jiang Zemin encouraged foreign investment, international donor support and domestic inputs into this project, which was also designed to offset the slow development and the 'backwardness' of the western provinces which was viewed as a severe limitation on rural growth and the creation of a rural market.[80] In a progress report conducted several years later in 2004, *China Business Review* concluded that the admittedly long-term strategy had mixed results: the infrastructural construction had significantly modernised parts of the region although transport networks were still unreliable and costs high; environmental awareness had improved but varied from region to region; industries based on the region's rich store of natural resources were growing but the necessary labour force skills were still slow in developing and incomes and living standards lagged behind the rest of the country.[81]

This slow development is largely because there is a shortage of central government funds for the project so that the campaign centres on cajoling better-off provinces, state banks and foreign donors and investors to make contributions. So far the pace of development has been insufficient to lure much in the way of foreign direct investment which despite incentives has fallen since 2000.[82] The state has also continued to dominate the economy and to retain ownership of assets which has provided little in the way of local stakeholding incentives. There are also accusations that there has been more emphasis on expensive infrastructural projects such as the Beijing to Lhasa railway and extensive pipelines rather than on the development of schools, health care and roads which tie isolated communities to markets.[83] There is a tension between the twin aims of the project, namely the extraction of natural resources including coal, oil and gas for the country's gain and the development of local economies for the benefit of local communities. The government may also be motivated by the threat of social and ethnic unrest including that by Muslim separatists and include policies which colonise this minority nationality at the same time as aiming to increase their incomes. All these facets may be relevant but the effect of these policies on local population has yet to be explored and in the meantime it would be a somewhat harsh judgment to ignore official commitment to the development of the western provinces and the reduction of inequality between them and other regions. Other lesser-developed regions besides the western provinces have also signalled that they too would like more government attention and investment. The most vociferous have been the central provinces which, with 36 per cent of the country's poor population, complain that they are likely to miss out as a result of the 'Go-West Campaign'.[84] In recent years the government has launched a new strategy to 'develop the central region' made up of Hunan, Hubei, Jiangxi, Henan, Anhui and Shanxi provinces which, containing 25 per cent of the population and accounting for 25 per cent of GDP, is one of China's main grain-producing regions.[85]

A second area of reform has to do with the extension of credit in the countryside and the reorganisation of the rural banking system. Although credit available in the countryside has expanded since 2002, agriculture still only receives 5 per cent of the financial system's loans although it makes 15 per cent of GDP.[86] This adverse trend has spurred the government to strengthen rural access to credit by reforming the rural credit co-operatives which comprise the only official channel in the countryside for either making deposits or acquiring loans. In 2004, there were serious concerns expressed that the 35,000 rural co-operatives were mismanaged, at risk from local government interference and that they constituted another financial black hole in the country's banking system. Together they control Y2.5 trillion or around 11.5 per cent of the entire financial system's deposits, making them nearly one-seventh of the size of the state-owned commercial banks. Given that their depositors are some of the country's poorest people, the government has little choice but to guarantee these deposits. But across the country, the government estimates that the rural co-operatives have an average non-performing loan ratio of 26 per cent, although most private estimates place the figure nearer to 50 per cent or even higher in poorer parts of China.[87] In the past 2 years, the government has aimed to create larger units to liberalise interest rates and introduce better management techniques. In this respect an immediate goal is to consolidate the highly decentralised 35,000 banks into 3,000 centres with branch offices which are managed at county level so as to improve regulatory mechanisms and reduce interference and mismanagement by local officials.[88] The government is currently testing lending-models based on a proper pricing of the costs and risks in the hope of getting more capital into the parts of the countryside where it is most needed and to poor farmers. Thus, in January 2004, the government initiated a programme in eight provinces to reform the rural credit co-operatives in which, in return for restructuring, reformed governance and a schedule for new and controlled commercialisation, the government agreed to write-off up to 50 per cent of their non-performing loans.[89] However without compensation for the high risk of lending to farmers who have little in the way of collateral, even rural banks are likely to continue to overlook the needs of farmers.

A third priority in terms of rural reform has been the introduction of new forms of village government and its financial support, although it has to be said that the call for reforms in village governance with greater village participation and transparency in local affairs is not new. Since the late 1980s, direct elections of local officials have been held in most of China's 800 to 900 thousand villages and there are many reports of successful village elections where the very process of electing new leaders has resulted in a raft of new and ably-led entrepreneurial and public activities. However in many cases, the elections themselves have been fraught occasions in that either the Party or higher-level administrative officials sought to influence the selection of the candidates for short-lists, votes were purchased, secret ballots interfered with or the persons elected by the villagers were refused official recognition. In 1999 it was reported from one village that a crowd of around 1,000 took to the streets to protest at vote-rigging by local officials.[90] In extreme cases rival candidates emerged which set appointed against elected candidates. More commonly perhaps, there is a general feeling that there has been very little change in the relations between local communities and lower-tier government as the result of the village democracy programme. In 2000, a study published by a researcher at Nankai University estimated that over 60 per cent of elected village committees did little more than carry out the orders of higher-level unelected governments.[91] In 2001, a very well-known and respected government researcher noted that despite the elections, there had been little change in rural administrative practices with the relations between elected committees and local party committees or higher-level rural governments remaining vague in definition so that elected officials often struggled with appointed party secretaries for control of village affairs and funds. He also observed that peasants in some areas were even more dissatisfied with their officials than they were before the elections in that although they seemed to have some semblance of control, the reality was often rival centres of power, administrative paralysis and fewer public services despite burgeoning local bureaucracies and increasing levies, fees and taxes.[92] As later chapters show, villagers have been known to demonstrate against unsatisfactory leaders imposed from above. Indeed the central government's recent official call for nation-wide efforts to promote openness and democracy in local decision-making at the grass-roots includes a sober admission that village elections have often meant changes in style rather than substance and have got in the way of developing rural prosperity.

> Only when the right to know, decision-making rights, rights to participate and supervision rights are ensured can village affairs, and in particular village financial affairs, be properly handled in the best of farmers' interests.[93]

This very recent call for further transparency, autonomy, supervision and accountability by the Central Committee of the CCP and State Council incorporated detailed guidelines for the revitalisation of rural democracy and only time will tell whether this aim can be achieved.

The government has had some success in reducing the number of taxes and fees levied by local governments. For some time it has been well aware that one way of lightening the 'farmers' burden' and increasing the cash 'in their pockets' would be to reform the administration and collection of local taxes and abolish the extra levies and fees imposed by local officials. In 2000, the government introduced a new tax-for-fees reform on an experimental basis in Anhui and other provinces which it then extended to a further eighteen provinces and municipalities in 2002.[94] With the new rural 'tax-for-fees' plan, a standardised tax was to gradually replace the range of taxes, fees and levies previously imposed on farmers in the main grain-producing and agricultural provinces in central and western China. Capped, this was expected to cut the financial burden on farmers by up to a third and thus release more of their income for consumption. Henceforth they were to pay a single agricultural tax limited to 7 per cent of farmers' cash incomes or a slightly higher special product tax and surcharge which, as before, were to cover the overheads of villages and salaries of village cadres as before but amount to a total of less than 20 per cent of the previous taxes and fees. Although the reform was first and foremost designed to lighten the burden on farmers, it was also expected to lead to a reduction in local revenues and thus lower the numbers of village and government functionaries receiving legal and illegal subsidies.[95] It was also anticipated that local officials, freed from the task of collecting fees, would have more time to serve local farmers. Overall the reduction in levies was heralded as a major milestone in the history of China's revolutionary and reform government. Indeed the deputy director of the State Council Development Research Centre thought that the tax-for-fees reform represented a third significant rural revolution in China of the same magnitude as the land reform of the 1950s and the adoption of the household responsibility system of the late 1970s.[96]

Whether the tax-for-fee reform turns out to be such a momentous step very much depends on several factors. Much of the long-term success of this reform will be dependent on the generation of alternative sources of revenue at local levels, either from village non-agricultural activities or additional revenue streams emanating from the central government. Certainly some township governments have met with financial difficulties after income from rural taxation fees was substantially lowered. In 2003 it was reported that each township government in the country owed an average debt of some Y4 million and that the root cause of the problem was that 'many rural government departments are overstaffed and consume too much'.[97] So far there has been some reduction in the numbers of local bureaucrats to be supported from local taxes. By 2004 it was estimated that the number of townships had been reduced from 46,400 to 38,136 and that there were 56,000 fewer township and village cadres.[98] The success in implementing the reform is also dependent on the degree to which local officials abide by central government policies and rules and actually reduce the levies imposed. In 2001 there was some evidence that the new local taxes might be higher than the sum of the previous fees and it is this trend which may be responsible for the very recent steps to abolish the agricultural taxes.[99] A senior researcher at the Agricultural Ministry's Rural Economy Research Institute recently stated that he thought that China was one of the last countries to tax agriculture and that the next step was to introduce a single income tax rate for both urban and rural residents.[100] As rural incomes derive less from agriculture and more from rural industry and migrant labour, there is some debate about whether the political and economic costs of levying the agricultural tax outweighs the benefits. The government not only abolished the tax on special products but also, at the 2004 National People's Congress, Premier Wen Jiabao promised an immediate reduction of 1 per cent in the agricultural tax and its total abolition within five years.[101] In February 2005, it was reported that in the previous year, 22 of China's 31 provinces had eliminated the 8.4 per cent farm tax.[102] Despite greater government attention and a raft of new reforms, stabilising rural livelihoods and improving rural incomes have proved to be difficult tasks. It is perhaps a sign of the magnitude of the task that although there is much talk of breaking the 'impasse' in rural development and investing in agriculture and raising rural incomes and standards of living, it is 'the peasant question' which continues to defy the government's best reform intentions.

The peasant question

Despite the new raft of rural reforms, it continues to be difficult to increase the cash incomes of much of the rural population, to boost rural consumption and reduce urban–rural differentials. In 2002, the deputy-director of a high-level party-government research office anticipated that the continuing problems of addressing low rural incomes, inequality and poverty would continue:

The per capita less-than-one mu (0.06 ha) farming land, the rocketing farming cost, the declining grain prices and the mutually-separated rural and urban economies have rendered it not only nearly impossible for farmers to increase their income through ploughing their meagre plot of land, but it is also very hard for them to benefit from China's rapid economic growth.[103]

Similarly in 2004, the Director of the National Economic Research Institute in Beijing reckoned that reversing the trends in the countryside would not be easy and that he did not 'see a reversal of the disparities in the next ten years because of the fundamentals'.[104] Only those in the countryside who 'have a way out' face the future with a degree of equanimity and expect to realise their ambition or aspirations. One optimistic farmer, living within two hours of the provincial capital of Guangzhou, thought he did have 'ways out' for at any time he could 'switch from grain to vegetables and duck farming or do both'.[105] There are many who have a range of options but for those with few alternatives or less of a 'way out', there is increasing frustration as they face rising costs, declining incomes and services and under- or uncertain employment. They feel themselves to be disadvantaged as they struggle to maintain their livelihoods in agriculture which continues to be the Cinderella of the economy and feel left behind or marginalised by the speed of reform and change. They can only dream of the types of lifestyles which remain the stuff of hearsay or television channels. One farmer speaks for many when he says, 'The government does not care about us farmers, only about economic development. There's no one to protect us anymore'.[106]

The plight of those 'left behind' or with 'no way out' was the subject of two recent and unlikely best-sellers. In 2004, one 460-page book, entitled *A Survey of Chinese Peasants*, reported first-hand the experiences of farmers and the persistent causes of rural poverty.[107] The two authors, both born in the countryside, wrote that they were shocked to find that despite much-acclaimed rural reforms, farming alone could no longer sustain a livelihood in most parts of China. They wanted to document the China beyond and behind city landscapes and urban skyscrapers; a China that consisted of primitive farming methods, economic exploitation, environmental degradation, tax burdens, social injustice and continuing poverty. As they wrote in the preface:

> We observed unimaginable poverty and unthinkable evil, we saw unimaginable suffering and unthinkable helplessness, unimagined resistance with incomprehensible silence and have been moved beyond imagination by unbelievable tragedy ...[108]

They argued that not only had poor farmers gained little from agrarian reform but that the successive cycles of reforms had themselves repeated relentless rhetorical cycles of incentive and oppression rather than fundamentally challenging the fatal flaws of the entire rural system which stood in the way of improving the lot of rural peasants. The authors concluded that the 'peasant question' is an economic, social and political crises which will deepen 'if we forget China's 900 million peasants' and fail to address reform 'at the systems level'. The book became an instant best-seller and was subsequently banned but not before its rural voices and critiques of rural policy sparked much debate on China's central media and in internet chat rooms. It has since been pirated and widely circulated. A second book, written by sociologist Cao Junqing and translated as *China Along the Yellow River: Reflections on Rural Society*, was similarly based on first-hand observations of livelihoods and rural living standards.[109] It too analysed rural China's future prospects and documented the mismanagement of agricultural policies, the land shortage, the low water table and the ever-increasing tax burden amounting to half of annual incomes. It too spoke of the new discontent now that more in the countryside are learning how poor they are in relation to others. Cao also concludes that it is the system rather than the individuals that must be held responsible for the corruption, over-staffing, nepotism and pocket-lining that he found everywhere and that only the promotion of debate and accountability would counter the importance attached to cultivating personal relationships and exchanging favours that bedevil rural socio-economic and political development.

To make similar points in visual terms, the painter Xin Dongwang has exhibited an oil-painting exhibition entitled 'Villagers' Biographies' which alongside the expressive paintings of single or groups of villagers features short but nuanced biographies of each of those portrayed. The paintings are finely-etched depictions of faces and bodies in which skin and eyes are textured with experience and emotions to depict the changing fate of peasants in the countryside. The main themes of the titles, paintings and captions include the exhaustion, the hopelessness, the under-employment, the mixture of hope and fear in changing times, the longings for and the reality of finding work in the cities and the 'deserted dreams' of migrants in countryside and city.[110] The exhibition, very much a visual village ethnography made up of paintings in the rough-hewn style of Lucien Freud or Francis Bacon has travelled to many of the major cities and in early 2006 in Shanghai, at no less a venue than the Shanghai Art Museum, it attracted large numbers of visitors. In 2004 and 2005 a number of documents and conferences on rural issues highlighted the government's determination to tackle 'difficult tasks' such as reducing rural taxes; introducing new grain policies and relaxing grain prices, purchases and sales; new rules and regulations inhibiting the appropriation of agricultural land for non-agricultural purposes; and the payment of wages owed to rural migrants. However, despite a considerable number of achievements, the government has stressed that maintaining the momentum of grain output and raising farmers' incomes would continue to be difficult.[111]

Perhaps the most serious and daunting obstacles to further rural economic growth and reform continue to be the high rates of under- and un-employment. There are many references to the high proportions of the rural labour force 'chronically unemployed', the millions that make up rural surplus labour and the difficulties which coastal and city labour markets would have in absorbing this surplus. The Director of the Rural Development Institute at the Chinese Academy of Social Sciences has argued that 'one of the most pressing economic issues facing the Chinese government at the present time' is the structural unemployment among the rural labour force.[112] Some estimates suggest that surplus rural labour amounts to more than a third of the rural population or between 300 and 400 million,[113] even though the proportion of China's population employed in agriculture fell by 20 per cent between 1978 and 2001.[114] There have been constant references to the 'massive unemployment' or 'massive idleness' in the countryside[115] which it is feared will be exacerbated by China's membership of the WTO. Hard-working peasants engaged in back-breaking work might rightly object to designations of 'idleness' but, according to official statistics, likely imports of wheat, corn, rice and cotton may well put a further 13 million farmers out of work.[116] It is also clear to the government that any development of off-farm sidelines or village and township enterprises may not be sufficient to absorb this labour force, especially in the central and western provinces. In these circumstances the two most common solutions mooted are the growth of the local tertiary or service sector and migration out to find work elsewhere. Recently China's leaders have made the case for the accelerated growth of the service sector in towns, small and new cities in order to absorb surplus village labour. Since the 1990s, local migration from village to town has been encouraged by the concentration of services and enterprises in small towns and cities and the movement of rural labourers to the small and county cities and townships. The successive changes in policy emphases in the countryside are reflected in a southern Jiangsu maxim: the 'building up' of fields in the 1970s, factories in the 1980s and towns in the 1990s.[117] Since 2000, the decline in township and village industries and the inability of the local and county towns and cities to develop fast enough to compensate for the rising numbers of under- and un-employed in the countryside has led to greater official support at all administrative levels for the idea of mass urbanisation or the unprecedented movement of millions to China's cities.

Mass urbanisation

Since 2000 much encouragement and support has been given to facilitating rural out-migration in an 'inexorable process of urbanisation' cited as a panacea for 'the peasant problem' and particularly for the high rates of rural under- and un-employment in the countryside. In 2003, a Xinhua commentary quoted a report to the Sixteenth National Party Congress which asserted that 'transferring surplus rural labourers to non-agricultural industries and to urban areas is the inexorable trend of industrialisation and modernisation'.[118] The report also suggested that the status change from surplus rural labourer to industrial worker and then to 'citizen' was part of the 'inexorable process of urbanisation'. Finally it calculated that if the targeted rate of 56 per cent urbanised by 2020 was to be achieved, then 13 million peasants would need to be transferred to urban areas each year. An alternative figure was mooted by the Academy of Social Sciences which suggested that China's modernisation called for 'about 10 million farmers to become urbanites each year in the next fifty years'.[119] To achieve such targets, government administrations at all levels have been encouraged to regard rural–urban migration as a 'major emergent industry'[120] with local governments further exhorted to increase investment and make new efforts to strengthen and expand the labour export industry:

> On the basis of reforming the system of household registration management, … [they] should lower the thresholds for peasant labourers to get urban residence registration, should give citizen treatment to the peasant labourers who have been working in urban areas for a long time, and should thoroughly remove the obstacles that prevent peasant labourers from getting jobs in urban areas … [in order] to quicken the pace of transferring surplus rural labourers to urban areas.[121]

More recently, in 2004, the scale and time-lines for such a massive move was anticipated by the Director of the National Economic Research Institute in Beijing:

> There are 300 million to 400 million surplus rural labourers who must leave the countryside, and that could take 10 or 20 years.[122]

Medium-sized Anhui province, an area half the size of Texas and home to 63 million people, has been one of the country's largest sources of migrant labour and became a model for assisted and large-scale migration. For example, the city of Shanghai reckons it has more workers from Anhui than from any other province and Anhui itself is reported to benefit substantially from migrant remittances which in 2002 amounted to more than Y24 billion.[123] In 2003, it was estimated by the Director of the Provincial Labour Bureau that so far the province had lost some 6 million migrant workers to the cities but that it still has 6 million more than the countryside can support. 'Without those migrants', he noted, 'under-employment in rural areas would be nearer 50 per cent' which meant that '12 million people or the equivalent of nearly half the population of Malaysia was unable to find work in the Anhui countryside'.[124] Although most migrants still rely on informal networks of kin and neighbours or private employment agencies to set up jobs, the provincial labour bureau also has a bevy of employment agencies both in Anhui and in cities such as Beijing, Shanghai and Shenzhen which liaise to pull workers out of the countryside and into factories and construction sites. They look for job openings in the cities, relay them back home to encourage the export of labour and provide mid- and short-term training where it is deemed necessary. For the Labour Bureau back in Hefei, the capital of Anhui province, migration is 'all about money and possibilities – the lack of them on the farmland and the chances of finding them in factories or building sites'.[125] As for the director of the Shanghai branch of the Anhui Labour Export Service Centre, he conceived of his role as 'to see people from my province getting richer, while people I introduced here are contributing to Shanghai's development'.[126] It has to be said however that not all towns and cities welcome this contribution.

Much of the international and internal debate has been about the possibility of achieving the national targets for movement out of the countryside and the mechanisms which might facilitate such a movement. Less attention has been given to the effect of this movement on towns and cities and the need for destination-management and new urban infrastructure to cope with the additional numbers of residents anticipated. As this study has already shown, there is a simultaneous rise in urban unemployment which has added to the fears that rural migrants may compete for the same jobs and make it much more difficult for urban labourers to find employment in their own cities. To some extent, as the previous chapter suggested, the labour markets are separate as rural migrants frequently have little education or skills training. This has its own problems, for it is estimated that 38 per cent of the rural work force has only primary school education or less, so that this plus their low-level skills also make it difficult for such farmers to find jobs outside farming and hinders their entry into the urban labour market.[127] However there is also growing evidence to suggest that, increasingly in the informal sector and in all but the lowest paid and most menial of jobs, there is now some competition for jobs. In many cities there is also much overcrowding of facilities and lack of affordable housing so that the addition of rural migrants on the scale envisaged makes for an additional pressure on both infrastructure and services, which generates some resentment in both small towns and the largest metropolitan cities. The growing presence of migrants in the cities has given rise to an array of negative perceptions and much discrimination against rural migrants. As the previous chapter has also shown, urban life for rural migrants is often beset with difficulties given that they do not have the same access as city residents to health and education services. If they do not return to their village homes, those who do not find work resort to begging, which is an increasing phenomenon in a number of cities. Migrant workers have little leverage or protection because, without technical qualifications, a stable job or fixed residence, they are not able to transfer hukou registration and acquire the necessary urban residential qualification which would allow them access to the same rights and services as city residents. It is also the case that many rural farmers themselves do not want to acquire urban registration or to move their families to the cities as they might lose their rights to village land, which still remains the most basic guarantee and important source of subsistence and security should hard times return. They fear that without their land, they might become 'three no peasants' with no land, no job and no income support. There are then a number of constraints which are likely to impede the scale and speed of mass urbanisation as a solution to China's rural impasse.

Outside China there is some debate about the efficacy of this policy of urbanisation. Although supported by the World Bank, some of us who have long experience of China doubt the capacity of the new or old cities to absorb such large numbers without major disruption and disorder. My own reservations derive from fears that too much attention is given to the abolition of the hukou registration and too little to the development of the urban infrastructure required to underpin such a policy and that the encouragement of movement out of rural areas will leave behind the most vulnerable, the elderly, women and children providing little impetus for hastening rural development. That said, it is also respectful to note that it is largely because both scholars and practitioners involved with rural reform and policy feel rural development to be at such an impasse that the only alternative to further rural impoverishment seems to be movement out or urbanisation. In December 2002, the deputy director of the Party Policy Research Office openly emphasised the importance of 'accelerated urbanisation' – reaching 50 per cent by 2050 – in addressing the problems of rural poverty, low rural incomes and inequality.[128] As Chapter 11 will show, just as this manuscript was being completed, there was some evidence that there may be a shift in the balance of official attention towards 'the construction of a new countryside' to counter the priority given to policies of urbanisation as the most important panacea. Whether the latter longer-term solution is feasible or correct remains to be seen, but in the meantime the livelihoods of many of China's 500 million farmers, although improving remain fragile. Despite the rise in incomes in 2005, it is unlikely that many will acquire much in the way of surplus cash to enjoy the 'modern' lifestyles to which they now aspire. That probably awaits not only some elements of urbanisation but also widespread rural development with stable and diverse livelihoods and a rise in village incomes, services and facilities to the benefit of all age-groups. The next section of the book profiles the population categories by age and suggests that not all generations are equally likely to become China's new consumers.

Part III
Profiling demand
The demographic pyramid

7 Children first

The indulgence factor

Children, alongside their parents, were one of China's first consumer groups to be targeted by both foreign and domestic marketing and manufacturing companies. Long-time observers like myself watched as first entire floors of city department stores and then whole department stores themselves were stocked with a colourful profusion of children's clothes, toys, foods and other goods. These were soon followed by single-designer or -branded shops in downtown shopping streets and malls. Children and their parents were also one of the first groups to be courted by television and other media advertisements publicising the educational, physical and other juvenile benefits of product after product – both foreign and domestic in origin. Indeed it can be argued that children rapidly became the single most important new category of consumers in China. That children and their parents early attracted international and national attention from manufacturers, retailers and advertisers is perhaps not surprising for it is now widely acknowledged across the continents that it is children who have become one of the most significant and determined of age-groups in generating and absorbing successive waves of new consumer goods. Advertisers the world over recognise that children comprise not one but three markets: they are a 'primary market' currently spending their own money on their own wants and needs; they are an 'influence market' that determines much of the spending of their parents; and they are a 'future market' given all the goods and services that will be purchased in their adult years.[1] Thus children are seen to have more market potential than any other demographic category and, in China too, children and their parents were early targeted by the major child-oriented global brands, such as Heinz, Johnson & Johnson, Disney and Gap, who were eager to enter China and take advantage of this large and fast-growing market. In the first decades of reform many such international companies and their products became widely known in China's metropolitan cities and their suburban hinterlands. In the mid-1990s, a director of a Hong Kong and Chinese advertising firm undertook a 5-month survey of Chinese children and concluded that the present expansion was but the beginning:

> Obviously everybody's interested in Chinese kids at the moment. Western marketeers are particularly interested in them because they have a whole range of global brands which have worked in other parts of the world, and they are interested to bring [these] to China.[2]

In addition to the global brands of Europe and America, Asian companies and manufacturers also produce and market children's foods, clothes and toys, many of which are cheaper and simpler versions of foreign-made goods and these too have proved popular in the fast-expanding China market made up of children and their parents. The initial interest in this new and potential market was fed by the untapped numbers of China's children, the single-child family policy and the ways in which newly-affluent families indulged and invested in their one child who became the focus of familial aspirations and spending. In total, China has the largest population of children in the world. It is estimated that there are around 400 million children under the age of 18 years[3] and, according to the Fifth National Population Census in 2000, there were 290 million between the ages of 0 and 14 years accounting for 22.9 per cent of the nation's population.[4] The census also suggested that approximately 12 million infants were born each year although some other estimates place the numbers born at between 20 and 28 million.[5] Whatever the exact numbers, the calculators have been busy. Many like the Canadian manager of Kooshies' diapers could not help but be impressed by the potential of such numbers.

> Twenty million babies are born a year and if one got 1% of the market that means 200,000 consumers and a million diapers a year. Now that's beautiful.[6]

It was not only the limitless opportunities offered by demographic projections which attracted attention to China's juvenile market but also the one-child family policy which placed the single child at the centre of family, national and international attention.

The single child

One of the most momentous policies introduced in the late 1970s and far-reaching in its demographic and social implications was the single-child family policy in which the government demanded that only in exceptional circumstances should couples have more than one child.[7] Initially this policy was distinguished by the stringency of the one-child rule, the economic sanctions taken against those not adhering to rules and the degree of state intervention in family affairs which it represented. However after a 5-year experiment, often conducted with considerable stringency and heartbreak, the government embarked on a series of modifications which permitted the birth of a second child in a range of circumstances. In 1984, the government modified the one-child regulations so that a family in rural areas could have a second birth if the first-born was a daughter and indeed, after that date, the one-child policy was most stringently implemented in the municipalities of Beijing, Shanghai, Tianjin and the largest cities while a two-child policy was implemented in much of the countryside and among many of the minority nationalities. It could be observed that village couples outside of city suburbs often had a third child where no son had yet been born. Indeed the policy was sometimes known as the 'relaxed one-child policy' or more often as 'the single-son policy'. In 2002 the first Population and Family Planning Law put in place a national legal framework which aimed to replace localised rules and regulations and extend the number of categories permitted to have a second or even a third child.[8] There have been a number of recent reports which suggest that, even in the largest cities, the government has modified its one child per couple policy to allow more parents to have two children.[9] Although many spokespersons in China still speak of a one-child policy as if it is still in place, the number and range of exceptions to the rule which have long been permitted mean that it has not been appropriate to speak of a national one-child policy for some time. Moreover current debates about the costs of supporting a rapidly ageing population suggest that the policy itself may be on the way out. Even so it is unlikely that the birth rate will show a dramatic rise as though the one-child policy has been decidedly unpopular, parents do now prefer to have two or at the most three children – largely so they can give them a good start to a better life.

One of the reasons for the many local variations in rules or practices and the incremental modifications of the one-child policy has been the unpopularity of the policy which has made it difficult to implement and to police. In the 1980s, several field studies of my own and others suggested that a two-child policy would have been more acceptable and that, left to their devices, many would have preferred to settle for this number. My own meetings with young women in villages years ago suggested that they were eager to learn of the ways to have fewer children than their mothers. In cities and towns, interviews and meetings suggested that two children, preferably a boy and a girl, was the ideal and that only a few hankered for more. Certainly the birth of my own son and daughter was the cause for congratulations and not a little envy. The desire for larger families has been considerably blunted by the rising costs of health care, education and housing so that, where two children are permitted, parents rarely exceed that number. Over past decades, the single-child rule has contributed to a rapid decline in fertility and family size in China which constitutes one of the most dramatic of demographic trends world-wide. Helped but not solely due to the single-child family, the fertility rate fell from 2.29 children per woman in 1980 to between 1.7 and 1.8 in 2004.[10] Although there is some debate about whether this is an under- or over-estimate, in the largest cities the majority of the young are single children while in much of the countryside it is still common for children to have at least one sibling. It is reported that of all the infants born in 1990 in Beijing and Shanghai, 87 and 86 per cent respectively were single children[11] while in the largest cities, it is estimated that more than 80 per cent of the children enrolled in primary schools, day-care centres and boarding nurseries are single children.[12] In these circumstances it is not surprising that it is this one child who has become the focus of family pleasure and parental aspiration.

Parenting

In the late 1970s and early 1980s, much of the early exhortation of parents to support the one-child policy included a campaign to substitute the 'quality' of the child for 'quantity' or additional children. Indeed, as I have already stated, it has always been my own view that the new and increasing opportunities for consumption went some way towards mitigating the opposition to this policy in the cities. In turn, a reduction in the number of children meant that the single child, or the child with a single sibling, became the focus of attention for two parents and four grandparents so that the so-called 4:2:1 or 4:2:2 family has become increasingly child-centred. Indeed child-raising or child development fast became a new and major pre-occupation of urban and suburban parents and there was a plethora of specialist parenting guides in both book and magazine form and a number of television programmes designed to teach and aid parents. One of the very interesting projects which I evaluated for UNICEF some years ago focused on the newly-established schools for parents which largely consisted of classes to help parents enhance the health and education of their single child. The immediate focus of family resources on the single child from the early 1980s earned them a new collective epithet which was to become well known internationally: 'the little Emperors of China'. There has been much social and psychological research into the characteristics of this apparently pampered generation of single children which suggests that these children are high achievers and self-confident but frequently spoiled and showered with attention, gifts and treats. The research is somewhat inconclusive but warnings against rearing little emperors or the 'dangers of drowning a child with love', are frequently discussed in the media. Nevertheless, as Cecilia Milwertz found in her field study in the cities of Beijing and Shenyang, city families tended to direct their attention to the cultivation of the 'perfect only child'.[13] A 3-year investigation of 1,800 Beijing families published in 1999 also concluded that parents 'pinned their hopes' on their only children and were prepared to make great sacrifices for their child's advancement.[14]

Child-rearing, as a project, was particularly dear to the hearts of many of the first post-revolutionary generation of parents and grandparents who very much wanted to compensate for the deprivations of their own childhoods. They had grown up in spartan times and many childhoods had been blighted by either the shortages of the Great Leap Forward in the late 1950s or the disruptions of the Cultural Revolution in the mid-1960s, both of which affected children's health, education and the quality of family life. Often dubbed the 'lost generation', and in part to compensate for their own years of hardship, this generation of parents seemed determined to give their offspring every possible advantage. One mother summarised the views of many when she said that 'no sacrifice is too great to give my child all the things I didn't have in order to ensure her happiness'.[15] For this first generation of reform parents any new opportunities to provide well for their children seemed like a 'second chance' to live 'a happiness which they themselves had not experienced'.[16] It might be their own second chance for happiness, but for many it was also their one chance to parent. Few city parents had a 'second chance' to try harder with another child should the first fail to fulfil expectations, hence they tended to invest all that they could in their first and often only child. In addition, children were often the focus of attention of two sets of grandparents as well as their parents. The 4:2:1 ratio of grandparents and parents to one child is often used to show the dependence ratio of the older generation on the younger generations on the future, but reversed, this ratio also reflects the indulgence of the one child in what is commonly called the 'six pockets, one child' syndrome. However if children frequently had first claim on the budgets of their parents and grandparents, some children have been more privileged by reform than others.

Generally sons are still more privileged than daughters although my own and other studies of city one-child families suggest that 'only daughters' are catching up fast. However, with fewer children and a continuing reliance on sons for economic support in old age, many rural and small-town parents still prefer to have at least one son for security and for the continuity of the family line. One of the consequences of a declining birth rate alongside a continuing reliance on son-support has been a rising imbalance in sex ratios at birth as parents deploy age-old methods or new ultrasound techniques to ensure the birth and survival of more sons than daughters. As a result of sex-selective abortion, infanticide and abandonment, the average sex ratios at or shortly after birth in *China today* are around 118 boys born to every 100 girls, which is well above the international norm of 106 boys to 100 girls.[17] In families with both a son and a daughter, the son often receives more attention and is newly favoured in the distribution of foods, medical care, toys, educational opportunities or recreational facilities as these become increasingly available. Fieldwork suggests that more sons attend and stay longer in school than daughters, that boys are more likely to be taken to hospital earlier or for less serious ailments and that their stay in hospital is likely to be more extensive and expensive. There are several letters and short stories which feature in the media or on school walls that have been written by or feature a disadvantaged sister – she frequently speaks of a smaller share of food or fewer years of schooling than her privileged brother. Interestingly though, where the single child is a daughter, she is as likely to receive the same privileges as a single son. Privilege has also been dependent on location and socio-economic background. In the metropolitan cities of Beijing and Shanghai, the costs of special nutritious or fast foods, school fees and extra-curricular classes, colourful or stylish clothes and toys or recreational activities can add up to a very expensive juvenile lifestyle.

While much attention has been drawn to the privileges and 'spoiling' of single children in the largest cities, around two-thirds of all children live in the countryside where they are less likely to enjoy such an expensive lifestyle. The new and rising affluence of the majority of China's population in the southern and eastern coastal regions in the first decades of reform meant that most parents were able to allocate a higher proportion of their rising cash incomes to their child or children who frequently had the first claim on family budgets. In poor families, school fees plus an extra snack, colourful jacket or plastic toy was likely to constitute a significant proportion of disposable family income and only in the poorest families did children still have insufficient food to eat or fail to enter school. In all families, child-oriented expenditure represented an investment in the future of the family and, in my own rural and urban field research, parents from quite different socio-economic backgrounds still had similar aspirations for their children and made great efforts to allocate as much of their income as possible to the education and well-being of the younger generation.

Surveys of a range of economic groups found that parents uniformly prioritised their children's needs and expenses.[18] In 1988 a Shanghai survey revealed that families were spending around one-third of their income on their child[19] and this trend has continued. In 1995 it was estimated that the average couple in urban China spent 40 to 50 per cent of their combined income on their one child,[20] while more detailed studies such as that in a Beijing factory showed that parents spent the equivalent of one salary per month or Y200 on their young children.[21] In Shanghai too, parents in the mid-1990s spent just more than Y500 per month on the 'basic needs' of their children and an additional Y100 per month to provide their only children with new clothes or treats which were increasingly seen as 'necessary' expenditure. Parents in this survey thought that each month they spent the equivalent of an adult salary on their children's tuition fees, toys, books, clothes, food and classes, which was certainly more than they spent on the adults of the family.[22] According to a survey of five cities conducted in 1998 under the auspices of the State Statistical Bureau, parents spent more than Y672 on their children (aged 1 to 2 years) with the highest amounts spent in Beijing (Y764) and Shanghai (Y736).[23] In 2001 the average monthly expenditure on children per urban household ranged from Y1,009 in Beijing to Y462 in Xian, representing a total collective expenditure of some Y9.6 and Y2.8 billion.[24] Even in the northeastern city of Shenyang which was hit by high rates of unemployment, it was reported in 2003 that 50 per cent of local families spent Y10,000 annually on their children, mostly on education, food and developing their skills.[25] In a variety of rural areas, my own fieldwork has shown that farmer families too spend a goodly proportion of their income to provide for and send their children to school. Most recently, in 2004, it was estimated that nationally a total of nearly 40 per cent of a typical family's income was spent on its children.[26] Given these amounts and familial priorities, it is perhaps not surprising that children and their parents rapidly became one of the fastest growing consumer markets in China and, just as for adults, it was the new styles and range of children's clothes which represented the first signs of affluence and consumer choice in the first years of reform.

Even during the 30 years of revolution, children's clothes were more varied in colour and style than the uniform blue-garb of adults and often provided the only splash of brightness on both city street and rural lane. With the onset of reform, new ranges of cheap, colourful and quality clothes for children rapidly became available in shops and on market stalls while in the metropolitan cities, international companies such as Gap and Children Pierre Cardin set up retail outlets. However designer clothes, shoes and sportswear are more likely to be the subject of billboard and television advertising than to be purchased and worn in the streets, at home and or at school. Although it is sometimes reported that parents will spend 20 to 30 per cent of their salary on buying a beautiful outfit for their children,[27] it can also be observed that children's clothes remain remarkably homogeneous and are largely mass-produced in China. Parents generally expect to purchase several new sets of clothing for their children per year and these purchases are normally made at New Year or on a birthday and, according to several mothers interviewed, the most important considerations in making such purchases are durability and price. Most children wear a uniform to school, and outside school or in schools where there are no uniforms, most children wear T-shirts and either shorts or skirts. For special occasions young girls may wear dresses which are often highly decorative and girls of all ages wear hair ornaments ranging in style from a single plastic grip to a glittered band or bow. In schools and on the street, there is evidence of some attempt to emphasise the individuality of children via their attire but, as in many other societies, what is more noticeable is the relative homogeneity of children's clothing with display and decoration confined to special occasions. In the metropolitan department stores, rack after rack of very attractive but expensive imported clothes with smart outfits, jackets and dresses each costing between Y300 and Y500 could be observed in December 2005. However, even at New Year in Shanghai there were few buyers despite the sales. Many more children's clothes were being purchased in the less-expensive shops and market stalls where outfits, jackets and dresses were still stylish but much cheaper. In addition to clothes, a new array of special and fast foods, toys, books and other recreational and educational aids have become observable attributes of juvenile lifestyles and are on sale across China's cities.

Foreign, snack and fast foods

By the 1980s there were substantial changes to the contents of the family food bowls of city, coastal and richer rural children, which still included rice, noodles, breads and vegetables but were supplemented by greater amounts of cooking oil, meat, poultry, fish and eggs. China's market reforms also brought an influx of foreign milk-formula companies which, enticed by the 28 million babies born each year, competed fiercely for a dominant market share in infant formula and toddler food products. It has been usual for almost all young infants in the countryside and around two-thirds of young city infants to be breast-fed for 3 to 4 months,[28] but now formulae, prepared cereals and other baby foods produced by both foreign and domestic companies have become popular as supplements or in some cases substitutes among city and suburban parents. With improved living standards, demanding work schedules and a faster pace of life, many mothers are no longer so keen to breast-feed or prepare cooked ground-rice and other baby foods for their infants despite the extra cost involved in purchasing substitutes. With good marketing and attractive packaging, it has been relatively easy for foreign-branded baby foods to find a niche market among China's rich and middle-income urban parents. Most of the marketing messages emphasise the nutritious components of these foods and the ways in which they represent advanced scientific knowledge, meet international standards and closely replicate breast milk. Parents who want to provide 'the best start for growing children' or want 'their infants to be the best' are influenced by such messages. In 1998, one survey found that just over a quarter of parents in the cities of Beijing, Shanghai, Guangzhou, Chengdu and Xian expressed a preference for purchasing foreign foodstuffs for their babies and toddlers.[29]

Research in a small 300-bed baby-friendly Beijing hospital revealed the degree to which the attraction of 'modern and scientific child rearing' had influenced the decisions of young mothers to purchase foreign milk formula despite the extra cost. For example a 26-year-old teacher chose a foreign infant formula because 'it seemed the best for our child's health' and this advantage more than made up for the high monthly cost.[30] Similarly a 25-year-old factory manager used foreign infant formula because she wanted to raise her son in 'the most modern, scientific way possible'. She thought it was more nutritious than a Chinese-made equivalent and was modern, scientific and conformed to international standards characteristics, all of which outweighed the additional costs.[31] Far away in southwest China, a 29-year-old worker in a state bank was also asked whether she would choose a Chinese or foreign-brand milk powder. She replied without hesitation: 'Of course, foreign. Almost all my friends buy foreign-brand baby food for their kids'. She and her friends placed more trust in foreign-branded baby foods: 'Yes, it's much more expensive, but you know, if parents can buy security and nutrition, they care less about the price'.[32] According to the Managing Director of China Dairy Foundation, 'there is little difference between foreign and Chinese milk powders' but 'so-called white- and gold-collar workers are prepared to pay almost three times more than the price of Chinese milk powder and cereal baby foods' because 'they believe in foreign-brands so much' and that foreign-branded baby food products meet 'more scientific' needs and are best for a growing child'.[33] However not all parents are able or wish to meet the additional costs of around Y200–Y300 per month, hence domestic milk-powder products still enjoy the major share of the milk-powder market although some recent scares about the safety of such products have influenced sales. It is also forecast that their share of the market, which is very much dependent on lower prices, is likely to be challenged by China's entry into the WTO.

In the cities, foreign baby-cereal products have become popular infant foods occupying some 90 per cent of the market share.[34] Of the major baby food brands, those of Heinz and Nestle have cornered much of the Chinese market in milk formula, cereals and other infant foods.[35] Heinz, one of the largest producers of cereal and baby-jar foods in the world, established a joint-venture with a United Food Enterprise (UFE) plant in the southern city of Guangzhou in 1984 to produce a rice cereal for China's infants. Heinz–UFE have endeavoured to associate their products with both nutritional growth and high achievement by establishing the Heinz Institute of Nutritional Science whose nutritional education programme was aimed at medical and child-care professionals.[36] Cleverly, it entered the China market via university towns and high-tech districts in the hope that the use of its products by these elite communities would stimulate others to follow their example. Prime-time television deployed scientists in white coats to present technical messages on vitamins and minerals, while cereal packaging featured the brand name in English but was accompanied by a line in Chinese characters emphasising the 'high protein' and 'nutritional' content. Advertising not only projected Heinz's Western and scientific credentials but also promoted the association of their products with advancing progress and a 'modern' way of life. As the President and Brand Director of Heinz–UFE Ltd noted:

> We are selling not only products, but also hope and confidence, calling on parents to rear the future generation in scientific ways.[37]

On the basis of such strategies, the company claimed in 2002 to have more than 50 per cent of the total share of baby-food products in China.[38] The one-child policy in the cities has caused parents, fearful of sickness, incapacity or even death, to become very anxious about the health of their only child. In these circumstances, the association of products with fostering children's health has meant that a whole range of nutritional supplements and medicinal tonics have enjoyed a ready market. As a result of television advertising, both Baby Essential (Wawasu) which is a tonic based on chicken embryos and a digestive drink known as Baby Laughter (Wawaka) are widely known and used to promote the health of children. It can be readily observed that the most crowded shops in urban high streets are those specialising in and signed 'Children's Foods', which sell an array of nutritious foods, supplements and snacks.

For older children, snack foods or 'small eats' (xiaochi) have become a common component of childhood diets. Made up of mass-produced sweets, cereal bars, crackers, crisps, cookies, ice cream and instant noodles, snack foods are readily and cheaply available from neighbourhood family-run convenience stores where they are purchased by both parents and children for juvenile consumption. Although snacks wrapped in machine-made packaging are associated with 'the West' or 'foreign' foods, most mass-produced snacks, whether they are foreign or domestic in brand, are produced in China's factories. A study of food diaries in Beijing suggest that factory-made or mass-produced snacks are consumed on a daily basis and that they are popular among children who follow snacking trends and the introduction of new snacks with great interest.[39] Many of the small family-run convenience stores are located near schools with snacks purchased by children on the way to and from school. Apparently the school-yard itself constitutes an important venue for the dissemination of knowledge about new snacks. As for snacking behaviour in the home, eating between meals is often a means of diversion when parents are busy or a snack may comprise a reward for good behaviour provided by either parents or grandparents. Snack production is a highly commercialised venture with constant market promotions of new product-types or flavours. There is clear evidence of the influence of advertising on children's snack purchases and of fast-changing preferences so that sales of a popular shrimp-chip snack may suddenly give way to an imported fruit candy followed by dried seaweed. The constant changes added to both the interest in and popularity of snack foods and, by 1993, it was estimated that around US$1.25 billion was spent on snack foods by and for children.[40] New snacks and snacking habits were not the only major change to children's diets in the first decades of reform for city children were also introduced to new Western-style fast-foods.

Fast-food outlets such as McDonalds and Kentucky Fried Chicken (KFC) were particularly successful in attracting the custom of children in China's largest urban cities. Both these restaurant chains benefited from their advertised association with the 'nutritious' as well as 'the foreign' and 'the modern' and both made a determined bid for the continuing custom of children and their families by introducing a number of child-specific marketing strategies. Billed as 'fun and exciting' places to eat, each chain introduced child-centred motifs, special children's hostesses, gift-giving, birthday parties, space for children's play and counters for selling toy and souvenirs. As elsewhere, the marketing strategies deployed by McDonalds have centred purposively on children both as primary customers now and as 'their future clientele'. In a 'Book of Little Honorary Guests', each child's name, address and birthday is recorded and acknowledged each year and, in 'Children's Paradises', birthday parties are celebrated with food, drink, games, presents and entertainment hosted by 'aunts and uncles' in ways designed to make the birthday child and friends feel special and important. McDonalds and KFC also promote 'learning for children' by celebrating school achievement, by developing partnerships with schools and by sponsoring drawing, essay and sporting competitions or themed experiences around the world's geography. Such moves to encourage children 'to achieve' and 'be modern' are popular with parents and children who have become an important category of fast-food consumers. These visits to foreign fast-food outlets or their domestic equivalents, even if confined to special occasions, have become a familiar component of city childhoods. However there is probably no more potent measure of the glaring inequality and different standards of living in China than that between the diets of poor rural and richer urban children.

In the poorer rural areas, diets still largely consist of grains and vegetables with perhaps a serving of eggs, pork or chicken on special occasions. In these poorer areas, the period of weaning is an especially vulnerable period in children's lives when inadequate supplementary foods such as watery porridge are likely to cause slower growth rates than in richer regions and the cities. Surveys have shown a substantial amount of mild to moderate malnutrition in rural areas[41] and one of the challenges of my own fieldwork in western regions has been to gauge the age of children. So under-nourished were they in the poorest regions that the incidence of stunting made it very easy to under-estimate the age of a child. In city children's diets on the other hand, grain and vegetables have given way to high-cholesterol foods such as eggs, chocolate and snack or fast foods so that overweight and obese children have been the predominant concern. Plumpness in children has always been a sign of plenty and prosperity in China as the unusual responses to my own children in the 1980s also attest, but now admiration for plumpness has given way to concern with child obesity. In this respect there is some talk of China's double burden of under- and over-nutrition giving rise to both underweight and obese children. It has certainly been evident to observers in the schools and in the streets that large numbers of city children are overweight. For years, one of my predominant impressions was that of neat-limbed and slim school children, which is in stark contrast to my more recent observations in schools and at Children's Day festivals when I have been struck by the number of children and in particular of boys who are overweight.

In the mid-1990s, a small survey in Beijing showed that the prevalence of obesity among children between 8 and 17 years was 13.2 per cent, with the rate for boys of the same age exceeding 20 per cent.[42] Two years later in 1997, another report suggested that every year an additional 10 per cent of urban children under the age of 7 years were classified as obese.[43] Certainly the government, medical profession and nutritionists have expressed concern at the rapid rise in rates of obesity in urban children and have launched popular campaigns to improve knowledge of nutrition and encourage more exercise. Indeed in the early 1990s, I often wondered if any single children under the age of 7 and 8 years had feet which touched the ground so often were they seen to be towed, wheeled or even carried by doting parents or grandparents. In 1997 it was reported that the problem of obesity was so acute in urban areas that summer camps had sprung up on the outskirts of many cities to help obese children shed their excess weight with the aid of doctors, dieticians and an exercise regime.[44] An added incentive to slimming was the exacting physical as well as academic standards for entry into the most selective and progressive high schools. However most children in the cities, suburbs and coastal regions have benefited from greater amounts and new varieties of children's foods which were not the only new attributes of a 'modern' childhood for play and leisure activities have also come to differentiate juvenile lifestyles across rural and urban China.

Toys and play

City children can now expect to own toys of a range and price not available previously while, in the countryside, children are more likely to have a make-shift or less expensive plastic toy purchased for a few cents at a market stall – unless a child has a generous migrant relative who may arrive home at Spring Festival with a large toy present. The variety of toys purchased for and by children now ranges from the simple and plastic to internationally-recognised brands and both can be purchased in specialised shops, general retail stores, malls and markets in China's cities and towns. Although children own toys to an extent previously unknown in that country and China is arguably now the world's largest maker and exporter of toys, it has proved to be much more difficult than expected to market expensive foreign toys within China. Certainly many of the toys familiar to children elsewhere and now manufactured in China, which include such perennial and favourite playroom-items as Lego, Duplo, Techno, building blocks, play-doh and variants of Disney and other cartoon characters, are all widely available in China's cities. A wide selection of dolls, video games, robots and model vehicles are also displayed in city shops as are Fisher Price and other well-known nursery and playroom brands. For some years now, foreign manufacturers have been anticipating a large market in China. In 1998 the general manager of a Canadian baby-product firm forecast a 'huge market' for toys ranging from visual cards to learning blocks and stacking toys which he thought was still 'relatively wide open for foreign manufacturers to tap'.[45] At the end of 2003, an article in *Far Eastern Economic Review* reported that the domestic toy market was expanding fast with annual sales expected to top US$1.21 billion in 2003–4 and to increase at a double-digit growth rate.[46] When Discovery Toys launched its products in a dozen cities in 2003, one executive forecast that China was 'a country ready to explode with a thirst for parenting knowledge and for educational toys'.[47]

In contrast, a survey conducted in China's main five cities in 1998 showed that a fifth of parents expressed some interest in imported toys, but most thought that these were too expensive to purchase.[48] Moreover many of the more classy foreign toys had their China-made equivalents which were sold at a much lower price. For example in the mid-1990s, elaborate Barbie sets sold at a price between Y128 and Y178, while a Chinese made clone, named Cindy, was available for as little as Y13.[49] Although Lego building-kits have become a popular purchase, a spokesperson for the company has noted that the main barriers for multinationals is that 'too many local toys of different quality and pricing, are competing through the same channels of departmental stores'.[50] Foreign toys are not as cheap as products made in China and parents often question the price and the utility of the expensive imports. While city parents do indulge their single child, toys have ranked low in priority after music and English language classes, Western fast foods and clothes. It has been observed that if they do buy a toy on impulse, the price is rarely more than Y20 to Y30 (US$2.40–US$3.60) and that this is because, despite a comfortable income amounting to some Y2,000 per month, kindergarten fees run to Y300 per month and now that rents and unemployment have increased, parents are much more cautious about spending money on toys.

> Now a lot of people are being laid off. So we are very careful about what we spend money on. When we spend money on something for her [his daughter], we like to get something useful – something to wear, or to eat. Something necessary.[51]

So on a Sunday afternoon in a spacious store containing many small stalls peddling everything from baby strollers to hot-rod cars, it is the winter clothing, thermoses, hats and mittens which are getting the most attention. Thus toy companies operating in China have had to struggle to build their brands and win a profitable market share and in 2003 it was reported that, so far, not one of some 6,000 toy companies operating in China has a significant market share.[52] My own observations in Shanghai in late 2005 suggest that it is the smaller and cheaper items that are purchased despite the fact that it is the more expensive and imported toys that attract the most attention from children and their parents.

Toys are primarily seen as sources of enjoyment and recreation for children up to age 7 years, but from 7 to 8 years of age, play gives way to learning and only toys and games that are perceived to be educational aids tend to find favour with parents. Hence toy manufacturers have learned to stress the ways in which their products help children develop their creativity and hand-to-eye co-ordination. In major cities such as Beijing and Shanghai, schools are introducing educational toys while parenting magazines feature toys and explain their educational value. One professor at the Early Childhood Education Institute in Shanghai suggested that the concept of a toy which was once considered to be an expensive gift has changed as 'people realise that kids learn and live and grow through games and toys'.[53] The President of BabyCare, a Beijing-based company started in 1998 by two American entrepreneurs to sell child-rearing services and products, concluded that the key to sales has been educating parents.

> People are ready to buy toys, but only if you really explain to them how a toy can be educational and if it will be fun for the child and the family.[54]

Some toy and educational games companies such as Discovery Toys and BabyCare have relied on direct-sales representatives as well as 'member' mothers to promote new toys and to directly educate potential buyers of their benefits. For example, one representative asked mothers at a 'toy party' to pick out a toy that their child might like so that she could then explain how each toy could help a child's development. She observed that though these toys costing up to US$35 each might be considered expensive, once parents could see the educational benefits and their superior quality, they more often than not made a purchase. One business mother in the private sector who grew up with few toys did not need much convincing of their benefits for her children: 'I buy the best for my kids. Whatever toys are available in the stores, they have'. She went on to say that she spent several thousand dollars a month on toys and clothes for her two daughters, which amounted to around two-thirds of the family's income.[55] With her income and her largesse, she may be something of an exception. However where there is a clear educational benefit, then parents are more likely to make a purchase. For instance, children of the rich and professional classes are now introduced to computing at an early age and it is probably not accidental that the Chinese translation for computer is 'electric brain' and it is the educational role of such a 'learning-facilitating machine' that is emphasised in promotional materials. Indeed it is not unknown for parents or grandparents to spend a 'chunk of their savings' on a computer, although their attitude towards computer games is not so forgiving. Although there has been a growing market for children's computer games, the chairman of a computer games company recently noted that to succeed he had to overcome a major cultural problem which was the attitude of Chinese parents towards their offspring's leisure time:

> To run an on-line games company in traditional Chinese culture is not easy; the people, they always ask their children to study; to be educated. Not to play games.[56]

In 2004, to help with the education of the young, the government earmarked £150 million to develop a 'healthy' on-line games industry which would wean teenagers away from the invasion of foreign violent computer games and towards China's own literary classics, myths and revolutionary stories featuring benevolent heroes and adventurers.[57]

It is not clear from conversations overheard in shops, however, that children agree with this arbitrary dividing line between play and education or that parental preferences always prevail. A visit to a toy shop is usually made in the company of an adult on special occasions such as a birthday, New Year, Children's Day or at the end of the school term or year as a reward for good grades, a special sporting or a cultural achievement. The mixing of play and education can be observed on the popular festivals of Children's Day (1 June), when children and their parents go to children's 'palaces', parks, schools and stadiums or other public spaces to visit the stands of many manufacturers who are using the opportunity to display the educational advantages of their wares. Many malls and stores also provide public play spaces for children where they can become familiar with toys, educational aids and video games. Children's toy departments are characterised by display-and-play desks and tables showing the ways in which various toys can provide both pleasure and educational value. When the renowned Japanese Yaoshan retail giant opened in the Pudong development zone of Shanghai, it provided an entertainment area the size of an in-field baseball diamond where any child under 1.3 metres could romp free of charge. At the centre of the play area, on a surface of synthetic grass, were slides and a running track while, along the periphery, alcoves were dedicated to quieter activities such as reading picture books, playing with Lego and listening to music. On the July morning in 1996 when scholars Deborah Davis Friedman and Julia Sesenbrenner visited, there were 25 to 30 infants, toddlers and primary-school-age boys and girls playing under the supervision of store employees. Downtown in the city centre, Shanghai's large department stores had less space but offered a similar range of consumer goods for children as well as areas dedicated to children's play. There, they observed 20 to 30 children playing video games, racing cars or buying toys.[58] Even in the mid-1990s, their studies suggested that the participation of children in the purchase of toys was 'striking' from a very young age.[59]

Perhaps the most potent of influences on children's preferences in China, as for their peers elsewhere, has been television and in particular series or programmes that have tie-in promotions and advertisements. Before the introduction of foreign films and programmes aimed at children, there was little brand association or recognition, but once television shows and films began to feature foreign and domestic characters, they became widely recognised and the subject of much merchandising. Many programmes and in particular children's cartoon series from abroad have been sold to Chinese television channels on the understanding that associated products and characters are directly tied into the promotional package. One scholar studied the craze for the Transformer range of toys which were linked to an American re-edited and rewritten version of original Japanese-associated cartoons. In the late 1980s, he observed that the Transformer range became the most successful toy ever launched on the Asian market and concluded that the factor most responsible for their surging popularity in China was the Hashno-sponsored series screened by both central and local television stations in the main cities. The show was an immediate success and the Transformer characters, ranging from Y10 to Y100 each, rapidly became the country's best-selling toy range in 1989, with queues forming outside Beijing's main Wangfujing's department store which sold tens of thousands of yuan worth each week.[60] This was the first of many waves of Western and Japanese television cartoon series with accompanying comic books, toys and clothes. Several years later, in 1996, the Disney film Toy Story had similar publicity and popularity among children with replicas of the heroes sold throughout the city. Two sociologists observed that in this era of globalisation, Disney's Toy Story had become as familiar to Shanghai's children as to their American peers.[61] Since the mid-1990s, branded cartoon and television series have brought segments of China's children into an international arena of global favourites. In 2005, Disney is reported to be looking to China for growth by organising a tour of Disney on Ice which featured the three favourites of Jungle Book, Tarzan and the Lion King and it also has high hopes of building a second theme-park in Shanghai to match that in Hong Kong which is already visited by many tourists from China.[62] Television series and films have also stimulated the sales of not just associated toys but also of books and magazines.

Reading and recreation

Before the mid-1990s, 30 or so publishing houses for children and youth controlled the lion's share of the children's book industry in China. They mainly published a limited range of textbooks and other reading materials that were either commissioned or permitted by the country's educational bureaux. A major change occurred in 1997 when, although still state-owned, domestic and foreign publishing giants were permitted to extend their operations and reach in China's domestic market. For example the Chinese Children's Press and Publication Group (CCPPG), the country's leading children's publishing house, joined forces with Belgian-based Customer EditionSA to launch a series of marketing bids to popularise the Tintin comic books. As CCPPG's Chairman noted, his publishing house aimed to 'introduce the best children's books worldwide to Chinese readers while striving to promote Chinese children's publications, which are a very important part of the Chinese culture, to the world'.[63] The company has been more successful in promoting foreign children's books in China, as in recent years these have increasingly dominated the China market. In 1998 more than 51 per cent of all children's books sold in China's largest book retail outlet, the Beijing Xidan Bookstore, were still published by China's own children and youth publishing houses, but by 2001 this proportion had declined to 28 per cent.[64] In September 2002, four Harry Potter books and the same number of Goosebump books dominated the lists of China's 10 best-selling children's books compiled by China's only market research company specialising in the book industry, Openbook.com.cn. The other two on the list were the Korean cartoon rabbit Mashimono and a Chinese education book.

In 2002, Tintin comic books also made the 'most popular' lists although the 'scary' Goosebumps books were considered the 'most cool and hip' by both Chinese children and by adults, among whom these American thrillers were also fashionable.[65] A combined readership of all ages was always fortuitous for as, the President of CCPPG noted, adults still purchase the major proportion of children's books:

> Now [on average] six adults rear one child, and they are ready to buy all kinds of publications that are good for the child's growth. Therefore it's a cake that everyone wants a bite of.[66]

Although adults may purchase the books, it is children themselves who exert an increasingly large influence over what is published and, if the 'best sellers' are an indication, they have tended to choose books that are 'fun' as opposed to those that are educational and the first choices of their parents. A recent *Guangming Daily* multiple-choice survey showed that parents preferred to purchase scientific encyclopaedias (62.5%) and fairy tales (50%) for their children. However children ranked fiction above both of these genres, while best-sellers tend to be translations of foreign children's fiction.[67] Nevertheless the President of the CCPPG is confident that the prevalence of foreign children's books in the Chinese market is but a temporary phenomenon and will come to an end as the fledgling domestic children's book industry matures.[68]

In addition to books, there are more than 250 children's newspapers and magazines and, here too, long-established Chinese publications are in direct competition with Chinese versions of Walt Disney's *Mickey Mouse Magazine* and other such comic books. The annual circulation figures of CCPPG's magazines and newspapers, which included the popular weekly newspapers for primary schools, fell behind the raft of new magazines and newspapers aiming primarily at entertainment rather than education.[69] The Children's Fun Publishing Co Ltd, a joint-venture with a Danish publishing house, has worked hard to introduce and distribute the Disney *Mickey Mouse Magazine* to boost the circulation of this 'healthy entertainment product' and 'give China's hard-studying kids a break'. In 2002, after 7 years of effort, 800,000 to 900,000 copies were sold each month, making China the single largest market for *Mickey Mouse Magazine* in the world. Encouraged by this success, the company began to distribute the bilingual Winnie the Pooh series in 2001 and, under licence for the BBC, a series of Teletubbies books written for children aged 0 to 4 years. The latter was an activity-book adapted for the Chinese market which was initially well received because, according to BBC WorldWide China, it had 'adopted a format familiar to children in China that also works well for the Teletubbies brand'.[70] One of the most successful routes to winning Disney magazine loyalty has been the establishment of Mickey Mouse or Disney corners complete with the whole line of Disney publications and colourful stuffed toys of Disney characters which can be found in bookstores, hypermarkets and schools in the major cities. In 2002, Teletubby corners displaying a wide range of branded merchandise set out to follow this example. However in recent years the promotion of new products has become much more difficult now that there is an increasingly competitive market in which discerning young customers exercise greater choice. As CCPPG's president wryly noted in 2002:

> Foreign magazines are powerful in that they attack from all flanks. After reading *Mickey Mouse Magazine*, the kids can play with Mickey Mouse toys and watch Mickey Mouse TV programmes. We really feel the pressure.[71]

Certainly Chinese children's magazine publishing houses rapidly learned lessons from foreign imported magazines and soon developed characters such as Du Du Bear with associated merchandising.

Similarly, China has developed a flourishing animation industry since the mid-1990s and some of the Chinese cartoon series have enjoyed wide popularity, with one of the first home-made cartoon characters, Blue Cat, soon rivalling Mickey Mouse. So far, five series of Blue Cat, with a total of 1,700 episodes have been completed and the cat, also designed to spread knowledge of science and technology to children, has enjoyed not only domestic but also some international success. The Blue Cat series has been translated into Russian, English and Hebrew and exported to some 13 countries including the USA, Korea, Hong Kong and Taiwan. This successful series has made its creators one of the largest television cartoon producers in the country and ushered in a flourishing domestic cartoon industry in which China's first cartoon cat has been joined by Pipi pig, Mimi sheep and Taqi or Xiaoren. Changsha city, the capital of Hunan province, has become the centre of a flourishing animation industry producing 70 per cent of the country's total cartoon programmes with an annual production value amounting to Y1.3 billion (US$157.1 million) and an export value exceeding US$1 million in 2003.[72] To encourage the development and investment in China's own animation enterprises, the State Administration of Radio, Film and Television set up a number of new national animation-industrial bases in 2004, one of which was to constitute a Digital Cartoon City complete with a cartoon garden, cultural gallery and fast music plaza. It also approved the establishment of three television channels given over to cartoons.[73] However, flourishing as it is, China's animation industry still only occupies 10 per cent of the country's market. In 2005, it was reported that 80 per cent of the Chinese market was occupied by Japanese companies and another 10 per cent by European and American companies.[74] Certainly Viacom, the US-based company that dominates children's programming in much of the world with its MTV and Nickelodeon network, is assiduously courting China's youngsters in the hope of capturing even a sliver of this market. It already has a station in Guangdong and programmes in Shanghai but much of its programming must be negotiated and modified to omit any disrespect to parents or other authority, hyperactivity or other unruly behaviour or bodily exhibitionism.[75] It also has to be said that parents are likely to be even more restrictive than the government. So keen are they for their children to achieve that television viewing is restricted and after-school time is filled by hours of homework and extra-curricular activities. Many of the children's programmes consist of quiz shows, team competitions and educational programmes or cartoons. Very recently the government announced a crack-down on all media deemed 'evil' or harmful to young people and attempted to impose new limits on production deals between foreign and domestic television and film companies, thus dashing the expansion plans of Viacom, Disney and Time Warner.[76]

Simultaneously a new range of recreational activities have become available to cater specifically for city children. Previously family outings were limited to visiting kin, strolls in parks and the occasional visit to a zoo, a museum, an acrobatic performance or Children's Day and other festive activities. Now family excursions may include visits to shopping malls, swimming pools, movies, performances, amusement parks, scenic spots, an aquarium or even further afield to a lake or beach. Some of these recreational activities are quite expensive and some charge admission fees amounting to many tens of yuan; others such as a visit to a shopping mall are ostensibly free of charge. I like the description of one foreign correspondent who observed how, on a Sunday afternoon in downtown Beijing, China's 'little emperors' can be seen 'hitting the streets' with parents in tow, one of whom, the parent of a 3-year-old playing in a Lego display area, described their usual Sunday afternoon pattern:

> We spend money on activities each weekend, but we don't always go to a store to buy things. We might go to a park, or to a restaurant to get something to eat, or just show her around the shops.[77]

Very recently, I observed children at play in a number of department stores on a Sunday afternoon in Shanghai. Most counters had display and activity tables where children could try out the toys or games at their leisure and some had a very good time but left with no purchase. The most popular counter was that which sold calculators, small computers and electronic games. Here fond families watched the young and nimble-fingered, admiring their numerate and other skills. There was some serious looking and questioning by parents with the most popular purchases a small toy vehicle, a doll, a calculator/computer or bicycle. Most of these were made in China and considerably cheaper, often as much as Y200 to Y300 cheaper, than their imported foreign counterparts. One little boy could not be persuaded to get off his China-made bicycle to the detriment of stands, toys and toes and I was interested to observe the tolerance of parents and shop staff at the speedy havoc of the journey and the price of the bicycle – Y289 – which was relatively cheap compared with other toys in the store. The higher the family income, the more a child is likely to have sampled the new range of leisure activities and particularly those that are perceived to have an educational component. During school holidays, older children too are more likely to visit the shops and amusement arcades on their own or in groups but, even in their younger years, school-aged children in China have less leisure than many of their counterparts elsewhere. Although parents are willing to allocate more resources than ever before to their children's leisure and entertainment, they together with poorer parents are even more anxious to further their children's education and make the most of the new and increasing educational opportunities widely available in China's cities, richer rural regions and even abroad.

Education, education, education

Whatever their location and income, parents want access to the best types and highest levels of education available in their location. The reform government has expended considerable effort to establish universal basic education and expand higher education. Since 1986, 9-year compulsory education has been regarded as the basic right of all Chinese citizens and, in 1992, the targets set by China's Education Reform and Development Plan aimed to eliminate illiteracy by the year 2000 and to provide nine-year compulsory education for all children by the early twenty-first century. Despite much progress, the achievement of these goals has so far remained elusive, but there has been much effort expended on improving schools and widening access in poor rural areas and on girls' education. Since 1999 much attention has also been directed to improving the quality of schooling by moving away from rote learning and injecting originality and creativeness into a knowledge-centred and examination-oriented education. China now has a 6-3-3-4 school structure, preceded in the cities and suburbs by pre-school education which is provided in nurseries and kindergartens that are organised and sponsored by either work-units, local communities or private companies. Primary school entry is at 6 or 7 years and lasts for 6 years while secondary education is divided into two 3-year stages of junior and senior middle school. Additionally there has been an increase in vocational or specialised secondary schools to train much-needed technical and professional workers or other middle-level staff.

Finally for higher education, there are large numbers of universities which in the mid-1990s were restructured and decentralised in an attempt to improve quality and promote economies of scale. Education is not free in China and tuition and other fees for education at all levels can amount to hundreds of thousands of yuan per year depending on level, quality and location. Despite attempts by the government to cap school fees at all levels and for all types of education in support of their aim of 'offering an educational system to all capable of receiving it',[78] all types of educational fees have risen incrementally over the years. This is largely because the financing of education has been decentralised and privatised with local governments, schools and universities increasingly looking to fees to make good the shortfalls in central government funding which are necessary to sustain their institutions let alone produce more and better education. The current cost-sharing framework is very uneven and has left many schools and especially those in local towns and rural villages short of funds. According to a survey conducted by the Development Research Centre of the State Council, the educational budget is shared between the township (78%), the county (9%), the provincial (11%) and the central government (2%).[79] Shortfalls in funding are largely made up from pupil or student fees which places a heavy burden on families in the cities, suburbs and countryside.

In the mid-1990s, a Gallup survey conducted nation-wide showed that about two-thirds of the families interviewed nominated financing children's education as a primary source of hardship and savings goal.[80] In many parts of China, the cost of education has superseded housing as one of the largest budget items for both rural and urban families. In 2001, a survey of 500 or so urban residents in three major cities and another of children up to 12 years of age in five major cities both showed that the costs of education were second only to those on food in calculating the total amounts spent on children.[81] In 2002, a survey by the National Statistics Bureau suggested that among the different reasons for saving, 'preparing for a child's education' was the most often cited.[82] References to 'deep pockets' and 'saving everything that can be saved in order to choose a good school is good for the child and his/her fortune' are popular sayings among parents.[83] Again in 2003, *China Today* reported that education constituted the major portion of consumption spending on children with 50 per cent of families spending Y10,000 on their child's education and food each year annually while 40 per cent of families had earmarked their savings for children's education.[84] In 2005, *The Economist* reported that in a recent survey on reasons for saving, education continued to come top of everyone's list.[85] My own field experiences in city and countryside over the years suggest that, whether residence is urban or rural or incomes high or low, providing for a better future for children and the costs of education are the most talked about items in conversation, interview and focus group. Farming and migrant families freely express their hopes and aspirations for their children and self-denial can be a way of life for those planning a better life for the next generation. Even when children are very young, parents talk of tending the fields or 'making money' far from home in order to save for their children's school and university fees:

> I want to support the children no matter how expensive it's going to be. I'll work hard. I'll be happy dying of exhaustion if my children are happy and successful.[86]

Hard-working parents did not relax until they had fees for the next term or year in hand, elder siblings worked to support the education of younger siblings and families often helped each other to meet the costs of schooling of a bright achieving child. One farmer thought he was 'unusual' in that he had been able to send all four of his children to middle school:

> Currently the greatest challenge facing farmers are the various kinds of heavy burdens which affect their children's education and their living standards.[87]

The extra effort required to meet the costs of schooling and any further education in rural villages is evident in the ways in which one farming family assumed the heavy financial burden of supporting their children in school. By labouring non-stop in slack and busy seasons, both parents cultivated four mu of agricultural land to achieve high yields of tobacco and sweet potato and sold candied sweet potato and bean curd in the market place even though this meant sleeping only 4 to 5 hours per night on some occasions. Their high-achieving children entered the only key middle school in the county where they boarded and studied hard to earn college places.[88] The chances of a bright achieving child progressing through the middle and higher-levels of education are very much determined by location and income.

In the countryside away from the richest suburbs and coastal regions and despite high enrolment rates, a goodly portion of school students do not graduate from primary school and the majority do not complete junior or senior middle school levels of education, largely because of availability, standards of schooling and the fees required or opportunity costs to families. In the very poor rural regions, children might be enrolled but this did not necessarily mean that they regularly attended primary school and many started late or dropped out early so that only a minority graduated from primary school. My own field work in very poor rural regions suggests that the majority, and especially girls, do not stay in school long enough to acquire, and most importantly, to maintain literacy leading to low literacy rates and other skills as outlined in earlier chapters on migration and employment. Schools may be very basic with four bare walls, rows of desks and teachers with minimal qualifications or even absentee teachers, but parents are still keen to have their children attend if they can afford the costs. An increasing number are completing the junior middle school years but even in the more privileged county towns only a minority reach senior middle school where the drop-out rate is high. Recently, the Research Institute for Rural Education found that the average drop-out rate of children in primary school in rural areas in 2004 was 40 per cent. For junior middle schools the drop out rate ranged from 40 per cent in county towns to 60 per cent in small towns; in less-developed areas and where there were long distances between home and school, drop-out rates reached 74 per cent.[90] Most students dropped out because they fell behind in their studies, wanted to earn a wage or were bored by the irrelevance of the rather old-fashioned rote and bench approaches to learning. Statistics show that only 23 per cent of gross educational expenditure in 2002 was allocated to rural areas inhabited by at least 60 per cent of the total population.[90] In 2004 and 2005, much government attention has been directed towards the need to improve or 'reinvigorate' rural education and of providing equal opportunities to migrant children for education in the cities.[91] In 2005, a Report on Research into Equity Issues in China's Education found that at all levels of education, city dwellers have significantly better opportunities than the rural population and drew attention to the lack of progress in the interior provinces in improving the resourcing, access to and the quality of schooling. In it there was also some talk of providing financial support to rural students or deferring school fees in order to reduce the drop-out rates.[92]

In the richer southern and coastal provinces and rural suburbs of cities, a high proportion of village children graduate into junior and senior middle school with a fortunate few attending university although often at great hardship to their families. According to a report in *Chinese Education Daily* in 2002, about 60 per cent of China's vocational college students come from rural areas although they are less likely to enter the premium and large-city colleges because of their inability to meet the costs of fees or acquire the entry standards necessary for the next level because of the poor quality of schooling.[93] In 2002, a staff member of Beijing University's Higher Education Institute estimated that a three-member rural family has to spend 70 per cent of its income to cover tuition so that 'education to some extent could mean real hardship'.[94] As one student, a freshman at the University of International Business and Economics, said in 2002, 'tuition was making his family starve'. Given that their total income was about Y6,000 and that only covered his tuition, his four-member family was in debt even though his 16-year-old sister had left school to find a temporary job in Shanghai to help provide support.[95] Another farmer's son was able to enter university in Beijing because he was awarded a scholarship as well as financial aid from several units and enterprises which was sufficient to pay the tuition fees. He also took on a number of part-time jobs, both to support himself and to help his younger brother have the same opportunities.[96] In 2004 it was estimated that some 20 per cent or 2.4 million of 12 million college students came from poor families.[97] In north China's Shanxi province alone, needy students suffering financial hardship in 2004 accounted for 30 per cent of the total enrolment, with 10 per cent so badly off that, even with tightening their belts and taking part-time jobs, they typically could only afford to spend Y12 to Y18 per month.[98]

In the cities and richer suburbs there is intense competition for entry into the key or better quality schools, facilities in the private sector and higher education of all types and levels. In 2002, research for the Municipal Bureau of Beijing estimated that on average Y160,000 was needed for a child's education from kindergarten to high school and, in Shenzhen, parents had to pay on average Y4,500 per year for a child's tuition.[99] There are major expenses in addition to regular tuition fees in that nearly every city school from kindergarten to high school also charges sponsorship fees. In Beijing in late 2002, the annual sponsorship fee for kindergarten ranged between Y5,000 and Y20,000, in primary school and junior middle schools sponsorship fees ranged from Y30,000 to Y50,000 and for senior middle schools from Y50,000 to Y100,000.[100] At each level of schooling, parents can pay extra fees to compensate for shortfalls in exam marks. For instance, in one of the best middle schools in Beijing in each of the 16 classes with 50 students there are reported to be around 10 per cent who paid Y100,000 to gain entry.[101] Given that the average annual income in urban areas tends to be around Y6,500 to Y7,000, these sums can be seen to represent hefty proportions of family incomes. Periodically there are major reports in the media about the rising numbers of students who are admitted to the better middle schools because they pay high fees rather than achieve sufficient examination scores. In 2002 it was estimated that around 25 per cent of Beijing's 791 middle schools supplemented their revenue by accepting high-fee-paying pupils who have failed to achieve the marks to enrol normally.[102] Parents report that they are paying tens of thousands of yuan to get their child enrolled and schools argue that if they are to cover costs then they have no choice but to both charge high fees of perhaps around Y30,000 and accept higher numbers, perhaps as many as 10 per cent more than permitted, thus making class sizes much larger than recommended. Parents who succeed in enrolling their children via this route consider the effort and expense to be well worth the satisfaction of having their child study at a key middle school which has better teaching, resources and facilities:

> The idea of a key kindergarten plus key experimental primary schools plus key middle school plus top university equals 'white-collar' is accepted by most parents as the way of life for their children.[103]

If it is the widespread hope of so many parents whether rich or poor that their children will be able to go to university, it is an unrealistic dream for most because of a number of educational and financial factors. Many, especially in the rural regions, will not have the opportunities to make the required academic standards and even for those who graduate from senior middle school, the number of university places falls short of demand, although China's higher education system has developed rapidly in recent years – so much so that *The Economist* reported in 2005 that 'China is engaged in the biggest university expansion in history'.[104] In 1994, only 2.4 per cent of all young persons aged between 18 and 22 years entered university, but since the mid-1990s a number of reforms have established new and expanded old universities enabling a total of 6 to 7 million students to attend university in 1999[105] and many more each year since. In 2005, the government expressed the hope that eventually 15 per cent of school leavers or a total of 16 million students would be able to enrol in higher education and that the best universities would be in the super-league to rival the best in the world.[106] The competition for places is still fierce, especially for the handful of premier universities such as Beijing, Tsinghua and Fudan, which are much sought after because of their status and the virtual guarantee of employment after graduation. However at the same time as there has been some expansion in university places, there has also been a parallel increase in tuition fees so that total fees at colleges and universities amount to many thousands of yuan which has made higher education a substantial burden for a fortunate minority and prohibitive for the majority. Within the space of one year, under-graduate tuition rose from an average of Y3,000 in 1999 to Y5,000 in 2000 and a poll conducted a year later by the National Statistics Bureau reported that 70 per cent of parents thought that Y5,000 was too expensive in relation to average annual incomes of between Y6,000 and Y7,000 and that they expected to accrue large debts.[107] In 2002, a National Statistics Bureau Report showed that university fees were rising faster than incomes.[108]

In 2005, it was reported that a student needed about Y10,000 per year for university study in Beijing to cover fees as well as living costs, transport and books, even though the Municipal government has attempted to cap fees.[109] Most of the capital's higher education institutions now keep their annual fees between Y4,200 and Y6,000 although more may be charged by key institutes and for popular subjects such as sciences, engineering, foreign languages and medicine.[110] These limits have been set because families of students struggle to pay the fees and because higher education is increasingly beyond the financial reach of a great number of Chinese students and particularly those from the countryside. However for all families, a high premium is placed on acquiring an educational achievement and parents are prepared to invest in and accord priority to their children's education because this investment is not just about brightening the prospects of a particular child but continues to be about the long-term security and future of the entire family. There is a centuries-long tradition in China of scrimping, saving and pooling of family incomes to educate a bright child for officialdom to enhance family status and advance longer-term family well-being and security. The continuing bid for high-quality education regardless of expense is such that some city parents have turned to the burgeoning private sector which in recent years has expanded to meet the demand for a quality education at all levels from pre-school to university.

A private education

In the cities, there is a growing interest in private pre-school education. Indeed the quest for quality education starts in early childhood as city parents have become more interested than ever before in the development of their only child. There is a ready literature on child rearing and as entry to the best kindergartens and primary schools is fiercely competitive, city parents are eager to give their child the best start possible long before they reach kindergarten-age. In the late 1990s, one enterprising young woman recognised and targeted this niche market by offering private education to children from 0 to 3 years of age. She had calculated the market potential of such a venture:

> Think about it. There are 70 million 0–3-year-old toddlers in China with over 10 million in more affluent urban areas. If their parents pay Y2,000 (US$241) for each of them every year to attend early education programmes like ours, the market size is around Y20 billion (US$2.4 billion).[111]

By September 2002, she had established 43 educational Oriental BabyCare stores in 32 cities nation-wide of which 10 were wholly owned by her company and the remaining 33 were franchised stores. Similarly, the registered capital of Y500,000 (US$60,240) that she invested in her pre-school had billowed into annual revenue of close to Y50 million (US$6 million) with a profit margin of up to 20 per cent. Although competition in the infant care and education market was much greater by 2002 so that in Beijing alone there were around 50 competitors, she still firmly believed in the vast potential of the market, the company's funding advantage and her own established reputation which would all help put in place at least 100 Oriental BabyCare stores across the country in the coming years.[112]

Residential week-day kindergartens have also become a lucrative business for parents working hard to make a living in the new market economy or to further their own education or vocational qualifications. Although the costs of sending toddlers to boarding kindergarten are a high Y1,500 amounting to one-fifth or a quarter of joint income, parents widely praise these kindergartens for giving their children a greater independence, social skills and a better start than care at home by doting grandparents or domestic maids from the countryside.[113] In Shanghai, about one-third of the 30 boarding kindergartens were owned by entrepreneurs in 2004.[114] One former radio-journalist who opened the first of several 'Good-time Kindergartens' in 2001, admitted that it was a profitable business with stable cash-flow opportunities despite the highly competitive market. Certainly there is competition for places and not just in the main cities of Shanghai, Beijing and Shenyang.[115] In one smaller city in northeast Shandong province, a residential kindergarten opened its doors to 15 pupils but within a year it had enrolled 300 children with an estimated 40 to 50 more on the waiting list. One parent who delighted in the learning and number skills taught, spoke for many when he said 'We've got only one child and we want to give him the perfect education'.[116] To help meet demand for quality in education, the government has also encouraged private education at all levels from primary school to universities. Although the ownership of the institutions is private, they are under the general guidance of government educational authorities with governing bodies overseeing financial management, curriculum development and the recruitment of teachers. In the late 1990s, there were reported to be more than 60,000 high-fee privately-owned educational institutions offering education to some ten million students. [117]

In addition to formal and expensive education provided by private schools, there are increasing numbers of education-related agencies or businesses in the private sector which offer various types of individual and extra-curricular tuition to help students enter schools of their choice. There has been significant familial investment in the private tuition of children in academic subjects and in extra-curricula activities such as art, music, calligraphy and the English language. Parents willingly pay fees for these classes which not only develop their children's skills and status but also help them gain entry into the school of their choice. During the revolutionary years, opportunities for such activities were limited to the privileged few selected for extra-curricular classes at Children's Palaces, but now private instructors offer the same or better opportunities in specialist or in one-to-one tuition – sometimes from a very early age. Several of the large shopping malls have floors devoted to 'Children's Education and Lifestyle'. On one in Shanghai labelled 'Children's Vogue Lifestyle and Education', several shop-fronts offering tuition and creative play could be observed which had signs including 'BabyArt', 'Music and Play', 'Gymboree' and 'Early MBA'. Most offered art and creative play although the early MBA, for 3 to 6-year-olds, promised integration, leadership, teamwork as well as creativity for 'fastrakids' in 'a globalised, market-demands world'. Such tuition is not cheap. In Shenzhen it was estimated that parents might pay Y3,280 for all kinds of after-school training in addition to the average fee of Y4,500 per year for a child's tuition.[118] However after-class academic and extra-curricular tutoring has almost become a pre-requisite for key school entry as a school's reputation and wealth very much hinges on the examination results of its students and the number of students with special musical, art, poetic and calligraphic skills. Indeed the attainment of high entry scores and extra-curricular skills can exempt pupils from paying the normal school fees and thus reduce the costs to parents. As one teacher noted:

> Parents spend enormously on kids after-class training courses partly to help their all-round growth and partly to save them more exorbitant sponsorship fees.[119]

Such is the popularity of these extra-curricular activities that there are substantial profits to be made in the educational market through providing private tuition, designing and producing educational software or establishing new schools and programmes. Some companies and regular teachers who moonlight have accrued considerable wealth. For example the head of a Beijing company that provides children with musical instruction and the head of China's largest English language training school are both known to be yuan millionaires several times over.[120] English language training is one of the 'hottest' sectors within the educational market, constituting a high-growth industry generating substantial profits. The best known institution, the New Oriental School in Beijing, provides basic English language and teaching in preparation for TOEFL and GRE tests for which there are known to be long waiting lists. Several English language schools have established partnerships with foreign software companies to develop multi-media language-learning tools. According to the China Manager of one of the American software companies developing English learning, 'the sky is the limit' for this sector as parents rush to educate their child:

> No matter how difficult their life is, Chinese parents always give first priority to the needs of their children especially education which largely decides a child's fate.[121]

Not only does mastery of the English language augment both educational and employment prospects within China, but also many of the richest official, professional and entrepreneurial families in China's cities are now turning to foreign boarding schools and universities to educate their children.

A foreign education

The increase in interest in a foreign boarding-school education is such that demand is reported to be growing steadily despite the high costs of fees. In 1998, British education fairs in Beijing for middle school students going abroad to study attracted 35,000 visitors.[122] By the turn of the century, tens of thousands of teenagers were studying at schools abroad and the number was growing despite the rise in costs to around £100,000 for 5 years of secondary schooling abroad. In Britain alone, demand is said to be 'soaring' despite the average boarding school fees of around £16,000 per year which amount to around 10 times the average annual income of an urban household in China.[123] Students from China are now the second largest category of new entrants to British private schools from abroad, which puts China just behind Hong Kong and ahead of Germany. According to ISIS calculations in 2001, there were more than 1,300 pupils from China attending public schools, with 525 new arrivals in the previous year. Most of these pupils were from high-ranking official and new entrepreneurial families in Beijing, Shanghai and Guangdong who were mostly sent to public schools such as Harrow, Charterhouse and Malvern.[124] Many more go to schools in Australia, New Zealand and Canada where fees are somewhat lower. In 2003 it was estimated that around 7,000 per year enter Australia for study at secondary level and the number was estimated to be growing at 10 per cent per year.[125] Most of the children sent abroad are single children from the larger cities and most of those sending their child abroad are either wealthy themselves or receive help or borrow from family members. It is often said that the single child studying abroad is likely to be supported by six pockets! Even in provinces such as Liaoning in the northeast where there is soaring unemployment, it was reported in a newspaper in 2003 that some 600 high school students go abroad to study each year and that this number was 'increasing rapidly'.[126] There are some suggestions that parents hope to use their children's bank accounts to accumulate funds abroad, but it is more likely that parents send their child abroad for other reasons. First they want to give a bright child a unique or a 'head start' and so increase the status of both child and family. One mother sent her son to a private school in Britain even though the cost of tuition, room and board was more than 10 times the cost of a private secondary school in China. As she said: 'I have only one child, I want him to have a bright future'.[127] In the years to come this 'bright future' may also be acquired in the new schools established in China by schools abroad including Britain's own Dulwich College. As for schooling abroad, this option is also a way of escaping the intense competition and stress experienced by many children and their families to gain entry to good schools and universities in China. As a result of both the shortage of places at prestigious universities and the increasing costs of higher education in China, there has also been a steady increase in the number of students from China studying at universities abroad.

If parents dream that their child may 'Go West',[128] many more achieve this dream at university rather than at school level. During the first decade of reform, most of the students studying abroad were sponsored either by China's government or by a number of scholarship programmes sponsored by K.C. Wang and the Chevening fund administered by the British Council. In contrast, by the late 1990s, there had been a rapid increase in the number of students going abroad who were funded privately by their families. In all, by the turn of the century some 300,000 Chinese students were studying abroad, mainly in the USA, Britain, Australia, Canada and New Zealand.[129] Initially the USA was the favourite destination and the bookstores of special English language schools overflowed with titles that guided pupils and their parents through the complex processes of applying to Ivy League Colleges. In 2001, a book entitled *The Harvard Girl*, detailing a Chinese sophomore's life at this holy grail of universities sold 1 million copies and spurred an industry of imitators including *The Harvard Guy*, *You Must Go to Harvard*, *Getting into Harvard* and *You can go to Harvard even if you don't have a Rich Father*.[130] However since 9/11 and the new visa restrictions in the USA, students from China have looked more favourably at higher education in the UK, Canada, Australia and New Zealand. Indeed universities in these countries have embarked on intensive recruitment campaigns to develop this lucrative overseas market. In the UK, the number of Chinese students in British higher education had increased to 18,000 by 2001–2, which represented a 30 per cent increase over the previous academic year.[131] In 2002, preliminary figures suggested a further increase of 67 per cent, taking the likely total to over 25,000 and making Chinese students the largest group of foreign students in Britain.[132] It was anticipated that, with this rate of increase which was the highest from any country, the number of Chinese students in Britain would probably exceed 30,000 in 2006–7.[133] While outside China, and especially in the UK and Australia, there is much talk of the potential numbers of overseas student fees, it is well to remember that China is also expanding and improving its own university system. Already there are signs that the numbers travelling abroad to attend university are declining. There have been several reports in the past year that the number of Chinese students going abroad is either stabilising or declining due to visa restriction, rising costs and stories of lax standards in both tuition and quality of student life at universities which perceive China's students as a source of profit.[134] However equally important is the expansion of China's own higher education system and the new and greater numbers of opportunities for students in China itself. Foreign degrees no longer bring with them the promise of a job now that many of China's own prestigious universities feature among the world's top universities in international league tables and attract students especially from other parts of Asia. Some of China's vocational, technical and senior middle school campuses are among the most modern and best equipped that I have seen anywhere. In sum, it might be concluded that, because children's education is of the highest priority and takes a substantial portion of most parental incomes and savings, there is frequently little left over for other child-oriented goods and services. Nevertheless the post-revolutionary generations of children also have their own small incomes and have become consumers in their own right.

The child consumer

Children themselves may now have money in their pockets to purchase their own small items of personal consumption which they choose themselves, albeit influenced by television, peers and parents. Children's 'income' is usually divided into regular pocket money made up of weekly and daily amounts for small needs or amounts given to children by parents and grandparents on special occasions such as birthdays, New Year and Children's Day. Several investigations around the turn of the century suggested that children in Beijing received as much as Y5 per day for their own consumption and around Y100 at New Year, on birthdays or as rewards for academic achievement.[135] In 1995, it was reckoned that the total of such allowances and gifts received by city children added up to an annual sum of US$35 billion – a sum which was also reported to be the rough equivalent of Mongolia's gross domestic product.[136] In 1998, *Beijing Youth Daily* polled 500 of the city's households and found that around New Year, children did well for they were given cash sums ranging from a few hundred to a few thousand yuan with the average hovering around Y500.[137] Such sums were much less in the countryside where pocket money was more likely to range between 50 fen and 3 yuan, paid on a daily or weekly basis.[138] Most pocket money in both city and countryside is spent on candy, drinks, crisps, instant noodles, cookies, chocolate, ice-cream, small toys and other such items. In one very detailed study conducted in the second half of the 1990s among 1,500 families in urban China, parents reported that their children had money of their own to spend from around the age of 4 years or so and that the sums received per week increased along with age, ranging from Y3.2 for 4-year-olds to Y21.1 for 12-year-olds. The primary sources of children's regular income were frequent small gifts from parents made on an as-needed basis (40%), an allowance (32%) and money gifts from other family members (22%), with the remainder earned from work in the home (3%) or from outside sources (3%). Children were said to regularly make small independent purchases en route to and from school or while shopping with parents and grandparents. Parents in this study estimated that the children spent their own money on snacks (21%), books and magazines (31%), school supplies (25%), clothing (10%), play items (8%), music (2%), sporting goods (2%) and electronics (1%). Children between 4 and 8 years spent more money on snacks and play items, while those aged between 9 and 12 years allocated significantly more to stationery, books, clothing and electronics. In total the investigation estimated that children in this study spent an average of US$1 per week or slightly more than US$50 per year and, on this basis, they calculated that the 100 million children of China spend at least US$5 billion per year on a relatively wide range of products in a relatively wide range of shopping environments.[139] Although this more detailed study was conducted a few years ago, observation suggests that similar trends operate today and that pocket money may not have risen as fast as family income as parents have become even more careful of their expenditure due to higher living costs and greater insecurity in employment.

In deciding how to spend their pocket money, the most important sources of information for children about new and popular products were the mass media, parents or peers and in-store advertising. A number of studies suggest that the mass media and especially television play the most important role in providing children with new product information. Television now reaches more than 90 per cent of China's households and there are some 400 stations with national and local channels which broadcast programmes specifically aimed at children from toddlers to teens and include cartoons, drama series and games or variety shows.[140] In 2004, in addition to the children's channel of China Central Television (CCTV), 24 provincial TV stations opened new children's channels.[141] There are also a number of radio stations which broadcast some after-school programmes for children and aim to combine both entertainment and education. Most of the newspapers for children, including the popular tabloid *Chinese Children's News* remain more educational than entertaining in purpose. In a survey of 2,288 Beijing children in 1998, the most popular media were television (89%), books (73%), newspapers (73%), tape cassettes (65%), the radio (61%), magazines (53%), computers (32%), electronic games (14%) and surfing the internet (7%).[142]

As elsewhere, marketing messages in the media aimed at children or the 'mini-me' generation are to be found in both the advertisements and programmes. Advertising in particular is intent on informing young persons about products and advocating the consumption of a range of domestic and foreign products from toys, special foods, beverages, snacks, school supplies, video games to toiletries while many children's programmes have merchandise tie-ins. A specialised service sector which includes domestic, foreign or joint-venture companies has emerged to foster a new promotional culture which keeps children in China surprisingly well informed about the attributes of new products. My own field evidence suggests that children in China, as elsewhere, can report on advertisements in some detail and it is very evident in the street, store, home and school playground that these are a major source of ready information.

Children learn about new products from their parents who may point them out or promise them as an incentive to further study, as well as from shops and in-store play areas where new products can be tried and tested by children themselves. Several studies have also shown how peer pressure in the street, playground and classroom strongly influences and spurs the acquisition of the latest new or 'must have' object, snack or experience by children anxious to keep up with their class- or play-mates. In interviews with school children, one researcher observed how the heavy or 'harsh' peer influence of classmates manifested itself in the competition and pressure to eat particular types of new snacks and prestige fast foods which were deemed to be 'up-to-date' or 'modern'.[143] In the playground, inclusion in peer culture and conversations can be dependent on consumer knowledge, exchange of information and one-upmanship. Indeed considerable scorn could be heaped upon the child who was out of touch or did not know of the trendy or latest must-have good and many a child experienced such 'loss of face'. One articulate schoolgirl noted that, following her first experience of peer exclusion, she made sure she was a step ahead:

> Once a classmate brought a package of New Continent ice cream to school. I said I had not seen this kind before. She said that the [commercial] market had been selling them for a long time; New Continent was the most famous – how could I not know? After school I went and bought one … [Now] Whenever there is a new product that I have not tried before, I buy it immediately. I hope to try new things. Otherwise when classmates are chatting, if everyone has tried something and you have not tried it, then you have nothing to say.[144]

In such ways children become the most informed and discerning of consumers as they choose and evaluate merchandise. Some very interesting research in the 1990s asked children to rank their three most important sources of information about new products: these included television (77%) followed by parents (47.7%), store-visits (41.3%) and friends (39.6%).[145] If parents have some influence on the consumer choices of their children, so also do children influence those of their parents.

It seems that China's children may have a great deal of influence on household purchases made by their parents and families. 'Pester power' is an international phenomenon and, as elsewhere, television and other media have consciously directed attention to child viewers in the hope that they will pester their parents for the latest 'must-have' toy, snack, item of clothing or even household good. China is no exception and there is plenty of evidence attesting to the power of the single child to direct family spending on themselves and on the household. Stories of parents queuing for hours to purchase the latest popular item for their child are not uncommon. In retail outlets, children and adults have been observed debating the value and evaluating the advantages or disadvantages of merchandise with children openly articulating their wants and exerting pressure to various degrees. In most cases, unless the child was particularly compliant, children influence or dominate the choice of purchase even it if was the most expensive of several options. Surveys in China in the mid- and late 1990s suggested that children from a very young age were active participants in and influenced family purchases and leisure activities.[146] Children were such a major source of consumer knowledge and exerted such influence that there was talk in the Chinese media of a 'new feedback model' from children to parents. One study of children's consumption in Beijing estimated that children influenced 68 per cent of household purchases in China compared with 45 per cent in the USA.[147] In China, children as young as 3 to 4 years old have been found to exercise influence on their family's choice of staples and snacks and in the case of food and beverage purchases, children in Beijing have been reported to have double the influence of their American counterparts.[148] This influence extends to many leisure-time activities including visits to parks, shops, restaurants and other entertainment venues.

In many stores and restaurants, parents openly admit that their children have influenced the choice of food and eating venues. On one occasion, many elder escorts interviewed in fast-food outlets said that they visited such restaurants between three and five times a month despite the fact that they ate these foods rather reluctantly and would have much sooner eaten elsewhere. Even if the parents did not enjoy the food, they said they fell in with their children's preferences and first choice of staples, snacks and restaurants. In McDonalds, one mother said that she had made great effort to adapt to the strange flavour of McDonalds' food so that twice a week her daughter could eat her 'most desired' food and could learn more about American culture.[149] A few years ago it was estimated that children in the large cities alone exerted direct influence on family purchases of over US$60 billion per year including food and beverages (US$50 billion), children's clothing (US$5 billion), school supplies (US$3 billion) and play items (US$3 billion). If these 'direct influence' purchases, which were overtly requested by children, were added to indirect influence purchases or those in which parents buy what they believe children like without being asked, then the combined value of direct and indirect influence was estimated to total some US$125 billion.[150] A study of kindergarten and school children in Beijing and Tianjin suggested to McNeal and Yeh, researchers with world-wide experience, that the average influence on family purchases by China's urban children substantially exceeded that of American children.[151] That families tend to be child-focused in their expenditure is not unusual in contemporary societies, but China is distinguished by the speed with which such a shift in familial hierarchies or to 'children first' has occurred.

Familial hierarchies

The new concentration of expenditure on children reflects the fact that in most families, children now have a major if not first claim on family budgets. Meeting the needs and satisfying the desires of children is not only likely to take up a significant proportion of incomes and savings in families of all income ranges, but frequently little is left over for other family members including parents and grandparents. Indeed the new concentration of concern and expenditure on children has led to growing competition for familial resources and a profound shift in familial priorities, not to mention inter-generational relations. In the words of one scholar, there has been 'a profound shift in decision-making power' within the family from senior to junior generations'.[152] Several field investigations of my own and of others have noted this shift in focus from senior to junior generations, especially in consumer-oriented urban China. In 2000, *China Daily* described the way in which the older generation has slipped from being 'the most revered and respected ones in the family' to become out of date as 'almost a flashy process'.[153] There has been a reversal in the generational hierarchies that were for centuries elder-oriented and characterised by filial piety; now it is the young who are revered and indulged. Symbolically and practically, this shift is most visible in the city and suburban birthday celebrations of the younger generation which have become increasingly elaborate as parents host meals and purchase large cakes and families offer cards, red envelopes and birthday gifts costing several hundred or even thousand yuan. One researcher has concluded that children have become 'little gods of longevity' for it is they who are now entitled to all the special respect previously reserved for the elderly or the 'old gods of longevity':[154]

> Birthday celebrations used to be simpler for children than for the elderly. Now the situation is reversed. One child after another has learned to act like a little god of longevity.

Although much has been made of the 'indulgence factor' or the 'six pockets' of the 6:4:1 or 6:4:2 ratio and the compensating sacrifice of this generation of parents, it is also true that parents consciously indulge or invest in their child in order to instil a sense of gratitude or even indebtedness which will ensure their own support and care in old age.

Parents very much hope that their child or children will prosper and provide well for their own and their family's future. Thus older generations frequently fall in with or gratify their children's requests in a bid to foster their attachment to and gratitude towards their parents. One field researcher in Beijing has shown clearly how the purchase of consumer goods for the single child has been motivated by a bid to increase the dependency and indebtedness of the child in order to secure both short-term appreciation or gratitude and long-term parent care. In perhaps the most explicit example of this, a mother purchased a piano to please her child on the grounds that 'a child who is grateful to parents should provide care'.[155] As a later chapter on the elderly will show, child care and investment is a continuing 'form of long-range self-interest'[156] in which parents deploy consumer goods and other resources in a bid to strengthen their bid for reciprocal care in old age. If it is clearly in the long-term interest of parents that their children prosper, it is not so certain that it is in the short-term interests of children. It is increasingly clear that present generations of children may be both advantaged and disadvantaged by this combination of familial indulgence and filial expectation. A child may bear the entire weight of parental hopes, expectations and aspirations and several field investigations have documented the heavy pressure placed by parents on children as young as 4, 5 or 6 years old and most especially on single children and those still in school. Bernadine Chee found in her study of young children that not only are children seen as a major asset contributing to a family's self-image and social standing but also their achievements can constitute the sole gauge measuring and reflecting the quality of parenting and the status of parents.[157] The most visible and important yardstick lies in children's school marks and other academic achievements. Children are encouraged to bring good marks home from school with all kinds of incentives and rewards, for parents know that marks not only reflect achievement but also facilitate entry into the best schools, reductions in fees and other financial rewards. As one mother of a fifth-grade daughter told Bernadine Chee:

> Parents know the competition is fierce now. Sometimes if [a child] misses one point – just half a point – then the difference is tremendous: some will go to better schools, and some will not be able to attend good schools.[158]

In a recent survey of children in Boston, Juliet Schor, alarmed by the way that children there have been drawn into the nexus of consumption, concluded that it is the consumer culture that is responsible for much depression, anxiety and lower self-esteem and many psychosomatic complaints.[159] In China too, there are reports of the increasing incidence of anxiety and depression among children and teenagers. One report by a senior official in the Health Ministry estimated that between 9 and 10 per cent of children under the age of 17 years suffered 'mental or behavioural difficulties' and quoted a survey in 22 provinces which revealed that 13 per cent of children and teenagers had behavioural problems while 16 per cent of college students suffered anxiety and depression.[160] It seems that it is the educational pressures on school children which are responsible for similar ills; certainly children fear that parents only care how well they do in school. A child who is not studying hard is continuously questioned or chided by parents and grandparents and sometimes called 'a white-eyed ghost' who is without respect for elders.[161] In a few well-publicised cases, the pressure is so intense that children rebel or commit suicide or murder. One case reported in the foreign press in 2000 involved a 17-year-old boy who struggled to meet his mother's demands that he be among the top ten in the class. When he came eighteenth in order his movement was curtailed and the resulting tension and conflict led to the murder of his mother.[162] This and other such cases have led to much debate in the Chinese press about the pressures on children to succeed in a highly competitive educational and familial environment.

The pressures have not lessened with time. Very recently, 14-year-old pupils in a Shanghai middle school told a *Guardian* correspondent about the intense pressure in their lives now that they do nothing but study: 'For us it's a hard life now ... the competition is intense'. Another also noted the pressure and went on to explain that parents 'put so much love on us that love becomes a reason to do everything'.[163] One young boy who had lived abroad reflected on the repercussions of such pressure:

> One of the things that happens in China, is that everything is focused on your grades, every aspect of expectation is forever on your grades. If you don't have good grades, you aren't a good child. Our parents sometimes do lots of things that we should be doing for ourselves because they want us to concentrate on our grades. For instance, my mom pushes my bike out of the door, presses the elevator button and waits for me to finish my breakfast and go out. It's just study, study, study, study and nothing else.[164]

He went on to note how parents want more and more – an A should be an A+ and an A+ should be A++. Another girl, who said her pocket money was stopped if she failed to excel, described the conversation at each New Year dinner:

> When we eat dinner, my grandmother, grandfather, uncle, aunt, parents and others always ask me, 'How is your study?' It is the only topic. There is not any other topic. They like to have this topic for a long time and I can't eat. When I get a bad mark in my examination, they always say, 'If you don't get good marks, your future is dark'.[165]

The headmaster of another Shanghai middle school also told of the intense parental pressure in his school which he thought was both widespread and 'unprecedented'.[166] However, although the pressure of mounting expectations on this generation of urban children is intense, their contribution to familial status and long-term security co-exists alongside observable warmth and much-valued parent–child bonds in which children are highly privileged and exercise an unprecedented degree of choice and influence. As one parent of a 15-year-old boy noted in 2000:

> The most distinguishing character of today's children compared with our generation is that they have the ability to influence their parents, while we had no such thing.[167]

Altogether, the evidence accumulated over the past twenty years suggests that the post-revolutionary period in China has seen the rise of a new and distinctive notion of childhood, perhaps paralleling an equivalent period in early modern Europe when childhood emerged as a separate phase of the life cycle with its own distinctive needs and interests.[168] In China, a similar emergence and the speed of recent change in the multi-faceted dimensions of childhood are inseparably intertwined with the rapid rise in consumption. For the first generations of children born into one- or two-child families and amid a consumer revolution, perhaps it is not surprising that childhood has been associated not so much with siblings as new forms and attributes of consumption. As an earlier chapter noted, in my own collections of children's drawings of 'their families', consumer items such as televisions and refrigerators feature prominently alongside their parents and their single selves. Commercially refrigerators are shaped as polar bears while promotional jingles in Shanghai's Orient department store laud the child as 'customer king'![169] Perhaps it is not surprising that a study of school children as consumers in Beijing and Tianjin concluded that the average influence of children on family purchases in China 'probably exceeds that of children anywhere in the world'.[170] So important are they that it can be argued that children have become the first generation or the largest and most-conspicuous sector of China's consumers during the past twenty years. As Yan Yunxiang observed in his fieldwork:

> Parental indulgence of children has become a national obsession making children and teenagers one of the most active groups of consumers.[171]

They are also the market of the future, for not only have the 1980s and 1990s witnessed the emergence of a child-specific culture of consumption that is both market-oriented and globalised, but also these highly discerning young customers have been socialised to consume from an early age and as they progress into their teens and young adulthood.

8   Chasing youthful dreams

Aspirations and alternatives

Perhaps there has been no more potent image of change in China's post-revolutionary years than the image of current generations of youth as they participate in new forms of recreation and entertainment, consume in the new world of goods and enter the global ranks of the 'young, hip and cosmopolitan'. As in much of Asia, not only have new youth styles emerged in China but also the very notion of youth has become a significant time-span between adolescence and marriage or childhood and adulthood, lasting from the late-teens to the late-twenties. Customarily childhood had ended on an early marriage when the full status of adulthood was acquired, while the stigma attached to late- or non-marriage was such that singles even in their late-twenties had little status, independence or autonomy. It was only in the twentieth century, in the decades of revolution before and after 1949, that youth acquired a new status as political activists and only in post-reform years that this age-category acquired a new socio-economic status. Now there are roughly 200 million young people in the late-teens to late-twenties age-group who are making the most of new educational and employment opportunities, are achieving independence of means and acquiring consumer aspirations to match their counterparts in much of Asia and elsewhere. The new opportunities for education, for employment and for mobility together with novel media, phone and wired facilities have generated new knowledge and aspirations among the modern young in the cities and among some in the countryside. In addition, broader contact with the 'outside' world, be it Western societies, Taiwan, Korea and Japan or China's own metropolitan cities, has generated and spread new ideas about youth, youth lifestyles and aspirations that are 'modern' and 'global', purposively distinctive or at least different from those of their parents and grandparents and undreamed of by generations of revolutionary young.

Above all, the reform generations of youth have experienced profound changes in life-course and lifestyle. Within two short decades that pace of change has been fast and it has been the openness to new ideas and new experiences by the young which has helped set the pace and contribute to new ways of thinking about the individual, the family or the future and about change itself. As one of China's young women authors noted, 'the pace at which China is moving now is really amazing'.

Changes happen so fast and there are so many young people yearning to make change happen even faster.[1]

Certainly the young have been at the forefront of many of the new fashions and activities, be they in the arts, popular culture or lifestyle choices. The notions of individual freedom, choice and independence as opposed to social and familial expectations lie at the centre of new youth styles and cultures. Young persons in talking of new opportunities and aspirations often say that they 'don't believe in the communist thing', the way their parents did and that they now have the freedom 'to choose their own life', 'to choose their own job' or are free to 'chase their dreams'.[2] In the words of a 25-year-old assistant engineer: 'What I most want is to do what I want to do';[3] a phrase that was almost exactly echoed by another young woman several years later: 'What I want to do is what I want to do'.[4] It is this newly-won freedom of choice which fuelled a determination to be different from parents and grandparents.

As to my parent's generation, they had no choice but to accept their fate. But I can't surrender. I will choose my future.[5]

Their thought was, everything they do should be for the country. Now we think about being beneficial to ourselves; of being useful to ourselves.[6]

Many did feel quite sympathetic with former generations who just did not have the same opportunities as themselves and therefore, as one Beijing youth said, 'they can't understand every single thing we do'.

We have the bars, we have clubs, we have everything here. If my friends and I talk about going to bars or clubbing, I think a lot of parents don't understand it. They can't understand it … They struggled pretty hard. They got hurt pretty bad.[7]

Post-revolutionary youth did not just understand or delight in differences from past generations, but wanted to enter new worlds that were metropolitan and cosmopolitan. They wanted to embrace ideas and social practices and emulate youth elsewhere in Asia and in Europe or North America. It has been observed many times that in these days of globalisation, China's youngsters are keen to belong to the 'international generation'.[8] As one young man observed, the young not only have the right to choose their own lives but now also have knowledge about the possibilities: 'we've got more information from outside now and can see that others live in a different way'.[9]

At the centre of the quest for the modern or the hip and the cosmopolitan deriving from the West and elsewhere in Asia is the search for wealth and happiness as well as self-expression. According to *Newsweek*, nowhere among Asia's 20-somethings is the desire to get rich as striking as it is in China.[10] In many interviews there are references by the young to the effect that 'all that matters is money', 'you've got to have money' or 'the only thing you can believe in is money' and certainly there is a great interest in money and material culture expressed by the young and entrepreneurial. If the desire to get rich is a very observable attribute in conversation and interview, so also is a personal search for 'happiness' which for long came second to social and socialist expectations. In this search, particularly evident among young women, there is a new interest in the quality of personal relationships with expectations that both these and a range of material goods define 'a good life' for the young. The quest for self-improvement takes many forms and includes further- or self-education, training, a new job, entrepreneurial experiment, migration and marriage. It is sometimes said that many of the young attempt to invent and re-invent their lives in order 'to make something different' of themselves not once but many times over.[11] As one correspondent noted, the younger generation are thriving with lives reinvented 'just as swiftly as the skyline'.[12] As *Newsweek* noted in 2001, as dramatic as the landscape changes are in Beijing, they hardly compare with the 'millions of individual makeovers that occur everyday in sprawling metropolises'.[13] Consumption has played a major part in this reinvention or make-over, and from the early 1990s many have observed that youth are 'the best consumers in the market', be it in clothes, goods or music and other entertainment industries. Much has been written about the pace of change and changing aspirations of the young in post-revolutionary China, but reforms have also created the spaces in which the young can adopt a range of 'linglei' or alternative lifestyles and sub-cultures that reject mainstream aspirations, defy convention and experiment with music and other forms of popular culture, sex and drugs. However these experiments fringe the main cities so that the majority of the young, in the mainstream, aspire to further and higher education and employment in a range of new occupations.

Youthful occupations

In 2004, it was reported that 43.5 per cent of 18 to 26-year-olds in China have more than 14 years of education[14] and, in recent years, the expansion of higher education has enabled many more of the young to continue their education into their late-teens and early twenties. In 2004, 2.8 million graduated from institutions of higher education in China which is more than twice as many as in 2002 and the numbers were expected to rise to 3.2 million in 2005.[15] In addition to the large numbers of universities, there is also a range of vocational and technical colleges offering computing, engineering and other technical courses. Visiting a large, new, spacious and well-equipped middle school and higher education campus in rural Shandong province a few years ago, the emphasis on computing and technological skills was an impressive sign of the growing opportunities for the technically-minded young. Again more recent visits to large and impressive campuses specialising in technology in southern China attest to the year-on-year graduation of new generations of well-trained and ambitious young graduates. Similarly for the northeast, Thomas Friedman was impressed by such facilities when he visited the nexus of universities, technical colleges and a massive software park in the far northern city of Dalian which, as he wrote in the *International Herald Tribune*, 'would stand out in Silicon Valley'.[16] It is not surprising to find that GE, Microsoft, Dell, Hewlett Packard and Accenture are taking advantage of such knowledge centres with their high-tech low-cost brain power.

In addition to such centres, and they are scattered across coastal and southern China, many young college and school students graduate in foreign languages, business and the social services. In 2004, it was estimated that some 26 per cent of 18 to 24-year-olds had mastered at least one foreign language and the number of MBA graduates who studied either within or outside China has grown incrementally in the past few years.[17] In 2001, an article in *Outlook Weekly* reported that youth themselves were increasing their spending on education.[18] Confronted with the challenges of a knowledge-based economy, many said that they were eager to take up any opportunity for further education and acquire qualifications before and after entering employment. A poll in Beijing conducted by the China Youth and Children's Research Centre showed that 65 per cent of those surveyed were taking various part-time classes to further their education and that half were paying for this education themselves. More and more young persons were also availing themselves of the new convenience of flexible online education, which has been developed by some of the most prestigious Chinese universities such as Tsinghua in Beijing.[19]

Whether young persons are graduates of primary school or of an illustrious university in China or abroad, the majority aspire to be gainfully employed in a job with an independent income and 'a good future'. Over the past 20 years, urban youth in the major metropolitan cities or large towns has enjoyed a new range of employment opportunities in the commercial, professional and service sectors as well as in manufacturing. There is a wide range of blue- and white-collar jobs not only in public-service occupations such as education, health and the civil service, but also in the rapidly expanding commercial, service and technical sectors. The private sector too, with new self-employed entrepreneurial opportunities in individual business and domestic, foreign and joint-venture companies, has produced a variety of additional employment opportunities for the city young. Although it is the successful young professionals in education, medicine, law and the civil service, or the engineering and computing technicians and entrepreneurial and office staff of the joint and other ventures in the metropolitan cities who have attracted the most attention, those living in cities that are heavily reliant on the state manufacturing sector have greater difficulties in finding a job locally. Instead many have turned to the expanding private or service sector for employment. As earlier chapters have noted, graduates too are not finding it as easy as in previous years to find well-paid and prestigious jobs with many having to accept jobs with lower pay and less status than they had hoped. Even in cities such as Shanghai the number of job opportunities has not been able to keep pace with the increase in number of graduates while, for the whole country, the summer of 2003 was a record year for graduate unemployment with a lower average starting salary for university graduates compared with previous years. Graduates tell of the difficulties of getting to the interview stage because of the number of applications for each job and those who are interviewed say they were asked how little they would work for![20] Others have accepted positions that make little use of the qualifications in the service sectors with the fortunate selling hamburgers in McDonalds and coffee in Starbucks.

One of the more observable sights in urban China is the numbers of girls in secondary and higher education, the chic young female clerical workers in small or large offices and the many professional and entrepreneurial women entering business, law or the commercial sector. Many young educated women have taken full advantage of every new opportunity to acquire and improve their skills, language or technical qualifications and, once in employment, they have been keen to further their qualifications, advance their job prospects in companies or set up their own enterprises. Perhaps this is because many of the company choices remain circumscribed by male privilege and preference. Some young women report that they find it difficult to get a 'good job' and face some gender discrimination in the workplace and in the professions. They report that they experience quite a shock after much encouragement in the home and at school to find that it is more difficult for young women to attain equal recruitment, remuneration and promotion in the workplace. It is also the case that generous maternity and other female-specific benefits have worked against their employment prospects so that work-units looking to recruit university graduate recruits much prefer a 'Beijing male student', leaving young women on the sidelines. A process which one young woman interviewed in *Beijing This Month* described as 'patently unfair'.[21] Another young woman interviewed in *Newsweek* observed:

> I looked through some ads in the newspapers and I was very upset to find some jobs actually say 'men only' (zhi xian nan xing) although any woman can do it just as well. A friend also told me that some companies would prefer a stupid man over an excellent woman. My parents worry a little bit about me for that reason – they know its not easy for a modern girl in this modern society.[23]

Several recent surveys suggest that the proportions of women experiencing some form of sexual harassment in the workplace were such that the Law on the Protection of the Rights and Interests of Women has been amended to make sexual harassment unlawful.[23]

As for rural youth, they work in the fields or are employed in local factories or services with the fortunate few recruited into local government or the army. Outside of the poorest regions where there are few alternatives to work in the fields and under-employment is common, greater numbers of young villagers have taken the opportunity to attend junior middle school which is often the pre-requisite for recruitment to local or distant factory work. Many of the rural young would happily swap the good earth for the good life and many migrate in search of alternative work. In the countryside, it has not been so easy to find employment for young men or women and a high proportion of those who migrate from the rural areas in search of work on construction sites, in the service sector or in small or large factories are young persons. Many of these young male and female migrants view migration not only as a chance to find a new job and gain an income but also as a route to self-improvement or to improve their 'life chances'. Around a third of the millions of migrants who travel in search of work in town, city or special economic zone are young women who range in age from late teens to late twenties. Most have had some schooling and nearly all find their first jobs through family, friends, local labour bureaux or the Women's Federation. Many start as housemaids or joint-venture factory workers and the fortunate few move on to work in retail, restaurants, kindergartens or office work. Most work long hours for low wages in the most menial of tasks but are determined to help their families by remitting a portion of their wages back home to support parents or siblings in school.

The majority of the young migrants also welcome the chance to experience city life and improve their own qualifications in the job and marriage market. In my own talks with more than 50 young and fashionably-dressed women at a migrant club for young women, they gave a number of reasons for migrating, which included improving their own situation, earning an income, acquiring skills, supporting their family and improving their marriage prospects. They were all attired in their Sunday best, ranging from sophisticated black lace to pussy-cat T-shirts and, in a relaxed atmosphere, they freely talked of their own experiences and hopes for the future. All the young women intended to acquire new skills in either dressmaking, retail, cooking, accounting, interior design or computing. However most of the young women who were housemaids found it very difficult to find sufficient time and funds for such courses and, what saddened me most, they found it difficult to find appropriate and regulated training courses which, as they are not tested or validated, often did not equip them properly or cheated them of their hard-earned money and their intentions to 'improve' themselves. So many felt fortunate to have the opportunity to earn a wage and live a better life than in the countryside, but they also regretted their lack of education which limited their choices and earnings, although not necessarily their dreams of living in a house of their own with a husband and child in the city. Although many wanted to stay and work in the cities, several also expressed a long-term wish to return to their villages with a new skill which would benefit themselves, their families and their community. Many openly hoped that they would meet a future husband in the city; a few had already met a partner of their choice; and several had been betrothed back home and had agreed rather reluctantly to marry a man chosen by their parents. The young women were unanimous in their view that travel and working in a city had widened their horizons, their expectations and sometimes their choices, although the life-changing experiences of migration did not always make it easy for them to contemplate returning and settling back in their villages. Several already had attempted to return to their villages but, rather unhappy there and without much to do, they had returned to the city where they hoped to acquire further education or skills, find a good job and enjoy the same independence and choices as their urban counterparts.

Youth lifestyles

The young have a strong sense of lifestyle, indeed the very notion of lifestyle is about difference and fashion so that any product can simultaneously signify choice, style, fashion and difference. At the centre of the pursuit of all these attributes lies consumption, which for the young in China is a new and individual pursuit centring on the personalised acquisition of clothes, adornment and entertainment, largely because almost all young persons, with the exception of migrants, continue to live at home with their parents before and often after marriage. Indeed there are few opportunities for the young and single to leave home and live separately from their parents either in the countryside or the cities due to the lack of alternative housing, costs in relation to income and the customary co-residence of the generations even after marriage. The co-residence of unmarried youth with the senior generations is still a marked characteristic of contemporary urban living in China's cities[24] and now that urban housing has been privatised, the ability of the young to acquire their own homes and live separately before and after marriage is as difficult as it was during the revolutionary years. The term 'kipper' (kids invading parents' pockets eroding retirement savings) or 'parasite singles' deployed respectively in Britain and Japan to refer to those grown children in their twenties who are still unmarried and live at home might be applied with some modification to the younger generation in China. For those not yet married and without filial responsibilities, there is a period between entering employment and saving for marriage when young singles have an independent source of income but normally continue to live at home and hence have a source of ready cash to spend on themselves. In China too, the spending of young singles and their lifestyle pursuits have attracted some media, marketing and research attention. From the early 1990s, many have observed that the potential of the youth market in China is such that it is important to understand the diversity and aspirations of this generation in order to overcome 'the difficulties of accurately pinning down the lifestyles of today's young adults'.[25] As with other social categories in China, the young are not homogeneous and vary in beliefs and behaviours according to location, socio-economic background, education and gender.

In 1992–3, China's Youth Research Centre led a large-scale investigation into the lifestyles of more than 4,700 youth in 10 different locations including Beijing, Shanghai, Guangzhou, Liaoning, Jilin, Heilongjiang, Shandong, Hainan, Guangxi and Hebei.[26] The questionnaires on quality of lifestyle, patterns of consumption and leisure activities revealed that generally there had been a marked improvement in the material living conditions of the young with many reaching 'remarkably well-off standards', although most could not be considered to have reached affluent levels. Many youths (42.5%), and especially those living near the coastal areas (53%), pursued a lifestyle characterised by good food, fashionable clothing and various kinds of entertainment, all of which reflected the more general rise in standards of living. Youth spent their money on purchasing drinks, cigarettes, food and CDs but the greatest growth area had been in the entertainment sector. The consumer durables that attracted their attention and which they hoped to either acquire or upgrade included a television set, stereo hi-fi, a personal computer and a telephone. For most, television programmes constituted a major form of entertainment and far outweighed other forms; close to 40 per cent did not keep books at home and only about 10 per cent of those surveyed set aside a fixed expenditure for books and periodicals. A more detailed study of a smaller sample in Beijing revealed that the major information channels of youth were television (27.5%), magazines (25.7%) and radio broadcasts (21%) with books at 0.8 per cent a long way behind. The survey also suggested that youth studied, did housework and enjoyed other recreational activities besides television and that only a low percentage (3.8%) took any exercise.

What is interesting is that the survey also revealed that this new and improving lifestyle came with an element of worry and pressure. The proportion who said that they were bored 'with nothing to do' was as high as 20 per cent, while worries about money dominated the list of pressures. A substantial number reported that they had money worries (31%) followed by smaller numbers with problems in personal relationships (10%), in finding employment (10%) or to do with housing (10%). The spending of a number of youths was far from realistic given their personal incomes and some had got into debt. Many could not find a job that offered satisfaction and about one-quarter of youths did not have 'a house to live in' or had 'very crowded living space'. Altogether more than half of the young surveyed 'felt the tension of daily living' so that they could 'barely get along in the same house'. Thus more than half of the youths surveyed (56%) listed 'comfortable lodgings' as the main item which could contribute to an improvement in their standard of living, followed by travel (22%) and new consumer durables (16%). The survey concluded that there was a big youth market for the construction of appropriate accommodation as well as for types of goods and services that would improve their standard of living, self-advancement and the more profitable use of leisure time.

Nearly 10 years later, in 2001, an article in *Outlook Weekly* reported on the 'enriched life' of Chinese youths.[27] As the cost of food had become cheaper, youth reported that they had increased their spending on education, housing, transportation, sports, travel and cars. Increasing their qualifications and skills was a top priority although the youth surveyed said that they spent more time and money on entertainment including books, newspapers, exhibitions and travel than previously. This is perhaps not surprising given that travel including the backpack variety had undergone a boom in recent years. Many also participated in old sports such as table tennis and snooker or new sports which included swimming, tennis, badminton and gymnastics which were all beginning to be associated with an investment in fitness and health and thus, it was forecast, were likely to rise in popularity. Although television and listening to music of all types comprised the favourite indoor recreational activities, the development of the internet had also proved popular in the cities with the average age of the 2.25 million users reported to be 27 years in 2001.[28] With a high 36 per cent of those internet users reported to be buying goods and services on-line, it was also forecast that on-line consumption may yet become 'a fashion for youth'.[29]

In 2004, the 'China Cool Heart' survey, polling 1,200 students aged between 18 and 22 years from 64 universities, set out to investigate their aspirations or dreams, their role models and their definition of 'cool'. The students' views of themselves make for interesting reading. Given that they described themselves as entrepreneurial (76%) and individual (26%), it is perhaps not surprising that about two-thirds hoped to eventually work for themselves rather than for a company. They also shared a confidence in themselves and their prospects with over half reporting that they usually manage 'to get what they want'. Although more than one-third took their parents as their main role models, a high 83 per cent agreed that 'it's better to follow my own ideas than to do exactly what my parents want me to do'. When asked what brands have 'cool' images, their list included Nike, Sony, Adidas, BMW, Microsoft, Coca-Cola, IBM, Nokia, Samsung, Ferrari and Christian Dior in that order, which were all chosen because they were 'unique, inspiring, empowering and show an individual style'. However they were also chosen not so much for their products – most of which were far beyond the pockets of the students – but because their brands represented a desirable and distinctive lifestyle. More than 60 per cent of the students polled spent more than Y500 or around a third of the average city income per month although it is not clear if this included board and basic living expenses. Because graduates could expect better-paid jobs, they were reported to be less inclined to save and, given their long-term earning potential, were more inclined to splash out, perhaps spending an entire month's salary on upgrading their mobile phones.[31]

According to Victor Yuan of Horizon Research, some only children have indeed grown up enjoying material benefits and can continue to expect cash hand-outs amounting to Y1,000 to Y2,000 from their parents, relatives and family friends which gives them considerable autonomy.[32] Take the case of a 24-year-old married office worker who chose to delay having children and continued to live with her parents – a decision which freed all the couple's earnings for their own spending. Within the space of one year, this affluent young couple in one of China's most prosperous cities bought a Nokia mobile phone, an IBM laptop computer and a made-in-China Citroen Fukong – the latter with a gift of Y30,000 (US$3,600) from their parents and a 5-year bank loan. Stories of such big spenders have been welcomed by foreign companies.[33] In 2004, the head of a public relations firm believed that the amount being spent by China's late-teens and early twenties was less important than the way they spent it, which suggests the emergence of 'a different kind of Chinese consumer' with 'a strong awareness of fashion, brands and quality'.[34] This impression was confirmed by a 2005 survey of city 'workplace tweens' or young adults with up to 2 years of work experience who were found to 'boast their own unique culture and consumer characteristics'. Compared with other groups they had fewer responsibilities, more carefree lives and showed a considerable capacity to consume that was based on newly-found salaried independence, a search for individual identity and peer recognition. They tended to spend all their income amounting to about Y1,180 per month and even accrue debt in the belief that 'now' is the right time to spend. Workplace tweens were found to be attracted by product appearance and to purchase goods that their peers believe reflect a high-status lifestyle. They like to be at the forefront of fashion trends and play an important role in the transformation of new fashion concepts into a commercial trend. Fashionable items include CDs, VCDs, books and magazines, followed by flowers and gifts, cosmetics and clothes. As far as digital products are concerned, mobile phones and MP3 players top the list, with many more planning to buy MP3 players, laptop computers and digital cameras in the future.

Workplace tweens also demonstrate a greater interest in leisure activities which may include recreational, entertainment and physical activities, video and internet games and some shop on-line.[35] On-line games and the internet is a growing form of popular entertainment among the young. Shinda, the on-line games firm based in Shanghai, reckons that its games attract an average of 1.7 million concurrent players, the majority of them young men aged 18 to 24 years.[36] Although the young long to travel and spend their wages, many find that they are so tired after working and commuting that they only have the energy to play video games or surf the internet. That said there is a vibrant restaurant, cafe and club scene in the metropolitan cities which attracts the affluent young in their leisure hours. In addition to the ubiquitous cheaper eating houses there are Starbucks, other boutique coffee and tea cafes and a variety of bars to cater for a range of income-groups among the young. For example in Shanghai's more exclusive XinTiandi complex there are minimalist and up-market bars owned by avant garde designers. One such bar advertised a belief in simplicity:

> We are minimalists. We think a bar should convey honesty, warmth, pleasure and modesty. Please strip to bear (sic) essentials and leave the complexities of life in a city of 15 million people behind. Switch your mobile phone to vibrate and indulge in the erotic potential of a chance encounter or a romantic rendezvous and enjoy the relaxing time and casual conversation and drinks.

In less exclusive venues and malls there are a variety of coffee, fast food and noodle outlets which are popular both for eating and relaxing among the young. However if it is the image of the more affluent, cosmopolitan and urban who dress with style, experiment with new ideas and goods and welcome new forms of entertainment and recreation that has become a potent symbol of China's successful reforms and modernisation or globalisation, this image is only one of the many that characterise today's youth.

As with other social categories in China, the range extends from the sophisticated urban, the rich of the eastern seaboard and those with higher educational qualifications including post-graduate MBAs to the barely literate with a smattering of primary school education and the poor or the remote of small town and rural village. Yet ethnographic studies across small cities, towns and villages show that only the poorest and marginalised remain isolated or untouched by 'outside things'. One survey of youth conducted in a medium-sized city in Hebei province far from the metropolitan centres, showed that even in 1994 the young were familiar with Hollywood movies, new-wave Chinese film directors and translations of Western books, new magazines and popular television programmes. Young persons preferred contemporary Chinese popular as well as foreign-cultural products and in particular Hong Kong or Taiwan and Western-made television programmes and films. They had developed their own views and preferences which differed from those of their parents and seemed quite willing to make or stand by their decisions and set their own life-course. Indeed the small-town survey showed that there was a clear generation gap in which the attitudes and expectations of the generations differed 'quite dramatically' with lack of privacy and lifestyle choices the main cause of inter-generational tension. However at the same time as they expressed support for their own independence and autonomy, the young also expressed widespread support for filial obligation, close familial bonds and even co-residence after marriage. Indeed they remained quite reliant on their parents for their basic needs and financial assistance. On average, parents interviewed in this survey thought that their children had received help in getting their first job (35–40%), in changing jobs (30–35%), finding a spouse (25–30%) and in obtaining housing (15–35%). A much larger proportion of the young had asked for and received advice from their parents, while 68 per cent of young persons had received gifts, either as cash or goods, from their parents. Hence family members still tended to pool their earnings and balance the consumption needs of all members. Although in the mid-1990s, it was the sense of filial and familial obligation that remained 'robust' for all generations, the researchers expected this to change as the young were acquiring a greater degree of independence.[37]

In my own rural fieldwork over the 1990s, a pattern which became very familiar was one in which young persons might contribute to the acquisition of family assets such as televisions but also spend a portion of their own cash on everyday needs such as shampoo, items of clothing, cigarettes, cosmetics, cassettes of Hong Kong and Taiwan pop stars, karaoke and other forms of local entertainment. Outside the poorest and most remote rural regions, young persons could be seen watching television, listening to pop music or playing billiards, snooker and basketball in their leisure hours. Even in villages well away from urban suburbs, young men were likely to be seen gathered around a pool table or a volleyball pitch. In medium-rich villages, the widespread use of scooters has given them a mobility and interests beyond the village. Throughout central, northern and coastal China, they tend to spend their own cash on shampoo, smart T-shirts, fancy clothes, leather shoes, cassettes of Hong Kong and Taiwan pop stars and cigarettes. Television is much in evidence and this, together with migrant stories, feed aspirations among the village young 'to be modern or fashionable'. One very fine ethnographic study conducted in a north China village by anthropologist Yan Yunxiang over the 1990s is suggestive of the youth cultures and lifestyle trends in rural mid-income regions.[38] Here young village youth tended to spend their spare time in small groups of close friends watching television, enjoying pop music, playing basketball or billiards. They liked to hang out in streets, display their new clothes and leather shoes and spend money on expensive cigarettes and cassettes, especially those featuring Taiwan and Hong Kong pop singers. A fortunate few had purchased a motor cycle or scooter.

Yan observed that more and more village youths had begun 'to define themselves and their quality of life in terms of consumption satisfaction'.[39] For this younger village generation, money was meant to be spent and goods to be enjoyed so that they spent much more on food and clothes than their parents and mostly on themselves, which became a source of both talk and tension in the family and village. One elderly woman could not understand why her grandson spent so much time in front of the mirror and why he wore good clothing and leather shoes even to herd the cows in the fields! More generally, older generations in the villages complained that today's young villagers were only interested in enjoying 'the good life' and shook their heads at the 'youth problem' by which they usually meant their laziness and lack of respect for filial obligations. In turn the young were often impatient or critical of the elderly who constantly lectured them on the virtues of thrift, hard work and familial obligation. Yan concluded that, in many ways, the generation gap seemed more acute in the countryside where the older generation had not been exposed to new ideas and lifestyles in the same ways as their urban counterparts so that inter-generational differences were likely to be greater and especially so between the spartan or 'stay-at-home' elderly and the materialist or mobile younger generation.[40]

Almost without exception, the young in Yan's village disliked working in the fields and tended to be much more interested in material comforts such as fashionable clothing, good housing and better jobs. In this respect, the young there exhibited a new sense of entitlement – that they should have the same lifestyles as their urban counterparts. Most rural youth in the village had either observed or experienced city life and even those who had not travelled were influenced by those who had or by new channels of information. Above all it was television which presented the most up-to-date and fashionable lifestyles to villagers and fostered aspirations among the young. Rural youth looked to the material benefits and fashionable urban lifestyles as an ideal or a model for a better life as they attempted 'to follow the mainstream culture of the cities, and to imitate the lifestyle of urbanites whom they regard as modern and fashionable'. On this basis, Yan concluded that 'their tastes in fashion and entertainment, their pursuit of individual independence and happiness, and their indulgence in material benefits would be regarded as moderate and thus "normal" in an urban context'.[41] However the constrained life-chances of rural youth tended to circumscribe their aspirations to approximate urban and modern lifestyles which, this village study suggests, led to some frustration and a sense of helplessness. If here the modern lifestyle of Hong Kong or Shanghai was at once so desirable yet unattainable, how much more must it be in poorer and more remote villages where any aspirations of the young are likely to be even more tempered by the struggle for subsistence and limits of village life. It is not surprising that many see movement out as their only hope of improving their own life-chances and the lifestyles of their families. In an equivalent mood but in very different circumstances, it has become fashionable among young city and rural backpackers to also move and organise their own adventure travel clubs and trips. So many young persons are starting to go backpacking not only because it is a cheaper mode of travel but also because it is flexible and 'free-spirited'. One young woman noted the attractions of such an individual form of travel:

> Independent travel is better than a tour because it's more flexible. I can go anywhere I want and stay as long as I wish and nobody will control me.[42]

Among the wide range of lifestyles between the young of the far western villages and the affluent young of China's metropolitan centres, there is one group that has received more attention than any other – the fashionable young urban miss. Perhaps more than any other social group, young and single city women have the time and income to desire, shop and spend on whatever is fashionable.

China's young misses

Some 90 million young single women work in offices, factories, businesses and the professions in the public, private and joint-venture sectors, they live at home and they have the earning opportunities and the time to take advantage of the latest consumer trends. Educated and salaried with a quest for style, self-improvement and the latest fashion, they are reported to be 'the savviest of customers'.[43] As in New York and Tokyo, they can be seen in the streets, the malls, the shops or the cafes and they are often photographed in the international media laden with an array of branded carrier bags. Throughout Asia and particularly in Japan, young and single women who are well employed, living at home, relatively wealthy and preoccupied with their self-image or future marriage prospects, have attracted considerable marketing attention. It was the estimated 10 million unmarried women in Japan who, aged between 15 and 29 years and working in offices, living at home and spending the bulk of their modest salaries on consumer goods and designer gear, first drew attention to this Asian phenomenon.[44] In 1998, the Hakuhodo Institute of Life and Living in Tokyo reckoned that there were three million young women living within an hour of the city's Shibuya shops who were poised ready to pounce on the latest fad. Reading consumer magazines and watching television to learn the latest trends and locations of items, be it the genuine designer article or counterfeit or cheaper designs, they were reported to be the only social category spending in hard times.[45] Even in the most difficult of times, these young women had continued to spend so that sales of women's clothes, accessories, shoes, handbags and cosmetics remained buoyant. Indeed when the country was struggling with an economic downturn and high unemployment, it was the continuing sales boom fuelled by the large disposable incomes of young women in sales of goods, luxury and otherwise which confounded retailers and business analysts alike.[46] As *The Economist* noted at the time, 'if the rest of Japan followed their example, Japan's economic woes would be over'.[47] As in Singapore, Hong Kong and other Asian cities, young women with similar attributes are to be seen in the malls, shops and streets of China's main cities. The international press frequently notes that the young women who 'parade the streets in downtown Shanghai' are as fashionably clad as in New York, London, Paris, Tokyo and Singapore and that the future of

China's market if not world trends in consumption lie in the hands of China's women, so great will be their bargaining power.[48]

For this category of young women there is a pervasive interest in fashioning and beautifying the body and new fashion, cosmetic and slimming industries have emerged to both meet and generate demand. Fashion is by definition subject to rapid and constant change and since the early years of reform, an absorbing goal of the young has been 'to stay fashionable'. What is 'new and fashionable' is immediately visible and, as noted in earlier chapters, the sequence of shifts in size of heels, length of skirt and trousers and the style of dress or blouse not to mention shape of hat, shawl and even the length of gloves has been an eye-catching feature of successive visits to China. Fashion and colour have been as quickly taken up as discarded. A few years ago, shopping for my daughter in a Beijing market with a much-admired London picture of a waist wrap-around shawl, I was not only fortunate to find the shawl but even more interested to find, on my return between the stalls, that all the young assistants themselves now sported a shawl wrapped around their waists! Similarly a short 'one-minute story', a genre traceable to ancient times, read several years ago memorably captures the mood of the times. Entitled 'Fashionable Summer Yellow', it is about a young girl's struggle to keep up with the constant turnover in fashion shades from 'deep yellow' to 'pure bright yellow' and 'brownish yellow' as each in turn moved from the fashionable to the 'unfashionable', the 'unsophisticated' and finally was discredited and discarded in favour of the colour mauve. In these fast-changing times, she concluded that it was 'so easy to be unfashionable'.[49] For others in this age-group 'looking fashionable' was more about the assertion of individual choice, a distinctive image and projection of personality. Clothes 'as a very individual thing' became a major mechanism for the expression of style, colour and personal choice and as such a source of empowerment for young women in the workplace, at home and in the streets. The young city women in China who are to be seen as fashionably clad as elsewhere are also as self-confident in their manner and independent in exercising consumer choice. As one English-language high-school junior noted at the turn of this century 'now we have the living standard and the confidence and the time to think about such things and there are so many pretty things to buy'.[50]

To help young women keep up with cutting-edge styles and trends, a wide variety of new fashion magazines have been published during the past couple of decades with a new array of glossy magazines displaying the latest visual images of young fashion, advising readers on what to wear and 'how to be stylish'. One of the earliest of the new magazines to guide the nascent connoisseur of fashion through the uncharted territory of style was the Beijing quarterly *Fashion* (Shizhuang). The very first issues introduced Parisian fashions and the latest new clothing collections from abroad and later issues featured those designed and produced in China. It fast became more daring – graduating from five ways to wear a scarf or the advantages of wearing skirts to depicting bolder leather outfits alongside the glamour and sophistication of new lifestyles.[51] At first, the very notion of fashion was aligned with the West and a number of Western magazines such as *Elle*, *Cosmopolitan* and *Marie Claire* were soon producing Chinese versions, however there were also large numbers of locally-produced glossy fashion magazines which compete with these and other high-street titles. The latest foreign glossy magazine to be launched is *Vogue China* which is especially written for the generation of Chinese professional women in their twenties and thirties who now have spending power and luxury brand aspirations. According to the editor, the format of the new magazine differs from its international sisters in that it is especially written for the Chinese market which 'vacuums up cosmetic products' and this market has a larger beauty section and more on dress sense and etiquette to play a 'pivotal role in educating taste'. The editor also has her own agenda not only to end the long love affair with the widely-worn ankle-length stocking but also to create leisured dreams after a hard day's work.

> Our role is to create dreams. When a woman comes home at the end of a hard day, she wants to be able to dream, and forget her troubles. I hope that *Vogue* can make people feel that tomorrow will be better.[52]

That the first edition sold a first print run of 300,000 copies in the first five days augured well for the future of *Vogue China*. Indeed the size of the print run of this and other such magazines testifies to their success among young female readers and there is little doubt that their visual images, articles and advertisements have had a pervasive influence on young women's emerging sense of themselves as feminine, modern and cosmopolitan.

These magazines were only one means of publicising new styles, for televised and live fashion shows have also proved popular showcases for European, American and Japanese designers. Contemporary designs from abroad can also be seen in the shop windows of the major fashion houses including Christian Dior, Gucci, Armani and Max Mara which have all opened outlets in Beijing, Shanghai and later other major cities. Local designer-clothes shops too have mushroomed in large cities as China itself has developed its own flourishing fashion industry. As one of Shanghai's designers noted, 'We're designing for the new office ladies who work for the big foreign companies'.[53] Although young designers want to move from China-cheap to *China Chic*, the title of a recent book by China-born New York fashion designer Vivienne Tam, it remains difficult to turn design creativity into a profitable commercial venture without the necessary infrastructure inclusive of trade shows, creative management, media support, the distribution system, independent retailers and sympathetic stores.[54] Where the ascendant labels are still foreign, it is their often embellished and certainly cheaper counterfeit copies which are readily available in the smaller shops and in market stalls where they are eagerly snapped up by young women shoppers. It seems that unlike some of their Asian counterparts, China's young city women may not have the same commitment to luxury labels or brands as Japan's young women, for it is readily observable that they tend to shop for cheaper versions or replica brand names which do not have the same cache but can be near-quality replicas of the original. Many search for the lower-priced version of fashionable goods and dress very stylishly but cheaply. China has been accorded the dubious status as 'the world's counterfeit capital'[55] with near-perfect copies of Gucci, Armani, Nike and Rolex labels easily obtainable. A survey in 2002 divided the young and single into successful and professional young women with purses to match, young office employees who largely shop for fashionable and cosmopolitan styles to acquire a distinctive modern image and factory workers who shop for cheaper practical versions on their day off. The underlying criteria for making their purchases were reported to fall into three equal categories according to individual and good taste (36%), the practical (31%) and the inexpensive (33%).[56] I am not so sure that in practice the categories can be so nearly separated, for my own observations suggest that young city women may combine the expensive, the cheap and the counterfeit in one set of attire. But the survey certainly confirmed that the young, well-educated, salaried women for whom individualism, good taste and good value are paramount constitute the main advocates of individualised consumption in the high street. For all young city women, fashion was part of a larger concern with personal appearance and a new interest in cosmetics, hairstyles and adorning the body.

Face and body

One of the first and a fast expanding area of consumer marketing in post-revolutionary China has been in cosmetics and other body-products. Absent during revolutionary years, the number of registered factories producing cosmetics doubled from 700 to 1,500 between 1986 and 1992. Then it was estimated that the domestic market alone was worth Y4 billion in output with the sales of the leading Xiafei cosmetics company alone totalling Y400 million.[57] International companies too, including the well-known Wella, Johnson & Johnson and Ponds brands, established joint-ventures in China and sold their products in city stores. China's beauty market soon displayed the status and price hierarchies characteristic elsewhere and range from the large foreign brand names sold in up-market boutiques, the major international hotels and joint-venture luxury department stores to middle-ranging foreign or joint-venture brands such as Pond's and Oil of Ulan. Although, by the mid-1990s, the latter were two of the most pervasive brand names on sale in department stores, Chinese brands also had their own hierarchy with Xiafei products competing with Aoqi, Ziluolan (Violet) and Ailisi (Alice) brands for first place. Both foreign and Chinese joint-venture companies widely advertised their products in magazines, television and billboards. On the television any time of the day or night, beautiful women swing their long hair to persuade viewers to 'please choose Huaizi, the Oriental wild type' or not to use ordinary shampoos but only Rejoice or Hazeline Snow, Ponds' OLC or Oil of Ulan. Some are persuaded and young women can be observed purchasing small sachets of shampoo alongside others spending large sums perhaps amounting to a month's salary on skin products and make-up. According to a 1998 report by Hong Kong-based Asian Strategies Ltd, cosmetics has proved to be one of the 'fastest growing sectors of the Chinese economy', with some consumers spending as much as 20 per cent of their incomes on personal care products.[58] Imported products, although more expensive, are valued for their quality and the top names have competed to set up counters in China's leading department stores, heating up a $2.6 billion market that has grown 30 per cent per year.[59] Although there has been some market interest in anti-ageing and anti-wrinkle creams, young women in their late teens and twenties have comprised the most important target market and the largest consumer group for cosmetics.

One international company which has made a determined bid for the custom of the young is the top-ranking French cosmetic firm of L'Oréal. It made a late entry into the China market in 1996 but since that time it has launched its principal brands with L'Oréal Paris, Lancôme and Maybelline all scoring some success. Within a short period of time and in the teeth of a consumer slowdown, Maybelline achieved the top two slots for lipsticks in China's largest cities while L'Oréal's Excellence became the number one hair-colouring product. China's most famous film star, Gongli, was recruited to promote L'Oréal brands and L'Oréal's China turnover grew from a mere US$3.5 million in 1996 to US$36 million in 1998.[60] Although the company hoped that sales would further increase by 40 per cent, such forecasts were usually tempered by the huge challenges of the China market.[61] The L'Oréal boss in China reckoned that not only was it unlike any other market in the world, but it was as much about creating as exploiting a market. The corporate objective has been to push sales at every level: L'Oréal Paris was to sell French chic and sophistication, Lancôme as the top luxury brand to be exclusively available at up-market department stores and Maybelline with its bright colours was aimed at attracting the young who wanted 'a New York sassy in-your-face look'. Maybelline is used aggressively as L'Oréal's entry ticket to capture each new and affluent generation eager to adopt a young American image. Indeed L'Oréal's president was quite clear that the role of the Maybelline brand was 'to put a little red lipstick in the hands of each Chinese woman in place of the [Chairman Mao's] Little Red Book'.[62] Although the average wage in Shanghai was around Y1,200 or about £100 per month in 1998, L'Oréal reckoned that its target female customer would spend more than 10 per cent of her pay packet on cosmetics. During a visit in the same year to a Nanjing Road department store in Shanghai, the L'Oréal commercial director pointed to a young woman mulling over a pair of jeans priced at £38:

> Look at her. She probably earns 1,500 RMB per month but she lives at home with her parents and probably eats at home or at work. All her money goes on consumer goods to make her look good and feel good.[63]

Feeling good is a very important part of the L'Oréal campaign world-wide which has been based on the now very well-known slogan, 'because I'm worth it'. Invented by a feisty, feminist New York female sign writer, the ubiquitous slogan was intended to be about self-respect and the exercise of choice and control by young women. At first, according to the L'Oréal boss, it was a difficult task to get his female staff in China to subscribe to this slogan for 'it was so against the grain of the communist ideal to say something so individualistic'.[64] Apparently his staff were quick learners and soon the assertive self-empowering L'Oréal slogan was taken up by the younger age-groups who had escaped the crushing conformity of the Cultural Revolution. In 2003, he described L'Oréal's Shanghai office as full of 'dynamos of energy in blue jeans and black dresses' who helped feed information about Chinese cosmetic tastes and hair-colour habits to their French employer. For this purpose a bathroom in the Shanghai office was equipped with a video camera and staff were invited to experiment with L'Oréal's new cosmetic and hair-care products.[65] For two of China's recent crazes, hair colouring and skin whitening, L'Oréal positioned itself well. L'Oréal Excellence became the number one hair-colouring product, well placed to take advantage of the new craze for hair colouring which over the past few years has become a significant item of young fashion in urban China. In hairdressing salons in down-town cities, young women can be observed as they sit patiently waiting for a perm or the hair dye applied to their black tresses to take and provide the desired brown streaks or red and purple tints. Page after page of fashion magazines display models with hair colours ranging from deep purple to bright copper framing a pale whitened skin.

A suntan associated with brown-skinned peasants working in the fields is no status symbol in China where a fair complexion is considered a sign of beauty. So L'Oréal sells Blanc Crystal, a skin whitener under the Lancôme brand, while sales of cheaper sun-blocking skin-care products are as hot an item as the sun outside. For young women, sun-creams have become an essential part of summer rituals. As one 25-year-old white-collar worker said: 'I would not think of going out in the sun without putting on sun-block first'.[66] In 2000, a beauty consultant with Mary Kay, the US-based cosmetic giant, said its sun-blocking creams and lotions sold like hot cakes each summer alongside mini-fans, cards to measure ultra-violet indicators exposure, sun glasses and umbrellas or parasols which have all become pre-requisites for the fashion-conscious young woman.[67] Certainly there have been widespread expectations that the cosmetics market will continue to expand. In 1999, representatives of China's largest international cosmetics and ornaments trade centre in Guangzhou anticipated that China's annual growth rate for cosmetics and ornament sales would be around 25 to 30 per cent. They expected that WTO membership would reduce the import duty and encourage greater numbers of foreign firms to enter China.[68] It was anticipated that China's total sales value, calculated in 2000 to be around Y30 billion (US$3.6 billion), would rise to Y80 billion (US$9.6 billion) in 2010 when China's improved standards of living and increased demand would make it the world's largest markets for cosmetics and ornaments after the USA and Japan.[69] As for L'Oréal, its domestic and international profile in 2004 was boosted by 5 years of consecutive growth above 50 per cent in China.[70] In addition to cosmetics, jewellery has also become a popular attribute of the fashionable city young. According to *Business Beijing* in 1999, China had become a boom market for diamond jewellery as retail sales of the 'girls' best friend' rose in value, making China the fifth largest market for diamond jewellery. Even though the average price of each item sold was the equivalent of US$500, the market was expected to expand and to take third place.[71] In 2005, it was reported that 'China added lustre to Anglo figures' as a result of a boom in engagement rings which had proved highly popular for the mining company Anglo-America which owns 45 per cent of de Beers.[72] The new interest in adornment was augmented by shows such as 'Miss World' which for the third successive year has been located on southern China's Hainan Island. Achieving and maintaining a slim and more attractive body became a common aspiration which occupied an important place in advertisements, magazine articles and advice columns.

During the reform years, young women received much advice on how to diet, exercise and become or stay thin or use cosmetic surgery to alter the shape of their eyes or enlarge their breasts. In 1999 the *International Herald Tribune* summed up the prevalent image of China's glossy magazines which 'are filled with only the skinniest of models and crammed with advertisements touting diet pills, diet teas and odd-looking weight-loss machines'.[73] Losing weight and shaping the body became very popular in the 1990s and many young women joined private women's clubs to shape their bodies for the fragile look. As weight loss became an exuberant growth industry, diet centres sprang up even in small towns and rural centres. For example, the Ying-dong Sanitary Weight Loss Centre opened ten sites in Beijing shortly after its founding in 1998.[74] While some shed pounds for health, many more pursued new notions of beauty – sometimes to dangerous extremes. Anorexia nervosa and bulimia, once virtually unknown in China, increased as new body-type ideals became new social pressures enjoining the late-teens to be beautiful as well as educated. A Beijing psychologist, one of a few doctors to treat eating disorders, reported in 1999 that every year she saw more and more girls, especially the young and well-educated, who absorbed the lessons of beauty contests and were influenced by advertisements for slimming drugs. She thought that it was hard for them 'not to feel the pressure to reduce, with ads screaming everywhere that fat is bad'.[75] There is also an unregulated diet industry with advertisements for herbal potions such as 'Slim and Pretty' which is purported to directly work on and dissolve fat cells. 'It's cold now and you will probably be shouting, "I've gained weight!" as you step on the scale', begins a magazine advertisement for the May Flower Tea and Drug Weight Loss Package of 18 diet tea bags and 72 diet pills.[76] Reports speak of a new frenzy for thinness and preoccupation with weight loss which thrives among schoolgirls and students and is part of the new urge for self-improvement or a make-over.[77]

A more extreme example of this urge is the growing use of cosmetic surgery to alter eyes and breasts. In 2001 Shenzhen's health authorities listed eye-widening as the most requested alteration with the city's 1,600 cosmetic surgeons opening an average of 8,000 pairs a week.[78] In one of 90 or so cosmetic surgery clinics in Shanghai around half the patients are students aged between 18 and 24 years who are convinced that 'a beautiful face and excellent figure' will enhance their career and marriage prospects. Currently the most popular adjustments there are the creation of double eyelids which costs between Y1,000 and Y3,000 and augmentation to create a high-bridged nose which costs up to Y10,000 depending on the implant quality.[79] One young well-groomed woman told a *Guardian* correspondent in 2004 that she had got her double eyelids done when she was 20 to help with husband- and job-hunting. 'My manager said, "I need a good-looker", so everything is good', she reported happily.[80] Minor cosmetic surgery may no longer be such a novelty in the major cities where even young men seek out plastic surgery,[81] but in recent years more extreme make-overs or 'man-made beauty' (renzao meinu) with guaranteed movie-star looks have received some publicity. In 2003, the progress of a fashion writer who announced a 6-month plastic surgery schedule 'to attain a movie-star look' was followed with interest in the media and inspired several to take the same route.[82] In 2004, one aspiring beauty queen who had enhanced her chances via a series of cosmetic operations was disqualified from the Beijing finals of the Miss Intercontinental Pageant on the grounds that she was 'a man-made beauty'.[83] The influence and effects of a competitive and unregulated plastic surgery industry which is not above attracting publicity with less than credible promises, is not only cause for official concern but also reflects the fact that promises of good looks and beauty via cosmetics, slimming aids and surgery fall on ready ears. Just as for Bridget Jones and young women elsewhere, an important goal of looking beautiful and of self-improvement for China's young women was to find a suitable and attractive marriage partner – a goal which has become as much a source of anxiety as of pleasure.

Matching and marrying

Marriage is well-nigh universal, with most young villagers marrying in the early-to-mid twenties so that those not yet married by their mid-to-late twenties are likely to experience some pressure from their families and friends. In the cities, the age of marriage is somewhat later with young persons experiencing a similar pressure around the late twenties to 30 years of age. As my own many years of field work have shown, marriages are no longer arranged in the customary sense, with parents choosing unseen brides or grooms, although they may still lend a 'helping hand' in presenting a suitable match for the consent or approval of the younger generation. In the cities, it is only those who are older than the normal age of marriage who are likely to turn to family members, peers or a marriage bureaux to act as matchmakers or go-betweens. However even the young who choose their own marriage partner are unlikely to completely disregard the opinions and wishes of their families as they are normally still dependent on their parents for help with the costs of the wedding celebrations, the associated gift exchanges and with post-marital housing. Over the decades, it has become much easier for young persons of the opposite sex to mix and match now that there is greater job choice, more mobility and a wider variety of recreational venues and leisure activities. For most young women, marriage to a suitable young man is viewed as the main route to personal happiness and also the best guarantee for a comfortable material life and long-term security. My own interviews and those of others also suggest that the search for a marriage partner is both an emotional and practical quest. Young women in particular dream of finding love, while marriage is seen to offer the best chance of combining such personal aspirations with practical interests in establishing a home, having children and securing a long-term future in either the city or the countryside.

In China's villages, most young women tend to get married at a younger age or in their early twenties. Most live at home and many of their families conduct marriage negotiations on their behalf, although an increasing number are meeting and choosing their own marriage partners prior to such negotiations. Previously mixing and matching was more difficult because of social norms discouraging dating or even marriage within the village, but now young persons conduct courtship on their own initiative or at the suggestion of their parents. The costs of marriage can be high for both the bride and groom's families who together pay for the marriage ceremony, housing, the furnishings, gifts and other goods. Thus the young remain reliant on the support of their parents and there are signs that an increasing number of young persons are also using marriage as an opportunity to acquire the maximum possible numbers of goods to set up a new household and lifestyle. In his study, Yan Yunxiang was quite shocked by the egocentric consumerism displayed by the young at marriage and the lack of respect for the interests of others and especially their elders.[84] Equally there have been reports from poorer regions about the ways in which marriage brokers roam the countryside either attracting daughters of impoverished farming families with good offers or offering such young women to poor peasant families who could not otherwise afford the costs of procuring and attracting a bride. Some of these brides have been abducted or even encouraged on false pretences while others seek out such marriage brokers in the hope of benefiting their own impoverished families. Sadly many of these young women do not find happiness with husbands and parents-in-law and no doubt contribute to the high suicide rate among rural women in the countryside which at around 30 in every 100,000 is among the highest in the world.[85] It is particularly high among young rural women who are left with their in-laws to cultivate the fields or tend the children and who have ready access to pesticides which are a ready and effective means. Others escape the prospect of an unfortunate marriage by migrating out of the village to work or to find a husband in the city.

In small towns and cities there is likely to be a wider range of potential marriage partners, but even here it is no easy matter. One small city in Anhui province with a population of 2 million or so is reported to have dozens of small private agencies which offer a triple service and have signs reading: 'Flat–Job–Marriage'. According to one of these agencies, many girls want to travel to Shanghai and seek husbands by taking advantage of the greater imbalance between young men and women in the large cities. Indeed one young woman client admitted that she was looking for a husband in Shanghai: 'Because it's not easy for a girl to get by. It's so complicated. Shanghai is a beautiful city and a dream. Everybody in China wants to go to Shanghai'.[86] Shanghai may be a city of dreams for those outside but there too, despite the fact that most young city girls fall in love with a young man in their mid-to-late twenties, it seems not to be so easy to 'find' a suitable husband, especially for educated women in their late twenties and older. Despite the new opportunities for meeting and matching provided by the new range of jobs and recreational spaces, many older single city girls in the largest cities say that they 'have given up on the idea of marriage' although some are 'still hopeful'. Some frequent the bars and cafes in Shanghai and Beijing in the hope of meeting Western men who will take care of the bill if not marriage and a passport. The author of *Shanghai Babe*, Wen Hui, who herself had a prolonged love affair with a European, observed that 'the women of Shanghai are very smart compared with other cities' for 'they steal both hearts and wallets'.[87] According to the *Sunday Times* correspondent who conducted the interview, she made it sound like an old Chinese proverb! Others prefer Western men because they tend to be respectful or experienced with women. One young woman, who worked in marketing in Discovery Asia and was dating an American who was her French tutor, told a *Guardian* reporter that she chose a foreign man 'because he thinks like me and doesn't try to control me'.[88] Another 28-year-old woman who had a high-profile job for a British company, told the same journalist that she had recently split up from her boyfriend and was nervous that she might not meet somebody before the age of 30 at which it was 'definitely not OK to be unmarried'. She was very aware that she was getting older and admitted that she saved a sum each month in the hope that she might 'meet a guy who understands her but who has a solid career and promising economic potential'.[89] These are the most common requirements of those taking advantage of the services offered by the many marriage bureaux in the cities where young men and women 'make their requirements known'. Perusing the applications in one of these bureaux in Shanghai, I noted that many young women hoped to meet an educated man with good job prospects and attractive physical features including height.

An increasing number of professional women in the capital and other main cities now say that they are not in a hurry to marry and prefer to defer marriage until they have enjoyed some career success, an independent income, the pleasures of a single life and have accrued sufficient wealth and independence to acquire a strong negotiating position in courtship and marriage. Li Jie, the 28-year-old author of six novels published under the pseudonym, 'Annie Baby', says that she writes for this new audience of young employed independent women and that her novels reflect the dilemmas of successful single women looking for a soul-mate:

> They like the characters in my books because they're persistent in their pursuit of independence, but in China now in the big cities there's a lot of depression because there's a difference between people's personal and working lives. People are busy at work and don't have time for relationships. My novels deal with this contradiction.[90]

Her books, which document the lifestyle of the young and unmarried as they search for Mr Right, like Bridget Jones, reflect the fact that most women marry later now that they 'can earn their own money' which makes them more demanding when it comes to choosing a husband. According to Li Jie:

> They want to have some real communication with men, they want real love and to be respected. It's no longer just about finding a rich and handsome husband.[91]

So confident and assertive are they by reputation that those with higher education, high incomes and high age are sometimes dubbed the 'three high women' and are said to have priced themselves out of the marriage market in which younger women with fewer qualifications and incomes less than their male peers are more prized. In an independent move, many of these 'older' single professional women are now purchasing their own house or apartment, which signals their own personal wealth and investment in their own future. According to real estate specialists, this category of women represent an increasing percentage of house purchasers in China's coastal areas.[92] Although this independent path is not necessarily one of their own choosing, they and others who now make such individual life-choices may well be paving the way for a greater acceptance of an independent and single female and male life-course.

For young men too, 'having prospects' is important when it comes to meeting girls, having a steady girlfriend and proposing marriage. In the countryside, their families will prepare for a son's marriage by renovating an old house or building a new one and accruing consumer durables all of which are aimed at improving the 'characteristics' of the groom's family and the young man's prospects of attracting a good match. Generally rural families are eager to have their sons marry in order to acquire a daughter-in-law to add to the labour resources of the household and continue the family line. In the cities, it is more likely to be the young men themselves who feel the pressure to increase 'their prospects' with a good match. As one young 26-year-old industrial researcher in Beijing admitted:

> We're under a lot of pressure. You've got to earn big money and get a big house – they are now standard criteria for women looking for a husband.[93]

Many of the lyrics of popular songs speak of the pressure on young men to reach the material standards required for matrimony. In the early years of reform, in rock star Cui Jian's famous song, 'Having Nothing', the young man is repeatedly turned down because he has nothing but his aspirations and love.

> I have endlessly asked when you will go with me
> But you always laugh at me having nothing
> I want to give you my aspirations and also my freedom
> But you always laugh at me having nothing.[95]

In the lyrics of 'Pretty Girl', written and sung by He Yong, he refers to her list of wishes: 'you want a car, you say you want a Western-style house …'.[94] Although this negates the oft-expressed aspirations of the young women who say they are looking mainly for love and personal happiness, it does express the ways in which rising standards of living have prompted material stirrings in both the rural and urban young as they go about setting themselves up for marriage, a home and a family. Indeed the accumulation of assets and the exchange of gifts at this time make it one of the most concentrated periods of consumption over a life-course and a very visible yardstick of success.

Song lyrics also suggest that this period is one of enormous stress when times, norms and measures of success and status are themselves changing but have to co-exist alongside older conventional and more conservative views. 'To change' was the message of a song called 'No More Nice Girls' by one of China's best-known all-girl bands, which tells girls that 'nice' is old-style 'quaint, shy and stupid' and that what is needed are more modern girls with modern defined as a matter of fashion and 'a way of thinking'.[96] Interestingly one of the constant observations of employers and the Women's Federation is that some young women take some persuading to assert their views and rights or 'take charge of their lives'. As a worker in the mass organisation for women noted, the Women's Federation needs 'to teach women they have a choice' and encourage women to 'learn self-reliance'.[97] Like previous younger generations in times of rapid change earlier in the twentieth century in China, many young women subscribe to both customary and modern attitudes and hover between the new and time-tested ways of relating and behaving. The young are encouraged both to change and also to conform to older norms which generates some confusion and anxiety. Many tell me in conversation that it is very difficult not to feel confused in these fast-changing lives. The avante garde author of the famed semi-autobiographical novel, *Shanghai Baby*, displayed the same ambivalence, even though she saw herself as feminist 'in helping her younger generation of urban sisters born in the 1970s to understand themselves as they search for an identity in a country of shifting values and dislocation'. Despite this bold stance, as the mounting criticism of her novel took its toll and she too headed home to her mother riven with doubts. As she told a foreign journalist 'sometimes I don't know who is right, maybe I am wrong'.[98] Several years later, she told another journalist that:

> the pace at which China is moving now is really amazing. On the one hand this is good, but on the other, people are experiencing much anxiety; they have nothing on which to attach their memories.[99]

This coincides with my own experience of the young which suggests that, cosseted or protected and idealistic or with little preparation for the details of life while very young, they can suddenly be faced with finding their own way in the world which may not be so smooth, caring or forgiving.

Although the younger generation now enjoy wider options in employment and greater opportunities for recreation and leisure than their predecessors, they also seem somewhat confused and anxious about the future as they worry about getting a good job which pays sufficient to acquire a home of their own, find a partner and repay their parents, not to mention supporting their burgeoning lifestyle aspirations. They often seem the least enthusiastic about the future and life does seem much more arduous now that the state does not pay university fees, allocate jobs or housing and parents arrange marriage partners. While they may not fully belong to the ranks of the 'Ipod generation' (Insecure, Pressured, Over-taxed and Debt-ridden) familiar elsewhere,[100] they do feel that they have a lot more commitments and that the younger generation is unlikely to benefit from any 'welfare bonanza' as they move into a pensionless future. As in many other societies too, confusion and some anxiety can slide into more chronic stress and depression. According to a Beijing psychiatrist interviewed recently in *China Daily*, the young are particularly affected by such a slippage:

> Society is full of pressure and competition, so young people, lacking experience in dealing with difficulties, tend to get depressed.[101]

A recent two-year survey revealed that more than 60 per cent of the 15,431 persons affected by depression were in their twenties and thirties and that suicide is one of the main causes of death among young urban as well as rural adults.[102] The fact that China has a 50 per cent higher suicide rate than the global average is reported to be due to the growing pressures to succeed in love, work and education in China's fast-changing society which lead to stress and depression among those aged between 20 and 35 and particularly among young urban intellectuals as well as the young rural women already referred to earlier in this chapter.[103] Newspapers periodically report the suicides of bright and wealthy college graduates who are almost all single children and fear that they cannot fulfil either their own or their family's aspirations. The numbers are not only rising but also take no account of the 2.5 to 3.5 million cases of attempted suicide each year.[104] If such cases represent an extreme response to failed aspirations, many more actively turn to music and other forms of popular culture which well express the aspirations of the young and their ambivalences about what constitutes a good life.

Popular culture

Perhaps no other contemporary phenomenon has enjoyed such wide support among the young as popular music which over the past two decades could be heard on radio and on television and in the cafes, shops and streets. It is sold on cassette, CDs and vidcotapes, discussed in newspapers and magazines, sung in the ubiquitous karaoke bars, danced to in discos and listened to at live events. More than any other activity it is Western pop music that has linked China's young to the global so that intermittent visits by Western bands, when permitted, have been eagerly awaited and enthusiastically welcomed by large audiences. According to one young man, it is this much-celebrated form of popular culture which has most helped China's young to feel that they had been deprived in the past and now belong to an international generation:

> We missed out on anything that was going on in the West. If you look back in the 50s and 70s, what was happening in China? Revolution, revolution, revolution. In the West you have Elvis Presley, the Beatles, the Rolling Stones, the Sex Pistols and so on. What did we have? Revolution. It's taken us this long just to catch up. It's very sad for a lot of people.[105]

The young gradually made good their lost opportunities and the successive preferences for different genres of popular music have reflected the different experiences and emotions of each post-reform generation. At first it was popular music derived from Hong Kong and Taiwan and in particular the soft-lilting love songs of the Taiwanese female singer Deng Lijun which captured imaginations and imitators. Soon a new generation of singers proliferated and with new cassette technology to make their original lyrics and music readily accessible, they were to be heard in homes, shops and cafes in the 1980s. By the end of that decade, and especially in Beijing, rock songs and bands had taken over as the voice or expression of the 'modern' and the 'cosmopolitan'.[106] During the unsettled years around the time of Tiananmen, rock singers and songs expressed some dissatisfaction and a desire for change that sometimes slid into criticism of a government that had permitted the isolation and backwardness of their country. Sung mainly in Beijing night clubs, bars and hotels, much of the performance and production of early rock was influenced by a handful of singers and rock bands.

Perhaps the best-known of song-writers and singers is Cui Jian, known as 'the grandfather of Chinese rock', who has sung fearlessly of a sense of frustration, loss and disillusionment. His songs came to represent the spiritual and material impoverishment felt by a generation of young intellectuals which erupted in Tiananmen Square in 1989. It was after this event that rock became an established part of urban youth culture. From the early 1990s, rock music was performed on a regular basis, spawning rock bands, 'rock clothes' (long hair, jeans, black leather coats), 'rock culture' (strongly associated with modernisation and Western values) and a 'rock spirit' suggestive of alternative hippie behaviour verging on the rebellious.[107] Certainly many of the lyrics featured disappointment, loneliness and disillusionment with life, love, society and politics to the extent that many ran the risk of and some did attract the attention of the government and were the subject of official disapproval. Rock concert tours, including some by foreign groups, were often banned or controlled closely so that during these years the more typical rock concert tended to be smaller-scale and 'underground' in pubs or nightclubs and attended by a few hundred urban youth, mainly university students and bohemian youth aged between 20 and 30 years alongside foreign journalists and their friends including myself on several memorable occasions.

Another of China's famed rock poets was Zhang Chu who was one of China's biggest rock stars until he took time out to reflect for a while on his own youthful approaches to life, work and politics. In the mid-1990s, Zhang Chu's songs drew widespread attention as much for the subtle power of their 'slice o'life lyrics' as for the arresting melodic simplicity of his songs. Described as more poet than musician, he shied away from black-and-white moralistic diatribes and grandiose imagery in favour of the infinitesimal wins and losses of everyday life that he thought had been overlooked in the typical epic-heroic material of Chinese rock music. His 1995 album features songs about 'ordinary' people such as Zhao Xiaojie (Miss Zhao) who lives with her parents, thinks she's not bad looking but lacks self-confidence especially with the opposite sex and therefore 'decides to just go shopping and buy some cheap things'.[108] Later, portraying himself as a 'cracked and hapless compass', he felt that he 'had lost direction for a while' and 'could not find himself'.

I got too mixed up with post-modernism ... at first it seemed to make a whole lot of sense, but eventually I started to doubt my own ability to discern what is good and valuable – what is worth doing. Everything started to seem questionable. Trying to find meaning through post-modernism is like the Chinese proverb, 'beidao ershi' – you pursue something but your back is facing the road you want to take, so you just get further and further away ... I think I just got too far away from my own road. But now I am getting back in touch with what I really want to be doing.[109]

After the mid-1990s, perhaps because of the diversion of youthful energies into consumption or new forms of recreation and away from politics and past troubles, there was a return to the 'softer', slower and more relaxing romantic songs of earlier days which dominated both the charts and sales. In terms of live music, it was the turn of the punk bands in the late 1990s and most weekends you could find a live punk show in Beijing. Listening to music, singing in karaoke bars and dancing in discos became popular forms of light entertainment replacing the idealism, resistance and protest of earlier days. Record companies from Hong Kong and Taiwan, well practised in the ways of the free market economy, supplied a steady stream of young singers and musicians who enjoyed a wide popularity, fostered huge market sales and were easily replicated in karaoke bars. In 2000, one record company executive noted the continuing predominance of Hong Kong and Taiwan in the music industry:

The total value of the music market is about RMB (yuan) 1 billion, of which popular music accounts for 80 per cent; and of the pop music market, Taiwan and Hong Kong products take four fifths of that. For ten years now, this structure has changed little.[110]

Like the rock scene, which was produced and performed almost exclusively by young men, the softened lilting lyrics and music are similarly male dominated although there has also been a number of very popular young female singers. Increasingly they have been joined by young female musicians and bands, the novelty of which still attracts much attention. One of the all-girl bands formed in 1997, Hang on the Box, played at several large US music festivals before returning to China and reinventing itself as a mixed rock band.[111] One young female singer who has become arguably the most famous woman in China is Li Yuchen, the winner of China's equivalent to Pop Idol called 'Mongolian Sour Yogurt Super Voice Girl', which attracted 400 million viewers in 2005. Known as Supergirl, her tomboy manner, spiky hair and self-confident certainty challenged the conventional feminine demeanour and introverted ideal of pretty-girl Chinese pop. Apparently she attracted a fan club of some millions of the rebellious young who identified with her and, according to a professor of gender studies in China, has empowered young women to feel that they too could be 'unique, creative and celebrated'. She observed that 'Supergirl provided an opportunity for ordinary young women to have extraordinary dreams'.[112] If popular music offered an important outlet for creativity and a vehicle for expressing the hopes or dreams and uncertainty or ambivalence of the younger generations, so too did the new literature and art.

The reform years also offered new opportunities to sample old and new Western literary works and for the first time generations of young were openly able to enjoy Shakespeare and Dickens alongside the more contemporary writings of Salinger, Greene and Amis, rather than relying on circulating underground copies. To serve them and encourage such reading, one young philosophy graduate from People's University opened a bookshop fronted by a corrugated-iron facade and plastered posters which repeated in rows were intentionally reminiscent of a building site in London or New York.[113] Hao Fang's bookshop was one of a number of alternative bookstores specialising in Chinese translations of post-1950 literature such as Salinger's *Catcher in the Rye*, Kerouac's *On the Road* or Rimbaud's poetry, which few of his customers had previously had the opportunity to read. He had not only read and liked books written by the authors Martin Amis and Will Self but he himself was also the author of two books. One he described as 'a philosophical look at the different phases of rock history and the ways in which Western rock'n'roll had responded to the pressure points of a modern liberalising society'. The other pieced together the life of Kurt Cobain and related the singer's personal experiences to the themes of his different songs. His bookstore was called 'New Ark' both because the Chinese characters were a play on Hao Fang's name and because the English translation suggested a place 'floating atop a sea of sameness going against tradition and orthodoxy and at the same time holding within it lots of different materials summoned together from the wild kingdom of arts and culture'.[114] His customers were mainly young students from nearby colleges, high schools and middle schools who came after class in the search for 'something different' or CDs and books not available elsewhere. Hao Fang has said that he quite consciously set out to foster the imagination and emotional sensibilities of those young people in order to help compensate for the pressures and rigidity of China's educational system.

The visual arts too have not been far behind in aiming to foster imagination and express emotional sensitivities. Many periodic exhibitions have attracted media and public attention because they pushed artistic boundaries, portrayed the new or expressed the ambivalent or seamy side of contemporary Chinese life. Like others, I can remember the furore surrounding the first portrayal of the nude and the first reproductions of 'everyday life' or the abstract as opposed to the socialist realism of previous years. Over past decades many young artists who have been exploring and experimenting with new subjects, new forms and materials, have gathered in collective work spaces created in derelict warehouses and other buildings on the outskirts of Beijing, Shanghai and other main cities. Their works could be seen in small and large galleries ranging from unofficial and anonymous exhibitions, which remained low profile or underground with artists mainly showing avant garde work, to large shows which attracted a wide audience and a great deal of media and market attention. Some of China's contemporary artists have become very well known, attracting the attention of collectors and critics in Hong Kong and abroad but there are many more known to smaller numbers of admirers within China. One young woman curator of art exhibitions, who purposively chose the English word 'Chaos' as her first name, tells how she sought to encourage improvisation, creativity and diversity and thus contribute to a vibrant arts scene.[115] Another curator feared that young artists now have 'no idea of art for art's sake – its art for the market'.[116] A young arts graduate too is very critical of the high-end art market for collectors from abroad, describing it as 'kissing foreigners' arses'.[117] However, whether for the foreign market or not, the arts scene has been vibrant and very much the centre of much cultural creativity and experiment by and for the young which feature not only in the private art galleries and exhibition spaces but also in major city art galleries and museums. In December 2005 there were several exhibitions on the top floors of the Shanghai Art Museum which featured work by the young and avant garde. Some large abstract colour ink washes had titles such as 'New Dreams', 'Springing from the Valley' and 'Reaching for the Sky'. Alongside was an exhibition entitled Metamorphoses which featured Italian Renaissance, French Salon and English portraiture all with Chinese faces. Yet another featured a young artist's portraits of his fellow villagers whose biographies were written into the rough-hewn textured bodies, perhaps reminiscent of Lucien Freud and Francis Bacon. Others took their art outside the galleries. For instance one young Shanghai artist, Xu Zhan, created a playful installation which set the Shanghai Museum clock hands spinning wildly out of control, while another, Yang Fudong, made a film evoking the disorientation of urban existence.[118] Such themes are echoed by many others in their works and appeal to the countless young who have been lured to the fast-changing cities with the promise of reinvention, cultural ferment and wealth. These fast-changing cities have also become the centres of a counter-culture or 'alternative' lifestyles extending beyond popular culture and the arts and into the deviant extremes of punk-hip, casual sex and hard drugs.

Alternative lifestyles

There is a fringe youth culture in which the participants have experimented with new interests, behaviours and substances with the intention of either pushing the boundaries of acceptable social behaviour or challenging social norms in the interests of self-expression and developing an alternative lifestyle The term 'linglei', meaning 'alternative', was originally and pejoratively used to describe unusual haircuts, flamboyant clothes and other forms of dissident apparel or behaviour which did not find favour with the authorities. However in the past few years 'being alternative' has become a source of pride among the young. As one young adherent dressed in battered black jeans and with long hair told a *Guardian* journalist in 2004:

> The Chinese still don't like to express themselves as much as other people do. As for me, I don't care what others think. Being linglei means doing what you think is right and going against the grain. And I think that there are many more people like me now.[119]

It was not only about self-expression, for those who described themselves as linglei also rejected consumerism and the relentless pursuit of the material and money-making that they saw all about them. As another 26-year-old man who worked in a coffee shop noted:

> To spend all you time worrying about how to make money is out of date. We should think more about what life is about. I just don't want to be part of all this.[120]

Perhaps the first groups dedicated to pursuing difference for difference's sake were Beijing's punks. In the late 1990s when it was cool to be punk, Beijing's punk underground produced both punk rock videos and tapes with serious lyrics and, played by a number of alternative bands, expressed a dark and alienated side. Some of these young underground musicians had travelled from other provinces and gathered to live in enclaves of shabby brick houses, attracted by cheap rents and the proximity to a semi-permanent underground music festival not unlike China's version of Woodstock. Together with local punk hipsters, they referred to themselves as the 'saw-gash' (dakou) generation after the smuggled gashed CDs and cassettes that they had purchased in Beijing music stores. Gashed with a saw in America, these products were 'destroyed' in the legal sense in order that they could be sold in China as waste plastic. The severed CDs and cassettes were easily spliced back together so that all but the last song was recycled and sold in informal outlets at bargain prices. Beijing's home-grown hipster culture, nourished on a diet of such CDs and cassettes, became known more generally as the 'saw-gash' generation.[121] The publication of a collection of collages, photographs, illustrations and reportage called the 'New Sound of Beijing' was designed to provide an accurate snapshot of this subset at the end of the century and 'in the fastest changing capital of the world'. Many had no official permits, were homeless and without jobs, attributes which were all a source of pride as well as of disappointment, disillusionment and regret. They described how they searched for saw-gash cassettes, talked to each other and were often depressed about their futures.

> We are a horde of hipsters infesting the edges of the city. We spend every day slacking. We like fiddling with two-deck cassette players in small rooms … We are brainless and unhappy. We are going to be spurned and buried. This bizarre age is going to cut a saw-gash in us. Our youth is cut with a saw-gash.[122]

For this generation, America's young Kurt Cobain, whose depression and alienation had resulted in suicide, became something of a cult hero. Hao Fang, the owner of the alternative bookshop, attributed the success of his biography of Kurt Cobain to the rebellion of the young against the tremendous pressure they felt from politically disillusioned parents who wanted them to take safe and predictable jobs. He himself viewed this generation gap and the growth of individualism among Chinese youth as an encouraging sign of progress or the 'first step toward a healthy democratic society'. As he said, 'Before we didn't have an I. We only had a we'.[123] The trouble as he saw it was that this subset saw no alternative future for the 'I' that was not materialistic and conformist. Hao though that they were 'after a deviant identity as a reaction against the control, conformity and "high-minded purpose" of previous generations of youth'.[124] Young, rebellious and seeking an alternative lifestyle, much of the antipathy of this and other alienated groups found an outlet in deviance from accepted norms or in promiscuity, casual sex and drugs.

After decades of sexual repression, sex mores have changed, with sexual relations becoming much more casual and pre-marital sex more common at least in the largest cities. In 1990, a study by the Chinese Academy of Social Sciences showed that virginity and chastity were highly prized. In contrast, a 2003 survey showed that nearly 70 per cent of the young had experienced sex before marriage compared with 16 per cent some 15 years earlier.[125] Concern about HIV/AIDS has pushed the government into sex education for the young and some advocacy of safe sex both among heterosexual couples and in the flourishing gay scenes tucked away in well-known corners of the major cities. However casual sex is still considered to be a deviant form of behaviour and frowned upon by the elder generation and the authorities. 'Sex is really casual these days', says Gao Shen, a 26-year-old former theatre school student who quit her advertising job to hang out in Beijing's sundry bars. 'People here have lots of boyfriends but don't know what love is'.[126] According to China's foremost family sociologist, the youth have been eager 'to imitate everything about Western society – including the stereotyped notion of pervasive casual sex'. She thought that it was the notion of constant change or the casual that was as attractive to the young as the sex.

> In the pursuit of freedom and profit, people think you shouldn't do anything for too long.
>   Advertising encourages you to change everything – including love and marriage.[127]

Wen Hui, the author of *Shanghai Baby*, has suggested that for the new generation who don't believe in 'the communist thing' like their parents, 'the only thing you can believe in is money or, of course, sex'.[128] Those who pursue sex in much of the literature indulge in a voracious rather joyless way which is largely about the self and a means of expressing difference, pursuing excitement or relieving boredom.

Sex is also for sale and, even in the early years of reform, it was obvious to the most casual of observers that prostitution had reappeared in China's cities after an interval of close on 40 years. Despite the fact that the reappearance of prostitution has been welcomed by the authorities it is widespread and considered deviant even though young sex workers turn to this occupation for a wide variety of socio-economic reasons. Bars, nightclubs or brothels sometimes employ up to 200 girls as sex workers, each of whom is often euphemistically referred to as 'xiaojie' or 'miss'. Many of the girls lined up on benches for client selection are either factory workers by day and moonlight in bars at night or they have travelled from the provinces such as those in the northeast where there is much unemployment. They can be glimpsed through open doorways by the curious and apparently are visited by a range of clients. The 'fortunate' make US$24 per client compared with an average wage of US$84 per month.[129] One of the young women moonlighting worked as a seamstress by day and another sitting next to her made toothpaste – both jobs without much reward or future. Some learned to sing and dance. A young female disco dancer, who came to Shanghai because she wanted 'to take control of her life', taught herself to dance and took Madonna and New York girls as models for they are 'sexy and avant garde'.[130] Others have a utilitarian purpose. 'I'm out here every night', says one 'I just do this to earn some spending money when I want to buy clothes'.[131] Some are motivated by dreams of saving up for their own business such as a beauty parlour and yet others hope to find a good husband or become a concubine.

The great prize for a few is marriage to a foreigner or, failing marriage, to become a mistress, second wife or concubine to a businessman from Hong Kong or Southeast Asia. Indeed the old position of concubine has gained a renewed notoriety in China today as wealthy officials and entrepreneurs seek out dalliances with attractive young women who in turn hope to improve their fortune. Some businessmen are reported to spend between US$700 and US$1,000 per month on mistresses, with around half used for rent and the rest for shopping.[132] One of China's anthropologists has argued that it is a rational economic choice. 'You can send money home, and tell people you're making it'.[133] In the Pearl River Delta, it is estimated that there are at least 100,000 mainland mistresses kept by Hong Kong and Taiwan executives, while boom towns such as Shenzhen and Shanghai have up-market enclaves known as 'concubine villages' where the residents are long-time mistresses visited once or twice a month and all the while 'earning' a few thousand yuan.[134] According to a reporter writing in *Newsweek*, there 'you can see dozens of fresh-faced mistresses who are girlish and hopeful of a new life' and who 'like hundreds and millions of striving citizens have found a way to get ahead in today's China'.[135] Without such a way to get ahead, a minority of the young without any form of support drift and drop out, sleeping during the day while they wait for a night-life that thrives on a form of escapism induced by sex and/or drugs.

Drug use, especially cheap and reliable heroin, is reported to be claiming hundreds of thousands of new addicts among the young in the booming mega-cities of coastal China as well as along the border with Myanmar where drugs are openly traded.[136] The manager of Beijing's 'Hot Spot' disco described his young customers as wanting 'drugs and money'.[137] A number of contemporary novels and short stories alerted observers to the recreational and other use of drugs by the city young. One reformed heroin addict, the Shanghai writer Mian Mian, has a book of short stories called *Ha Ha Ha* which describes the drugged-out night club world made up of bad relationships and loose or casual sex.[138] Several new novels written in the 1990s by glamorous and much-photographed young female authors in their twenties depict the lifestyles of the disaffected young who mix drugs and sex. Perhaps the best-known of the novels, dubbed 'pretty women literature', which touches on many social issues long taboo in Chinese literature, is that of *Shanghai Baby*, written by Wen Hui who has been quoted several times already in this study. Published in 2000, the novel immediately became a cult book as its themes of sex, drugs and rock'n'roll struck a responsive chord among westernised youngsters keen to escape the stifling attributes of their parents and the strait-jacketing and social conformity expected by the government.[139] In one interview, Wen Hui admitted that she herself is intrigued by sex and that the heroine Coco, a young waitress who simultaneously falls for an impotent drug addict and a married German businessman, is to some extent based on her own life and those of some of her girlfriends who have love affairs, casual sex and take or push drugs. She thinks that this is the first book that aims 'to tell young modern girls how to face sex'.[140] On a more abstract level, Wen Hui noted that the inspiration for her book also derived from Henry Miller, Allen Ginsburg and Jack Kerouac who in their own societies were avant garde in breaking down sexual and social barriers. Other novels include Annie Wang's *Lili: A Life of Tiananmen* which documents the brutal experience of a beautiful young woman who slipped into a Beijing underworld of sex and violence, eventually falling in love with and cohabiting with an American journalist. In this novel, the heroine Lili is obsessed with shocking her intellectual parents: 'I love to upset those old Confucians'.[141] Such characters frequently upset more than their parents. Wen Hai, the 27-year-old daughter of an army officer and shop-worker mother, had no inkling of the storm the booming sales of *Shanghai Baby* would cause. Although the book was denounced by the authorities as decadent and debauched and was soon subsequently banned and copies burned, this was not before a total of 13 million or so underground copies had been sold in the first 18 months.[142]

In 2001, some 75 per cent of drug-users were said to be under the age of 25 years[143] and in late 2003, there were reported to be more than a million registered drug-users of whom more than 72 per cent were young people.[144] The increase among young persons is linked to growing drug use in recreational venues.[145] Young migrants are thought to be at particular risk as they may resort to drugs when feeling adrift and homesick in China's fast-paced and booming cities to which they have been drawn by the promise of wealth and success. Instead, uprooted and far from home, many, like the young man from Shandong province who travelled to Beijing with dreams of becoming a rock musician, turn to heroin 'to forget their problems'.[146] In a similar case, a young girl dancer who had left her village home in Sichuan to 'see what she could achieve' in metropolitan Guangdong, had only been able to find work singing in a karaoke bar where she was pressed into prostitution. Finally, tired, defeated and homesick and to forget all her problems, she was introduced to heroin. In yet another case, a young woman from the poor Guizhou province sent most of her earnings home, but following a succession of eighteen-hour working days, she fell ill and, miserably cut-off from her family, she was introduced to heroin. She too soon became addicted and henceforth spent her entire earnings on the drug.[147] Without regular earnings, addicts may turn to crime; drug-related incidents are reported to have led to a rise in the number of crimes committed by juveniles individually and in groups. In general, independent researchers estimate that the crime rate tripled between 1978 and 1998 and that nearly three-quarters of these were committed by young people between 14 and 25 years old.[148] Drugs is only one factor which has fed the juvenile crime wave. Criminologists put at the top of their lists the 'little emperor' factor, which has given rise to spoiled and self-centred children, the intense pressure to succeed at school and the growing desire for wealth and material goods, all of which may encourage many to play truant or turn to sharp practice which may include an element of deviant or criminal behaviour. There are also cases where juvenile gangs operating in large cities like Beijing and Shanghai and in some rural areas are thought to have started in schools as informal protection societies against bullying and then turned to pursuing their own ends via robbery and assault.[149] With corporal punishment common, the Chinese authorities take a rather unforgiving line on any form of deviant behaviour including drugs and crime and only very small numbers cross the line between adopting an alternative lifestyle and resorting to more extreme deviant or criminal behaviour.

Indeed it would also be easy to exaggerate the numbers and social importance of those pursuing a linglei or alternative lifestyle. For most it is a phase in their young lives which they later abandon in favour of more conventional styles. As one young man said, 'I have no choice, I have to live in society as it is'.[150] Another, also describing himself as linglei, noticed that friends of his change, acquiring jobs and suits and shrugged at the thought that maybe 'I'll change too'.[151] In terms of numbers, those who frequent the clubs in pursuit of cheap sex, foreign men or drugs recognise that they too represent a small – although growing – group. Li Jie, the young authoress, has expressed concern that books such as *Shanghai Baby*, *Beijing Doll* and *Candy* depict this 'dissolute' lifestyle and give foreign readers a misleading impression of what Chinese women are like:

> My books don't have much sex in them and the men are just the backdrop. The women in my books are more spiritual, their inner world is more important to them than having a boyfriend or going shopping.[152]

The author Annie Wang concurred. She noted that so many of the books about nightclubs, sex and drugs 'only look at the cosmetic changes in China' and that 'reading them is like buying a counterfeit handbag'.[153] For the majority who do not drop out or lead an alternative lifestyle, the growing desire for wealth and prosperity and a lifestyle to match is based on hard work, not a little leisure and as much consumption as possible, aspiring not just to live a life but to live 'a better life' or to have 'a brighter future'. The majority are taking advantage of new opportunities to individually aspire to be independent and modern but, simultaneously, they are also not a little daunted by the constancy of change and the practical challenges of finding permanent and promising employment, a marriage partner and establishing a houschold prior to having their own children. In the meantime, uniquely placed between full-time education and family responsibilities and with their own income made all the more disposable by living at home, they have opportunities to earn, spend and save that are unique to current generations of China's youth.

Just as the final version of this manuscript was to be posted to the publishers, the astute *Times* correspondent, Jane Macartney, filed an interesting report on the importance of China's young women consumers which very clearly expressed many of their contemporary priorities.[154] She wrote that though they may have more choices and freedoms to follow their own fancies than any generation before them, they experience the same pressures common elsewhere: between pursuing a successful career, attaining new goals and standards and having a home and family the structures for which remain conventional. She quotes a recent study which reveals that the expectations which young women have show some confusion about the two opposing stereotypes: the 'loving kind angel' and the 'working warrior'.[155] Jane Macartney's report also quoted from several interviews which she herself had conducted which reflect this paradox and show the conflicting emotions among young women who have embarked on demanding and high-flying careers but also want 'to be loved and to love'. Interestingly, in pursuit of their ambitions, several of the young professional women interviewed said that shopping for designer clothing was now low on their list of priorities and now they preferred to save rather than to spend. Macartney notes that this is an attitude common among China's newly better-off women who proclaim that it is 'better to be financially prudent and to invest in a career or in a husband'. As many improve their qualifications and help themselves up the career ladder, they have little time or inclination to do more than allow themselves the odd treats. As one said, 'You never know when times will get difficult so its important to economise. That's how many people think in China'.[156] Despite the noticeable trends to save and invest in the future, it has been both the numbers of China's young and the propensity to embrace new ideas, to try new things and spend on themselves that have attracted the attention of both domestic and foreign firms marketing jeans, trainers, fashion attire, electronic gadgets and computers. However demographic projections are such that the numbers in this age-group may already have peaked, suggesting that in an ageing society the youth market may attract less attention than China's new elderly or 'greying' market.

9   The greying generations

Shifting needs

World-wide, there is a general consensus that the rise in the proportion of the Earth's elderly will be the defining demographic feature of the twenty-first century. Population projections in many countries have caused serious concern about old-age support in the future and simultaneously aroused hopes of a large and growing 'grey market'. Already in 2000, the proportions of elderly in Japan (23%) and in the OECD (on average 18.6%) were high and projected to rise to 34 and 30 per cent respectively between 2000 and 2050.[1] For the USA, the 70 million or so persons over the age of 50 years in 2004 were expected to increase to 108 million by 2015.[2] However, it is China that is expected to age faster than any other country and to have the largest number of older people by 2030 and 2050. The percentage of the population aged 65 years and older is expected to rise from the current level of 7 per cent to near 12 per cent by 2020 so that by the middle of the century, the number of people in this age-category is expected to exceed 400 million.[3] Over past decades too, life expectancy has doubled and by the mid-1990s was just more than 70 years.[4] Indeed, this single-country rise in the numbers of those over the age of 65 years suggests that the speed of China's ageing is without parallel. Very recently, in 2005, Asian Demographics, a research organisation, predicted that the decline in China's total population under 40 years and the increase in numbers older than 40 and 60 years will amount to nothing less than 'a demographic earthquake'.[5] China is also unique because as it is often said, it is growing old before it gets rich. This rapid and unprecedented rise in both the world's and China's elderly has not only drawn attention to high dependency ratios and the likely inadequacy of support systems to cope with their care but also to the potential of new 'greying markets' which might be expected to augment consumer demand as they have already done in Europe and North America.

Greying markets

There are many who expect that populous and ageing China will follow in the footsteps of North America, Europe and Australia where growing and greying markets have already attracted considerable commercial interest as large cohorts of healthy and wealthy 'baby boomers' reach their fifties and sixties and look forward to 15 to 20 years of a retirement lifestyle. In these societies, many have the resources or accumulated wealth and income-pension to support a lifestyle that includes good living, leisure activities and travel. World-wide, it is estimated that the over-fifties hold 80 per cent of private wealth and they are 'the fastest growing sector' of consumer populations.[6] According to Senioragency International, a consultancy firm specialising in marketing to the elderly, the over-fifties in developed countries own three-quarters of all financial assets and account for half of all discretionary spending. Most retire with a pension and more than two-thirds own their own homes mostly without a mortgage, control four-fifths of the money in savings and own two-thirds of all shares on the stock market.[7] Jean-Paul Treguer, the French founder of Senioragency International and author of *50+ Marketing* (Palgrave 2002), recounts how, not so long ago, European company executives would laugh when he tried to convince them they should pay more attention to older consumers. 'Now', he says, 'everybody is talking about them but no one knows what to do'.[8] Similarly the 'Second50Years' website encourages companies to focus on the over-fifties because, according to the most recent US census statistics, the over-fifties number 78 million and control 67 per cent of America's wealth, amounting to US$28,000 trillion.[9] The census data also showed that those between 70 and 74 years are by far the most affluent in America with a median net wealth of US$120,000 compared with just US$7,240 for the under-34 age group.[10] Joanne Fritz, owner of the Second50Years website and founder of an Arizona consulting firm that specialises in the older market, has also pointed out that the over-fifties market is growing by 40 per cent per year and hence much faster than the prized youth market which has long been the Holy Grail of advertising executives on Madison Avenue.[11] Numerous newspaper articles report that Americans are retiring at any point between the ages of 40 to 75, depending on their wealth, inclination and fondness of work – and that they are proving to be tireless shoppers.[12] According to marketing research, the elder generation are interested in 'an extended middle-age' or even the recapturing of youth by embracing creature comforts, status symbols and anti-ageing products.[13]

Increasingly and world-wide, the idea of a major new lifestyle concept based on elder health, wealth and leisure is coming to the attention of manufacturers, entrepreneurs, retailers and advertisers. Those in the USA are probably a few years ahead of Europe in developing a better understanding of the 'greying' market. For instance the Centre of Mature Consumer Studies at Georgia State University segments the elderly into four groups according to health and activity: 'healthy hermits', 'ailing outgoers', 'healthy indulgers' and 'frail reclusives'.[14] The author of *Age Power: How the 21st Century will be Ruled by the New Old* (Putnam 1999), prefers to segment them according to the phases in the family cycle from 'empty nesters' to grandparents and sometimes single again.[15] In the past few years a slew of new marketing campaigns in the USA have been aimed at ageing consumers who, becoming richer and more adventurous, now feature in advertisements on television screens in the USA and Britain. These feature new 'second-lifestyle' images, products and services that have been developed to meet the needs or even demands of older consumers. In 2004, *Marketing Magazine* organised a conference of executives to 'challenge your perceptions of the over-fifties market'.[16] According to a recent *Wall Street Journal* article, senior managers at Proctor and Gamble were ordered to watch a video depicting a day in the life of an 'older consumer'.[17] Ford is reported to be developing a new car, the 'Five Hundred', for the so-called 'empty nesters' while the American department store Target has introduced a new multi-functional wardrobe for the older, 'fairly active' and above-average-income baby boomers or 'zoomers' as the company calls them.[18] The co-founders of the 2young2retire website describe baby boomers as 'the richest, best educated, healthiest and most long-lived generation ever seen' who 'are increasingly demanding goods and services that would have been unthinkable only a few years ago. And this is opening a whole new market for entrepreneurs who are able to spot the opportunities'.[19]

If the opportunities are being spotted in Europe, Japan and North America, it would not be surprising to find, given the numbers of elderly and the pace of economic growth in recent decades, that there is a similar trend in China or at least in the major cities. However it has taken most marketeers some time to shift their focus from the trend-setting youth of China to the potential of the elderly and factor China's ageing into their long-term plans. They are now doing so, albeit slowly. A spokesperson for the ad agency, J Walter Thompson, has observed that while the ageing of China is well known in principle, 'none of my clients are talking about it yet'.[20] Other marketing firms say that they are beginning to take note of the 'large and dramatic change in the demographics of China'. For example a marketing executive for Proctor and Gamble China recently noted that they are considering the 'greying issue' as 'China's ageing population will be a significant market'.[21] Demographic trends are an important factor and there has never been a shortage of calculations where China is concerned – but a closer examination of livelihoods and lifestyles of the elderly in contemporary China suggests that the idea of 'the new old' and the development of a 'grey market' as in Europe and North America may not be an appropriate analogy. This is largely because the elderly normally continue to work into old age, few retire with a pension, savings or a modicum of economic independence and because, instead of empty nests, the post-60 age group are likely to live with or rely on the younger generation and invest almost all their time, energy and wealth in their families. Even in the cities where retirement until very recently conferred pension rights and privileges, there has been a shift in patterns of work, old-age support and welfare provision that make for less independence, leisure and greater reliance on the family. For most of China, it can be argued that the concept of retirement, as it is known elsewhere, is either unknown or less than applicable to the lifestyles of the elderly, whether they reside in the city or in the countryside. Hence this chapter is less about consumption or lifestyle and more about shifting familial hierarchies and the changing needs of the greying generations in both city and countryside.

Village elderly

In rural China, where some 70 per cent of the country's over-sixties reside, elderly men and women have long continued to labour in the fields or in non-agricultural main or sideline occupations such as animal raising, fruit growing, fish farming and carpentry or other handicraft activities. Those who had earlier left the land and worked in local factories or migrated further afield in their early and middle working years also tended to return to the village as they aged – either to farm or participate in other household-based activities. With increasing old age and so long as they were able-bodied, they progressively moved into less arduous activities that were not so physically demanding, perhaps undertaking small farm activities or some form of domestic labour. Indeed field work suggests that it is the elderly who care for the very young, shop, cook, sweep or grow vegetables and raise the chickens. I have never forgotten how one village grandmother described herself as 'too old to work in the fields' and who was now 'only able to do her bit by cooking the meals, taking care of the grandsons and raising two pigs and a chicken'. What she neglected to add was that the sale of the pigs, chickens and eggs amounted to Y300 which then formed just under half of the total cash income of the household. For recreation, the very old may gather to chat and smoke in the sun, play cards, chess or mahjong and visit the local market or teashop. For the most part, the rural elderly are almost entirely reliant on their families for material and all other forms of support and they think it entirely natural to continue to contribute to the support of the household and thus to family income and well-being in the absence of pensions and alternative forms of individual economic support. Only those with no ability to work and no alternative income or family support are eligible for social assistance. In these circumstances, support takes the form of 'five guarantees' comprising minimal clothing, shelter, food, medical care and burial expenses.

One study of a rural county in central Shaanxi province conducted in the late 1990s found that the economic well-being of the 1,200 or so elderly informants was somewhat lower than that of younger generations.[22] They were more likely to reside in poor or average income households, have few personal assets and about 90 per cent did not possess a television set at home. A high 80 per cent lived with their adult children who provided financial support and physical care for their elderly parents and, in turn, the parents helped with child care and housework. The rest continued to live in separate establishments, either with their spouses or alone, but they all resided near their adult children from whom they received some form of support. Again nearly 80 per cent of those surveyed said that they were entirely supported by their adult children and that this support was mainly provided by sons; the remainder either received practical assistance from their children or had their own resources. About one quarter had between Y50 and Y100 to spend each month which compared well with the average monthly per capita cash income of Y85 in the region. A very small proportion (2.3%) received Y100 per month as opposed to three-quarters of the elderly who had Y50 or less to spend per month which mainly derived from their own small earnings or family support. These amounts suggested to the investigators that the resources at the disposal of most of the elderly were barely sufficient to cover the minimum living costs. As for the elderly themselves, most felt that their living standards had improved but that they were entirely dependent on the bounty of their children which eroded their own autonomy and influence in decision-making. Many children voluntarily and with great affection provide care and cash for their parents, especially if they are still active and can contribute to the well-being of the household, but there are also cases where resentment at providing for the needs of the very old and ill can spill over into conflict and neglect. In some rural areas, the practice has been established whereby the younger generation sign contracts with the government which promise care for parents in return for inheriting the house and other assets.[23] The reliance of the elderly on family support is not new and continues a long-established practice in China's villages despite various attempts during the revolutionary and reform years to provide supplementary or alternative forms of support and care.

In some of the richer peri-urban and coastal regions, communes did supplement family support during the revolutionary decades and, since that time, township and village governments have attempted to establish a rural pension plan that might provide the elderly with some semblance of support. In 1991, the Ministry of Civil Affairs introduced a voluntary pension insurance system for farmers and workers in town and village enterprises on an experimental basis in more than one thousand counties, mainly located in richer rural areas along the coast and nearby. After three years in operation, it was estimated in 1995 that some 50 million rural workers were participating in the scheme and that a fund of Y4 billion had been accumulated.[24] In 1999, some 80 million farmers had joined a voluntary state pension scheme in which farmers contributed up to 50 per cent of the payments.[25] This rural pension plan encouraged workers to contribute to retirement savings accounts which were turned over to local officials to match and invest in treasury bonds, bank deposits or in special trust arrangements with banks. Each year the individual accounts were credited with interest payments which might be as high as 12 per cent, although in some years the returns might be less than the rate of inflation. Ordinarily the funds could not be withdrawn until retirement when it was turned into an annuity which, supplemented by any annuity purchased with a lump-sum payment, was intended to last a lifetime. However the average accumulation per participant across the pilot counties amounted to a mere Y80 which at the time was unlikely to generate more than a 5 per cent replacement rate of income after retirement. In 1997 it was estimated that 510,000 rural-based people were receiving pensions, most of which had been paid for by lump-sum payments. However for those without lump sums at their disposal, the amounts contributed were miniscule while local governments without township and village enterprise income could ill-afford to match such contributions.[26] By the late 1990s, the government gave up promoting the scheme. In poorer areas, farmers could ill afford even the minimum contribution of Y2 and local governments certainly had no spare funds to add matching contributions; in richer regions, farmers could see no point in making contributions once interest rates on bank deposits fell to around 2 per cent and government bonds yielded a low 3 per cent.[27] Not only did any mooted scheme fail to provide the elderly with a replacement income sufficient for even the most basic standards of living, but farmers also worried that any pension funds they accumulated would disappear into the coffers of corrupt officials. Altogether only some 10 per cent had bothered to pay into the funds[28] and although there have been a number of periodic attempts to devise such schemes, few of China's 800 million rural dwellers retire or receive any pension or benefits.[29] Recently it has been estimated that around 94 per cent of the rural elderly have no pension or alternative form of support to the family and that most work long into their old age without any thought of retirement.[30] In the cities, the concept of retirement is much better known, although the prospect of a funded retirement is decreasing as the conditions making for a comfortable retirement have changed dramatically in the past two decades of reform.

City elderly

The concept of retirement was more than notional in China's cities during revolutionary and early reform years when, until the mid-1980s, the majority of urban workers could look forward to some form of pension support once they retired. After the age of 60, most retired workers returned to their work-units to pick up their pension payments each month and continued to receive the same housing, medical and other benefits as before. My own field work in city households during the 1980s and early 1990s revealed that the receipt of pensions after a life-time of employment was very much seen as a reward for years of hard work. It was a welcome source of support and independence for the elderly and was sufficient to allow most to provide for their own daily needs, make small consumer purchases and enjoy their own leisure to an unusual degree in a still-poor third-world country. For instance, one of the surprising findings of my own survey of urban employment of domestic maids in the mid-1980s showed that the most common category of employers was not dual-career families with young children as might be expected – but grandmothers. On retirement, they frequently used their pension to employ domestic servants to undertake the domestic labour and child care that ordinarily might be required of them now that they were no longer in employment. Many then used their new leisure to enjoy and care for their grandchildren, exercise or dance in the park, learn new skills, take up new hobbies or participate in community organisations and just sit in the street chatting with their neighbours, keep pet birds or join in chess, cards or mahjong games. Their wants were few and their financial support secure, largely due to the widespread pension system during revolutionary and the early reform years.

In the cities, pensions for the majority of urban labourers who had worked until retirement age, 60 years for men and 55 years for women, were generous, perhaps constituting as much as 70 to 75 per cent of their pre-retirement wages. The pension system operating in the state enterprise, government units or in non-profit and party organisations was funded exclusively by contributions from the enterprises on a pay-as-you-go basis so that each enterprise or organisation paid the pensions of its retired employees out of current revenues. When the economic reforms began in 1978, the State Council issued new pension regulations to unify the pension system and extend it to include a larger range of members including those employed in collectively-owned enterprises. The prevailing retirement ages of 60 for men and 55 for women were reaffirmed, although a number of incentives were introduced to encourage early retirement and thus create jobs for the large numbers of young entrants into the urban labour force. These incentives included new and higher retirement benefits, a lowering of the minimum years of service required to qualify for retirement pensions and benefits, and for a time, the guarantee of a replacement job for a worker's child following his or her retirement. Under these new and generous terms, 20 years of continuous service earned 75 per cent of the standard wage, 15 to 20 years earned 70 per cent while 10 to 15 years deserved a 60 per cent pension.[31] Perhaps it is not surprising to find that the numbers of retirees increased five-fold between 1978 and 1985 and that pension costs rose from 2.8 to 10.6 per cent of the urban wage bill.[32] Although not all urban elderly and especially older women who worked outside the state sector received the same levels of support, the proportion of urban residents over the age of 60 who received a pension had steadily risen so that by the mid-1980s the majority received some support, albeit of varying amounts. Since pensions had grown at the same rate as wages, retirees with high-level pensions were often better off than younger workers. Since the mid-1980s however, the pension and benefit schemes underlying the independence and leisure associated with retirement in the cities has been eroded by the new economic reforms.

Although during the early years of reform there were frequent complaints by pensioners that inflation had diminished the value of their retirement benefits, the pension system remained intact and work-units were still obliged to meet the pension costs of retirees. However many work-units found it increasingly difficult to meet these costs as market reforms placed state-owned enterprises on a new and individualised profits-and-loss basis. Instead of central planning with state responsibility for resources, profits and pensions, enterprises were to be responsible for their own income and expenditure, expected to show a profit and at the same time meet the welfare costs of workers and retirees. The increase in loss-making and bankrupt state enterprises and the sale of some state enterprises meant that many were unable to continue to meet their obligations to the retired. Even where the core business of an enterprise proved profitable, the capacity of state-owned enterprises to expand was inhibited by the costs of welfare and pensions. With marketisation too, employment growth in the state enterprise sector slowed so that the number of pensioners relative to current employees rose, which frequently made it more difficult for state-owned enterprises to manage the burden of pensions. The government became increasingly aware that these problems were inhibiting both the profitability of state-owned enterprises and the stability of pension schemes. It introduced new regulations in the mid-1980s to establish pension pools, first across cities and then across provinces, to which enterprises were invited to contribute according to a set formula. In 1991 new regulations called for an expansion of pooling to include collectively-owned enterprises, joint-ventures and foreign enterprises and for the establishment of three tiers in the pension system in which contributions by the state, the enterprise and the individual were designed to place the pension system on a sound financial footing.[33] However these reforms remained fragmentary as many individual enterprises found it increasingly difficult to make pension payments to their retired workers.[34]

Even before the raft of exacting reforms put in place by Zhu Rongji at the Fifteenth Party Congress and the National People's Congress in 1997–8 which further stretched the demands on the remaining resources of the state-enterprise sector, it was evident that these enterprises were finding it difficult to continue to fund enterprise-based pensions and medical or other social services both for their current workforce and their dependants as well as for retirees. For instance in the large cities of Shanghai and Shenyang, the ratio of employees to retirees in state enterprises was reported to have fallen to around 2 to 1.[35] In some of the older enterprises, the number of retirees had increased so rapidly that the ratio of pensioners to workers worsened so that some now had more pensioners than workers.[36] A more-detailed study of one machinery factory showed the changing ratios of workers to retirees. Established in the 1950s, it had employed three generations of workers, most of whom were still alive and, until the last decade, all profits had been transferred to the state which in turn had looked after both working and retired workers. After the industrial reforms of 1995, the workers bought the company from the government and successfully made the transition to a private company, but it was hampered in its development by continuing obligations to the growing population of retired workers and the fact that the previous pay-as-you go system meant the absence of any pension fund. The factory now had to pay out pensions to support 890 employees of whom 220 were workers, 420 retired and 250 'laid off' or on medical leave.[37] As former and present state enterprises struggled simultaneously to meet salary and benefit bills of current employees in an unforgiving market place, the pensions and benefits due to retirees became a secondary concern and many no longer received the pensions and benefits due to them. By the end of the century, the late, partial and non-payment of both pensions and benefits to retired state enterprise workers had become commonplace in China's cities. The result was a profound change in the lives of the urban elderly, many of whom have responded loudly and publicly.

Since the mid-1950s, the receipt of a pension in retirement was the defining prerogative and privilege of state-enterprise workers, distinguishing them from less-privileged social categories. Many of these retirees, who had earned and received pensions previously and who were now suffering reduced or non-payment, have taken to the streets to air their grievances. Throughout the 1990s, so-called 'pension protests' played a prominent part in the surge of urban demonstrations in the largest metropolitan cities and especially those in the northeast. In Liaoning's capital, Shenyang, under-funding of enterprises became such a serious problem causing lay-offs and shortfalls in pension payments that 27 per cent of the city's state enterprises had simply stopped making pension payments by 1998. There were waves of protests until the municipal finance and labour departments stepped in with a Y240 million bail-out.[38] In Shanghai too, retirees could be seen obstructing roads and holding demonstrations outside government offices and factories to protest against pension arrears and to demand that 'missing' or inadequate pension payments be made good. Reports also suggested that these protests were supported widely and by current generations of urban workers who considered that non-payment of pensions constituted a fundamental breach of the social contract or the long-term employment bargain between state or enterprise and worker. At the same time there was a rise in the numbers who, prematurely retired or laid-off, had very little prospect of a work-related pension. As enterprises became more concerned to maintain their solvency and local governments more concerned to create jobs for the young, the employment span of older workers was shortened, resulting in a decline in the mean retirement age. Many of the women in their forties and men in their fifties who were laid-off had a minimal allowance and some benefits but very little likelihood of ever returning to work while others of similar age were officially and involuntarily retired.

As a result of the market reforms, the rules of employment and retirement had begun to change with drastic consequences for both the elderly and not-so-elderly. In much of urban China then, and for the first time in a generation, elderly skilled and other workers in state enterprise and other sectors began to experience a new insecurity as reductions in or the absence of state-supported pensions and benefits jeopardised the very notion of a supported retirement promising adequate standards of living, health care and a degree of independence. Aware of their own worsening plight, many elderly interviewed reported that they felt worse off than any other generation and that 'retirement, once the expected golden age of one's life is now mixed with uncertainties and anxieties'.[39] Studies showed that, in this uncertain terrain, retirement is no longer such a privileged life-phase:

> Retirement, once a privilege that provided a secure income, guaranteed health care and respected social status is now associated with elemental risks of income slippage and less secure benefits.[40]

In terms of retirement then, most of China's urban elderly had to come to terms with a new set of circumstances in which they could not count on retaining their jobs until the formal age of retirement, finding new jobs to replace lost earnings or even receiving pension payments for which they were eligible. Without a pension or the promise of a pension, it became very difficult for any urban employee to anticipate a life-time's employment or plan for a secure retirement.

Pension planning

In China's cities, securing a pension and planning for retirement has become the privilege of a minority in Party, government, management and a few industrial and manufacturing sectors. If for most, the promise of pensions and retirement benefits belong to the privileged past, the problems of providing support for growing numbers of elderly are widely recognised and one of the most formidable challenges facing China's government continues to be the daunting task of establishing a nation-wide or inclusive pension plan at a cost which the country can both afford and sustain. It is not only expected that the elderly population will constitute some 200 to 300 million in the next 20 years, but that the dependency ratios will become increasingly unfavourable with the numbers in the workforce supporting the elderly declining from 10 workers per retiree in 2000 to three per retiree in 2050.[41] There is general government concern that, unless some adequate provision is made, it will be difficult to avoid a 'pensions backlash' or 'pensions crisis' and escalation of protest with the potential to threaten social order. It is widely acknowledged outside of China that pension reform is one of China's most urgent and immediate problems:

> What China needs most is to tackle its social welfare system and quicken the reform of the systems of pensions for the aged.[42]

The challenge facing reformers has been to meet the needs of a growing population of elderly within current institutional and fiscal constraints and accommodate all enterprises covered under pre-existing separate plans together with those in the non-state sector who are presently excluded: in short, to establish a single system with common standards across the country. Since the mid-1990s, there have been a series of new pension reforms which have attempted to put in place a unified system, extend coverage, reduce costs and establish individual funded accounts within a strong regulatory framework. Quite how these objectives can be achieved has been the subject of much policy debate within and outside China.

There is a general consensus about the need to reduce the costs of any pension system by adjusting the retirement age, wage replacement ratios and pension indexation. To this end there have been attempts to raise the retirement age to 65 to take account of longer life expectancy and shorten the average duration of retirement which today is over 16 years. This, it is agreed, would have the added advantages of lowering contribution rates for a given level of benefit, increasing the viability of an expanded pension system and reducing the loss of skilled personnel to early retirement. In addition, the existing pension levels at more than 80 per cent of wages plus housing, medical and other benefits are thought to be much more generous than in other societies where wage-replacement rates are more likely to be between 40 and 60 per cent. In line with international practice, it is also argued that a more appropriate means for reducing the pension burden in coming years would be to index pensions to the consumer price index rather than to wages which are expected to rise and be affected by future dependency ratios. Finally and perhaps most importantly, it is widely advocated that there should be some movement from a pay-as-you-go system based on pension payments out of current revenues to some form of partial accumulation based on fully-funded individual accounts. Without this shift, officials forecast that the pay-as-you-go system runs the risk of requiring very high contribution rates of around 39 per cent by 2030 which could lead to high rates of evasion by enterprises and place an enormous burden on society.[43] Thus the government favours funded individual accounts which would shift much of the burden to current workers who would save and manage their own accounts, ensuring that enterprises make their contribution and that fund managers maximise the rate of return on pension funds. Much debate has centred around the respective roles and balance of state-organised and market-generated schemes and the degree of redistribution necessary or desirable to incorporate both economic efficiency and social equity. With the help of the World Bank, a growing consensus has emerged within China around a shift to a three-tiered or three-pillared system which includes compulsory pensions organised by the state which are both basic and earnings-related, supplementary occupational pensions which may be optional or semi-compulsory and individual pension schemes which are entirely voluntary.[44] So far the reforms in place have established the principle that individual employees should share in the costs, that responsibility should be shifted from enterprise to the provincial governments and that provincially-managed funds derived from firm and employee contributions should be invested well in a range of financial institutions.

Although the broad directives of reform have become clear, their implementation has proved to be much more difficult. Nearly half of urban employees, not to mention farmers and migrants, remain almost entirely excluded and there is much evasion of the new contributions required of both employers and employees. So far individual and personal accounts are little more than notional as accumulated funds do not yield sufficient rates of return to transform them into an adequate pension and they are continuously raided to meet existing liabilities and pay present-day pensioners. According to the *21st Century Business Herald* in 2004, a state-owned newspaper, the funds accumulated in personal accounts should have amounted to around Y480 billion by the end of 2002. However an official who deals with social security matters reckons that there is probably only about Y100 billion in them and that only six or seven out of 31 provincial governments have pension funds in the black.[45] Even in Liaoning province, which is the acknowledged leader in pension reform, there is evidence to suggest that in places where provincial authorities have taken over the pension liabilities from over-stretched firms, retirement funds show large shortfalls consisting of many billions of yuan.[46] The government too has scaled back its contributions to the central social security fund so that this 'fund of last resort' is still too small to provide much in the way of 'comfort' or reassurance for today's pensioners.[47] Certainly trust that any pension contributions and funds will be well-managed and yield rates of return better than ordinary bank savings is low.

Many of China's policy makers acknowledge the shortcomings of present schemes but they have not yet devised a practical way to fund individual accounts and pay current pensions at the same time. One of the suggestions proposed by *The Economist*, which has recently concluded that China's pension system is still 'in a mess', is for the government to assume the burden of the old-system's liabilities, transfer administration of the personal accounts to independent asset managers and allow investment of these funds in domestic and foreign capital markets.[48] What gives urgency to deciding on these options is the limited window of opportunity over the next 15 years or so in which China can take advantage of both high rates of economic growth and a still lower proportion of elderly. After this time, the numbers of elderly will rise sharply, which means that the costs will be higher and the capacity to bear these costs lower than in other countries that have made similar transitions. In the meantime however, and in the foreseeable future, the spread and speed of reform is such that it is unlikely that a pension system will lead to acceptable levels of replacement income or that the state will be in a position to provide more than minimal or residual support for those outside the system. In these circumstances the very notion of retirement previously associated with full urban employment, a secure pension and other benefits making for independence and leisure has come to be questioned. Some will retain pensions and privileges, but the majority of urban residents including those in the fast-expanding private, joint-venture and foreign enterprises as well as those remaining in the state-enterprise sector may well have to look for alternative forms of support. In the foreseeable future, the majority are unlikely to acquire the pensions and privileges that once distinguished state-sector employment and the lifestyles of the urban elderly. Increasingly as urban pensions and privileges associated with retirement have declined and are less secure, the urban elderly have become more like their rural counterparts in that they too continue to work, to earn extra sources of income and to look to alternative sources of individual, community and familial support in old age.

Self-support

Increasingly, as in the countryside, a significant proportion of urban retirees continue to work beyond the formal retirement ages. Already there are signs that the elderly are attempting to prolong their employment span, find new jobs once 'retired' or adopt the 'portfolio lifestyle', mixing part-time work with some benefits or pension entitlement. One very interesting study of a smaller Chinese city in the mid-1990s showed how older city residents had sought to remain employed or find new work after retirement once the employment-based financial security of a guaranteed pension enjoyed by older urban residents had been eroded.[49] The study found that one-third of all male respondents aged between 60 and 64 were working and that many of those of retirement age now regarded retirement as 'a requirement' or something to be avoided rather than a privilege. Indeed privilege was now associated with the opportunity to continue in employment with 'the focus now' on 'how to stay on in the labour force or return to work after retirement'.[50] To delay retirement had become a privilege that was 'reserved for those who occupy important positions in the pre-existing social, political and economic hierarchy'.[51] In all cities and especially in Beijing, those who are members of the Communist Party and work in a government office are much more likely to enjoy the privilege of extending employment beyond the retirement age. That said, those in the service or private sector are more likely to have opportunities for re-employment in contrast to state and manufacturing employees who are more than four times as likely to be retired early and to find it difficult to join the growing trend towards re-employment. Retirement earnings were not only welcome but now necessary for the increasing numbers on fixed incomes, reduced pensions or with little more than subsistence support.[52] Thus China's urbanites, old and young, are looking for alternative and effective ways to secure an independent and comfortable old age.

In addition to staying on or returning to the labour force, many have saved for their old age. Indeed the importance of savings as a form of insurance for old age cannot be over-estimated and bank savings remain the most popular means of safeguarding the future for those with surplus income. In recent years substantial numbers have also turned to life insurance as an alternative form of self-generated support for old age. Interestingly in the late 1950s, the government had abolished life insurance as unnecessary, but since the introduction of the new economic reforms there has been a burgeoning insurance industry. Throughout the 1990s, new forms of life insurance designed to guarantee economic support for the elderly became increasingly popular as a means of relieving fears and anxieties about old age in the face of reduced state and family support. Even for those with every prospect of family support and a son or sons, the idea of insurance was welcome. In the early years of reform, one woman was tempted by the likely stability of such an arrangement: 'Now the money a son gives his parents every month is 30 odd yuan at most. But after we joined an insurance company we got more than Y200 for an elderly pension. This is much more than a son's Y30. So it is more reliable than relying on a son for old age'.[53] Another, younger 31-year-old mother of an only daughter who had arranged a monthly retirement payment of Y80 was heard to ask 'so why do I have to rely on a son when I am old?'[54] Within the context of family planning, parents have been encouraged to purchase insurance as an alternative to dependence on sons. Indeed in 2003, a Beijing researcher on family issues noted that endowment insurance for rural residents was having a far-reaching influence on farmers' attitudes towards the number of wanted children.[55] More widely, and certainly during the 1990s, as fears about pension provision and other benefits mounted, the selling of life insurance has increased and led to the expansion of the life insurance industry. One study suggested that around 20 per cent of those over the age of 60 now expected insurance to play a part in old-age support.[56] According to Swiss Re, a re-insurer, life insurance premiums rose from Y70 billion to Y220 billion between 1998 and 2002 and for the first three months of 2003 were 39 per cent higher than in the same period in 2002.[57] China's oldest and largest insurance company, the People's Insurance Company of China (PICC), has enjoyed steady growth as the demand for life insurance has increased and continues to dominate the insurance market for domestic insurance, property and casualty but, in addition, a number of new domestic and international companies have entered the market.[58]

Today, China Life, with a wider distribution network and stronger brand recognition than its competitors, is the country's biggest life insurer with a 45 per cent share of the market,[59] while the second largest life insurer, with a 28 per cent share of the market, the Ping-An Company, enjoys great popularity in Beijing and Shanghai.[60] Since the mid-1990s, foreign insurers too have eyed the new 1.3 billion market 'where life insurance is growing fast'.[61] In previous years they have only been permitted to establish joint-ventures with domestic partners but, under the terms of China's entry into the WTO, all foreign insurers have the option to obtain a license and operate nationally by 2005. American International Group, the first foreign insurer to do business in China, owns 10 per cent of PICC; British-based Prudential too is already in the market alongside such giants as Metropolitan Life and ING Group. Altogether up to one hundred other contenders are reported to be poised to jump into China's life insurance market where there is evidence of an increasing need and desire for old-age support, especially in the cities.[62] Chinese companies also recognise that the demand for insurance is likely to increase due to the decline in numbers of children and fall in state-enterprise provisioning. In 2003, Ping-An's chief executive forecast that the sale of life insurance policies 'has great potential' and is likely to constitute a major area of growth as China's population of all ages seek new guarantees for an independent and secure old age.[63] However it is still the case that, for life insurance companies, investment returns are low, largely because they are circumscribed by a limiting regulatory framework requiring them to invest in Chinese banks and government bonds rather than overseas equities and corporate bonds. In addition there is the constant fear that funds will be mismanaged or that corruption will lead to the depletion of funds. It will take some time to establish sufficient trust to woo the majority of China's residents into life insurance schemes and away from bank savings which are deemed to be safe despite the fragility of the banking system discussed in Part IV. Should there be any loss of trust in the banks and fears that savings are not well-invested and safe, then retirees would certainly petition and demonstrate in what would amount to a massive exercise of 'grey power'. Thus as later chapters assert, the government will do its utmost to avoid such a situation, not least because neither the state nor the community has the means to step in and support the elderly should savings and other individual forms of support fail.

Community assistance

The role of the state in providing support for the elderly remains minimal and is largely confined to providing residential forms of social security and support via local government and community assistance. These safety nets mostly take the form of limited subsidies or services and are targeted at those who are destitute or without any surviving family members capable of providing support. In the majority of China's villages there is little more than a minimal safety net for the childless elderly who, as stated earlier, are eligible for the 'five guarantees' (clothing, shelter, food, medical care and burial expenses) which are funded centrally by the state and perhaps supplemented by local services and subsidies. The scale and scope of any supplements are very much dependent on local resources now that social welfare responsibilities have been devolved to township and village governments. In the wealthier coastal, suburban and delta locations, local governments have been able to make allowances available or even establish homes for the retired which are supported from the proceeds of local township and village enterprises. In the mid-1990s, it was estimated that around two-thirds of townships across China had more than 6,000 homes for the aged which altogether housed a total of 600,000 residents or around 20 per cent of the 3 million elderly eligible for the five guarantees.[64] My own extensive fieldwork trips in the 1990s suggested that such community assistance was almost entirely dependent on the presence of local industries and that there was a strong correlation between the profitability of such enterprises and local government funds or community services. Hence in poor regions without or with ailing local enterprises, there were unlikely to be any local services beyond the state-funded guarantees. What has changed in the past few years however, is that even in richer regions, local government funds have dwindled as township- and village-owned enterprises have declined. Field studies in a variety of rural venues suggest that, in the absence or decline of local-enterprise familial subsidies, any security, services or assistance for the village elderly is now of mounting and widespread concern. Of course it has always been the case that it is kin, neighbours and friends who have provided informal help for lone-elderly by providing meals and undertaking small domestic tasks and this is still forthcoming although there are fewer sources now increased production responsibility and migration are more common in the countryside.

In the cities too, state subsidies are rigorously means-tested and mainly confined to urban residents in the 'san wu' or 'three withouts' category consisting of the elderly, orphans and the disabled who have no familial or alternative means of support. Implementing this system of residual welfare is mainly the responsibility of the Ministry of Civil Affairs which devolves responsibility for social and community assistance to local street and residents' committees. These committees have been encouraged to take responsibility for and establish home-help and other community services which provide laundry, meal delivery and shopping services and in some cases old-age day centres and homes. However during the 1990s, increased demand alongside rising costs and the absence of additional central-government funding have stretched the resources of urban and residents' committees and thus the continuation of such services.[65] The government, itself suffering short-falls in central funds, has encouraged local-enterprise support for the development of urban community services and welfare enterprises by introducing favourable tax reductions or exemptions to those who allocate a portion of their income to such causes. Central policy directives, such as 'Views on Speeding Up the Development of Community Services' in 1993, confirmed the government's support for developing community industries as the foundation for funding and supporting community services which were then to be made available to urban residents either at market prices or at little or no extra cost to the elderly, disabled and infirm.[66] Without extra-budgetary sources of funding, many local residents committees have been forced to mediate mounting demand and fiscal constraints by introducing fees for community services, which has meant that access has increasingly rested on ability to pay. In addition to user fees and enterprise-funded welfare, the government has also promoted care for the aged by non-government organisations, foundations, charities and individuals in an attempt to diversify both public and private support for old-age community services and care.

Most elderly remain home-based and very few move into sheltered housing or old-age homes, even in advanced years. Old-age residential homes are mostly state-run welfare homes with minimal facilities and, as in the past, they are mainly used as a last resort by those without any form of alternative support. The 1990s saw the development of new private retirement homes and hospices which were established by enterprising individuals and charged admission fees of around Y350 to Y5,000 plus monthly care and food charges between Y780 and Y1,430.[67] In 2002, it was estimated that only about one million elderly lived in state-owned establishments in the cities, while a mere 24,000 residents were housed in 1,100 privately-operated homes.[68] In 2004 it was reported that homes for the elderly, including those state-run and owned or managed by neighbourhood committees, enterprises or individuals, had increased to number 437 in Shanghai, 308 in Beijing, 300 or so in Tianjin and 187 in Guangzhou. Apart from a few welfare exceptions, most residents were self-paying with the fees ranging between Y400 and Y600 per month.[69] A recent study of 526 elderly residents across different types of homes in the mid-Yangtze city of Wuhan showed that they were almost all more than 70 years of age, widowed and could no longer care for themselves. Around 70 per cent had a pension which covered costs and the remainder received partial or total help from their families. Some said that they had entered the homes because of a lack of family care, housing shortage and strained family relations, while others stressed that it was more a case of exercising choice in that they had the means to pay the fees and had sought company of their own age.[70] For the same reasons 1,500 residents had chosen to live in the new and comfortable 'Long Life' complex of buildings and gardens in southern Guangzhou city which, although owned by the local authority, charged fees that were 'exorbitant by local standards' and only within the reach of the elite.[71] To exercise such a choice required a substantial income, pension or savings and it is usually only retired officials, high-income professionals and entrepreneurs who have such an option.[72] The founder of Pine Tree Hall, China's first hospice, was very aware that such homes only cater for the wealthy and that the majority cannot benefit from these initiatives.[73] Indeed most are not full – both because of the costs and the shame that still surrounds the idea of residence and care outside of the family. Although government, community and private initiatives have provided more in the way of community assistance for the retired in the cities, so far neither the state nor the community has been able to fill the gap and provide comfortable or affordable substitutes for home-based family care.

Familial support

For centuries, the Confucian precept of filial piety or reverence and support for parents was extolled as the highest virtue so that caring for elderly parents, especially by sons, was regarded as a most important and practical obligation. This age-old precept underlying an inter-generational contract which embraced both child-care and parent-care has continued to play a central role in the physical and material support of the elderly, especially but not only in the countryside. In rural villages, it is customary for elderly parents to reside with or in close proximity to an adult child or children. In 2000, it was estimated that between 70 and 80 per cent of rural elderly lived with their children while the remainder normally live in neighbouring households or at the very least in the same village.[74] Such proximity makes for close inter-generational ties characterised by a two-way flow of resources with each generation having responsibility and caring for the other. In the cities during revolutionary years, the widespread introduction of a pension system, state-allocated housing and well-established child care and canteen facilities reduced the need for daily interaction between the generations, although the acute housing shortage in some cities meant that there was still some co-residence. Now in the post-reform years the threats to pensions and other social services, such as child care plus privatised housing in the cities, mean that there is a greater need for this flow of resources including services, money and goods between the generations. A recent small-city study suggested that the inter-generational contract with its emphasis on parent- and child-care and support was 'robustly intact' in that it was no inherited relic but a vibrant core of both old and new household forms.[75] Although there has been an increase in smaller nuclear or two-generational households in the cities, the majority of the elderly in the city too are still likely to move in with or live in close proximity to their adult children in old age. In the cities, it has been estimated that around 80 per cent of urban elderly parents were not so much empty-nesters as co-resident with adult children.[76] Commonly, there are two patterns which lead to such high rates of co-residence in both city and countryside: either the younger generation marry and continue to reside with elderly parents or they establish a separate household at the time of marriage, the birth of children or following household division into which elderly or widowed parents move at a later date. The first is the predominant sequence in the countryside and the second is more common in the cities.

Where the generations do live in separate households in the cities, they are also likely to reside in the same neighbourhood or city, making for constant contact and support. Studies of old-age care in China suggest that living near as opposed to with children does not necessarily mean that there is less support or flow of resources between the generations. Indeed such are the exchanges between these separate households that field workers refer to the 'virtual Chinese extended family',[77] the 'networked' urban family'[78] or the 'aggregate' rural family[79] to emphasise the co-operation and interdependence of these separate but close kin-related nuclear households. What both high rates of co-residence and inter-dependent separate households suggest is that familial resource flows continue to be the most important source of support for the elderly. However there are also widespread fears among the elderly that this support is not as secure as it was in former times and that there are fewer guarantees attached to continuing familial support than they would like. My own interviews and conversations with the elderly in very different regions of China suggest that they feel their own authority and security to be at increasing risk as a result of a widening generation gap and a decline in respect shown to the senior generation as households become more child-centred. Concertedly, too they perceive their expectations of familial support and security to be jeopardised by the diminution of family size, the migration of family members and the unemployment of adult children.

The average family size in both rural and urban China is shrinking quite significantly as household numbers range between three to four persons with an average of one to two or at the most three children. Due to birth control policies and especially the one- to two-child family policy, it is estimated that there are 300 million fewer offspring available to provide support for the older generations.[80] Reversed, the 4:2:1 ratio means that one child may have to support two parents and four grandparents. Overall, the decline in family size has threatened if not eroded the time-honoured ways in which siblings have co-operated to jointly support their parents. This dependence on children and sibling co-operation for continuing old-age support is one of the major reasons why there has been so much opposition to the single-child policy in rural China. My own field work and that of others in a wide range of rural villages showed that it was the risk to old-age support and care that was most responsible for the very great opposition to birth control policies in the countryside. It is still a folk truism that only the birth and survival of a son can guarantee old-age support; thus individual and village resistance to birth control policies is defended in simple terms: no state support or security for old age, no support for birth control policies. Such opposition has been responsible for the continuing modification of the single-child rule to permit two- to three-child families or at least one son in much of the countryside and increasingly in the cities. In addition the continuation of familial support for parents is also threatened by the large-scale migration of the younger generation from the countryside to the cities.

What has shaken the expectations of the rural elderly and made their care and support seem more uncertain in recent years are the new patterns of migration in which the younger generation leave the village in search of work, an independent income and the 'modern' experience of city life. In rural regions and especially in the poor central and western and northern provinces, increasing numbers of the younger generation migrate to small towns or the largest cities, leaving their parents behind to housekeep, farm and care for any grandchildren. Although the cash remittances sent home to parents may go some way to supporting those back home, remittances are as likely to be used for education of siblings or of children, for upgrading or building new houses or for investment in agricultural inputs, all of which may less directly benefit the elderly. My own field work has also suggested that if the younger generation become permanent migrants and marry and establish their own households in the cities, then the transfer of remittances to folks back home is often less generous and regular or may even stop altogether. In the cities too, the expansion of high-rise suburbs and a more flexible job and housing market have combined to reduce the residential proximity of the generations, stoking the fears of the elderly that contact may become more intermittent and support or care less certain. However one of the most immediate threats to the familial and financial support of urban elderly derives from the lay-off or unemployment of their adult children. Current suggestions that the elderly should be able to rely on their children and families in the absence of state or community forms of support does not take into account the rates of unemployment, lay-offs or any backlog of unpaid wages in the manufacturing sector. In these circumstances not only can retirees not rely on their children for financial support but, in many cases, these adult children have become reliant on their aged parents for support or help in establishing or buying into new businesses or other substitute economic activities. The plight of the elderly with laid-off progeny has attracted increasing attention in the Chinese press. In 2000, a journal published for the elderly detailed the travails of an extended family now reliant on the secure and reliable pension of a retired cadre who could not be properly taken care of by his laid-off children.[81] In these conditions, adult children are less likely to be able to provide any additional resources to contribute to the living costs or medical expenses of their parents, although they may have more time to provide physical care.

The changing circumstances of reform suggests that the old – and the not-so-old – worry that the capacity and commitment of the younger generation will not be sufficient to support them in old age and that this commitment and capacity is increasingly jeopardised by new pressures on familial resources and parental priorities. As young parents or the middle generation attempt to rear and educate their own school-age children, purchase their own housing, invest in a career and take advantage of new income-generating opportunities afforded by market reforms, there is clear evidence that families have become increasingly child-centred. Indeed, as Chapter 7 suggested, the costs of children's education, marriage and housing frequently take a disproportionate portion of pooled family income, require long-term savings and in some circumstances even the sale of family assets, leaving little for other expenses including those for parents and grandparents. In these circumstances of new couple- and child-centred family priorities, there has been an increase in the flow of resources to children which has led to increasing competition for attention, care and cash. This new competition has also meant that the middle generation, simultaneously young parents and adult children, have increasingly become the 'sandwiched' or 'pincer' generation, caught as they are between the dual and conflicting demands of investing in children and supporting parents.[82] In the resulting competition for family resources between the generations, the older generation is not only more likely to feel disadvantaged and less sanguine about future support, but also more likely than ever before to direct any of their own discretionary income, savings, time and energy towards the well-being of their children and grandchildren in the hope of securing short- or long-term reciprocal care.

Familial investment

Although members of the older generations emphasise the duties of the younger generation, they are also less assured of their old-age entitlements and, to compensate, they have taken a number of compensatory steps to ensure their own immediate or short- and long-term care. These strategies include an intensification of investment in their young children, a lengthening of investment to include adult children and the spread of investment to include daughters as well as sons. As an earlier chapter has already shown, parents invest much in their young children, spending increasing amounts on more and better education, clothing, toys, recreational and extra-curricular activities, not only for the success and pleasure of their children but also in the hope that these investments will pay dividends in later life. Regardless of the different levels of familial wealth, spending on children in both poor and rich families is frequently rationalised as both an expression of affection and sign of devotion and a strategic nurturing of gratitude and indebtedness to parents which has been described as 'a long-range form of self-interest'.[83] In a memorable example worth quoting again, one professional urban mother sets out to purchase a piano not only in order that her 5-year-old daughter might learn to play but also to show her that they were 'saving money in order to specifically please her' and that her gratitude and debt to her parents should be repaid in later life.[84] In less privileged settings, it may be smaller items such as an article of clothing, a toy or an extra year at school which is accompanied by similar expectations of long-term gratitude and support. However, a widening fear among parents pursuing this strategy and investing in young children has been that there is no guarantee that these long-term and delayed returns will be honoured. One way to reduce the odds and increase the likelihood of filial returns or repayment by the younger generation has been for older parents to contribute to the support of their adult children.

The advantage to ageing parents of lengthening their investment in support of adult children is all too clear: returns would be more direct and short-term. Ethnographic evidence suggests that because of the new uncertainty and greater insecurity, parental contributions to the well-being of adult children and their children's children have assumed a new importance and that the elderly direct more time and energy to providing services for their families than ever before. The tasks which elderly parents undertake for adult children, frequently now both employed full-time and for long hours in village and city occupations, include domestic labour, minding grandchildren, marketing or guarding and caring for property. Despite the numbers of nurseries and availability of migrant domestic help, the potential of grandparents as the ideal of 'best' child minders providing the cheapest and most convenient yet most responsible form of child care in the earliest years, appears to be the most valued form of assistance the older generation can give in all but the most ambitious of families preferring professional or educational forms of child care. It might be argued that this is hardly a new trend in that elderly parents have always provided such help, but my own field studies suggest that this help has increased, is now more purposive and has spread to urban locations where it is now quite common for the elderly to play a major domestic role. The work of others also suggests that retired parents are working harder than ever before and, in urban China, hard-worked elderly have been heard to sigh and say to each other rather resignedly, 'For the children …'.[85] As for adult children, they say that they welcome this help especially in the cities where familial and socio-economic changes in the market place have increased the demands on parental time, energy and purse as they extend their own education, take up full-time employment, get married, rear children, acquire homes and manage their own households in a market economy without the same state support as hitherto. To meet these greater needs and with rising costs of goods and services, younger generations have increasingly turned to their parents for material and non-material forms of support which more often than not they readily receive.

Evidence that the younger generation have a renewed appreciation of the support of the older generation and recognise this support as more of 'a family resource' than 'a family burden', is to be found in the degree to which the younger generation openly state and currently show their support for filial obligation in both word and deed. In recent surveys in China, upwards of 85 to 90 per cent of youth expressed their support for 'filial' obligations and there is a general consensus that, far from an erosion or weakening of filial obligations due to the growing generation gap in other attitudes and behaviours, filial support remains strong.[86] There is also some evidence to suggest that these expressions of support are stronger among older youth who are at an age when they are approaching marriage and parenthood themselves.[87] Many of the young start worrying about taking care of the old at quite a young age. One young woman wondered if she would have children given the responsibilities she would have for her parents and, with this in mind, she planned to purchase a flat nearby.[88] Several young married friends of mine have had their parents move in or very near to them once they had a child. A young 22-year-old graduate was already thinking of how to repay his parents given the costs of his education:

> It's a huge burden for us to take care of our mother and father. At our age, you have to start thinking about that. When I get married, my wife and I will have to take care of four old people, so I am deliberately screening out certain jobs already. That's the kind of thing we have to think about, before we think about our own interests. There is a saying: if you are a good student, you earn money for your parents. This has become part of our consciousness.[89]

Certainly it is not lost on the elderly that those of their number who are materially able to help financially and are physically able to provide services for their children are in turn more central to their families and more likely to be consulted, respected and supported. Put quite simply, those who help get helped! Similarly, in field studies, it is often suggested that any cases of old-age neglect by children have their origins in past tensions or conflict over lack of parental assistance or the allocation of familial resources. There are likely to be more of these cases if the less 'civil' behaviour of the village young referred to previously becomes widespread. In short, continuing parental contributions to their offspring are more likely to generate reciprocal services and security in a circular pattern of care and affection between the generations. Another bargaining strategy open to parents with savings, property and other assets is to transfer these assets to adult children prior to their death in exchange for immediate or guarantees of immediate old-age support. It has become more common for elderly parents to give or promise property to the members of the next generation with whom they expect to live or from whom they expect to receive most support in their old age, who in some cases may not be their direct descendents. Although almost all in the countryside and increasingly those in the cities live in housing which is privately-owned and thus transferable to the next generation, only a very small proportion of China's elderly population have other assets that are substantial. Many have savings, although there is some evidence that the elderly in both city and countryside are increasingly likely to have depleted or exhausted their savings due to their spending on adult children and grandchildren.

In addition to intensifying and lengthening investments in their young and adult children, a third new strategy is for parents to spread their investment more evenly between sons and daughters. Sons have customarily been preferred over daughters, largely because they have been the single most important source of long-term old-age support. Unlike sons, daughters move away on marriage and thus are less likely than sons to remain within the same household or neighbourhood to support or provide care for parents in old age. For this reason daughters were often perceived as burdens, with the expenses incurred in their upbringing, education and marriage dowries sometimes likened to 'water spilled outside the door'. These differences in the roles and returns from daughters and sons led to a pronounced bias in familial investment and resource allocation which has favoured boys and disadvantaged girls. However in recent years, ethnographic studies suggest that, although son preference and under-investment in daughters still exists and, as this study has shown, discrimination against girls can still take extreme forms, there has been a slight but gradual spread of parental investment to include daughters. Indeed in the cities, there is an emerging consensus that there is an untapped potential for daughter-support necessary now that fewer sons are born in the one- or two-child family and that longer-living parents may require more in the way of physical care which might be better provided by daughters than daughters-in-law. Both rising life expectancy and the epidemiological transition have resulted not only in a prolonged old age but also in more degenerative and chronic disease profiles. At the same time, it follows that the separate residence of the younger generation in their own households after marriage better facilitates the ease with which daughters can continue to care for their parents. In urban China in particular, it has become apparent in conversation and interview that daughters are increasingly regarded as a major source of physical care and emotional support and that, more independent that hitherto, they may also have the means to contribute materially to the well-being of parents. A surprising fieldwork finding by the knowledgeable and experienced sociologist, Martin King Whyte, was the similarity in filial expressions of support for the elderly by both daughters and sons.[90] In this respect it is quite clear that daughters are being groomed in single-child families to take the place of absent sons and that, even in the more common two-child families, parents are also starting to appreciate and invest in daughters as a source of old-age care and support.

What is perhaps the most significant feature of all these investment strategies is the degree of purpose of both generations and their consciousness of the importance of these inter-generational contracts for securing mutual assistance. If all this sounds very instrumental, the inter-generational contract is also accompanied by a great deal of mutual appreciation, affection and devotion in most families. However, perhaps it is not surprising to find that, in a society where both generations are increasingly totally reliant on their families for care, services and support, these relations have another more practical side. It is also true that much more is likely to be required of family support in the future as life expectancy, demographic and epidemiological transitions increase the numbers and life-span of the elderly, reduce the ratio of younger to older generations and lead to more chronic and degenerative disease profiles. In the face of these new demographic and social challenges, the government is unlikely to abandon the principle of 'care by the family first' or have the capacity to develop and finance a more comprehensive state-sponsored social support system for the elderly. Given current social trends which seem to threaten the maintenance of filial obligation and recognising a new sense of insecurity among the elderly, the government has concluded that the only option given its resource capacity is to enhance state support for family care. This support has taken legislative, rhetorical and practical forms.

In the past there have been general legislative requirements obliging the younger generation to provide support for their ageing parents but, in 1996, the government enacted a special law on the Protection of the Rights and Interests of the Elderly. This law specifically reiterated the responsibility of adult children to support their parents as well as parents-in-law and prescribed familial obligations for taking care of the financial, medical, housing and social needs of the elderly.[91] The oversight and enforcement of these family obligations is the responsibility of city neighbourhoods, village and work-unit mediation services and there are a number of penalties for failure of duty to do with inheriting smaller shares or the confiscation of family assets. The government has also turned to traditional belief systems to boost rhetorical support for filial commitments and obligations. There have been a number of nation-wide educational campaigns reviving Confucian ethics and in particular the concept of filial support. My own field work in a number of scattered small towns in the late 1990s suggested that these responsibilities of the younger generation constituted the focus of much legal and family education in schools and in pre-marital counselling classes. However it is worth noting that in 2003, the Minister of Civil Affairs, acting on the instruction from the State Council, reported on the necessity to safeguard the rights and interests of China's senior citizens, He referred to the growing numbers of the elderly and the increasing demands of their medical and nursing care, both of which meant that China's 'geriatric' age structure was emerging as a 'serious social problem'.[92]

Practically, the government has taken or is considering taking steps to establish supplementary voluntary services which both aid and encourage families to care for the aged. In addition to the policies encouraging local governments to provide a variety of community services including day care centres and homes for the aged, there has been a new initiative based on the development of voluntary services for single, poor or frail elderly, those in low-income families and those living in households where all the adults are in full-time employment and therefore not available for daily care. Although one of the unexpected consequences of the high numbers of unemployed and laid-off workers has been their greater availability to provide physical care for their parents, many elderly are left at home for long hours each day. In the countryside, villagers have been encouraged to guarantee responsibility for the care of the elderly left alone because of migration. So far however in both city and countryside neither the state nor voluntary informal or formal community services have been able to provide full support and, in these circumstances, it is not surprising to find that both the old and not-so-old continue to rely on and invest in the family and that individual retirement plans continue to centre on the family:

> The net result is that many people are fundamentally insecure about the future and relatively few have personal plans outside the framework of planning for their children's future.[93]

It is the familial orientation of these personal plans and investment strategies that dominates the spending of the older generations and leaves little that is surplus or for their own small everyday purchases and pleasures.

Small pleasures

With little surplus cash and many familial demands on that cash, the elderly over the ages of 60 and 65 are more likely to make do with small pleasures for themselves which may include special foods, a new suit of clothes, a small domestic appliance and a television set. Indeed most of the elderly in the southern, eastern and northern provinces and cities now have access to and enjoy television. They may also contribute to the family purchase of larger items and, in the cities, most live in households which have accumulated some of the widely-available and longer-existing goods, although fewer have the opportunity to either upgrade or experiment with new products. Interviews with retirees suggest that they usually take a great interest in new goods and frequent the newer and cooler shopping malls, although more for window shopping than purchasing. A small minority enjoy the highest standards of living, leisure activities and the means to travel. In the countryside, those residing in the richer village households and suburbs may watch larger television screens, enjoy the use of white goods such as a washing machine or refrigerator and have access to some form of mechanised transport, in contrast to those in the central, western and poorer regions who still have few opportunities to sample a wide range of consumer goods and services.

A small number of goods and services have particular appeal to the elderly. In the interests of self-reliance and reducing financial insecurity, there has been a growing interest in life insurance and other monetary services among those with the means and who want to ensure that their savings, investments and insurances are safe.[94] In 2004 several reports in *China Daily* suggested that the elderly are increasingly investing in the rather shaky stock exchange but are somewhat oblivious of the fact that stocks can fall in value as well as rise. Apparently several had fainted on discovering that their portfolios had depreciated, leading one official to suggest that the elderly should be prohibited from trading in shares![95] More widespread is a long-standing interest in traditional medicines and also in pharmaceutical products to ensure good health and a long life. In addition to well-trusted remedies, sales of Pfizer's cholesterol-lowering and anti-hypertension medicines are reported to be growing rapidly and according to Pfizer's Asian President, China 'is rising up the agenda of big drug firms'.[96] One domestic company that has long recognised this potential interest among the young is China's own Shenyang Jinlong Healthcare Products Company which, in 1992, set up as a joint-venture with Hong Kong-based New Wellon to target China's elderly population with products such as 'Longevity Ginseng'.[97] In 1998, First Eastern Investment also expressed a growing interest and planned to launch a wellness magazine in the hope of creating markets for senior education, leisure clubs and nursing homes. There is evidence of a new but limited 'grey' market especially for the middle-aged or younger old, although many of these services are only likely to appeal to those with above-average incomes.

One set of services which has attracted an elderly clientele with means is the Silver Hair Project which offers comprehensive home-help to retirement-age residents of Shanghai. For a fee of Y20, they can purchase a book of coupons which offers discounts on a range of services from hair-dressing to group tours, restaurants and housekeeping. Several items are also provided free of charge including hotlines for medical emergencies and other assistance, appliance-maintenance services, banking and legal services as well as free film tickets. The subject of television documentaries as well as magazine, newspaper, television and internet advertisements, the Silver Hair Project has attracted wide support in Shanghai from both individuals and some state enterprises which issue the coupons to their retired employees in lieu of offering their own benefits. One grateful retiree-client impressed by the services and coupons noted the substitution:

> Originally the government took care of us, but now we're supposed to look after ourselves. And you can't always rely on your friends for help.[99]

Initially, the founder of the project, Huang Shuo-zhu had hoped that his project would 'help fill the gap between what the state provides and what is needed'.[100] So successful has it proved that in 1998 he went on to launch a new membership plan called the Fuleshou Golden Card which, in return for a Y2,800 fee reduced to Y800 after the first 2 years, gives members services valued at Y4,000. These included newspaper subscriptions, birthday cards and delivery services, annual medical check-ups, tickets to 10 films, travel insurance of up to Y100,000, priority admission to old people's homes, a free gift, a hot-line service, a telephone chat-line and home visits by Silver Hair staff. At the time of launching, Huang planned to liaise with foreign and domestic manufacturers to provide product-lines such as calcium-enriched teas, sugar-free wine, special foods and a range of health-care products designed for the elderly under the Silver Hair brand name. His ambition was to expand and set up an integrated national network of Silver Hair brand products and services in 200 cities across the country because he thought that there was a fortune to be made by creating a viable market of old people:

> No one has really investigated what old people want in terms of sizes, colours and products that they like. This is an incredible market for goods and services.[101]

To those of us who have studied social developments in China for some years, it is not clear that the elderly will prove to be such 'an incredible market', largely because of several attributes pertaining to current generations of elderly and the increasing reliance on their families for security and well-being.

If some of the previous guarantees for support in old age are seen to be at increasing risk, so also many of the elderly feel that some of the benefits of reform are passing them by. Not for them the opportunities to make entrepreneurial fortunes; rather with little in the way of pension or alternative individual economic support to their families, many struggle to meet the increasing costs of old age, especially if their later years are marked by illness or other family misfortune. Not only do many members of the older generations feel that they are missing out on the fruits of economic growth and reform for all the reasons already outlined, but also it can be argued that this generation of elderly has borne a disproportionate cost of the decades of revolution and reform which in addition to affecting their own life chances have influenced their attitudes towards consumption. The present generation of retirees and those nearing retirement are scarred by their history of struggle and misfortune. In the late 1950s their health was likely to have been damaged by the deprivation and starvation common during the 3-year famine, in the early 1960s many urban youth were sent to the countryside to work, and in the mid-1960s the Cultural Revolution disrupted primary and secondary education. During the reform years, the working lives of many have been foreshortened by economic restructuring or down-sizing and, with little education and skill, they were ill-equipped to take advantage of any new economic opportunities beyond those in the most informal and unstable of sectors. Many also married late and the strictures of subsequent birth-control and one-child policies have limited the number of children permissible. Peng Xizhe, Director of the Institute of Population Research at Fudan University, has noted that it is China's baby boomers with a mediocre education, interrupted working lives and reduced savings who will find themselves facing a pensionless old age with only one child to support them. He argues that the plight of this 'lost generation' is likely to pose the most intractable ageing problem anywhere in the world.[102]

Not only was this generation of elderly less equipped than the younger cohorts to withstand the economic shocks and insecurities of their later years, but some have also found it difficult to adjust to the market economy with its array of consumer goods, advertisements and materialism in which money has assumed prime importance. A spokesperson for J Walter Thompson suggests that this generation is 'battle weary' and given to viewing commercial slogans and advertisements as an 'evil' of modern times.[103] This is perhaps an extreme conclusion but certainly they perceive much of the new materialism with some regret and find it difficult to adjust and entirely discard previous inhibitions about commercialism, materialism and individualism. Although it might have been imagined that, with the deprivations of the past decades, this age-group would gladly embrace any opportunity to indulge themselves, it has been observed that the elderly still 'want to hang on to their money':

> If they spend, they want to know what they're getting for their money, and they're reluctant to indulge themselves.[104]

For this generation too, it is also probably fair to conclude that they tend not to have a highly-developed sense of self or of their own individual needs. Although this may be changing for the not-so-old urban professionals who have their hair done, have a facial, join a gym, dance class or a tea house group, many of this generation do have more money than ever before but it is still less likely that they will spend it on themselves. Indeed a spokesperson for the advertising agency, Ogilvy and Mather, has noted that 'the selflessness of older people is a real marketing challenge'.[105] Whether they are empty-nesters or not, it is not surprising, given the absence of state- or community-sponsored alternatives, that the old and not-so-old continue to invest in and contribute to the family's well-being and that few have pursued or have individual plans 'outside the framework of planning for their children's future'.[106] Thus it is the familial orientation of these personal plans which dominates any spending of the older generation who may well contribute to major family expenses such as the purchase and furnishing of the homes of the younger generation or the education, extra-curricular or recreational activities of grandchildren, both of which have benefits in which they expect to share.

If the older generation are more likely to make financial contributions to their families rather than to directly purchase for themselves, it is their younger-generation kin who are now increasingly encouraged by media advertisements to give gifts to parents and grandparents:

> The best way to reach China's older generation, as most local companies and, increasingly, many foreign ones are starting to realise, may be indirectly, by appealing to Confucian values of respect for family elders.[107]

Many companies, such as Nestlé, encourage grown-up children to purchase products such as fortified milk powders and food supplements to look after the health of their parents. One advertisement asks if sons know the date of their father's birthday.[108] Another shows a would-be son-in-law stopping on his way home from work to buy a package of Longevity Ginseng for his future mother-in-law. Those marketing Longevity Ginseng say that they highlight its appeal as a gift because they recognise that usually 'the purchasers are not old people themselves but people who buy ginseng for them'.[109] One of the target groups for Silver Hair and the Fuleshou Golden Card are wealthy overseas Chinese who have elderly parents living in China:[110] perhaps not so much a greying market as a market aimed at the young for the grey.

In the decades to come, the support of the younger generation for the old is increasingly likely to be required by the elderly and not just for gifts, for the continuing dependence of the old on the young in the countryside and the increasing dependence of the old on the young in the cities – alongside the ageing of the population – is a major socio-demographic feature of twenty-first-century China. In these circumstances, the elderly tend to sacrifice personal wealth and welfare and take less interest in pension plans and life insurance than in spending on their children and grandchildren. Indeed it might be argued that the well-being of their family is their life insurance, but for how long? That is the question that the elderly ask themselves as they watch the middle generation working long hours or not at all, the migration of family members to distant places and the birth of fewer grandchildren, the raising of which take a major share of family resources. The ensuing reduction in the number of junior-generation siblings and thus the all-important sibling sharing of elder care due to one- to two-child families alongside projected rises in numbers of elderly, poses a formidable challenge not just to China's government but also to each family as it attempts to meet the impending financial and long-term care needs of the elderly with fewer children. One member of the younger generation noted in 2001 that 'we need to figure out who is going to take care of our parents and grandparents'.[111] The increasing sense of insecurity of the elderly in the face of any threat to family support is understandable given the minimal role of the state, which is largely confined to providing residual forms of social support and security. It is difficult not to conclude that the escalation in numbers and needs of the elderly in the next decades means that even those living within families may be at risk unless both generations maintain the will and the resources to nurture the inter-generational familial contract. In these circumstances it is likely to be many years before the elderly have the pensions and services that would boost their spending power and encourage them to have the confidence to do more than invest in their families.

Part IV

Present trends

Future demand

10 Consumer confidence

Stability and security?

In order to expedite the growth of domestic demand, China's government has continued to introduce a steady stream of measures to encourage consumption. The government continues to hope that if it can get people to spend 'furiously', it can make consumption the new engine for China's growth. It is well aware that consumption only accounts for about half of China's GDP compared with two-thirds in most developed economies and that 'for every yuan the government can get the consumer to spend boosting GDP, that's one less yuan it has to spend'.[1] The government deploys a variety of strategies to encourage spending. It is still extending holiday shopping-days punctuated by decorative festivals that are both Chinese and Western in origin. My friends in Beijing talk about 'holiday economics' or 'economic holidays' now that the government has created week-long holidays around the main national festivals of New Year and National Day. Other holidays too have been extended and Western festivals such as Christmas and Valentine's Day have become the subject of fashionable celebrations. At Christmas, shops, offices and other buildings are festooned with fairy lights and other colourful decorations are much in evidence as young affluent white-collar workers enjoy the opportunity to spend, exchange gifts and party. Valentine's Day too is increasingly the occasion for popular celebration especially among the urban young and romantic. In 2002, a survey conducted on Valentine's Day in China's three major cities of Beijing, Shanghai and Guangzhou revealed average spending of around Y192 (US$23) per person which is close to the US$25 per person spent by Americans. Many city yuppie couples celebrate the day with flowers and dining out, while more than half the respondents, aged 15 to 44, sent gifts including flowers, chocolates, ties, belts, cosmetics and handbags.[2]

To encourage China's host of savers to spend rather than save, there has been a succession of interest-rate cuts which reduced interest rates to 2.75 per cent in 2001 while a new tax on interest income was also designed to make saving less attractive.[3] To cater for those who want to maintain their savings and also spend, the government and the banks have taken several steps to push the idea of 'credit consumption' to finance the purchase of houses, cars or other goods. As *BusinessWeek* noted in 2001:

> China's economic planners are hoping to unleash decades of pent-up consumer demand for houses, cars and smaller purchases funded by bank

loans. Beijing hopes that if it can get people spending furiously, it can make them the new engine of China's growth.[4]

For a while it looked as if their plan might work. In the first 10 months of 2000, individual consumption loans increased significantly amounting to a total of Y194.9 billion so that personal loans accounted for more than 40 per cent of the total lending increase in that period.[5] In the same year, China's *Business Weekly* had headlines such as 'Borrowed Money Gains Credit in Cities'.[6] One survey of 2,100 citizens in China's seven largest cities in 2000 suggested that 'credit consumption' was becoming increasingly popular with 20 per cent of the respondents having bought products on borrowed money in the previous 6 months while 33 per cent said that they had plans to do so in the next 6 months. Altogether an average of Y30,000 in credit purchases had been made by each family interviewed during the previous 6 months.[7] One of the main advocates for expanding consumer credit were the banks which, with high proportions of bad loans, welcomed individual customers who were deemed less of a risk than loss-making state-owned enterprises. In addition to earning the fees and commissions attached to credit cards which were the most profitable form of consumer loans, China's banks also wanted to establish their share of this lucrative business before foreign banks were allowed to compete for the same clients in 2007. Indeed there was talk of a whole new mindset and a 'whole new way of financing the boom'.[8] Instead of the virtues of the model worker that were extolled some 20 years previously, now it was more likely to be the attributes of 'the model borrower' or 'someone willing to fearlessly pile on debt for a piece of the Chinese dream' which were likely to be cited for emulation. Take the example of Yao Lan, a 26-year-old assistant at the Russian News Agency Interfax, who, right out of college, had bought a new US$40,000 apartment with a 20-year mortgage at 5.58 per cent from the China Construction Bank. She herself was said to be in no doubt that this was a good investment: 'Where would I find so much money in such a short time without a loan?'.[9] As Beijing sees it, the more Yaolans there are the better and the plan was reported to be working well but, after an initial splurge, credit consumption declined.

According to China's central bank, card-spending accounted for only 2.7 per cent of overall consumer spending in 2001 and only about 5 per cent of Chinese cardholders revolve credit.[10] From 2001 the government encouraged consumer spending by allowing credit cards, mortgages and car loans available to their customers. Again in 2003, and with an eye on Olympic Games visitors and future foreign competition, the government once again attempted to persuade China's banks and shops to encourage consumers to accept and use credit cards.[11] In addition to increasing their spread and ease of use, the government also attempted to improve the credit infrastructure by simplifying application procedures and improving credit-recording systems. At present these are often location-specific and inhibit the use of credit cards by out-of-towners while, in town, both shop owners and consumers remain wary about using credit to finance purchases. The number of consumers with mortgages and other loans had increased by 2003 but only around one million had credit cards with another 24 million were reported to have debit cards that offered limited borrowing.[12] Since early 2004 there has been a tightening of the availability of credit or loans so that a tenth of all outstanding bank loans or around Y2 trillion is now owed by consumers, with most defaulting on mortgage repayments followed by car loans. Apparently thousands stopped paying after the government tightened credit.[13] In 2005, *The Economist* reported that only 12 million bank cards are genuine credit cards and that mortgages, car and education loans now make up 11 per cent of the total and 26 per cent of new lending.[14] Although the government can be said to have alternated between the expansion and contraction of lending for consumer items, depending on whether or not it was determined to cool an overheating economy, its overall ambition to get more plastic into people's wallets has not been realised. With the exception of the high-income spenders, the lack of enthusiasm for credit consumption has been attributed to on-going technical hurdles which inhibit the development of a nation-wide credit-card system that is easily and widely used in all locations. Just as formidable, however, has been the resistance of consumers to spending on credit. Although many are increasingly comfortable with the idea of borrowing for a mortgage, most still prefer to wait and use ready cash rather than credit for other purchases. Moreover inhibitions about borrowing against future earnings or savings were part of a much larger and continuing consumer reluctance to spend on unnecessary items, largely because of a persistent sense of insecurity and lack of confidence in the future.

Confidence indices

Consumer confidence, whether it is used as a measure or as an explanatory term, is now a much-discussed feature of any economy and recognised to be a significant factor encouraging or facilitating consumption. Internationally, the interest in defining and measuring consumer confidence has drawn attention to the importance of eliciting customers' opinions not just on products and purchasing habits, but also on their sense of confidence both in the future of the economy and in government policies.[15] Thus a number of confidence indices are based on consumer attitudes towards their current finances and their future prospects with the aim of assessing willingness to spend, borrow, risk or save. One of the largest international polling exercises designed to measure 'expectations about the future and its prospects' was that conducted in 29 countries for *The Economist* in 1998. The results indicated that Asia was the most 'optimistic region' with five out of the top 10 countries located in Asia. Malaysia, South Korea, Thailand, China and Taiwan topped the poll in that order and because of the concentration of expectations that the future would get better on that continent, *The Economist* was minded to dub 'optimism' another Asian value alongside Confucianism, conservatism, family values and respect for authority.[16] China was seventh in ranking, although less than a quarter of respondents were satisfied with their current quality of life. The Mastercard International Survey, carried out twice a year in 13 countries and regions of the Asian Pacific Area, also aims to investigate how consumers feel about economic trends. More particularly it sets out to ascertain their views on five indices which include employment, the economy, regular income, the stock market and quality of life. In summer 2000, the survey conducted among 5,469 customers in the 13 Asian Pacific markets suggested that Chinese consumers were optimistic about the economy and their future standards of living; they were upbeat about their regular income and the stock market, although more were cautious about 'the future of employment' index. According to the country-manager of Mastercard China, this is the only market where the Masterindex or a composite measure of the five indices has kept rising.[17] However, a different picture emerged two years later. In 2002, an international consumer confidence index, compiled by a research consultancy firm and based on questions relating to whether respondents expected their personal economic situation to improve and to purchase goods over the next 12 months, placed China fifteenth out of 25 countries listed. Only 10 of the 25 fell into a positive category so that the remaining 15 did not expect their present economic situation to improve and did not think that the present was a good time to purchase any goods they might want or need.[18]

In China too, there have been reports of a number of surveys of consumer confidence which have revealed some wariness, lack of confidence and insecurity regarding the future. In a set of random interviews with 5,670 adult residents in a number of China's cities including Beijing, Shanghai and many of the provincial capitals reported in *China Daily* in 1999, 7 per cent said that they were 'very satisfied' with their quality of life over the previous year, 63 per cent were 'fairly satisfied' and 23 per cent were 'not so happy'. The degree of satisfaction varied with age, career and educational background, with those between 18 and 24 years and over the age of 55 showing the most satisfaction with their quality of life, mainly because of continuing economic growth, abundant career opportunities and greater consumer choice. It may be that despite many of the problems of the elderly, their living standards were still higher than any they could have anticipated while, for the young, there was still hope for improvement. Those aged between 35 and 54 were much less satisfied and expressed many concerns about a slack labour market, corruption, social security or pensions and environmental pollution. However almost half of respondents (47%) expressed confidence that life would improve considerably over the next 5 years with 12 per cent expecting a 'big leap forward'.[19] Four years later in 2002, the National Bureau of Statistics reported that consumer confidence had slowed down in the spring of that year despite a short burst of spending at New Year. The official Xinhua News Agency associated this burst of consumer spending with an increase in incomes and stable prices which caused consumers to 'feel better briefly about the economy'.[20] However the *Far Eastern Economic Review* surveys of high-income earners over several years suggested that even 'feeling better about the economy' did not necessarily translate into consumer confidence or consumer spending.

The 6-year 'Survey of China's Elite', conducted and analysed in the *Far Eastern Economic Review* which was reported on in some detail in Chapter 4, showed that there was a general optimism about the 'bright' future and 'excellent prospects' of the country with some confidence expressed in their own individual futures especially but not only among the highest earners. However it also showed a decline in spending with more saving than ever before between 1998 and 2002. The decline in spending did not reflect slowing income growth, a decrease in income, a downturn in the country's economic growth or fears about entry into the WTO so much as careful and cautionary planning to meet the anticipated costs of securing a better future for themselves and for their children. The future might be 'bright', but it was by no means certain, hence much of the spending too was about securing and investing in the future as Chapter 4 noted. Although those surveyed might have had a number of unprecedented consumer choices, they preferred to purchase money products, insurances and education either for their children or for themselves. Uniformly they thought that in the future they would have 'to look out for themselves' as a result of rising unemployment levels and the sharp decline in many government or work-unit benefits such as housing, medical care, education and pensions. Hence a certain incongruity in the findings which juxtaposed confidence in the future alongside more saving than ever before and greater priority accorded to investing in and improving the future than indulging the present.[21] Over the 6-year period, the practical actions of elite informants suggested a mixture of hope or optimism and some caution and uncertainty about the future.

This ambivalence about the future among the elite evident in this and other surveys reflected a more widespread mood among all social categories which combined pride in the achievements of reform and China's economic development alongside anxieties about the pace of change and the shape of the future. This ambivalence was particularly evident around the time of the death of Deng Xiaoping who was acknowledged widely as the 'father' or 'architect' of reform. Within China, there was genuine appreciation of his role in ending the excesses of the Cultural Revolution in the 1970s, in opening doors to the Western and global and in generating change and choice. At the time of his death, a young and yuppie worker in the Bank of China expressed confidence that his generation was ready and 'could change China for the better'.[22] Those who had taken advantage of the many opportunities for new livelihoods and lifestyles would echo the sentiments of an independent and relatively wealthy stall holder selling goods to Russian traders. In 1997, he noted that 'without reforms, he would have stayed on the buses as a conductor all his life – just like his father'. He lived better than average, had enough savings and was hopeful that, with good health and the government's continuing light touch, the future would brighten still further, although he was also mindful that 'change is not easy in China'.[23] Some, including many state workers and older members of society who felt that they had lost out in the reform process, were not so confident that the future would improve and instead hankered for the cradle-to-grave security of the past and the seductive socialist promises of a bright future. For instance, a middle-ranking official in a textile factory would prefer to return to the more secure conditions of the past. He did not have too many fears for himself but he felt gloomy on behalf of the next generation and thought that an increasing number of the poor would not benefit from economic reform or get help from the government:

> The life of my children will be harder than mine. They have to take care of themselves and pay everything from their own pockets.[24]

A retired primary school teacher, who thought that life was much better than before when she had to worry about food and clothes, was also concerned about the social security in the future and the problems ahead for those who are not able to make the necessary changes and take advantage of future opportunities.[25] If the prevailing mood then was mixed, intertwining both hopes and fears, most from professors to farmers expressed the view that there was no escaping change and that their country was on an inexorable development path without a certain or even knowable destination. A bookish history professor reflected the view of many when he noted that although economic reforms may be irreversible, it is a transitional period in China when there is much change and even disorder during which people 'are waiting for something new'.[26] At the same time as farmers were grateful for the first years of reform, prosperity and new freedoms to move and improve themselves, they too knew that they were integrally linked to the market and outside world over which they had little control. They also did not know what the future held but acknowledged that there was no going back. 'We can't return to central policy. We must keep moving ahead'.[27]

Since the death of Deng Xiaoping, there is a tendency to be both emboldened and intimidated by the pace of change, further reforms, new opportunities and uncertain times. Even those earning high and steady incomes report that 'no matter how much money they make now, their mind is never easy'.[28] For some there has been a trade-off: new choices and freedoms in return for less guaranteed employment and long-term security. Many have taken advantage of the opportunities and appreciate the benefits, while others, and in particular state workers and the elderly, feel that they have lost out in the reform process. For such persons, the certainty and security of a lifetime's 'iron rice bowl' has become was a seductive memory. One elderly couple noted that 'when Chairman Mao was alive, life was good', but life 'was not so good now that they had lost their jobs'. They expressed some nostalgia for the days when Mao would have 'looked after them and not assigned them to the streets like this government'.[29] Such a view is not only expressed by some of the unemployed, farmers and migrants who feel left behind by the reforms, for even those who were still in employment frequently felt uncomfortable at the sight and presence of those less fortunate than themselves. One primary school teacher noted that 'Mao would have found jobs for the unemployed',[30] while those in the countryside made comparisons with Mao's war on the diseases and the inaction of the present government which 'only cares about economic development' and 'there's no-one to protect us anymore'.[31] In December 2003, the one hundred and tenth anniversary of Mao's birth was widely celebrated with a variety of lectures, exhibitions, television programmes and concerts honouring the Chairman's achievements.[32] If the 'have-nots' or those who feel that they have lost out as a result of reform might have special reason to look to the past as a golden-age of security, the majority have taken the view that the present is unimaginably better than the arduous years of revolution. They are encouraged by their leaders and an official press to make the contrast between revolution and reform, a poorer and richer country or a closed and open China – and to leave the past behind. For the most part there is widespread support for the government mantra that 'reforms are good' and have 'delivered the goods'. When Beijing's National Museum of Chinese History announced an exhibition on the modernisation of China, word was that thousands of citizens sent in 'reform artefacts' or ration coupons and other symbols of deprivation as a reminder of the advances of the 'modern' present over the 'backward' past. Commercials too remind television viewers that life has never been better. Two recent advertising campaigns for sportswear had the names 'goodbye' and 'anything is possible' to encourage the belief that final goodbyes can safely be said to the past in favour of the limitless opportunities of the present.[33] However for most it is not the contrast between the past and the present which is at issue but that between the present and the future. Today, although pride in the pace of China's economic development and its growing international voice and vote in world affairs continues and has been enhanced by the prospect of the coming Olympics, expectations of reform are still guarded and tempered with some anxiety, fears of insecurity and instability. In my own view there is no question that for the majority, the pace of change has intensified uncertainty and anxiety about the future. Informally, in shops, cafes and on the streets, it has been my own observation that despite surface talk of new opportunities for their country and themselves, there are many signs of lack of confidence in individual futures. 'Nobody has confidence any more' is a common refrain heard from friends and acquaintances with both stable and less stable incomes in Beijing and in other cities. This observable trend is well-expressed by a young author who, on the eve of the new century, thought that though real and dramatic changes in China were under way, China's future remained unpredictable. He suggested that in the short term, access to the internet and China's membership of the WTO might be cause for optimism but, in the longer term, he remained pessimistic because of the serious political and economic problems facing China. He thought that 'every conscientious intellectual is worried and that many are really pessimistic about the future'.[34] In 2005, the fast-paced lifestyle, heavy pressures and concerns for the future were reported to have led to greater stress, anxiety and a rapid increase in 'the number of people suffering from mental disorders'. In Shanghai, for example, 16,000 were said to be suffering severe mental illness and 600,000 emotional disorders such as depression and insomnia.[35] Whether it is anxiety, pessimism or a more general mood of uncertainty, widespread concerns to do with social instability and personal insecurity have led to lower levels of consumer confidence than might have been expected.

Social instability

There is general concern and some would say even some fear that China's very stability is at risk. Anxiety that the numerous protests in China today will lead to widespread social instability is expressed by the government, the media and individuals in interviews or in conversation. There have been many reports of local unrest, protests or demonstrations in the national and international press that highlight the increasing social tensions across the country, the difficulty in exercising many entitlements and rights in practice and a new readiness to take local action against instances of injustice and disadvantage. A young intellectual interviewed also feared that with the large and worsening gap between the rich and poor, the have-nots were breeding resentment against the rich and that this anger could well turn to violence'.[36] Official reports suggest that the numbers of incidents have been increasing over successive years and amounted to some 58,000 protests involving more than 3 million people in 2003, to some 74,000 protests involving 3.76 million people in 2004 and a reported 87,000 protests, riots and other 'mass incidents' in 2005.[37] According to a leading domestic commentator, most of these low-level riots are a 'manifestation of the ever-worsening conflict between the haves and have-nots, the powerful and the exploited, the governors and the governed'. He thought that the threat from low-level riots was so great that it 'could become a source of regional or even national social unrest', while Wen Jiabao has very recently warned of growing social instability.[38] Certainly several incidents reported in the international press during 2005 suggested that a single incident can spark a collective expression of general resentment. In one example reported in June 2005, what began as a traffic accident in a city in Anhui province expanded into a very large riot involving 10,000 or so people. Apparently the riot started after four men in a sedan ran over and beat up a teenage pedestrian which, leading to the firing of the sedan, public cars and the storming of a local police station,[39] suggests a degree of local resentment simmering just below the surface and a lack of formal outlets either institutional or in print for venting criticism and frustrations. The majority of such explosive incidents that have been reported, seem to involve specific grievances to do with environmental pollution, local government inaction or instances of corruption by local officials.

As city residents see their incomes rise and experience greater pollution, they are increasingly aware that the quality of the air and water can potentially affect both their health and their lifestyle, while in the countryside the very livelihoods of villagers may be threatened by environmental degradation. Newspapers increasingly write about environmental problems, stimulating public debate, while numerous non-government 'green' groups together with a number of well-known individual campaigners promote public education, public opinion and local actions that test the boundaries of permitted activism. As *Business Week* noted: 'As Beijing's leaders try to balance the needs of development with the imperative to clean up, it may well be the citizens who lead the way'.[40] In the cities, the quality of city air is a common talking point, with so many of China's largest cities showing unacceptable levels of pollution. Factories which continue to belch out smoke can be easily observed and together with the smoke from coal-fired power stations and domestic coal burners, this hangs pall-like above many of the cities. According to the World Bank, China has 16 of the world's 20 most polluted cities and the world's highest emissions of sulphur dioxide, while a high prevalence of acid rain affects up to a quarter of the country.[41] In 2002, a study of some 300 of China's cities found that the air quality in about two-thirds of these cities failed the standards set by the WHO.[42] In the surveys of high-income earners reported in the *Far Eastern Economic Review* between 1998 and 2003, the quality of the environment emerged as an important factor affecting confidence in the future. For example, in 2002, a survey of more than 1,000 high-income residents in the three main cities revealed that more than 80 per cent (and close to 100 per cent of Beijingers) thought that the country risked environmental problems. The investigator concluded that there was 'a high awareness of the potential environmental problems that the country faces' and that this finding 'constituted a clear sign that information is flowing more freely than in the past'.[43] In an unusual occurrence, one resident of Beijing raised concern in the local media that the plastic sheeting being laid on the often-dry lake bed at the Summer Palace would have adverse repercussions for the environment. The ensuing public debate in the competitive tabloid press resulted in the halting of the project, the organisation of a high-profile hearing to which critics of the scheme were invited and an apology by the severely-embarrassed local district government involved.[44]

In the countryside, the effects of water pollution and waste much more directly affect both livelihoods and lives and these have become significant causes for protest, unrest and even violence. It is estimated that about half of China's population have water supplies that are contaminated by untreated factory, animal or human waste because of industrial dumping, inadequate treatment infrastructure and insufficient investment.[45] In 2003, more than half of China's waterways were reported to have excessive levels of chemical and biological pollutants;[46] in 2004, one study found that 70 per cent of the water in five of China's seven major river systems was unsuitable for human contact.[47] There are many stories of river pollution causing the deaths of fish, ducks and wildlife or inducing illness and disease among humans and animals. One of the most severe examples occurred on the Huai River, one of China's seven major rivers, when a 133-metre long black and brown plume was reported to have swept along the river, killing millions of fish and devastating wildlife.[48] On a smaller scale, but one of many cases telling a similar story, a local river in northern Guangdong province threatened both lives and livelihoods as small private mines shed their toxic waste directly into the river, raising lead levels to 44 times the permitted rates, turning the water to an alarming rust-red and poisoning crops, ducks and farmers alike.[49] In 2005, there were several similar examples in which local media reports drew attention to the ways in which over-farming, the increasing use of pesticides or chemical fertilisers and industrial waste or accidents have polluted rivers and lakes, affecting fish, wildlife, livelihoods and water supplies.[50] A major report revealed that all seven major rivers as well as 25 out of the country's 27 major lakes were polluted and some seriously, that soil erosion affected a third of China's surface areas and that waste treatment facilities in all of China's cities were 'quite inadequate'.[51] If soil erosion and desertification are added to the list of environmental problems affecting lives, livelihoods and lifestyles then the list of concerns is long. Adding it all up, the World Bank has concluded that, if the impact on crop yields, manufacturing output, urban health, compensation, and disaster relief is added to the less direct long-term costs of resource depletion, then pollution is costing China between 8 and 12 per cent of its US$1.4 billion GDP in direct damage.[52] Although not all would agree with Elizabeth Economy, the author of *The River Runs Black*, that environmental problems 'have the potential to bring the country to its knees economically',[53] the continuing threat to the physical environment is of concern to many. Perhaps the most widely-reported incident in 2005 was the explosion at a petrochemical factory which released a vast 50-mile slick of carcinogenic benzene into the Songhua river, which feeds the water supplies of Harbin city with 9 million inhabitants.[54] With their water supplies cut off and little or no information, it can only be time before an accumulation of such incidents concentrate the minds of many and spark a political response.

Several incidents involving protest against unacceptable levels of pollution have led to unrest and violence as farmers have taken matters into their own hands. In April 2005, the local old-age people's association in several villages in Zhejiang province established road blocks and kept a 24-hour vigil for 2 weeks outside a chemical factory in a nearby industrial park, which they blamed for 'the contamination of the local river, ruined crops and malformed babies'. The local residents said that they had demonstrated after losing faith in the authorities because the village chief had refused to listen to their grievances and their attempts to petition the central government had proved fruitless. When the riot-police arrived to remove the demonstrators, they were set upon by the villagers who sent them running after a prolonged battle. Once word spread quickly to nearby towns and cities, their actions aroused the interest if not admiration of thousands of well-wishers and sightseers.[55] Again in June 2005, in a village 150 kilometres from Shanghai, hundreds of residents took over a local factory, locking in the workers amid accusations that lead poisoning from the factory, one of China's largest manufacturers of batteries for electric bicycles, was responsible for bouts of sickness among the village's 200 children who were 'all getting sick'. As one father said, 'they are polluting the air and it has been going on for years'.[56] As in so many cases of political unrest and violence, the passivity or even connivance of local officials who more often than not personally benefited or received bribes from the offending parties, was responsible for the outrage of local residents. Throughout the reform years, corruption has been a perennial hot topic railed against by leader, populace and foreigner alike. It played a part in the Tiananmen protests of June 1989 and for years President Jiang Zemin compared corruption to a 'cancer' in the Chinese body politic and, on one occasion, Zhu Rongji told an American senator that corruption, if not tackled, would very likely develop to such a serious extent that it would pose a clear threat to the government.[57] For the population at large, nothing unites them so much as a common dislike of bribery and corruption.

Some of the most popular novels and television series which have attracted a large readership or nightly audience-figures of hundreds of thousands have been those exposing high-level corruption, crooked government officials who were promoted and real-life whistle-blowers. Over the past decade, successful novelists, including Zhou Meisen and Lu Tianming, have written several anti-corruption novels which have become best-sellers. The latest hot-seller, entitled *Sex and Stocks*, exposes the capers and corruption in the banking world as it follows the fortunes of an investment banker and his ties with a vice-mayor who is eager to translate power and position into profit.[58] Major cases of embezzlement and bribery repeatedly make headlines in the media. As Chapter 4 suggested, many of the powerful and well-connected are suspected of making their wealth by grabbing state-controlled assets and commodities to their own advantage. In 1998, it was reckoned that such insider dealings had diverted millions of yuan from the national budget and done much to end public confidence in the reform process.[59] In the same year, the author of *China's Pitfall*, He Qinglian, analysed a host of such cases and referred to the 'wholesale plunder of public wealth' by officials who throughout China had used their power to grab shares of state companies listed on the stock market, to develop large real estate projects and to secure loans from state banks. Though it is not easy to determine the real cost of corruption, the cheap sale of state assets and corrupt property deals, He Qinglian estimated that more than US$3.7 trillion or some four times more than annual GDP has been transferred from state coffers into private hands as officials have acquired a taste for new riches as a result of property, foreign exchange and other deals.[60] Many officials who do not enter such transactions themselves provide protection for and benefit from the favours of those that do. For example, according to a local newspaper, the director of a shopping centre in the northern city of Harbin embezzled more than US$5 million under the protection of the city's vice-mayor who had deflected the attention of the tax authorities in return for favours. Interestingly when police raided the home of the vice-mayor, they uncovered US$225,000 in cash, 19 cameras, an assortment of 29 televisions and VCD players, 77 watches, 31 diamond bracelets and 100 designer shirts.[61] In 2000 in southern Guangxi, central Hebei, Fujian and northern Heilongjiang, high-level party bosses and city managers in property speculations were convicted of taking bribes and kickbacks, smuggling or amassing illegal gains often worth millions of yuan.[62] Since this time a number of major cases have grabbed the headlines but studies of the local press and fieldwork investigations also suggest that such cases are also replicated on a lesser scale in local urban and rural communities where some have resulted in demonstrations and violent incidents.

In the past 5 years there have been rising numbers of public demonstrations in the cities with urban dwellers protesting at housing scams, corruption, investment swindles or forced relocation and the difficulties in exercising lawful rights and pursuing cases through the law courts. Official participation or collusion in such schemes has infuriated many ordinary people who have been lured by get-rich schemes that have turned out to be scams.[63] City-dwellers too have to suffer from petty forms of everyday bribery. According to friends, 'money and gifts talk' and just getting an ordinary everyday permit requires a gift or extra payment. One laid-off construction worker noted ruefully that 'to keep your job you have to pay off your boss'.[64] Even admission officers at universities are said to have 'lucrative' posts in that they demand or are offered bribes by over-eager parents and others.[65] Increasingly it is protests against forced relocation which have stolen the headlines. For every new city skyscraper development there is a story of reluctant resettlement, lack of compensation or of official connivance for personal gain. In the countryside there have been sporadic and local protests at the exaction of illegal fees by local officials, often for their own purposes and pockets. Farmers in one county in Anhui province who had first petitioned the government to expose the corruption of local village chiefs and the heavy taxes they imposed, eventually protested and kidnapped the officials.[66] In 2005 there were a number of reports in the international press of local protests caused by the confiscation of land which had been aided and abetted by local officials who often stood to benefit personally. In one long-standing case in Hebei province, farmers who lost their prize vegetable-growing land when it was confiscated by the local government for road, office and residential development were offered compensation that fell far below the value of the land to either the developers or local officials. After many attempts to sue the officials who had seized their land in the courts, the farmers felt they were left with little option but to take matters into their own hands.[67] It is often the failings of and interference in the local judicial systems which forces people onto the streets. In another similar instance, angry farmers who had occupied their land to prevent it being handed over to a state-owned power plant were attacked by a gang armed with shovels and poles. They had been hired by local officials who had agreed to and no doubt benefited from the handover. The angry scenes, which resulted in a number of deaths and injuries on both sides, were recorded with a video camera by a resident and given to the *Washington Post*.[68]

In a similar case in Inner Mongolia, a telephone call to the *Guardian* newspaper led to international reports about 2,000 protesters who had seized the equipment and blocked the construction of a motorway that was being built on their land without adequate compensation for their houses and crops. They claimed that they had received a fraction of the compensation promised and that they only wanted 'our land and fairness'. In defence of these claims and no doubt suspicious that officials had siphoned off the funds for compensation, they sacked the local government office and held the party secretary and another official hostage and engaged in a 6-hour battle, eventually driving off the 100 or so police sent to empty the site and arrest the ringleaders.[69] What is interesting about these very recent reports is that in circumstances where it can still be difficult to criticise or protest at official misdeeds, these events were recorded either by video, mobile phone or in telephone calls to the international press. Perhaps this is a sign of what is to come but it certainly shows a growing awareness of the power of the press. In turn, the government has become increasingly aware that the ways in which leading cadres have taken advantage of their position to embezzle money and accept bribes, abuse their power for illicit profit or trade power for money, affects the power and prestige of the Party and trust in its ability to govern. Nevertheless it is still difficult for individuals and their lawyers to bring officials to trial. In the meantime, communication of such incidents by word-of-mouth, on the internet and in the national and international press, has contributed to a general fear of rising instability which, when supplemented by a wide array of direct or indirect threats to livelihoods and lifestyles from the physical, political and social environment, make for a widespread sense of personal insecurity.

Personal insecurity

Even among those with stable incomes there is a sense of insecurity about managing the future in the face of rising unemployment, uncertain social safety nets or support and the rising costs of public services for health care and education. It is not only the scale of recent lay-offs and unemployment that causes widespread fears about job security among both the employed and unemployed, but also it is the forecasts about job creation in the coming years which provide little in the way of reassurance for the future. At present, even conservative estimates suggest that the number of urban and rural unemployed amount to some 200 million persons and that this figure is likely to be much higher when seasonal, partial and under-employed workers are included.[70] In total, most Chinese analysts consistently place the unemployment rate, including the laid-off, at around 8 to 10 per cent in urban areas. A survey of five large cities conducted by academics at the University of Michigan and the Chinese Academy of Social Sciences found that unemployment rose overall from 7.2 to 12.9 per cent between 1996 and 2001.[71] In some regions in the northeast and in mining towns dependent on only a few industries, the 2004 rates were estimated to be a high 40 per cent.[72] Although many of those who lost their jobs do not remain unemployed, their new jobs rarely combine the same income and benefits that were attached to their previous employment. Indeed finding any job for all the unemployed and laid-off will be difficult unless millions of new jobs are created. More recent forecasts about future employment also suggest an upward trend, at least in the short-term, due to further reform of the state-owned enterprise sector, membership of the WTO and the numbers of young people entering the work force each year. Despite the loss of a staggering 24 million workers or 10 per cent of the urban labour force between 1998 and 2002 mentioned in earlier chapters, closures and lay-offs in the state-owned sector have continued.[73] In autumn 2004, it was reported that some 2,500 state-owned mines and large enterprises with a total staff of more than 5 million were due to be shut within the next 4 years.[74]

Official newspapers also report that substantial lay-offs are imminent at some of the country's state-owned commercial banks which have already shed some 250,000 staff and closed 45,000 offices since the late 1990s.[75] In April 2005, it was reported that a total of 13 million laid-off workers were looking for jobs.[76] There are fears that China's entry into the WTO will prove to be a double-edged sword, simultaneously creating and destroying jobs.[77] A Green Paper on Population and Labour published in Beijing in May 2002 predicted that, as a result of China's accession to the WTO, domestic urban unemployment would rise by some three to four million, pushing up the unemployment rate by about 2 per cent – even though in the long term job opportunities were expected to rise.[78] In the initial period of WTO accession (3–5 years), it was anticipated that traditional trades and agriculture which have low technical content and weak competitiveness would be the most affected. A national meeting on employment held in September 2004 noted that 'the scale of the unemployment problem was a huge one' and that 'resolving it would be a difficult and long-term task'.[79] Increasingly such reports have also noted that the pressure on jobs is exacerbated by the numbers of young persons entering the workforce each year.

According to most reports, there are approximately 12 to 13 million new entrants into the labour force each year so within each 5-year period there could be more than 60 million or so new entrants into the labour force – a sum which far exceeded the number of new jobs likely to become available in that period.[80] In 2005, the total number of new entrants into the urban labour force was expected to reach 11 million, including 3.38 million university graduates.[81] The number of graduates has almost tripled since 2000 to total 2.8 million graduates in 2004[82] and in the past couple of years there have been numerous reports of widespread graduate unemployment, with the result that graduates, after making countless applications and begging for interviews, accept jobs with lower status and pay than they had expected. In the summer of 2003, the average starting salary for university graduates was reported to have dropped by 40 per cent compared with 2002.[83] In some of the largest cities, job fairs held to help laid-off labourers, peasants and migrants find work have been attended by graduates in their search for any kind of employment. In Wuhan, the organisers of one such job fair estimated that one-third of the applicants were university graduates.[84] What is new is that growing numbers of graduates are returning from abroad who, increasing at an annual rate of over 40 per cent, are also having to compete for jobs.[85] In Shanghai more than 7,000 'sea turtles', as those who have returned from overseas are called, were reported to be waiting for jobs in 2004. Compared to former times when job offers were plentiful and salaries high, sea turtles too have had to accept jobs of lower status and lower pay or incomes between Y2,000 and Y3,000 per month rather than the Y10,000 to Y12,000 that they might have once expected. Several employers say that, without up-to-date experience of their own society, those returning from abroad 'do not have much in the way of comparative advantages when compared with their homegrown counterparts'.[86] There are reports that at interviews they are asked to name the lowest salary they would find acceptable or they are laid off after a period of unpaid probation when their free labour is taken advantage of by employers who recruit such staff regularly without any intention of giving them a contract.[87] Unless the graduate market shows some sign of improvement in the near future, the expectations of the younger generations are also likely to be dashed, leading to some disillusionment and resentment. Although the government has attempted to reassure its citizens that there will be sufficient jobs in the long term, it has been difficult to persuade them that there will be less unemployment in the future and allay their very considerable fears and anxieties that livelihoods are less than secure. These present-day fears and anxieties are exacerbated by the continuing lack of short- and long-term safety nets in China today.

In China's cities, urban populations continue to worry about short-term support in the event of industrial accident, unemployment and long-term security in retirement. In factories and mines there is the risk that poor working conditions and disregard for health and safety rules will lead to sickness and industrial accidents. Much publicity is given to the high accident and death rates of China's mines, but many private companies violate the basic rights of employees and take no responsibility in the event of workplace injury. A government survey of more than 2,000 private companies in 2005 found that 80 per cent refused to sign contracts and that even when urban employment contracts did exist they more often protected the rights of employers than employees, with some of the contracts specifically stating that the company was not responsible for any employee illness or workplace injury.[88] For those who are laid off but remain attached to their work-units and receive benefits or find alternative and additional sources of informal income, the new terms and conditions of employment rarely match those offered by their previous work-units. Their work-units may continue to act as a shelter against the vagaries of unemployment, sickness and old age, but with their decline many urban workers feel adrift and insecure. As of 2000, the ratio of urban jobless workers covered by unemployment insurance was less than 50 per cent and since that time the year-on-year rise has been modest;[89] many of the benefits received were inadequate or insufficient to cover basic living costs, while growing numbers of self-employed and migrant labourers remain outside of any such insurance arrangements.

The government is firmly of the view that social security is desirable and in the interests of all employees and many of the policies are now in place. It makes constant reference to the guarantees which include subsistence allowances for laid-off workers from state-owned enterprises, unemployment insurance and guaranteed minimum living allowances of urban residents. Although spending on social security has increased, implementing and funding insurance or income-support for the unemployed has not proved to be an easy task. Similarly the government has attempted to implement the long-term social security system funded by workers and employers outlined in earlier chapters. However the establishment of these new pension systems continues to be plagued by several problems, chief of which is that many of the debt-ridden, poorly-managed and over-staffed state-owned enterprises are still unable to meet past obligations, let alone take on any new responsibilities. In 2002 it was estimated that more than one-third of all urban workers no longer received their rightful pensions even though many of the present workers' retirement contributions have been switched to pay the pensions of current retirees or used for other purposes by hard-up local governments.[90] Significantly, it was reported at the end of 2001 that more than RMB200 billion had been looted from pension funds and that this figure, increasing rather than declining, constituted 'a ticking time-bomb'.[91] Again in 2005, it was reported that basic pension coverage was low, with less than half the estimated numbers paying into final pension schemes.[92] No wonder city residents, old and young, are anxious about secure employment, secure support in old age and the lack of a working social security system.

In addition, city and country populations continue to worry about the rising costs of essential public services which increasingly take large proportions of their current incomes. In the streets of the cities and lanes of the villages, it is the costs of education and health and to a lesser extent housing that comprise the fastest-growing constituents of household budgets and are still the main topics of conversation and causes for anxiety. In 2000, and in absolute terms, consumers paid nearly three times as much for healthcare and more than double for housing and education as they had in 1994[93] and, as the following pages show, the costs of all three have been rising since then. Although the availability and quality of urban housing has increased, subsidies have been reduced or removed so that rents in both the public and private sector have increased greatly as have the costs of owning one's own home which still remain beyond the reach of those with low incomes despite the increase in mortgage lending. The purchase price of a city or modern apartment on the open market ranges from 10 to 20 times the average annual income and affordable new housing is still in short supply. Most of the apartments in the luxury blocks built in the main cities over the past few years have been purchased by non-residents for investment.[94] Speculators account for 30 to 50 per cent of the market in some areas. However the new rules and taxes that came into force during 2005 are likely to see a slowdown in developers' speculation and a fall in prices by 10 to 30 per cent as the steam comes out of the market.[95] If renting or purchasing urban housing and utilities have generated some concern, these costs are less pervasive than the escalating costs of health care and education in both city and countryside.

It is a truism that there will be less spending in high streets so long as consumers are worried about meeting the costs of education and health care. For most of China's households the costs of health care have continued to rise in both city and countryside as government spending on health has declined, as charges for services and prescription drugs have increased and as previous subsidies, benefits and insurance schemes have all but disappeared so that overall central government spending on health has declined by around 50 per cent.[96] Even in 2000, a WHO study ranking public health systems inclusive of access and costs of 191 member countries placed China one hundred and forty-fourth, behind India, Indonesia and Bangladesh and some of Africa's poorest countries.[97] In 2004, urban hospitals received only 10 per cent or so of their operational funds from the state so that they had to generate revenue themselves to meet the remainder, largely through charging entrance fees, service charges and selling treatments and medicines some of which are unlicensed.[98] Indeed income from medicine sales alone is reported to typically account for more than 60 per cent of the revenue.[99] Many of the hospital lobbies are dominated by notice boards giving lists of costs and tellers so that you could be forgiven for thinking you were entering a bank. Where the facilities of city and county hospitals have improved they have done so at a cost which is not always affordable to the patient. In August 2005, the Health Minister himself referred to the 'profit-chasing' of China's hospitals and criticised them for 'being too greedy and putting profit ahead of social function', and thus 'adding to the burdens of patients and undermining the image of medical personnel and public health departments'.[100] He has also admitted that China's health care system could not meet demand and that the difficulty and high cost of getting access to medical treatment was 'of greatest concern to the people'.[101]

In both urban and rural hospitals, fees are normally charged up-front or on entry and added to at each stage so that families have a choice of depleting their savings, going into debt or avoiding treatment altogether. Family stories and a perusal of hospital records both tell a similar story – for all but the wealthy, the costs of the state health-care system are very high in relation to income and there is little help with fees and charges now that many of the former insurance schemes are no longer in operation. In the cities, long-term or expensive medical treatment can cost several months' salary while in the countryside just the removal of an appendix is said to be 'a year's farming up the spout'.[102] In an ordinary year with no major illness, one-tenth of a family's annual income might be spent on medical expenses and much of that may well be red-envelope cash to bribe the doctors who otherwise might prescribe more expensive medicines or treatment.[103] In the cities it was estimated in 2004 that only 110 million or roughly one-sixth of the total urban working population was covered by medical insurance which can considerably lower out-of-pocket expenses. In the countryside around 67 million or less than 10 per cent of the rural population is covered by any insurance scheme and they still have to pay the costs of treatment for less serious illnesses and can only be partially reimbursed for the cost of more expensive medical treatment.[104] Certainly in the face of prohibitive costs, many delay treatment or avoid hospitals with serious repercussions not only for their own health and life-span but also for the spread of disease. A government survey in 2004 found that nearly 50 per cent of rural residents avoided hospitals altogether because of the expense and that nearly 30 per cent of city residents referred for hospitalisation refused to be admitted with some 70 per cent citing the cost as the main reason.[105] The result has been that disappearing diseases such as tuberculosis, measles and snail fever have returned on a substantial scale and that the morbidity rate and the number of people suffering from illness in both the urban and rural sector is rising.[106] It is often said that if it is the fear of illness which is one of the main reasons for high savings rates in China, it is the costs of education which are probably the biggest drain on all family cash incomes and, in recent years, education is said to constitute the most important cause responsible for eroding consumer confidence.[107]

Education fees of various kinds, including tuition fees, costs of books, uniforms, food and other sundry expenses, remain very high in relation to urban and rural cash incomes and continue to be major topics of everyday concern and anxiety. In much of rural China, the fees for educating children in primary school still have to be saved and scrimped for by families with school-aged children. In official documents and in the media considerable attention has been given to the difficulties which rural children face and the gap between the attainment of rural and urban children at all educational levels including primary and secondary education. In 2005, it was reported that a very high proportion or 93 per cent of the rural population only received primary or junior secondary education with 0.2 per cent graduating from junior college and no more than 0.02 per cent from university. This contrasts dramatically with the cities where 11.1 per cent of the population attended junior college and 5.63 per cent had a university education.[108] There are great differences between the quality of schooling including curriculum content and student–teacher ratios with drop-out rates linked to rising costs of education plus opportunity costs for rural households. In the cities, where entry into the best schools is fiercely competitive, education fees take a major proportion of family budgets and parents frequently take evening jobs to meet the extra costs. In 2003, it was estimated that the families of the nearly 10 million college students and 250 million middle-school students who can be expected to graduate in the coming 10 years will spend around Y26 to 27 trillion for their education – a sum which does not begin to match their savings valued at Y8 trillion.[109] In these circumstances, it is not surprising to find that education still requires 'deep pockets' and that in a 2005 survey of people's reasons for savings, education came top.[110] The costs of educating children and grandchildren, alongside fears for health care in the event of illness or accident, the lack of safety nets and the spectre of unemployment, have all generated a degree of personal insecurity or uncertainty about the future so that, instead of spending on goods and services, many have opted to accumulate savings in other forms of monetary security.

Monetary support

The new importance attached to money during the reform period is sometimes described as the arrival of 'money worship'. If the idea of money as newly important seems a surprising statement to make it is because, during the revolutionary years, cash wages were very low and most goods and services were allocated by state-sponsored units according to need and simply were not available for purchase by the general public. The few items in the shops were either small and cheap or rare and very expensive requiring savings made over a number of months or years; such was the dearth of goods that there was very little everyday need or use for money for purchase and savings often accumulated due to lack of any purchases or exchanges. Indeed, as I have argued elsewhere, it was words rather than money that constituted the most significant coinage of exchange, such was the premium placed upon and privileges attached to the prior acquisition of pertinent information.[111] All this was to change with reform when money became not only important for the exchange of goods but also a pre-requisite for the exchange of information and of services. It is a surprising feature of so many of China's contemporary films that the answer to even the simplest question by young or old requires the passage of money or the promise of a monetary exchange. Money and its exchange has also become essential to procuring even the smallest of services, a permit or a bribe in return for a blind eye. Monetary exchanges have altered the nature of relationships between individuals, households or communities and officials so that it is sometimes said that 'now as long as you have money that is all that counts' and that 'if you don't have money you can't have power'. Foreigners resident in China often comment on the widespread importance of and belief in making money and, in 2005, the *Observer* also noted the readiness to place trust in money, 'Freedom in China is a pocketful of money'.[112] Money and its accumulation have not just become a source of status and power but also a pre-requisite for achieving or maintaining a better life and having confidence in the future.

If money has become the new form of security so household savings and insurance have become important means for managing risk and uncertainty.

The transfer of risk from state and work-unit to family and individual and the importance of money in managing risk is one of the reasons why urban saving is still around a high 25 per cent and still rising despite attempts by the government to increase incentives to spend rather than save.[113] As earlier chapters have shown, those with both high and low earnings are keen to save to take care of a future in which they anticipate that each person will 'have to look out for themselves'.[114] In a recent study of saving, the factors identified as responsible for the high savings rates included fears for old-age support in the context of the one-child family, the weakness of social security safety nets, expensive health care, the costs of education and relative lack of credit.[115] Since 2000, the country's overall savings rate – already the world's highest by far – remained at about 40 per cent of GDP until 2002 when it rose sharply to nearly 50 per cent of GDP.[116] In 2004, savings deposits were estimated to amount to Y20 trillion of which around Y12 trillion is held by individuals and Y8 trillion by companies.[117] Indeed household saving, at around 25 per cent of disposable income and rising, is astonishingly high by international standards.[118] If savings are perceived to be the most important of individual and familial safety nets then it can be argued that any lack of confidence in the safety of savings and a run on the banks could be the one factor that might spark nation-wide unrest. It is very noticeable that any hint of such trouble has effected an immediate response on the part of the central and provincial governments. When queues formed outside the local banks of an obscure branch of the Bank of China in Guangdong province as a result of a rumoured theft of US$725 million in 2001, the provincial government spared no effort to truck in sufficient cash to meet demand and contain the panic.[119] If the government in Beijing needed any reminder of the importance of safeguarding the deposits of hundreds of millions of hard-working savers, it only had to observe the popular unrest in the wake of the collapse of a co-operative share credit system offering higher rates of interest in Fujian province where buildings were looted and burned in large street demonstrations in what was described as 'an orgy of vengeance'.[120] In July 2005 there were reports of runs on a number of rural co-operative banks as depositors attempted to withdraw their savings.[121] Although informal credit associations which have a long history in many parts of China, have enjoyed a revival and savers have few alternatives to state-owned bank deposits, a relatively new option lies in the purchase of insurance products and there is evidence of increasing demand for life and property insurance.

To offset an increasing ambivalence about the future, many households have turned anew to the burgeoning insurance industry to offset the most obvious threats to their livelihoods and lifestyles. As earlier chapters have shown, the achievement of higher living standards, the accumulation of assets, the onset of new risks and the loss of security provided by the 'iron rice bowl' have all generated a new interest in insurance. This is especially so in the cities and central provinces where the take-up of life insurance, health insurance and insurance protection for property and vehicles have all led to the rapid growth of the insurance business to around twenty or so domestic companies. Today China's insurance market is dominated by a small number of domestic insurance companies which operate nation-wide and account for a high proportion of total premium income. China's three leading insurers, China's Life Insurance Company (CLIC), the Pingan Insurance Company (PAIC) and the People's Insurance Company (PICC), have all either become or are planning to become listed on overseas stock exchanges in the near future. At present, China's Life Insurance Company is the largest enjoying 60 per cent of the market while China's second largest life insurance, the Pingan Insurance Company, controls about one-third of the Beijing and Shanghai markets.[122] Foreign life insurance companies too have eyed the China market and at present around 22 foreign-owned life insurance companies and 16 foreign-owned casualty insurance companies have offices in China – but so far their business is restricted in scope and to certain locations such as the cities of Shanghai and Guangzhou.[123] At present foreign companies conducting life-insurance business in China are required to do so through joint-venture companies in which they hold no more than one-quarter of domestic insurance company accounts; however, once these restrictions are reduced in line with the terms of China's entry into the WTO, it is widely anticipated that a large share of this 'virgin market' will fall to foreign insurance companies. They plan to move into China at an unprecedented rate and, with their superior management capabilities, range of products and regulatory mechanisms, it is feared that they may well better meet the professional, personalised and diversified needs of customers in China.

As increasing numbers of households become accustomed to acquiring assets and 'looking out for themselves', there is evidence of a rising demand for personal insurance products. In 2003, it was reported that the premium income of China's insurance sector rose by 45 per cent over the previous year to Y305.31 billion, that life insurance premiums rose by 33.8 per cent to Y53.48 billion and that property insurance premiums climbed by 28.1 per cent to Y8.32 billion. At the same time, penetration of China's insurance market was estimated to be just 1 per cent.[124] A State Council survey of more than 22,000 households in 46 cities the year before showed that only 6 per cent of households felt they had a good knowledge of insurance. However purchasing insurance products did rank fifth in expenditure items after savings, real estate purchase and the like and nearly 50 per cent of households stated that they would consider purchasing insurance products, particularly health and life insurance, during the next 5 years.[125] Although the potential seemed enormous, only the high earners in the main cities and the densely-settled eastern and coastal provinces thought they could can afford to purchase such policies. For those outside these locations, insurance products are still relatively novel and not widely available due, among other factors, to the lack of adequate distributive networks and falling capacity to maintain the premiums. A recent study suggests that even where insurance products have become popular, there has been a pronounced rise in the number of people either cancelling policies or invalidating their policies through non-payment, which the investigators directly linked to the falling rate of increase in incomes and rise in unemployment.[126] Despite regulations and new regulatory bodics to supervise the industry, leading to delays in processing claims and making compensatory or other payments, insurance companies too may lack capital or be poorly managed, all of which may discourage clients from renewing or taking out new or additional insurances policies. It might be said that placing one's savings in an insurance scheme still requires long-term faith that funds are safe and payments will be honoured and, although it is too soon to assess the returns of many insurance schemes, there are sufficient reports of scams to justify fears that savings and/or insurance policies are not without their risks. As one retired blacksmith with modest savings noted, 'no matter how much money you make now, your mind is never easy'.[127] For an easier mind and to offset some of these worries, increasing numbers have turned for reassurance to the non-material or to religion as an alternative or additional source of personal support and security.

Spiritual solace

For Asia as a whole, and not just for China, it has been observed that rapid social and economic change have sent many in search of the certainties of religion.[128] Asia-wide, new and old religions alike have acquired a new popularity: the number of Christians has risen, there has been a revival of Buddhism and many visit Confucian and other religious temples to pray for good fortune both instantaneously and for the future. Most Asian societies have changed rapidly as secular governments have pursued a policy of modernisation so that Westernisation or globalisation leading to a decline in their own socio-cultural norms has seemed to many to be an unstoppable process despite periodic economic crises. Some scholars have suggested that these international and secular processes have led to a feeling of 'rootlessness', 'personal crises' and 'broken society' during which many have turned to old and new religions for spiritual solace and security. Alan Chan, a professor in the philosophy at the National University of Singapore is one such scholar:

> In places like China and Korea and other countries experiencing rapid change, there seems to be a general spiritual void as these countries develop, which is why religions have enjoyed a comeback.[129]

The spiritual void is perhaps most observable in China because of the previous role of the socialist and communist ideology during the revolution which had provided a belief system which very much focused on and invested in the certainty of a better future. Indeed, as I have argued in another study, the deprivations of the present were made tolerable in the face of deferred hopes and rewards of the socialist future which itself would certainly be better, albeit some decades or even centuries hence.[130] Such a supportive belief system had for many years inspired a widespread and nation-wide fervour normally associated with some of the more evangelical of religions. However after the first years that seemed to be full of promise, the confidence invested in the leadership and policies of Mao Zedong to achieve this future soon gave way to fears that life would never get better, especially in the aftermath of the Cultural Revolution.

In my own view, it was the erosion of this hope or confidence as much as any other factor that brought the 30 years of revolution to an end. The result was an

ensuing ideological vacuum caused by the decline of socialist belief, rapid socio-
economic change and, perhaps most of all, uncertainty or lack of confidence
in the path and outcomes of reform. The loss of such a unifying belief in the
shared destination of reform during a period of rapid socio-economic change
has led to an absence of faith, identity and sense of moral and spiritual vacuum,
accentuated by the new importance attached to money during the reform period
which has caused considerable government and media concern. With some
support, China's reform government did attempt to counter the onset of a new
materialism by initiating a number of campaigns in the 1980s which advocated
'socialism with Chinese characteristics', a return to China's ideological roots or a
spiritual civilisation and love of the motherland, loyalty to the Party, diligence at
work and care of fellow-citizens. Such campaigns to revive socialist characteristics
and Chinese values were designed to counter spiritual pollution emanating from
the West which were held responsible for such ills such as individualism, crime,
corruption and collapsing family values. These campaigns were also intended to
renew faith in Party rule, but this has been a much more difficult goal to achieve.
Just as in the latter years of the Revolution, the pace and fall-out of reform and
particularly the hypocrisy and corruption of many Party officials had chipped
away at the religious-like faith in the power of the Party to determine China's
future. The government has also turned to Confucius and his classical learning to
help in the re-introduction of socialist morals and values feared lost in the tide of
materialism. Confucian writings have re-entered the school curriculum and the
book of Confucian fables for school children specially commissioned by President
Jiang Zemin sold 8 million copies.[131]

At a more personal level and as the lack of certainty in the new fast-moving
economy became more unsettling, the pace of change more bewildering and the
disadvantages wrought by reform for the 'have nots' increasingly clear, many have
turned to temples, churches or mosques for an answer to their needs. During
the revolution itself, China's leadership had always assumed that religious beliefs
and practices would fade as socialism developed and, although they may have
faded, believers and 'house churches' did not completely disappear during the
years of revolution. During recent years many have reappeared as old and new
religious beliefs and practices have flourished. The reform government too has
eased its controls on religious practice and officially recognised the five faiths
of Buddhism, Protestantism, Catholicism, Islam and Daoism and has tolerated
religious activity conducted within State-sponsored churches and organisations. It
is estimated that more than 10,000 Buddhist temples and monasteries have been
rebuilt in the past twenty years while Islamic peoples in Beijing and the northwest
provinces maintain their mosques and customs.[132] Both mosques and temples are
well attended on religious and festival occasions. The Catholic Church has long
had an official organisation, the Catholic Patriotic Association of China, which
still oversees many churches and open houses that are well attended for worship.
Relations between the Vatican and China's government are effectively frozen,
with differences of opinion mainly centred around existing ties with Taiwan
and authority to appoint bishops. Although negotiations about allegiance to the

Vatican remain delicate, the present Chair of the official Catholic Church thought that 'the situation of Catholics in China has never been as good as it is now'.[133] For example, as he noted in 2004, the number of new churches opened was 300, the new faithful admitted to the church each year number 100,000 and the total number of adherents could be anywhere between 5 and 10 million. On New Year's Day 2006, I observed mass at the Catholic church of St Ignatius, the second largest cathedral in southeastern China. Shrouded in darkness outside, it was in stark contrast to the crowded neon-lit cathedrals of consumption next door – with all their brightly lit decorations – that at first I thought it was shut. At the entrance, there were pictures of the present Pope, Benedict XVI, while television screens attached to each pillar showed episodes from the life of popular Pope John Paul. The congregation of 300 to 400 worshippers comprised all age-groups in varied attire, ranging from jeans and leather jackets to dark cloth coats and anoraks.

For Protestants, the China Christian Council was set up in 1980 to co-ordinate all the churches and there are many denominations including Anglicans, Presbyterians, Methodists and other networks embracing several provinces, groups and inter-denominational sites for worship in China.[134] Just as for other groups, so for Protestants too there has been an increase in numbers, with the government advocating the establishment of more state churches to accommodate the spread of Christianity and to prevent undue overseas influence. Protestant groups account for the largest share of growth, largely due to a wave of religious revival in the countryside in the 1990s which later spread to the cities embracing workers, entrepreneurs and young professionals.[135] One young businesswoman spoke for many when she said that her Protestant faith had provided her with 'comfort and confidence' in the face of difficulties in her life and work.[136] In 2003, Premier Wen Jiabao estimated that there were 100 million religious followers and 100,000 religious sites in China,[137] although unofficial estimates of China's religious believers placed their numbers much higher at Protestants (25m), Catholics (4m), Moslems (20m), Buddhists (150m) and Daoists (5.5m).[138] Still more recent estimates suggest that the number of Catholics lies somewhere between the government figure of 5 million and the 10.5 or 11 million estimated by foreign and Chinese scholars. Similarly the number of Protestants is now estimated to be 35 million, which is more than twice the government estimates of 15 or 16 million.[139] In addition to the State churches there are also charismatic and evangelical churches or 'underground' forms of worship which are reported to have become increasingly popular among China's Christians. If these underground house-churches and secretive or unorthodox syncretic cults combining elements of indigenous or folk religion with those of evangelical Christianity and faith healing, are included then the numbers turning to religious movements run to hundreds of millions. Perhaps the best-known and most-developed of these popular religious and spiritual movements is that of the Falungong.

The Falungong movement draws on meditative traditions from both Buddhism and Taoism combined with deep-breathing techniques and shadow-boxing routines from the traditional martial arts. Founded by Li Hongzhi, a long-time resident in the USA, it teaches truth and benevolence and aims to achieve better states of physical and spiritual fitness. The movement is widespread in China, with estimated numbers ranging from the government's admitted two million to the 60 or 70 million claimed by the movement itself.[140] What brought Falungong to national and international attention was the secret, sudden and unexpected demonstration in 1999 when between 10,000 and 20,000 Falungong followers surrounded the leadership compound in central Beijing to ask for official recognition. One newspaper report described how soundlessly and silently Falungong's faithful, made up of 'many ordinary folk', slipped right past the network of plain-clothed policemen, informers and uniformed guards who patrol the city centre to surround three sides of the central leadership compound at Zhongnanhai in Beijing before vanishing out of the centre and into the night.[141] Three days later the government proclaimed that this kind of gathering was detrimental to the maintenance of social order and should be banished. Indeed the demonstration of 25/4 has been branded as the most serious political incident since June 1989 in Tiananmen Square and, far from gaining official recognition, the movement has been banned and many of its members detained and imprisoned. Perhaps the authorities needed no reminder that it was similar Buddhist and Taoist religious movements and health-related martial-art disciplines which for centuries played a major role in challenging and even ending dynastic rule. Moreover the ways in which Falungong adherents persistently defy the ban and challenge the authorities in a small but steady flow of demonstrations in Tiananmen Square and other locations reveals its continuing importance and the tenacity of its members in their long-standing bid for recognition.

One of the many reasons why the Falungong is viewed by the government with some suspicion is that it brings together a number of disparate disadvantaged groups into the one movement. An internal report outlining the government's findings on Falungong reveals that the average age was 40 plus years and that the membership was largely female (60%) and belonged to both urban and rural low-income groups (70%). The report noted that it had attracted the support of three groups: the poorest, laid-off workers and marginalised professionals including a number of intellectuals and individuals from the highest echelons of the Party and the army.[142] The fact that most of the members are middle-aged and more suggest that the movement has had particular appeal for the generation that was born during or soon after a devastating anti-Japanese war, grew up on few calories and were sustained mainly by communist promises. Given that their hopes for a proper schooling had been dashed by the Cultural Revolution, their family size limited by the one-child policy and their job and pension security ended by state-sector reform, it is perhaps not surprising that it is members of this generation who feel most disillusioned now that their life-long goals and years of arduous work have been discarded as a result of reform. As an *Economist* reporter noted, the Falun protesters outside Zhongnanhai may 'have looked fearless for their own safety' because they 'probably had little more to lose'.[143] This might be an exaggeration, but there is a consensus that many of Falungong's members look to the movement both for spiritual solutions to ameliorate physical health problems and for spiritual guidance and solace in the absence of alternative routes to a certain and secure future.[144] It is sometimes claimed, both within and outside of China, that the Falungong movement not only illustrates the bankruptcy of Party ideology and its inability to guide and satisfy China's people[145] but also poses the biggest challenge to China's one-party rule.[146] However so far Falungong does not seem to have expressed any such ambitions to become a substitute for Party rule but, alongside other religions and religious groups, it does continue to provide non-material or spiritual support, comfort and security in uncertain times.

Managing uncertainty

For China's leadership, the management of this uncertainty and maintaining popular faith in its ability to shape the future has become an increasing political challenge crucial to its bid to sustain economic growth and expand its own domestic market. What has become increasingly apparent is that old-style Communist Party campaigns in support of an ideological or spiritual revival in socialist or communist faith, with or without a touch of Confucianism, have had less effect than it would have liked. There is much evidence that, for many, even the mantra 'socialism with Chinese characteristics' has come to have a rather hollow ring to it in the days of unemployment and corruption which have both contributed to some loss of confidence and even cynicism about the efficacy of socialist material and spiritual values. In 2000, a 10,000-word essay in *China Society*, a magazine produced by the Ministry of Civil Affairs, attracted considerable attention when it admitted that there was a wide-ranging moral vacuum apparent in post-revolutionary China:

> In today's China, the most profound challenge is not unemployment, inflation or corruption, the most powerful challenge is that there is no effective ideology.[147]

In 2001, on the occasion of the eightieth birthday of the Party, it was reported to be 'suffering a crisis of faith, identity and legitimacy'.[148] In recent decades the government has also turned to consumption and consumer aspirations as instruments or incentives in order to elicit support for further reform and to compensate for unpopular policies. Initially the very premise of reform itself was introduced and sold on the platform of increased consumption. As *China Daily* noted in 1997, 'Deng's revolution' might itself be called 'a revolution in rising expectations'.[149] In the 1980s, as a previous chapter has noted, it was apparent from my own fieldwork then that one of the reasons the single-child family policy was introduced and implemented with less opposition than might have been expected was due to the simultaneous and spiralling opportunities for consumption and a better or 'quality' life for both parents and child. In 1990 too, it was observable that the government instantaneously and strategically encouraged consumption following the events of Tiananmen Square when a sudden flurry of retail and recreational opportunities and facilities were directed towards distracting the attention of the young.

The question to be asked now is: can the government similarly turn to consumption or to political campaigns in the event of an economic downturn or widespread popular unrest? The government's own greatest fear remains social instability caused by the 'joining up' of the many single demonstrations and protests which presently remain issue-centred and location-specific. The fear of social instability or widespread unrest, exacerbated by the memories of the Cultural Revolution and by the fragmentation following the break-up of the former Soviet Union, is widespread. There is a fear that instability and even the fragmentation of China could follow if there was a series of economic downturns which would make it difficult for the government to retain sufficient authority to placate the disaffected and maintain social order. This fear is well expressed by a young author who thinks that the degree and direction of social and political change could mean the difference between degenerating into violence and a viable future. He thought that, during the first 25 years of this century, the country will either follow the route chartered by Taiwan and reform politically or the Party's morale will deteriorate, exacerbating corruption and widening the gap between rich and poor, leading to social instability with nationalism defining the future.[150] A fear commonly expressed both within and outside of China is that, if there is widespread evaporation of an official and shared ideology and consumption does not do the trick, then the government may be left with no alternative but to turn to nationalism to maintain support. Certainly, the street demonstrations in the main cities following the bombing of the Chinese Embassy in Belgrade and the American spy-plane incident were evidence that patriotic fervour could be aroused easily in the face of any perceived threat to sovereignty and national dignity. As an *International Herald Tribune* headline had it in 2001, 'Nationalism is on the Rise in China's Ideological Emptiness':

> Of the many revelations resulting from the incident of the American spy plane which landed in China, the most important was the intense reaction of the Chinese public, especially young people.[151]

The combination of patriotic sentiment and nationalist indignation is also reflected in the periodic anti-Japanese demonstrations and boycotts largely aimed at opposing Japan's denial of its war record on Chinese soil. The most recent of these large and angry demonstrations took place in Beijing and other main cities in April 2005 when the eloquent and astute commentator, Isabel Hilton, was minded to write of the dual role of nationalism in China today:

> Nationalism is the last shred of Maoist ideology for a ruling party that has abandoned its socialist roots ... nationalism is also the only safe political outlet for new generations. To direct the political frustration of young Chinese on to Japan may seem like a safety valve for a ruling group nervous of the growing political frustrations of its population.[152]

Whether the demonstrations are actually government sponsored or merely tolerated, China's leaders, despite their anger at Mr Koizumi's visits to the

Yasakuni Shrine in Tokyo which honours Japan's war dead, have not so far lent any substantive or sustained support to these demonstrations, perhaps because they value China's image and international reputation as a responsible world power and because they fear that such demonstrations may become less of a safety valve and might spiral out of control.[153] Certainly if they were fuelled by the widespread discontent of the disadvantaged and disillusioned as they attempt to exercise their legal rights then they could turn against the government.

The government only has to look to the huge 'nationalist' demonstrations and 'colour revolutions' (named after the colour and flower symbols adopted by protesters in their bid for greater democratic freedoms in the former Soviet Union and Central Asia) to take heed of the dangers of large-scale street demonstrations and the potential role of the international media, which is one reason for the ban on foreign newspapers to print in China.[154] Present experience suggests that widespread political and social instability can probably be avoided so long as economic growth continues and that only if its political authority is threatened, is the government likely to turn to nationalism, perhaps in a last bid to maintain legitimacy. It is my own view that, barring unforeseen external circumstances, China is not set on a course of self-destruction, fragmentation or melt-down not only because of the general and popular fear of instability but also because the government itself is concerned for and takes constant steps to ameliorate social problems that underlie the most common causes of personal insecurity and political instability. A persistent theme in all government speeches, national conventions and everyday conversations is the stress on social stability with its preconditions of continuing economic growth and prosperity. This is not a new theme, but what is new is the amount of attention that the government is directing towards the notion of the 'social' as well as to 'stability'. It is the array of serious contemporary social problems outlined here and affecting popular perceptions and aspirations in China itself which has caused the government to introduce new policies and to give more attention to 'the social' in balancing the benefits and costs of economic development.

11 Developing demand

From trickle to transition

Outside China, awe is expressed at the economic growth miracle and the productivity boom produced by the reforms and the unprecedented scale of foreign investment over the past two decades. Today most observers assume that China's economy will continue to expand or at least remain at growth rates of between 8 and 10 per cent due to the significant restraints still in the system and the government's commitment to further reform. Indeed for most outsiders, China has an aura of invincibility largely based on the assumption that this dragon-like country will continue to experience an economic boom, all the while importing raw materials and exporting manufactured goods in ways which inexorably affect global markets, prices and the location of work. Although it is a fair guess that economic growth will continue at high rates and that exports will continue to expand to include commodities and goods at the high end of technology, this aura of invincibility is not necessarily shared by China's leaders. While taking pride in the country's economic growth and achievements, China's leaders have successively become less sanguine and more ready to admit that present rates of economic growth may not be sustainable and that the quality of growth is deteriorating. As the introductory chapter suggested, the importance of continuing economic growth alongside maintaining the physical environment and social stability is now emphasised by China's leaders as new concerns for the costs of economic growth have emerged. The gradual acknowledgement of the social costs and environmental problems associated with rapid economic growth is aptly illustrated by the contrast between Zhu Rongji's speeches at the beginning and at the end of his premiership. In 1998 when Zhu Rongji took office, he pledged that 'no matter what is waiting for me – whether it be landmines or an abyss, I will blaze my trail'. Four years later, nearing the end of his tenure in 2002, his 2-hour speech emphasised less of the trail blazing and more of the 'new difficulties' and 'severe challenges' which had worsened in recent years.[1] In 2004, Premier Wen Jiabao, in a widely reported speech to top officials, emphasised that China was entering a new stage of development:

> The development process of many countries shows that during this stage, two developmental results may appear. In one scenario, a country successfully industrialises and modernizes. In another, growing economic gaps and

social tensions cause development to stagnate or even result in turmoil and repression.[2]

In April 2005, Hu Jintao's main message to the Politburo emphasised that social stability and harmony could only be secured by practising a modern 'scientific' concept of development that aimed to promote 'fast and good' economic and social development in order to build a solid foundation for building a prosperous society. He reiterated the importance of a co-ordinated, sustainable and people-oriented approach to ensure that development benefited all social categories and went on to outline 'the number of profound economic and political challenges' that China faced.[3] Recognition of these challenges also underlay a State Council document, 'Opinions on Deepening Economic Structural Reform' which, issued the following month, suggested that China's reform programme faced an imminent and 'crucial battle' to resolve serious economic and political contradictions. It went on to suggest that so far reforms remained superficial, tentative and flawed and that, given the fragmentation, competing claims of multiple interest groups and the high degree of risk, it could be said that reform had never been more complex or difficult than it is now.[4] Such statements confirm the commitment of the new leadership to reducing regional and income disparities and the environmental and social costs of the China's go-for-growth policies and to the redefinition of development to include care for the social and physical environment alongside economic growth. The socio-economic and environmental problems outlined in the previous chapter are not only admitted by the government and commonly discussed in the workplace, at home and in the streets and market places across China but also are the subject of new and continuing policies to balance economic and social development.

Balancing development

Currently the new stress on social development, designed to address popular concerns and reduce the causes of protest or unrest, has meant giving priority to creating new employment opportunities, putting in place effective social security and public service provisions, reducing corruption and improving the physical environment. Creating sufficient jobs and matching China's labour resources to the changing needs of the labour market is a daunting task for any government and, as Chapters 5 and 10 have illustrated, to both maintain economic growth and provide greater employment opportunities for its people, the country needs to create millions of new jobs per year to meet demand from the urban unemployed, laid-off, new entrants and migrants and rural un- and under-employed. At a national meeting on employment held in September 2004, Wen Jiabao accorded employment and re-employment the highest priority in China's economic and social development programme.[5] He also pointed out that the employment problem was 'huge' and that resolving it would be a 'difficult and long-term task'.[6] To maintain the status quo in the labour market over the next decade, it is estimated by the World Bank that China will have to create 100 million new jobs, although according to the Chinese Academy of Social Sciences it will be necessary to create 300 million new jobs.[7] For several years now, the government has given a prominent place to expanding employment and re-employment opportunities in small and medium-sized enterprises but it is very likely that a major portion of these jobs will be in the fast-growing service sector. The expanding numbers of restaurants, bars, shops and private educational, professional and leisure services are there for all to see. However this expansion is also hampered by uneven and onerous regulations, lack of approved standards and less government encouragement and foreign investment than in the manufacturing sector which is also losing jobs to cheaper countries such as Vietnam. Although there is much private initiative and many job-creation schemes, it has not been easy to create sufficient employment in the cities let alone in the countryside and, as previous chapters have shown, the scale of under-employment in the countryside and the difficulties of creating jobs there are such that the long-term solution most often mooted is to move the 150 million or so surplus rural labourers into small towns and larger cities. As Chapter 6 has noted already, this policy is fraught with difficulties to do with the logistics of movement, subsequent job creation or establishing new livelihoods and improving standards of living following relocation. At the time of China's first space mission, it was widely quoted in China's press that one university professor had told his students that 'to send one man into space was easy for 1.3 billion people compared to telling half the population in agriculture to do something else and to move 60 per cent of rural people to the cities'.[8] Fears are expressed both within and outside of China that, 'in the current difficult situation', the creation of new jobs is unlikely to meet the country's needs and constitutes a long-term task that is 'hugely difficult' with 'no short-term solutions'.[9] The continuing necessity to keep creating more jobs is one of the reasons why the government finds itself on a treadmill and has no choice but to maintain high rates of economic growth. Even so, according to Morgan Stanley, job creation had already slowed by 2004 with 'only half as many jobs created in the most recent five years as in the previous five years'.[10]

The government does not just intend to expand job opportunities in the low-cost production sector but also to expand the numbers of skilled labourers, technically-qualified personnel and managers in order to develop sophisticated technical innovation and a range of well-managed global brands. One of the most prominent constraints on further economic growth is the critical shortage of experienced highly-skilled managers for the 25,000 or so state companies and the 4.3 million private firms, not to mention foreign and joint-venture companies which are all reported to be competing for a limited supply of senior managers.[11] The government is expanding the opportunities for business training including establishing a new raft of MBAs to enhance the management pool. At present such is the competition for skilled and experienced managers that many firms report that they spend an inordinate amount of time and energy recruiting, training and retaining managers while experienced managers and local chief executives have seen their salaries double alongside competitive benefit packages. So long as demand outstrips the supply of mid- to top-level managers with the requisite skills and experience in project management, human resources, sales and banking divisions, large and foreign firms have to rely on expatriate staff from their home countries and other parts of Asia while domestic firms flounder for lack of appropriate leadership. It is not only a matter of the requisite qualifications, for as a Chinese partner in the Shanghai office of the human resources firm, Heidrick and Struggles, noted, one of the problems for local senior managers in any type of Chinese company is their lack of experience in a fast-changing society:

> The speed of market change, foreign markets and internal markets, all those things are really becoming much more complex than even a couple of years ago. People on the ground haven't experienced those kinds of complexities.[12]

In addition to coping with fast change, many older managers spent their early years following the rules and practices of the planned economy in which production for quotas had little to do with consumer demand or making a profit. The older age-group also had their education disrupted by the Cultural Revolution while China's present education system itself is only just beginning to encourage creativity, initiative and risk-taking. In a government-sponsored survey of 5,000 Chief Executive Officers and Chairmen, just 40 per cent said that they had attended college.[13] The Dean of Tsinghua School of Economics and Management in Beijing, in an interview in 2005, said that he thought China was even farther behind in terms of management than in some other scientific and technological fields.[14] The consulting firm McKinsey and Co has forecast that even the relatively small number of Chinese companies trying to expand abroad will need up to 75,000 internationally experienced leaders if they want to continue to grow over the next 10 to 15 years. They estimate that currently there are between 3,000 to 5,000 such men and women in China[15] and there are many plans to rectify this shortage although it is still more difficult for women to obtain the necessary experience and qualifications for senior management positions. To support the bid of the northeastern provinces to promote private business and develop high-tech 'pattern' industries, the government has initiated a variety of training courses in software engineering, management and Japanese language skills.[16] Whether this shortage of trained and experienced managers will continue remains to be seen – certainly the rise in numbers of young graduates suggests that there is a young and educated cohort eager to have the opportunity to acquire both further training and experience.

As important as increasing China's level of economic and export growth for improving job opportunities for increasing numbers of labourers, are maintaining China's advantageous low production prices and a cheap labour force. In this respect a second set of shortages widely reported within and outside China is that of low-skilled migrant labourers who are willing to work in the sweatshops of southern China with their long hours, poor and harsh work conditions, piece work and low pay, and of skilled workers for the increasingly technically-sophisticated work-place. For many years poor rural workers flocked to the sweatshops despite such working conditions but in the past couple of years there have been reports that they are voting with their feet and either staying at home or looking elsewhere for better jobs, pay and working conditions. A report of the Ministry of Labour and Social Security issued in June 2005 found that such labour shortages had occurred in South China's Pearl River Delta and East China's Yangtze River Delta since 2003 and that in these two regions there is a present shortfall of some 2 million workers and particularly of women aged between 18 and 30 who are badly needed in factories and companies in these two regions.[17] One important repercussion of such shortages is that factory pay and conditions may improve and increase product prices. According to the deputy-president of the Ministry's Institute of Labour Research, companies that pay less than Y700 (US$84) per month have much more trouble filling vacancies than do those paying more than Y1,000 (US$120) per month.[18] He also urged all local governments to increase their minimum-pay benchmarks and authorise migrants to ask their bosses for more money, better treatment and the same rights to equal pay, housing, education and health care as city residents. Indeed there are many labour regulations in place to protect the rights of workers, notices in the official media ordering employers to grant better pay and working conditions and some evidence that employers in the Pear River Delta have started to offer more attractive benefits – including better pay and improved living conditions – in order to attract and retain workers.[19] Although many factories have widened their search for labourers to the poorer inland provinces, there is also another possible scenario – that as more factories expand and require additional such labourers, then not only will pay income and conditions improve but higher labour costs will also feed back into the 'China price' which may no longer depress production prices world-wide.[20]

To mitigate any skilled labour shortages, the government has embarked on a new set of policies to train migrant workers in order to provide peasant migrants with the skills required for an increasingly sophisticated workplace. In late 2003, six ministries issued a 7-year plan to provide pre-employment training for 60 million rural labourers in advance of their transfer to urban employment as well as 'professional training' for over 200 million rural workers who had already found jobs in the cities. The plan anticipated that increasingly the migrant workers now employed in housekeeping, catering, hotels, construction and manufacturing would, with development, need up-graded educational, occupational or 'professional' skills. Already in manufacturing, many of the new factories look more like a modern manufacturing machine-led enterprise than sweatshops.[21] Several observers have commented on the increasingly sophisticated technology and management on display in China's large factories. In one, the Fuan Textile Complex in southern China which has 6,000 employees, 400,000 square metres of factory floor with 1,600 knitting machines, dying vats and dyers, the hundreds of workers are described not as 'machine minders' but 'lab technicians'. They test fibres on computerised monitors, try new fabrics in sweat simulators or in dozens of different washing machines and are engaged in any number of other high-end technological processes.[22] As well as entering a new technical age, China will soon enter a new demographic phase in which the number of young people entering the labour market will slowly decline in the next 15 years and with it the supply of entry-level, low-skilled industrial and migrant workers. It is possible that the workers themselves will enjoy more bargaining power and that, at the same time, the declining supply of younger recruits may create more employment opportunities for the older laid-off and under- or un-employed.

In the meantime, individual and family insecurity in the event of unemployment or loss of livelihood at any age is exacerbated by the continuing lack of short- or long-term safety nets for the majority of China's population. In October 2003, the Party Central Committee re-emphasised its commitment to accelerating the establishment of a system of social support and 'to advance welfare through improvements in social security arrangements'.[23] A major event of 2004 was the publication of a White Paper on 'China's Social Security and its Policy' by the State Council. It was divided into 10 major sections: old age insurance, unemployment insurance, medical insurance, insurance of work-related injuries, maternity insurance, social welfare, special care and placement, social relief, housing security and social security in rural areas.[24] Since that time there have been various reports on the increase in budgetary allocations to social security and the numbers that are now covered by the various social security and support schemes and modifications to the schemes themselves. In this respect one of the interesting pension reforms designed to generate trust and reduce shortfalls or raids on pension funds has been the separation out and safeguarding of personal accounts so that they remain untouched until they are paid to the retiree.[25] In addition to safeguarding pensions, the government has set new minimum wages for employees and minimum subsistence payments in both urban and rural areas for all those in need. For example in July 2004, it was reported that all of China's provinces had set up minimum wage levels for all employees in various organisations, enterprises, government offices and small family businesses. The highest minimum wage levels have been set for Shenzhen (Y600 per month), Shanghai (Y570 per month) and Beijing (Y495 per month).[26] In 2004 too, the government proudly announced that the total number of urban residents in receipt of minimum income relief from the government had risen to 22.5 million.[27]

For the security of the retired, the government has re-committed itself to a combination of overall social planning and individual accounts to provide basic old-age insurance for all those employed in cities and towns. For the unemployed, the government has also re-committed itself to developing a social system of unemployment insurance as the means to best provide basic subsistence support for laid-off staff and workers of state-owned enterprises. However in each case, these new systems are predicated on a combination of mandatory contributions by the individual, the state and the work-unit which does not take account of the continuing resource shortfalls which have impeded the establishment of new support and security programmes. Few schemes have been implemented successfully and it can be argued that urban residents have joined villagers in increasingly looking to family support and accumulated savings to accommodate the on-going transfer of risk from the state and work-units to individual workers and their families noted earlier.[28] To help families and individuals manage this risk and reduce a source of much anxiety which also affects level of savings and consumer confidence, the government has also attempted to stabilise the costs of public services and in particular those of health care.

There is no expectation that health care provision will abandon the 'fee-for-service' principle, rather contemporary government reforms have focused on consolidating insurance schemes already introduced to help meet individual and family costs of health care and on shifting the costs of health care from the state to the private sector. The government has continued with a number of pilot programmes to experiment with locally-administered health insurance schemes in 59 cities, in which basic medical expenses would be covered by individual insurance accounts funded by employer and employee contributions to be accumulated in new social funds managed by employers and municipal governments.[29] Such insurance entitlements were to be capped with catastrophic illnesses such as cancer and HIV/AIDS covered by commercial health insurance although, so far, there are few such schemes available. By 2003 it was estimated that local insurance schemes covered some 50 million urban residents, insurance provided through the workplace covered another 50 million and that some 600 million workers or 85 per cent of the labour force still had no health insurance.[30] In 2003, however, the SARS outbreak demonstrated the potential costs of neglected government attention to health systems and increased the government's commitment to improving access to health care especially in the countryside where a new co-operative medical system with funding shared between participants, local and central governments has been piloted in 300 or some 10 per cent of China's counties with a view to nation-wide expansion by 2010.[31] In addition, a new insurance scheme paid for by central and local governments has been introduced for the poorest of urban and rural families to cover the cost of serious illnesses and it is planned that this scheme too will be expanded nation-wide. For the 80,000 or so AIDS patients and more than ten times that number of HIV-infected, the government has introduced new support services and treatment, making free anti-retroviral drugs available to all infected persons in the countryside and the urban poor. However despite such good intentions and the fact that the numbers of HIV/AIDS cases are less than originally feared, there is still a shortage of drugs and treatment centres so that only 15,000 presently receive the anti-retroviral drugs.[32]

The private sector has also been mobilised to compensate for the shortfalls in government resourcing and there are several new schemes aiming at concentrating government resources in certain key hospitals and letting the private sector provide and charge for health services. There is a broad consensus that both domestic and foreign private providers can play a role, although there is less agreement on how to implement a privatised health-care programme that does not reduce accessibility for the poor. So far private investment has been used to construct new hospitals and a number of existing hospitals have been sold or leased to private investors or new hospitals built with private-sector funds. However a health-care programme consisting of some privatised care which may limit accessibility remains controversial, hence the government has attempted to regulate the pace and degree of privatisation by limiting it to second-tier hospitals and by minimising the role of drug companies in privatisation programmes.[33] Both the government and health professionals are attempting to improve the quality of health care and at the same time equalise access or at least avoid a situation in which only the affluent can afford treatment. The Ministry of Health has been busy revising rules and guidelines to encourage better medical and management practices and to regulate drug makers but in recent months there has been a renewed call for the need for further reforms in the health care sector, largely as a result of acknowledged shortcomings in the present system which include inefficiency, high costs, corruption, low standards and poor service.[34] Again these problems were specifically recognised in a hard-hitting report written by a government think-tank in early 2005, which described medical reforms as 'basically a failure'.[35] One of the authors of this critique said that the post-Mao public health system had 'run into a dead end'.[36] Today there is little evidence that the price of health care has fallen and most of the schemes to finance health care are hampered by the general reluctance and/or inability of local governments to make their required contributions and by widespread misgivings that any individual insurance contributions are more likely to line official pockets than provide for any health care in the future. In these circumstances rising medical costs remain a central source of anxiety for both the sick and the healthy who, fearful of illness or accident, dare not reduce or place their savings at any risk.

As for education, most government reforms aim to increase supply, make for greater accessibility and reduce costs for certain categories of the population – the rural, the migrant and the poor. In 2004, Wen Jiabao stated that new measures were to be introduced to 'reinvigorate education' with a focus on compulsory education particularly in the rural areas.[37] The State Council gave top priority to improving and expanding rural schooling and vocational education in 2005 when it promised new central and county funding to expand provision, raise standards and provide financial help for poor students by reducing or abolishing fees for textbooks, heating and boarding. At the same time, the Vice-Minister of Education announced that the government would adopt a system of free nine-year compulsory education for the country's rural children, starting with China's poorest counties in 2006.[38] In 2005, the government also promised more state schooling opportunities for migrant children in the cities in addition to introducing new regulations to stop primary and middle schools from charging extra fees to migrant children who do not have a permanent residence permit.[39] This is particularly important to migrant parents who frequently deprive themselves to save for their children's fees and fulfil their ambitions to have their children leave the countryside and become professional and 'white-collar workers' in the cities. For higher education, not only has there been considerable expansion in the number of universities but China is also determined to create a super-league to rival the best-known elsewhere. Poor college students are to be offered special state grants and further opportunities to defer their tuition payments.[40] For all students, the government is attempting to cap tuition fees and reduce the illegal and informal exaction of excess fees.[41] Parents and students are eager to take advantage of any new opportunity for further education, although the rising costs at all levels remain a much-debated topic in China. In the cities and even in the countryside, regular tuition fees are not likely to be reduced in the near future and are likely to be saved and scrimped for as in the past. However the government is attempting to reduce illegal and other informal fees in education, and as part of a more general attempt by the government to reduce and end bribery and corruption.

The government has continued to head a number of public campaigns against corruption. Zhu Rongji had set in motion a series of anti-corruption campaigns following his nemesis during the floods of 1998 when he witnessed dykes crumbling 'like bean curd' because the steel reinforcing beams were missing as a consequence of the misuse of construction funds. Apparently it was a very shocked Zhu Rongji who expressed his determination then and there to squeeze corruption out of the system, to spread a far-flung net from which there could be no escape and to rein in provincial or other leaders whose cosy insider dealings had milked millions from the national budget.[42] As a result of these campaigns, there were more high-profile arrests, but there was also some scepticism expressed that it was only the 'small' rather than the 'big fish' who were being exposed and punished.[43] Despite periodic crackdowns and the leadership's apparent commitment to excising corruption, it was admitted in 2000 that perhaps corruption had 'never before been bigger in China'.[44] Again in 2004 and 2005, the government has reaffirmed its commitment to stamp out bribery, embezzlement and other forms of corruption. In 2004, an article on problems of discipline and corruption within the Party warned cadres not to interfere in or bid for construction projects, involve themselves in the transfer of land-use rights and other real-estate activities or use their authority to accept cash, negotiable securities or other forms of payment from units or individuals.[45] In 2005, the government warned them against fraud, falsification of documents, abuse of power and other corrupt practices and a total of 115,000 Communist Party members are reported to have been punished for bribery, influence peddling and other offences.[46] As well as embarking on an education campaign to remind Party members of their duty,[47] the government has taken more stringent measures and strengthened the National Audit Office which, led by the 'iron-faced' auditor Li Jinhua, is credited in China's press with 'stirring a storm' across China's cumbersome government departments and putting 'huge' pressure on anti-corruption agencies to take concrete action.[48] Each of the annual reports of the National Audit Office have received increasing attention in the media as they make public cases of high-level embezzlement and misuse of public funds. In 2003, four central government departments were criticised for severe budget embezzlement as were the managers of disaster-relief funds and the China State Power Company.[49] In 2004, the National Audit Office reported that 41 out of 55 government departments investigated had misused a total of US$170 million which was largely intended for poverty alleviation, disaster relief and the construction of basic infrastructure. In also reported that, since 1999, a total of Y130 million allocated to the Chinese Olympic committee had been siphoned off to officials and developers.[50]

The 2005 report was even more extensive and was widely reported and discussed in the national press. In that report, Li Jinhua reported that, over the previous year, a total of Y9.1 billion (US$1.1 billion) had been misused by 38 central government departments including the Ministry of Land and Resources and National Tourism Administration. He went on to detail cases of embezzlement and misuse of funds across departments and relating to hospitals, universities, water projects, highway construction and scientific research. Major cases highlighted in the press included the misappropriation of Y4.9 billion in water-project investment, Y4.1 billion of rural highway subsidies, and Y669 million of scientific research funds. In addition, eighteen central government department-owned universities were found to have collected irregular fees amounting to Y868 million in 2003 and, in 10 Beijing-based hospitals, patients paid extra fees amounting to Y11.3 million in 2003 and 2004. At the same time, the report also noted that new measures to deal with such practices had been adopted, leading to savings of over Y1 billion and that many of those responsible for budget transgressions had been administratively punished or had their cases transferred to the courts.[51] These so-called 'audit storms', the dismissal of national and local leaders and a string of national and local court cases, all confirm that China's battle with corruption is far from over. Even for the showcase Olympics, the associate director of the information office of the Beijing Olympic Research Association has said it is unrealistic to expect Beijing to host a corruption-free Olympics:

> As the amount of people and the money involved in the games is so huge, corruption is almost unavoidable. What the government can do is to reduce the number of corruption cases: that's more practical.[52]

In December 2005, Li Jinhua announced that he is to extend his hunt for corruption in the lead up to the Olympic Games.[53]

Such cases of corruption and bribery extended to provincial levels of government administration and one very recent case led to the decimation of the top levels of a provincial administration. At the local levels too, it is everyday 'petty' bribes to 'get things done' or services performed that impoverish the poor disproportionately, cause widespread hardship and corrode the very public services put in place to contribute to their well-being.[55] As the previous chapter has shown, petty bribery is part of everyday life as local officials and service personnel, who are often paid low wages, regularly expect to benefit from negotiating contracts or granting permissions and papers. At this level, defining bribery and corruption in today's China is a complex process given the importance of guanxi or connexions in a relations-based system of socio-economic trading and political trust which is highly personalised and makes reform more difficult. Market reforms spread at a time when there was no rules-based system incorporating contracts, legislation and the judiciary and, instead, the reforms took advantage of and accentuated personalised exchanges of materials and resources to facilitate production, trading and trust. This relations-based trading system has not only commoditified and cemented personalised exchanges and gifts but also created economic distortions through gift-giving or bribery, crony-credit and the misallocation of resources. It could be said that the government is belatedly attempting to switch from relations-based to rules-based governance by trying to push through stringent economic and legal reforms. In the meantime the extra-budgetary passage of cash and goods frequently remains the best means for getting anything done. That said, there is no other term but rampant corruption for the siphoning off of public funds and stripping of assets for private gain which has taken place at all administrative levels and it is this feature which, more than any other, continues to threaten the long-term popular support for the government. It is very noticeable that within China it is not pleas for a change of political system or democracy that abound, so much as the demand for good governance including transparency and accountability.

Another cause for government concern and one likely to influence both future rates of economic growth and individual well-being has to do with the physical environment and now there is a new and concerted effort to meet China's environmental challenges. At the very top, in Beijing, the government has set up the State Environmental Protection Administration (SEPA) as the country's watchdog ministry with a brief to counter pollution, enforce standards and impose fines. In 2005, the government committed itself to spending close on US$85 billion on environmental protection inclusive of reducing emissions of coal-fired power plants and industrial treatment and disposal plants.[56] There is also some external pressure to meet a number of international targets and China's government has signed the Kyoto protocol. There are also many new policies and some tough laws in place – such as those regulating emissions and demanding environmental impact assessments on all new infrastructural projects. Across the country, environmental protection and in particular pollution reduction is becoming an industry estimated to be worth an annual US$20 billion and to be growing by roughly 20 per cent per year. This industry has attracted a lot of interest from foreign companies who are already deploying their techniques and skills to aid and profit from China's clean up.[57] Indeed the deputy director of a Beijing trade group, the China Association of Environmental Protection Industry, predicted in 2003 that 'the next five to ten years will be a golden era for environmental protection in China'.[58] Certainly notices and facilities in the main cities suggest that there is a new interest in improving public hygiene and the environment. The city of Beijing had led the way, for in its bid to host the Olympics in 2008 the capital had to promise huge improvements in air and water quality and is in the process of building new sewerage treatment plants, converting furnaces to gas and introducing strict new limits on vehicle emissions. As the deputy-director of the Beijing municipal government Bureau of Environmental Protection said 'it puts heavy pressure on us, but we will try our hardest to achieve our targets'.[59] In support of their targets, the city has pledged to allocate 4 per cent of the city's gross domestic product or some US$1.5 billion annually to environmental protection.[60] It has gone further and there is even popular talk of a 'Green Olympics' or the 'Greening of China'. More recently in 2005, the government has signed a multi-billion contract to design and build a string of 'eco-cities', which will be self-sustaining in energy, water and most food products.[61]

Despite some serious attention, show-case examples and popular slogans, it has to be said that very often environmental administrations and watchdogs have neither the resources nor the power to over-ride or penalise local governments or private companies which are often the largest culprits. Some of the regulations in place have sweeping goals but are vaguely worded and often difficult to implement or enforce, especially at local levels. In 2005, the suspension of several large construction projects that failed to comply on environmental impact assessments was regarded as a major victory for SEPA.[62] However local authorities, with other priorities ranging from concern about jobs and raising tax revenues to establishing services, often turn a blind eye to the environmental downside of any new industries that they have agreed to attract to the region. To discourage local officials, Hu Jintao has endorsed a new attempt to devise and implement an elaborate points system that, adding up to a 'Green GDP', both determines the careers of local officials, integrates environmental costs into local growth figures and mitigates against reckless showcase projects.[63] In July 2005, the State Council issued a circular calling for the creation of a 'conservation-oriented society' based on protecting energy, water, materials and land.[64] In the following months, Hu Jintao and Wen Jiabao continued to make constant references in their speeches both at home and abroad to the importance of cleansing and protecting the environment. This is not an easy task for as industry expands and as living standards rise, farmers are likely to use more pesticides and fertilisers, city dwellers to purchase more cars and manufacturing to cause more pollution. In sum, the Vice-Director of SEPA has warned that the deterioration of China's environment could multiply five or six times if an imbalanced development strategy is allowed to continue.[65] Thus there is likely to be some conflict between the goals of continuing economic growth and the protection and cleaning-up of the environment or between short-term windfalls and long-term costs of denuding the environment. In the continuing pursuit of balanced and sustainable economic and social development, the government has been faced by a repeated constraint – the procuring of sufficient resources to implement the very policies that are intended both to safeguard livelihoods and to lead to a better quality of life.

Resourcing development

One of the main impediments to economic and social development in emerging economies is an underdeveloped financial system and, for China too, it is the weakness of the financial system which endangers continuing economic growth and social development. In 2004, China's financial system was described as 'frail, dysfunctional or sclerotic', largely because of the failure to invest or allocate capital efficiently, collect sufficient revenues and reform a banking system crippled by high ratios of non-performing loans.[66] Since the onset of reform, the government has stated many times that it hopes to improve the overall financial environment in ways appropriate to and encouraging of a market-oriented economy. It could also be argued that, to some degree, the flood of foreign direct investment has camouflaged the weaknesses of China's own financial sector. If there is one outstanding feature underlying China's rapid development, it is the high level of foreign direct investment over the past three decades which is unprecedented and continues to soar as Western businesses seek to cash in on cheap labour, the expanding consumer market and opportunities for infrastructural investment. With fixed investments making up 40 per cent of GDP and the accumulation of foreign exchange reserves at the phenomenal pace of US$10 billion per month in recent years, China has been described as experiencing the 'most staggering investment boom in recorded history'.[67] It is all there to be seen with a quarter of the world's cranes now working in China's cities as construction and reconstruction abounds or in building the forty new airport terminals likely to come into operation within the next few years.[68] Enabling as such foreign investment is, it has also led to some over-investment in property, automobiles and steel production. Moreover the failure to allocate capital efficiently and avoid falling returns has meant that increasing amounts have had to be invested to generate the same amount of growth.[69] The flood of foreign direct investment that flows into the country, pumping up money supply has allowed China's banks to direct loans towards such wasteful projects as the concreting of paddy fields to establish economic zones, the building of luxury blocks which have no purchasers or investing in enterprises that produce goods that nobody wants.[70] These trends are likely to continue so long as provincial and local governments view foreign direct investment as the favoured route to rapid development and to winning favours in Beijing. Even though there are signs that the flow of foreign direct investment may be slowing, the desire of foreigners to invest in China is not likely to dry up.[71] Within China too, the bias towards foreign direct investment is likely to continue if only because of the under-development of China's own public finances, a functioning national taxation system and an efficient banking sector.

Previous chapters have noted time and again that, since the onset of market reforms, one of the constraints inhibiting the implementation of new policies to contribute to social security and public goods has been the shortfall in government funds to finance new and necessary infrastructure and services. Without adequate tax revenues, any government has difficulty in delivering its legislative programme, providing public goods, investing in education or health and in redistributing wealth. In China, the introduction of a nation-wide and efficient taxation system based on individual and corporate contributions has not proved to be an easy task, partly because of a lack of precedent or habit and the competition between the various administrative levels for existing taxation revenues. There is something of a Catch 22 situation in which there is both a shortage of government funds reaching local levels and a shortage of local revenues reaching the centre. The government attempted to centralise the taxation system in 1994 when, for the first time, it gave the central government first claim on the revenues collected in the provinces but it has required enormous effort to tax and collect adequate amounts. That said, the total amounts of tax collected have climbed steadily to reach 13 per cent of GDP in 2000 which was a step in the right direction but was still low in comparison to other countries such as the USA where it amounted to just over 30 per cent of GDP.[72] In 2004, it was estimated that tax collection had risen to 18 per cent[73] and to 19 to 20 per cent in 2005.[74] Even so, it was reported in 2004 that individual income tax revenue was Y141.8 billion or a 'mere' 6.5 per cent of total revenue, which still fell far short of the amounts required to finance infrastructure and service development.[75] Many of the shortfalls in the provision of local assets and services, the costs of access and the informal levies and fees are due to shortages of local, regional and national funds. In the countryside, both the absence of services and the high costs of any services provided are due to the low levels of government funds reaching township and village governments, many of which themselves have considerable debts. Indeed, as previous chapters also suggest, much rural unrest is due to the leverage of informal fees and taxes often for low or non-existent services. In the cities, new sources and levels of taxation will be necessary to clean up the environment and if the benefits and services previously provided by state-owned enterprises are to be replaced and extended to all citizens. As in the collection of most levies, a working taxation system is very much dependent on the ability of China's government to tax and spend transparently and to win trust in the government and its financial systems at the centre of which lie the large banks.

China's banking system is beset by many problems which are likely to continue so long as they constitute an arm of the government subject to political policies and practices rather than economic regulation and proper risk assessment. Political influence by party bosses and officials occurs at all administrative levels and it is sometimes said that bank managers have greater ties horizontally with local officials than with their own managers in the bank's hierarchy! What most ails the present banking system, which still provides China's businesses with around 90 per cent of its funding, are the high rates of non-performing loans, pervasive political interference and poor or sometimes corrupt governance.[76] In 2003, it was estimated that around 60 per cent of bank lending was still being made to state-owned enterprises, a substantial number of which were failing.[77] It is this bias towards state enterprises that has not only reduced the availability of credit for the private sector, but has also allowed the banking system to build up a mountain of non-performing loans. It is estimated that the ratio of non-performing loans of the four largest state-owned banks, the Bank of China, the Chinese Construction Bank, the Industrial and Commercial Bank and the Agricultural Bank, amount to about half of bank lending.[78] Standard and Poor, in a report entitled 'China Banking Outlook 2003–4', argued that the state banks are technically insolvent and in the short term are incapable of reducing their non-performing loan ratio of nearly 50 per cent and that it will take up to 40 per cent of the country's GDP to help deal with bad loans.[79] There is a general consensus both within and outside of China that the banking system, crippled by political loans and bad debts, is fragile and in urgent need of reform.[80]

In these circumstances, it is no surprise to find that China's government has placed the reform of the banks high on its financial agenda. Since 1998 there have been a number of attempts to reduce the ratio of bad loans in the banking system including a number of capital injections from China's foreign and other reserves.[81] However there has also been an increasing awareness that continuing bail-outs will require ever-increasing sums, perhaps amounting to as much as 30 or 40 per cent of GDP and that if welfare and unfunded pension liabilities were added then the central government's total liabilities could well be in excess of China's total GDP.[82] One of the reasons why past capital injections have not had the desired effect is that loans have continued to be made to state-owned enterprises so as not to increase unemployment or reduce social welfare to unacceptable levels. Indeed it was a new lending bout of 2002–3 which added to the stock of bad loans that convinced the government that more stringent banking reforms were a top priority.[83] At a central financial conference held in 2003, the government announced a new set of policies to stabilise the monetary system and safeguard financial risks.[84] Again, in 2004, the government announced a massive US$45 billion bail-out of two of its main banks and pushed banks to move billions of dollars of bad loans off their books, reign in lending to dubious projects and improve risk-management systems.[85] In an important policy shift, the state-owned asset-management firm set up to manage the bad-debt problem of the big four banks announced that it would auction off bad loans to foreign-owned banks. The 'Big Four' began to prepare to list their shares overseas and to make the requisite reforms. This time, in a reversal of previous procedures, the banks were not just to promise reform but to show evidence of high standards of corporate governance and make rapid progress in reducing non-performing loans before they received any further injections of capital and won approval for listing domestically and in Hong Kong. During 2004, Standard and Poor estimated that non-performing loans at the Bank of China dropped from 16.2 per cent of assets to 5.46 per cent with those at the China Construction Bank alone declining from 9.12 per cent to 3.08 per cent during the same period. This led Standard and Poor to reckon that for the banking sector as a whole, the percentage of non-performing loans had dropped from 50 per cent in 2002 to 35 per cent in 2004.[86] Official statistics within China have been more optimistic, putting bad loans at around 13 per cent,[87] but the fall in the ratios of non-performing loans may also be due to the rise in numbers of new loans, thus reducing the ratio of bad loans to the total, and it is not yet clear if or how many of the new loans will turn sour.

What is clearer is that the large national banks have worked to tighten their own structure and lines of command in order to reduce undue outside influence. The government, showing a new resolve to reform and regularise the banking sector, has also appointed an independent regulator and enlisted foreign expertise and capital for help in reforming and revitalising China's banks. An advisory panel of prominent bankers from a number of foreign cities has been appointed by the government for consultation, while individual foreign banks have been queuing to purchase stakes in China's banks of all sizes in a bid to gain access to a market where there are hundreds of billions of yuan savings.[88] Foreign banks are now permitted to hold up to a 20 per cent share in China's smaller banks but in return have to provide foreign capital, technology and management skills. In the past few years there have been several rounds of vexed negotiations, including those by HSBC, IFC, Citibank, JP Morgan, Goldman Sachs and the Royal Bank of Scotland with a number of Chinese banks in Shanghai and Shenzhen some of which have provided their foreign partners with a limited foothold in the China market which is now increasing at such a rate that it is forecast that foreign banks and investors could control one-sixth of China's banking system before they are formally permitted to offer full customer banking in 2007.[89] In the meantime the government hopes that a foreign presence will reduce reliance on local political support, increase efficiency and bring discipline to the operations; in addition it hopes that the new independent bank regulator will help China's banks pursue debtors and that it can cool China's economy and withstand foreign pressure to devalue beyond what it deems appropriate. In 2004, the government also raised interest rates for the first time for 9 years in a concerted effort to stop undue borrowing and to slow down or cool the economy. Opinions vary as to the efficacy of the new measures for reducing the fragility of China's banking system.[90] Some conclude that they 'have never seen such a rapid change in China's banking history'. For instance, Andrew Roth who is China-country head at CLSA Asia Pacific Markets, noted the effects of the new banking reforms with some optimism:

> You've got a banking system that's owned, operated and regulated by the state. But it's also a banking system that now stands a decent chance of being fixed.[91]

Others argue that the change from administrative to market-based measures is still more spin than substance and that the battle for bank reform will be won or lost in the branches.[92] In 2004, Nicholas Lardy estimated that the liabilities of China's government were 'still huge', with the bailing out of the banking system set to cost a high Y3.3 trillion or 30 per cent of GDP over the next few years. In addition, he argued, setting up a pension and welfare system will cost an additional 70 per cent of GDP or more, so that even conservative estimates of China's liabilities could add up to 100 per cent of GDP.[93] It is certainly true that, so far, administrative measures controlling the quantity of credit rather than its price have proved to be rather a blunt instrument in the allocation of credit in a system where the criteria for lending still leans towards the political. However, it is also true, as a recent study by UBS found, that the banking environment has changed radically over the past ten years with better regulation and supervision.[94] Nevertheless, the government continues to face a series of dilemmas: if it reduces loans to the failing state-owned sector it risks increasing job losses and social upheaval; any increase in interest rates will mainly affect mortgages and consumer credit which constitute a rising proportion of banking business; while thirdly, if it succumbs to foreign pressure and floats its exchange rate further, then it risks increasing the fragility of its own banking system. Indeed within China itself, there is some criticism that China is selling the family silver too cheaply and letting the foreign banks in at discount prices, which has led the government to reaffirm strict controls on foreign banks.[95] The government finds itself in a difficult situation. It has an iron commitment to reform if only because it understands that China's economic development depends on a healthy banking system and will face intensive competition and pressure from foreign banks with their sophisticated technological and management systems after new

WTO regulations come into force after 2006. At the same time, however, the government is also determined to proceed at its own pace and reform the banking system and state-owned enterprises in such a way that will not unduly increase the number of disadvantaged and thus further contribute to uneven development.

Uneven development

China's age-old pattern of uneven development has been exacerbated by the reform process which has benefited some physical locations and social categories more than others so that the resulting gaps are the subject of increasing international, government, media and popular concern. Outside China, the current disparities are often described as a 'chasm' or 'yawning gap' and there is concern that the accepted international measure of income inequality, the Gini coefficient, is rising incrementally to 0.48 or beyond the international limit of around 0.45.[96] In 2004, James Wolfensohn, then head of the World Bank, warned that China was fast becoming 'the most unequal society in the world'[97] and, in 2005, the United Nations Human Development Report on China also concluded that China's 'urban–rural income inequality gap is perhaps the highest in the world'.[98] This view echoes that of China's own Academy of Social Sciences, which for some time has argued that in no other country have income disparities increased to such an extent and that the resulting gap is potentially destabilising.[99] It is true that, at the very outset of reform, the government had anticipated that a minority would get rich first, to be followed by the majority. Indeed Deng Xiaoping's favourite maxim: 'Let some people get rich first, then try to achieve the common prosperity in society', was repeated in various phrases by subsequent leaders. For example, Jiang Zemin, in his 2003 address to the Sixteenth Party Congress reiterated this premise when he suggested that 'the well-off life we are lacking is still at a low level; it is not all-inclusive and is very uneven'.

> We need to emphasize and pay attention to the less-developed regions and the professions or the people who are experiencing difficulties. Especially, we should guarantee the basic living of the poor people, and actively help them to get employed and to improve their living conditions. We should let them feel the warmth of a socialist society. This is what we mean by getting rich together.[100]

The most recent generation of leaders have taken a broader and more inclusive view of development than their predecessors, while, at the same time, the second of the three-phased development plan which aimed at achieving a 'xiaokang' or 'better-off' quality of life for all by the year 2000 has been extended, with the target date for this phase pushed much further into the future. It is certainly the case now that only the minority may be defined as rich, that the majority can be classified as poor and that many feel themselves to have been impoverished by the process of reform despite an overall rise in the standard of living for most. In 2005, Li Xiaoxi, the head of the Economic and Resource Management Institute at Beijing Normal University, emphasised the two gaps that most needed to be addressed by the government:

> The first is the very wide gap between different social groups; the other is the astonishing economic development gap between regions.[101]

Whether China is divided between village, town and metropolis or eastern coast, centre and western interior, there are major divisions in resources, incomes and services between rural and urban China and within city and countryside which have widened in recent years. Regionally, much of the development has taken place in the cities, the suburbs, the coastal and river plains and eastern and southern provinces. It cannot be emphasised too often that behind the high growth rates and the economic boom of these regions, be they the modern metropolises of Beijing, Shanghai, Tianjin and Guangzhou or the manufacturing belts making up the Pear River Delta, the Yangtze Plains and special economic zones, lie the interior rural, remote and mountainous regions of the western provinces, the barren aridity of the northeastern provinces and the impoverished northeastern cities which have lost much of their manufacturing base. On any measure, whether it be GDP, the Human Development Index or the World Bank's gross national income index, the regions of China span the categories. Per capita GDP passed the US$1,000 mark for the first time in 2004, but some regions of China's 'fourth' world, such as Guizhou, Gansu, Shaanxi, Guangxi and Tibet, nowhere near reach this amount and rank very low within China or on any international index. According to the World Bank's gross national income (GNI) index which takes into account gross national income converted to international dollars using purchasing power parity rates, China ranks one hunred and twenty-fourth among 206 nations and remains in the lower-middle economy band with a purchasing power parity (PPP) GNI of US$4,600. Disaggregation within China shows that 2.2 per cent of China's population, or those living in cities like Shenzhen, Shanghai and Beijing, have reached a high economy income set at a PPP GNI of US$27,770; 21.8 per cent or a large proportion of those residing in coastal regions have reached an upper-middle economy level or a PPP GNI of US$9,210; while 26 per cent live in the lower-middle economy level and 50 per cent, mainly those in western and central regions, have a PPP GNI below US$1,980 which parallels the poorest regions in the world.[102] In terms of the United Nationa Development Program (UNDP) Human Development Index (HDI), a universal indexation that measures per capita GDP, education attainment and life expectancy, China is ranked at 96 among the 174 countries and regions. Shanghai, Beijing and Tianjin at 0.8 fall into 'high development regions' and are ranked 32, 33 and 48 in the world. The HDI figures for Guangdong, Liaoning, Zhejiang and Jiangsu reached 0.75 or higher, which put these provinces into the high end of the medium human development band and among the best 70 regions, while the central and western provinces ranked below 100.[103]

In terms of the wealth gap, the most recent figures suggest that, despite some increase in income levels, income disparities are large and growing at an exponential rate. The ratio of income inequality between city and countryside has increased incrementally over the years, with the latest income figures for 2004 showing a per capita cash disposable income of Y9,422 for urban residents and an average per capita net income of Y2,936 for rural residents, giving an income difference of 3.2:1.[104] According to the National Bureau of Statistics reported by Xinhua News Agency in 2005, 10 per cent of China's richest enjoy 45 per cent of the country's wealth leaving China's poorest 10 per cent with just 1.4 per cent of the nation's wealth. The survey, which polled 54,000 urban and rural households, found that the richest 10 per cent had a disposable income 11.8 times as great as the lowest 10 per cent compared with 10.9 times for the same period during the previous year.[105] The notable disparity between rich and poor households has continued to widen as the disposable income of the richest 10 per cent rose 15.7 per cent to Y8,800 compared with that for the lowest 10 per cent which rose 7.6 per cent to Y755 over the previous year.[106] Although on average, disposable income growth rates could be reduced from 11.3 per cent to 8.6 per cent if inflation was factored in, these gaps in income between either the rich and poor or rural and urban are not expected to diminish in the near future. As Fan Gang, a leading economist at the National Research Institute of China told Xinhua:

> The income-gap issue will not become smaller in the next 10 years, but probably will increasingly widen.[107]

If the trends which are briefly summarised here are added to those already presented in previous chapters, then there is little prospect of evening out development gains or much upward mobility. As previous chapters suggested, of 300 million or so city residents around 3 million may be classified as rich and 37 million as poor with the rest placed somewhere between the two extremes and increasingly impoverished; of the countryside's 800 or so million farmers, around 20 per cent live below the poverty line set by the government, more than 60 per cent have reached or just exceeded this line, 10 per cent are well above this line and only 5 per cent or so can be classed as relatively affluent and wealthy.[108] Just as the Academy of Social Sciences studies suggested in 2002 that there was little movement upwards with fewer joining the middle classes than anticipated,[109] so in 2005 the middle classes are still described in China's press as 'just a sliver of the population' numbering some 100 million.[110] Others place the numbers with discretionary spending at near 300 million, largely because households have just one child and hence more to spend.[111] The widening gap and proportions of rich to poor suggest that China's present pyramid shape is unlikely to be replaced by the more conventional diamond shape common in Asia and anticipated for China. The very evident income and regional disparities and the widening wealth gap keeps directing the attention of the new leadership towards rural development. Very recently, in the autumn of 2005, there has been much talk about the 'building of a new countryside' or 'constructing a new socialist countryside' and introducing measures to accelerate rural development in the interests of achieving balanced development. At a Central Conference on Rural Work held in December 2005, Wen Jiabao admitted that agricultural and rural development was still 'an uphill climb' although the formal abolition of the 2,600-year-old agricultural tax by a Standing Committee of the National People's Congress in the last days of 2005 was heralded as an important step in redistributing resources and 'giving more and taking less from the farmers and helping the countryside catch up with cities and thus the achievement of a balanced and harmonious society'.[112] Although much of this effort is aimed at maintaining social stability in the countryside, these policy innovations also have an economic rationale in that they are deemed essential to increasing domestic demand. While maintaining social stability does remain at the top of the government's agenda, it is not lost on the leadership that uneven development also begets uneven demand.

Uneven demand

As this study has shown time and again, an exacerbated pattern of uneven development has led to and is reflected in accompanying differentials in demand across China. So long as growth continues to be investment-driven rather than consumption-led and demand for consumer goods is very uneven then consumption is unlikely to rise fast enough to satisfy internal and external expectations. Domestic private consumption is still a relatively small proportion of GDP in China which, amounting to 45.1 per cent in 2002, was low in comparison to 70.5 per cent in the USA and 64 per cent in the EU.[113] The rise in retail sales from 9.1 per cent in 2003 to 10.7 per cent in the first quarter of 2004, was not enough of an increase to draw down inventory stockpiles and soak up excess supply.[114] Retail sales strengthened slightly throughout 2004, but the consumer mini-boom that analysts had been expecting did not materialise. China's per capita income may have crossed the US$1,000 threshold in 2004,[115] but food prices also rose in the same year as did the demands placed on that income by health care, education, housing, pensions and other services no longer provided by the government. In the face of continuing uncertainty and insecurity, the latest figures for household savings of urban and rural residents showed that these totalled Y12,620 billion, up 14 per cent over the previous year.[116] Throughout 2005 too, there was much talk of rapidly rising excess capacity, growing exports and fading domestic demand.[117] Despite the fact that most industries already suffered from the over-capacity outlined in previous chapters, corporations and companies continued to invest in spite of falling sales and profit margins – in the belief like many before them that there was an ever-expanding market in which they would share. With the exception of manufacturing for infrastructural developments, professional English language, legal and financial services, air travel, fast foods and a few other like items, supply has continued to exceed demand, resulting in stockpiles of unsold goods produced by domestic, foreign and joint-venture firms, cut-throat competition and falling profits.

There continues to be signs of the well-worn cycle leading to a mismatch between supply and demand whereby an initial supply of goods enjoys a first flush of sales and generates high hopes of a limitless market based on exaggerated expectations only to be followed by excess production, lower prices and falling profits. This has continued to be so for television sets, mobile phones and automobiles. In June 2004,

China's optimistic television manufacturers were reported to still have four times more capacity than they needed[118] and air-conditioners and microwaves followed a similar trajectory.[119] Even the more recent and rapid growth in mobile phone sales showed a decrease in 2004, suggesting to analysts of the global phone market that, despite expectations that the China market represents the 'biggest growth opportunity', sales had levelled off.[120] Not only were there fewer replacement sales than expected but, even though market penetration was still only 20 per cent, it seemed that most people who could afford a mobile phone already owned one. However the number of China mobile customers purchasing cheaper and locally manufactured varieties is expected to rise.[121] Similarly for cars, there has been a strong slow-down as car sales and profits, particularly of American and European manufacturers and for larger cars and jeeps, were reported in 2005 to be ailing or 'seriously hurting'.[122]

> The China auto-market, the best source of growth and profits in recent years for Western manufacturers like General Motors and Volkswagen, is turning into a quagmire of falling prices, over capacity and slowing sales. For example, GM and Daimler Chrysler both halved their shipments to China to reduce inventory of unsold vehicles while for Volkswagen, the most popular model and company, profits in China are lower in 2005 than in 2004 which in turn are half of 2003 profits.[123]

There are some exceptions to the slowing of retail automobile sales which include GM's basic, cheap and small lightweight trucks, Honda's mid-size Accord and Hyundai's roomy mid-sized Elantra sold at a compact-car price which all had a low baseline.[124]

Foreign car-makers increasingly rely on China to compensate for market saturation elsewhere and, despite the price wars there, continue with their plans to expand production. In 2005, foreign-car firms and their local joint-venture partners planned to invest a total of US$15 billion to triple output to over 7 million cars by 2008.[125] Such plans are based on the fact that car ownership in China is still minuscule in per capita terms at 7 or 8 out of every 1,000 compared with the global average of 120 and more than 600 in America.[126] Recently a spokesperson for Ford, which had a low 2 per cent share of the market in 2004, estimated that there were 450 million people in eastern China with purchasing power of over US$7,000 per year which is US$1,000 higher than the US$6,000 threshold at which car ownership usually takes off.[127] It is this rise in purchasing power and the gap in car ownership between Western nations and China and China's supposed millions of potential buyers which still underlies the dreams of manufacturers despite growing losses as fierce competition for falling numbers squeeze margins. In May 2004, the *Far Eastern Economic Review* predicted that by the end of that year, China would have auto-capacity for 6 million more sedans compared with demand for only 3 million.[128] There is no shortage of explanations for excess supply to do with the credit squeeze, government intervention and high prices, but the most likely explanation is that demand was less pent-up and smaller than anticipated so that the market got ahead of itself and quickly exhausted any capacity for expansion or growth. The quick success with the affluent passed as producers encountered a fragmented or impoverished customer base, fierce competition, lower prices and falling profits. Outside China there is still some reluctance to recognise that the limitations on the growth of China's domestic car market may include not only excess supply but also the lack of a large and growing middle-class. Few dare to admit to themselves that everyone who can afford a car already has one and few conduct a close sociological examination of the China market or study the very contemporary characteristics of China's demand pyramid.

The demand pyramid

In 2005, it cannot be said that the mass of China's population have become consumers in the accepted sense and it would be premature to speak of mass demand, mass consumption or the People's Republic of Consumers which is the by-line of some commentators. Rather China is a mosaic made up of 'consumption hot spots' amid a sea of slowish or some would say 'sluggish' consumption. If the demand pyramid very much mirrors or replicates the wealth pyramid outlined in previous chapters then the consumption hot spots lie at the top of the pyramid and are made up of the mega-rich and the rich of the main cities whose affluent lifestyles or homes, cars, array of durables, travel and recreational activities are much reported in the international and national media. In a sluggish global market, the main hopes of the world's luxury brands and manufacturers continue to include the potential lucrative opportunities presented by new top-end consumers in the emerging markets and especially in China. As the *Financial Times* noted in 2005, 'The luxury goods industry is in thrall to the US and China, the world's present and future super-powers'. It went on to observe that although strong US demand is welcome, the main hopes of high-end manufactures and retailers are on the 'huge potential of China'.[129] These ambitious forecasts for luxury goods are based on the numbers of 'cathedrals of consumption' that have opened in response to the country's growing wealth and on demographics, which it is argued 'speak for themselves'. Research published in March 2005 by Morgan Stanley, which considered the growth prospects of five quoted luxury goods over the next 10 years, also acknowledged the importance of China as a source of growth for these products:

> We believe that the luxury goods industry has already globalised, leaving the most important remaining opportunities from Chinese consumers – either as tourists or in mainland China – and eventually from eastern Europe.[130]

An analyst at Merrill Lynch estimated in 2005 that China's consumers already accounted for 11 per cent of worldwide revenues of luxury goods (although most of the purchases occurred outside China) and forecast that the big appetite for top luxury brands was such that, by 2014, China's consumers would have overtaken American and Japanese consumers to become the world's leading luxury shoppers, yielding 24 per cent of global revenues.[131] Not all of those purveying luxury goods are so confident. Two veterans seduced by the demographics and by the vast stores opened by Western luxury goods groups that are 'beautiful' and seductive, cautioned that there was 'still a gap between when it starts to be meaningful and when the meaningful develops in to real money' and that it should not be forgotten that 'we fight from customer to customer'.[132] Most of the businessmen accompanying Prime Minister Tony Blair to China in September 2005 expressed hopes that they would soon move on from manufacturing in China to selling their products there. For example, the Chairman of Alba, a consumer-electronics company, said that he was 'looking for business partners to sell our Grundig products' for 'we have global brands and it is time to capitalise on it'.[133] The director-general of the Confederation of British Industry, also accompanying the Prime Minister, argued that EU protectionism is an own-goal in that Britain understands that you 'off-shore production of low-value goods and that by doing so you're creating incomes for people who can buy our high-value goods'.[134]

Such continuing hopes that the top-earners will buy no end of high-value goods are not borne out by my own recent studies of the retail landscape of Shanghai, rated the most commercial of China's cities. This study of several of the main shopping clusters there, including Nanjing Road, Pudong, Xuhuijia, Huaihui Road and Xintiandi, suggested that the city retail sector is as stratified as the country-wide picture is fragmented. At the top-end are the large luxury malls with several-storey-high spaces lined with the most exclusive of world-wide brands including Armani, Bulgari, Dior, Gucci and a host of others. With minimalist displays suggesting luxury and exclusivity, they stand in stark contrast to the foyers which feature the most elaborate of festive tableaux and decorations. They really are temples or cathedrals of consumption from whose high atrium or domed roof spaces drift mobiles of ostentatious proportions. At Christmas, giant icicles float, Christmas trees soar, reindeer run, Father Christmas flies with or without a trapeze and sacks or wheels of wrapped or unwrapped gifts turn.

A study of the consumer base on both weekdays and the New Year's Sunday showed that the shops are much emptier than the mall escalators and avenues where many jostle and cameras flash as friends and families photograph each other using the Christmas stage-sets as a colourful backdrop. Several of the shop assistants said that there were few customers, probably, they thought, because the items displayed were so expensive. On New Year's Sunday, one of two or three most popular shopping days of the year, some of the luxury brand shops had as many as two or three visitors at any one time, although many had none. After browsing, many of the visitors left the shop without making a purchase and the tell-tale carrier-bags were few; instead many enjoyed a recreational window-shopping or sight-seeing experience. Similarly it could be observed in the luxury boutiques in high-end retail sections of Nanjing or Huaihui Road or in courtyards such as Xintaindi that customers were fewer than browsers and passers-by. These venues are known for their 'fine class and elegant stores' featuring internationally-famous brands and as a 'paradise for visitors from home and abroad'. Unlike the exclusive malls which were mainly visited by the sightseer and the curious and described by many of those in the professional and other classes as 'not relevant to them', the more up-market street-outlets benefited from their proximity to cheaper shops, restaurants and kiosks which drew more of a crowd, although not necessarily of purchasers. The juxtaposition of brand and bargain was also a feature of the middle-malls and department stores. Here a few of the luxury and more of the less exclusive international brands co-existed alongside their cheaper and cheerful China-owned equivalents. A study of these malls and department stores suggested that a number of well-established Chinese brands in clothes, accessories and white or brown goods provided opportunities for shoppers to purchase goods that are similar in quality, material and design to their foreign counterparts at a much lower price. A wide range of these brands and products are promoted and demonstrated in shop windows, interiors and entrances with similar skill and aplomb, although less minimalism and suggestion of exclusivity. Many retail outlets at the high-end of these middle-malls and stores display a range of cheaper products or mixed racks of clothes including trays and baskets of cheaper items which, clearly visible at entrances or in centre barrows, draw the customers in. The same principle applies in the middle-malls and department stores in which no space at the top of an escalator, on the ground floor or in the lobby is without a bargain counter or stall. This is where the crowds collect, examining the knock-down value of each item in turn. This range of items enables customers to adopt a popular shopping strategy which is to mix and match their purchases, be it in fashion, household goods or children's items and thus combine selective up-market purchases alongside cheaper garments or goods.

It is clear from observing and interviewing customers, including young women with high disposable incomes, that they may make one up-market, middle or 'extravagant' purchase made all the more affordable by a range of cheaper purchases. At any one time they may possess the one 'fashionable' garment or accessory of the season, maybe a handbag or a pair of boots to mention the current favourites, or have one up-market outfit which they wear frequently to signify their individual taste, modernity or social status. It is also evident that, as for cars and homes, shoppers rarely upgrade their existing items and instead those both at the top and middle of the pyramid are tending to spend as much on leisure services and personal enjoyment as on goods or fashion. In some ways consumption could be said to have become less about purchase and possession of goods than the pursuit of sport or health fitness, travel, new types of home or club and restaurant entertainment. Certainly one of the cutting-edge advertising firms marketing interactive entertainment for homes and bars is not alone in openly admitting that they are 'targeting people who want to enjoy life'.[135] The courtyards of Xintiandi include a number of up-market clubs and restaurants with names such as The Ark, La Maison, Coffee Bean and Tea Leaf, Rendezvous, K2 Jazz, T8, which all have their distinctive style and popular offerings and are suggestive of the new forms that 'the pleasure business' are taking in today's China.

Middle and lower-end malls and stores also have a range of fast-food restaurants, coffee shops and entertainment venues to attract the crowds. Those at the middle and lower-end of the mall-store spectrum have numerous restaurants and perhaps a movie theatre, ice rink or other major attraction. In one such mall in Pudong, I counted at least 15 restaurants plus half as many coffee and fast-food restaurants which were cheap, cheery and mostly full at weekday lunch and weekend meal-times. Perhaps it is this same combination of both expensive and cheap goods and range of services which has been responsible for the growing popularity of multi-range one-stop supermarkets and hypermarkets. Many buy the cheaper range of food products in supermarkets because they feel that these goods are of higher standards and subject to better quality controls than their outdoor-market equivalents. Due to the popularity of the hypermarkets, Wal-Mart and Carrefour expect to have 50 to 60 outlets respectively in the near future. Their Chinese chain one-stop equivalents and in particular the Guomei electrical stores which also have a wide range of products including cheaper bargain models and more expensive Chinese brands, have also expanded at a rapid pace. The findings of this Shanghai study point to the increasing popularity of China's own cheaper and stylish products, the stratification of retail clusters and the success of mixed range venues. These findings for Shanghai are confirmed by both my own observations and those of others elsewhere.

In Guangdong, it has been observed that consumers are no longer so interested in foreign brands or products and that many of these are struggling to retain their original position or acquire a share of the market now that China's own products are seen to be better value with good-enough or matching quality at lower prices. As one shopper told a reporter from the *International Herald Tribune* in 2005: 'Maybe some people thought that American brands are better than Chinese brands or had better after-sales service. Now they don't think so'.[136] In Beijing, the main characteristics of the top-end of the demand pyramid are confirmed by a very recent appraisal of the customer base at the new and enormous Golden Resources Shopping Mall dubbed 'the Great Mall of China'.[137] This trendy steel and glass giant neon-lit mall is reported to be the largest in the world, equivalent to 100 football pitches and with 1,000 shops in its 6 million square feet floor area which is four times the size of the Great Hall of the People. The mall promises a 'perfect shopping experience' and provides arcades of shops for international, national and local Chinese brands aspiring to the same showcase status; visitors include the rich shoppers, typically professionals in their thirties who with their children arrive in imported cars and spend in the supermarkets and shops – but not to the levels anticipated or desired. A shop assistant in a costume jewellery shop which sells pendants for up to Y1,000 and jewellery boxes between Y400 and Y600, admits that business has been slow: 'To be honest business has not been too good'. Most Beijingers can't afford to shop in the mall and those that visit the mall say that they come to while away their time window-shopping for luxury goods. A young couple strolling in the mall told one correspondent that they never bought anything from the shopping centre because it was too expensive: 'It's a nice place to look at things and spend your spare time'. Migrants working in the mall observed that one item of clothing was easily several times their wage and that 'only the rich come here'. The migrants might recognise that 'we can't compare ourselves to them' but they also find some comfort in the thought that maybe their hard-earned money will enable their children to get educated so that they too can shop in the Great Mall:

> I just hope our children won't have to do what we do. I hope in the future they'll be the people who are shopping here as opposed to working here.[138]

What is interesting about China's present wealth and demand pyramid is that those at the bottom still believe that the whole nation is getting wealthier so that the rich are simply those who got there first and that others will follow in their footsteps via hard work and further education. In the meantime most of China's population is not getting rich enough fast enough to snap up all the luxury brands or the China-made goods flooding the shelves. In the luxury-goods markets, there is some debate about how quickly luxury-good groups can build their presence in China and how soon more than a tiny percentage of China's population will afford and purchase imported items. Internationally, the luxury market hopes that 'creative marketing' will both retain existing customers made up of the wealthy few and expand to include more middle-income earners:

> The new business model for luxury relies on ever-finer segmentation to find new groups of consumers, identify unmet needs and locate unexploited sales opportunities and develop offerings for customised and localised appetites based on frequent consumer feedback.[139]

In China, as elsewhere, much depends on the speed of rising income levels, the spread of middle-class lifestyles and the scale and speed of the 'trickle-down' effect.

The conventional basis for the spread of mass consumption or the normal route to a consumer revolution has been a 'trickle-down' effect, a phrase deriving from the early works on conspicuous consumption and on the role of goods in the emulative and competitive processes of status-making and/or status-claiming by Veblen[140] and Simmel.[141] The premise underlying this approach is that the most efficacious point of entry is to insinuate goods into the lifestyles of the upper class in the hope that they will 'trickle down' to the less affluent and lower-income groups. Practically and symbolically, China's elite are seen to be living the good life to which all may aspire – very much in line with Deng Xiaoping's dictum of encouraging some to get rich first – or it might be added to shop first! Despite the concentration of centuries of change in consumer habits elsewhere into a few decades in China and reports that 'as prosperity spreads, more and more Chinese people are able to start affording life's little luxuries'[142] or of a much-hyped expanding middle class, it is becoming increasingly clear that not only are goods not trickling down fast enough to satisfy expectations but also that even at the point of entry – at the top-end of the market – consumption, conspicuous or not, is faltering. As this study has also suggested, the expansion of the elite and the emergence of more than a sliver of a middle class may be some time in coming and it is perhaps important to note that China's retail companies are not waiting.

Instead they are offering a wide range of cheap and expensive products and services to meet segmented demand. For instance, Shanghai's Brilliance Group operates a total of five department stores in the same busy retail and tourist zone (Nanjing Road), which are designed to cover all consumer bases from 'upscale' to 'mid- and upper-range' and 'lower level' shoppers. As their spokesman stated, 'we hope to attract all kinds of shoppers to our stores through different positioning'.[143] Conversations with friends and shoppers in Shanghai at the close of 2005 suggested that they too could position the clusters of malls, streets and markets very clearly; they knew where the different income-levels shopped and why their favourite mall or store was appropriate to their own income and lifestyle. If urban demand is segmented and city shops stratified with very few at the top-end or in the middle of the demand pyramid, the market is also polarising between the affluent at the top and the majority of China's urban and rural population who remain in the low-income brackets and at the bottom of the pyramid.

The pyramid base

In emphasising the expansion of domestic demand and as they hope to move from being the world's factory to the world's market, China's leaders anticipate that it is China's countryside that will play a key role. In April 2004, Wen Jiabao told top officials that to 'always take increasing domestic demand as the starting point in our economic development' means placing rural development at the centre of the government's agenda.

> The key to boosting domestic demand lies in the vast and largely untapped markets of China's countryside. Urban markets have been saturated with most consumer durables for years, while many rural areas still lack the income levels or basic infrastructure – roads, water and electricity – to get or use them.[144]

In the context of rural development and expanding demand internally, there has long been some questioning of the conventional sequence or 'trickle down effect' from the rich to the poor. It is now mooted that to penetrate rural markets may not only require infrastructural development, a rise in incomes and the expansion of distributive and retail networks but also some redefinition of demand. If the concept of development has been debated and redefined over the decades to substitute the participation and empowerment of the poor for top–down paradigms, so similarly has demand become the subject of new analyses. Currently and in ways reminiscent of previous shifts in thinking about development, long-standing perceptions of demand are being questioned Instead of a preoccupation with increasing wealth, conspicuous consumption by the rich or top–down seduction, the sophistication of products and services and the spread or speed of trickle-down, there is now a new global interest in the low-income and poorer consumers, low-price goods, downmarket retail and local distributive networks among the poor and the rural. As one very recent *Newsweek* commentary argued, 'consumer goods-makers are realising that they only have one direction to go for growth – down-market'.[145] Several analysts and multinational company spokespersons are making the business case for turning to low-income groups: 'companies that turn up their noses at low-income consumers are snubbing their own potential for growth'; 'the great white spot in the world economy is the lower-income market'; or 'all over the world, the low income market is the market'.[146]

One analyst who has done much to publicise the potential of the poor as consumers in emerging markets and to encourage the idea that small can be as beautiful in demand as well as in development is C.K. Prahalad who introduced his recent book entitled, *Bottom of the Pyramid: Eradicating Poverty through Profits*,[147] with a simple proposition:

> If we stop thinking of the poor as victims or as a burden and start recognising them as resilient and creative entrepreneurs and value-conscious consumers, a whole new world of opportunity will open up.[148]

He goes on to argue that wealth can be created at the bottom of the pyramid, a phrase he shortens to BOP to contrast with the wealthy customers at the TOP. He suggests that at the TOP, the selling of over-priced wares to the few phenomenally rich at the top and the thin wafer of middle class just below is to sell in a market in which quality foreign brands as well as top-tier domestic-made goods is soon saturated or spoken for. Instead he argues that firms should focus on the colossal plinth of poor folks who have nothing or little more than just their dreams. Not only does he firmly criticise top–down thinking on aid, but he ascribes agency and independence to the poor as both producers and consumers and argues that the involvement of big business, crucial to eradicating poverty, is best guaranteed by sustained investment in BOP markets. Indeed Mr Prahalad reckons there is a huge economic opportunity and potential profits amounting to some US$13 trillion per year to be made from serving the 4 to 5 billion people earning less than US$2 a day.[149] Although Mr Prahalad thinks the win for big business is self-evident, he also argues that building BOP markets is not cost free and requires new simple low-cost but nevertheless technically-sophisticated small-unit packages which have no or low on-going costs, high value and need new distributive networks to make up for low margins per unit. He argues that the benefits for the poor include empowerment deriving from exercising choice and the freedom from paying the widespread 'poverty penalty' or the premium that the poor pay on everything from rice to credit, which can be between 5 and 25 times that paid by the rich in relation to their income.[150] He concludes that reducing these premiums can make serving the BOP more profitable than serving the TOP. In support of his arguments he cites a number of case studies.

Perhaps the best known of Prahalad's examples is that of Hindustan Lever, a 51 per cent subsidiary of Unilever the Anglo-Dutch consumer goods giant, which has become a model of how to do business in the vast and complicated markets of rural India. That it has become the country's largest 'fast-moving consumer goods' firm with a growth in sales of over 12 per cent per year for the 5-year period prior to 2000 was helped by its sale of single-serving shampoo sachets in small rural villages which at two cents could be afforded out of pocket money rather than denting the household budget to buy a whole bottle costing US$2.[151] Although Hindustan Lever had a recent blip in sales due to internal competition, a poor marketing ploy and failed monsoons which reduced spending money, particularly on items of personal care which lost out to the increasing popularity of mobile phones and other durables. However, such was the perceived potential for growth in rural India that Hindustan Lever has continued to invest heavily in advertising and in new marketing mechanisms. One of these, called shakti, extends marketing through self-help groups which offer tiny loans to support a direct-to-home distribution network – a form of micro-credit to help demand if you like or micro-consumption. It is expected that by 2005 there will be 25,000 shakti entrepreneurs covering 100,000 villages and 100 million rural consumers.[152]

C.K. Prahalad cites other such cases in India as well as in Brazil and South Africa which have also been the subject of some discussion in the international press. For instance in 2004, the month of May was depicted in *Newsweek* as a watershed in the Brazilian economy largely because low-income consumers had flooded shops on Mothers' Day to snap up 1.5 million basic cut-rate-call phones that operated on prepaid phone cards costing as little as US$3 per month. These basic phones soon amounted to 78 per cent of the 20 million mobile phones purchased between 2002 and 2004, taking the entire market to 5.3 million. According to *Newsweek*, these low-income customers represented such 'a new consumer vanguard' or a 'battalion of buyers with shallow pockets but a keen eye for a deal', that now makers of other basic or low-price goods from bicycles to bouillon cubes were scrambling to serve 'these most modest of consumers'.[153] Factories in Brazil are reported to have retooled to provide simplified floor fans, single-door refrigerators and air conditioners and washing machines that are basic and cheap for low-income customers. Brazil's best-known department store, Casia Baha, with more than 350 branches, operated on the premise of a hassle-free instalment plan that let low-income buyers pay off goods for a few dollars a month. Brazil's biggest private bank, Banco Postal Brandesco, defied sceptics and invested US$100 million to set up bare-bones teller services in under-used post offices. Although most of the new depositors earned US$65 or less, Banco Postal had already captured 1.6 million new accounts by 2004 and was expected to break even 2 years ahead of schedule.[154]

When South Africa opened its doors to global enterprise in the early 1990s, mobile phone companies found their sales limited to the small moneyed class of urban sophisticates until they introduced low-price handsets and pre-paid phone cards costing less than US$5. Then mobile phone purchase exploded, making Africa with 51.8 million handsets the fastest growing of the world's cell phone markets.[155] Such examples are not confined to low-income countries for, even in the USA, the value-price or small-dollar stores show the fastest growth of any of the major retail sectors, outpacing those which focus on luxury goods or cater for middle-tier consumers. The objective is not only to reduce the costs of products but also to make it possible for lower-income customers to enter the market and pay a little at a time. According to an analyst from Pyramid Reach in London, profiting from fast growth in rural markets is not so much about how much something costs, but about lowering the entry barrier to consumers and giving them control over cash flow.[156] In a move similar to that within development, micro-credit has been deployed not only to increase production but also to encourage micro-consumption and to effect a demand transition. Just as for development, so in analysing demand, it may be that the 'bottom-up' approach, micro-credit, participation, stake-holders, inclusiveness and empowerment will become some of the more common buzz words.

China too, as much of this study has shown, is not only a country of low-cost or low-price producers but also of low-income or low-price consumers. Many of China's own entrepreneurs have recognised the limits of high-end consumption there and said very early on that they would leave the luxury high-value goods and large profit margins to the foreigners and concentrate on the lower end of the market. One successful businessman, who has specialised in building low-price affordable housing with low profit margins, reckoned in 1997 that he had a two-to-three year advantage over any competition from Hong Kong or elsewhere as 'they want the elite'.[157] Most of China's small firms include or focus on the low-income consumer and even China's best-known brands are sold at the lower end of the market. For instance the stylish, simple and cheap products of the Kelon and Haier brands have given these companies a long-time advantage at the cheaper end of the domestic market. Another entrepreneur who has concentrated on the parts of China not easily reached is Mr Huang Guangyu who founded GuoMei Electrical Appliances, now China's largest electric retailer chain. From small beginnings, when he rented a shabby market stall and hawked cheap household electronic appliances, he has recently been named the richest businessman in China and the first retailer to head China's rich list. He himself says that he has steadily built his retailing empire through a single but tested formula: 'small profits but large sales'.[158] At the last count, the GuoMei retail chain had more than 160 stores across China with a workforce of 10,000 employees and in cities such as Tianjin it dominates the local market, attracting 70 per cent of the city's customers. Mr Huang is aiming to set up a further 600 GuoMei stores in all Chinese cities with a population of between 400,000 and 500,000 and to extend his retailing network into the vast countryside. Some observers think that profits from many of his household electric goods could be as low as 1 per cent and he readily admits to slashing prices to gain a larger share of the market. He is also emphatic that it is adaptation to the customer base which is the key to market expansion and dominance and this is where he thinks foreigners may have to learn more about the local conditions of the China market:

> If foreign retailers want to enter China they will have to really understand how the market works here. It's not only about investment of money. It's more to do with your mindset or perception. Retailing is different from other sectors, technology for instance. Foreign operators will have to go through what I call a 'naturalisation' process first. They are not coming to China to

change the consumer society here. Success or failure depends on whether they can seamlessly interact with Chinese society.[159]

Several foreign firms have had the type of interaction recommended by Mr Huang. One is General Motors whose general manager, back in the late 1990s, was reputedly the only multinational automaker to have spotted the potential among small business owners and affluent farmers, not prosperous enough to afford the latest Western models, for small and inexpensive fuel-sipping cars, minivans or pick-ups. These have a quarter of the horsepower of American minivans, weak acceleration, a top speed of 81 miles per hour and seats a third of the normal thickness and sell for US$5,000. These practical little minivans which GM builds in a joint-venture with a Chinese partner have become a hot new formula, helping GM sales jump 41.3 per cent in one year[160] and climb faster than its rivals to sell more than 172,000 vehicles in the first half of 2005, surpassing Volkswagen which has dominated sales in China for two decades and earning US$176 million to turn China into GM's biggest centre of automotive profit.[161] According to the President of Automotive Resources Asia, a consulting firm based in Beijing and Bangkok, this venture was 'impressive' and 'strategically very smart'.[162] Whirlpool, the country's largest appliance maker, has found it 'much harder' to take on domestic models in the countryside as it, unlike Nokia, Proctor and Gamble or Unilever, has not adjusted its product mix but relied instead on an increase in after-sales services to sell middle- and high-end washing machines in small provincial cities.[163]

When Nokia faced a decline in its urban market share, it stemmed the decline by producing cheaper phones and introducing pre-paid services for low-income users.[164] In China as in India, small one-wash sachets of shampoo abound and are widely purchased. Both Proctor and Gamble and Unilever have adjusted their small laundry and personal care products to the rural market. When Proctor and Gamble, an early and successful participant in the China market, found its share declining at the turn of the century it turned from selling to the wealthiest 8 per cent at the top of the three-tier pyramid it uses to categorise the Chinese laundry market to the low-income urban and rural market. It no longer shipped common US products for sale in China and instead has modified the properties of both detergent and toothpaste to provide a range from basic cheap to multi-function expensive versions of the same product in an attempt to crack the low-income market and use its global pharmaceutical and health care expertise to out-class and compete with popular locally-made brands.[165] Unilever too is committed 'to work the entire pyramid' by also 'building the market from the bottom' in order to expand its share of the China market. In diversifying its products and giving consumers what they could afford, the head of Unilever for Asia and Africa is adamant that although the return might be less than some top-of-the-range products, Unilever's centre of international gravity has shifted south and east and that Unilever 'is building markets, not parachuting in foreign products'.[166] China's leaders are also into building markets, although the priority to be accorded to the transition to domestic demand as opposed to developing export markets is still a matter of some debate and dissension within China.

The demand transition

In emphasising the expansion of domestic demand, China's leaders seem determined to counter China's over-dependence on overseas export markets which, together with imports of capital, technology, energy and raw materials, have tied it into the global economy in ways that render it more vulnerable than ever before to world market fluctuations and outside trade rules. It is hard to believe, even for the most optimistic, that China's manufactured exports can keep on growing at present rates, especially if China revalues its currency or its prices rise, if the American economy slows or if there is a glut of cheap manufactured goods on the world market. However, despite an overall commitment to harmonious development and the raising of living standards, there is still some internal debate on how best to achieve the economic growth essential to creating jobs and continuing development. The central question at issue is how much of China's future lies in the potential of its own domestic market or on further exports and thus which of these two should lead economic development. There is evidence that even within the Politburo there is some disagreement and fierce debate over precisely how and when to dampen down the economy.[167] Perhaps the most interesting aspect of this debate, as far as this study is concerned, revolves around disagreements as to whether to continue the emphasis on exports, leading to fast growth and fast returns as favoured by some at the centre and many of the regional provincial officials who alike object to any government policy which threatens immediate and short-term returns. They argue that China can withstand any downturn in the consumer economies of North America and Europe for, although China's economy is trade-dependent, its ratio of exports to GDP stands at around 30 per cent which is high by the standards of America and Japan but not if comparisons are made with Europe and East Asian societies. They point to Japan, which never really made the shift from export-led to consumer-led growth, and they argue that even if there is to be a shift then it is likely to take many years. Apparently the Chinese leadership includes such an influential 'export bloc' that has 'hitched its wagon to export growth', is less supportive of China's WTO accession and does not welcome the on-going appreciation of the yuan for fear that it will reduce exports and profits.[168]

Others in the Politburo are reported to favour policies which may reduce growth in the short term but lead to longer-term and sustainable development that is not so dependent on external factors over which China has little control. Certainly most of the speeches of Hu Jintao and Wen Jiabao emphasise the importance of all-round or balanced development and of expanding domestic demand alongside economic growth. In almost every policy preamble, whether it be about economic growth or development more generally, the provision of social security and public service or the reduction in costs and illegal fees, a most important and explicit rationale for the new policy is the expansion of domestic demand. One of the most recent lists of 10 major tasks for China's government included the promotion of incomes in order 'to boost consumption' and, in late 2005, the rationale behind building a new socialist countryside included 'ensuring sustainable development and the continuous expansion of domestic demand'.[169] The two leaders seem determined to counter China's over-dependence on overseas export markets and, in particular, its reliance on the continuing spending of the American and British consumer. Politically, the large and growing bilateral trade deficits and the likely doubling of China's exports have generated widespread fears and if recent EU and American attempts to limit imports from China are anything to go by then the chances of avoiding a protectionist backlash do not seem high. Even a minor advertisement in London's Sunday papers in 2005 featured a label in red, white and blue letters, 'Not Made in China'.[170]

The resolution of this conflict is of more than national interest as the spectres of either excess capacity and growing exports not just of cheap and low-end products but also of sophisticated technologies and commodities flooding international markets or of the sudden collapse of the market for China's exports both fuel international anxiety. There is an emerging international consensus that China should look to the growth of the domestic market as a third arm alongside investment and export. In late 2004, the *Financial Times* noted with approval that the obsession with attracting foreign direct investment and with exports is being questioned by some domestic officials and experts as they turn to developing and emphasising domestic demand.[171] In late 2005, the US Treasury began to exert pressure on China's government not only to devalue its currency but also to rely less on demand elsewhere and to boost domestic consumption in order to shift the economy away from reliance on exports and talk of protectionism.[172] As with many other issues, the resolution of this conflict within the Politburo between the export and domestic demand blocs is not likely to be resolved before the Seventeenth Party Congress in 2007 when it is expected that support for the present leaders may well increase within the Politburo. In the meantime the leaders not only emphasise the importance of economic growth and all-round development for raising domestic demand but also, in an accompanying mantra, reverse this order and emphasise the importance of accelerated domestic demand for sustaining all-round development. Not only can development beget demand, but perhaps increased demand may also beget or speed development.

In thinking about the relationship between development and demand, there is a precedent for hastening demand and not awaiting development. In a parallel relationship between demography and development there is also a conventional sequence from increased development to declining death and birth rates effecting what is called a demographic transition to the lower population growth rates of most high-income countries. In China, the radical birth control and single-child policies of the 1970s and 1980s were designed to hasten the demographic transition by reducing fertility as a fast route towards – rather than awaiting – development. China's government, given the sum total of its population and projected population growth rates, felt it had no choice but to intervene and speed the demographic transition if the country was to ever effect economic growth and development. Now in an equivalent move, the government shows every sign of attempting to speed a demand transition in the interests of development. The creation of a 'unitary nation-wide mass market'[173] is one of the means to achieving a balanced', 'harmonious' and sustained social development. To a large extent the legitimacy of the present leaders rests upon improving the general standard of living of the population. Certainly Hu Jintao and Wen Jiabao have succeeded in conveying the hope that China's growth is moving fast enough to lift the majority of the population into the middle classes. Popular hopes for and dreams of riches still pervade the lower levels of the wealth pyramid and are encouraged at every opportunity.

On a very recent trip to Shanghai, I was struck once again by the number of times the word 'dream' kept appearing and reappearing in both expected and unexpected contexts – in the newspaper, on the mall and street billboard, in television advertisements and in the theatre and at art exhibitions. In Shanghai in the last days of 2005, audiences were entranced by the multi-media high-tech artistic music-and-dance production 'Dream' which explored the variety of and uncertainty around different dreams. Typical too was the layered abstract painting 'New Dream' by artist Wang Wucius which, exhibited in the Shanghai Art Gallery at the same time, featured shaded squares and merging dots with glimmers of brightness and clouds that were both light and dark, portraying stretched horizons simultaneously unlimited and constrained. A New Year's Count-down party at Shanghai's Xintiandi (New Heaven and Earth), a fashion and club hub, had the theme 'As You Dream, You Shall Become'. Dreams were either overt and focused or dormant and at the very least deferred and invested in the next generation. Perhaps for many, as this book suggests, it is still the dream of the future rather than the present destination which fuels hopes and expectations and it is how these expectations can be managed and realised not only within but also outside China that has been the subject of this study. It set out to examine the demand patterns, paradoxes and pyramids that are necessary to understanding China's domestic market, to managing foreign expectations of China's domestic market outside China and to fulfilling the hopes and dreams of China's own population and government within China. If these goals can be realised, then China's domestic market may yet number some 1.3 billion people and realise long-held hopes and expectations, not least those within China itself where it is hoped that accelerating both domestic demand and social development will build 'a well-off society in an all-round way'.

References

1 Increasing demand

1 *China Daily*, 24 March 1998.
2 *The Economist*, 14 August 1999.
3 Xinhua (New China News Agency), 24 April 2002.
4 *China Daily*, 3 April 2003.
5 Ibid., 31 March 2003.
6 Xinhua (New China News Agency), 4 March 2004, 4 April 2004, 16 April 2005; *Renmin Ribao* (People's Daily), 13 May 2005; Xinhua (New China News Agency), 16 May 2005, 5 July 2005.
7 *Financial Times*, 30 September 2003.
8 Yiren Rong, 'China: Moving Towards the Twenty-first Century', in F. Itoh (ed.), *China in the Twenty-First Century: Politics, Economy and Society*, United Nations University Press, Tokyo, 1997.
9 *BusinessWeek* (Beijing), 8 December 2003.
10 *Sunday Times* (London), 27 July 2003.
11 *Financial Times* (London), 24 December 2003.
12 *Sunday Times*, 18 January 2004.
13 *The Times*, 17 September 2005.
14 *Wall Street Journal*, 11 November 2005.
15 *Far Eastern Economic Review*, May 2005.
16 *Financial Times*, 24 June 2003, 9 December 2003.
17 *The Economist*, 14 August 1999.
18 Ibid., 25 August 2001.
19 *Time*, 3 December 2001.
20 *The Times*, 28 September 2001.
21 *Sunday Times*, 23 December 2001.
22 Ibid., 16 March 2003.
23 *Evening Standard*, 17 October 2002.
24 *Sunday Times*, 16 March 2003.
25 *The Economist*, 11 January 2003.
26 *Sunday Times*, 16 March 2003.
27 *BusinessWeek*, 11 April 2005; *The Economist*, 8 October 2005; *Newsweek*, 21 November 2005; *Observer* (London), 1 January 2006.
28 *BusinessWeek*, 8 December 2003.
29 *Sunday Times*, 18 August 2001.
30 *International Herald Tribune*, 8 April 2002.
31 Ibid.
32 Ibid.
33 *The Economist*, 11 October 2003.

34 *Far Eastern Economic Review*, 9 January 2003.
35 *The Economist*, 25 May 2002.
36 *Far Eastern Economic Review*, 9 January 2003.
37 *The Economist*, 15 October 2005.
38 C. Mackerras, *Western Images of China*, Oxford University Press, Hong Kong, 1991, p. 19.
39 Ibid., p. 39.
40 Ibid., p. 43.
41 *The Economist*, 19 July 1997.
42 Mackerras, op. cit., p. 113.
43 Joe Studwell, *The China Dream: The Elusive Quest for the Greatest Untapped Market on Earth*, Profile Books, London, 2002.
44 Carl Crow, *China's 400 Million Customers*, Hamish Hamilton, London, 1937, p. 304.
45 Ibid., p. 202.
46 Ibid., p. 314.
47 Studwell, op. cit., p. ix.
48 Ibid., p. 23.
49 Ibid., p. 24.
50 Ibid., p. 63.
51 *The Economist*, 25 September 1999.
52 *Newsweek*, 7 December 1998.
53 *Observer*, 27 February 1994.
54 *Newsweek*, 29 September 1999.
55 *China Daily*, 14 September 2000.
56 *Newsweek*, 29 September 1998.
57 *The Economist*, 10 March 2001.
58 *Newsweek*, 29 June 1998.
59 *China Daily*, 13 December 1999, 14 September 2000, 10 September 2001.
60 Ibid., 13 September 2000.
61 *Beijing This Month*, 1 February 2000.
62 *Sunday Times*, 27 July 2003.
63 *The Times*, 19 August 2003.
64 *The Economist*, 20 July 2003, 20 September 2003, 15 November 2003.
65 *Sunday Times*, 9 January 2005.
66 Studwell, op. cit., p. x.
67 J.K. Fairbank, *The United States and China*, Harvard University Press, Cambridge, MA, 1971 edn, p. 324.
68 *Sunday Times*, 26 January 2003.
69 *International Herald Tribune*, 29–30 March 2003.
70 *The Economist*, 10 March 2004.
71 Ibid., 8 April 2000.
72 Elisabeth Croll, *The Family Rice Bowl: Food and the Domestic Economy*, UNRISD/Zed Press, London, 1983.
73 *The Economist*, 20 April 2002.
74 Ibid., 16 December 2002; *International Herald Tribune*, 13 December 2002.
75 *The Economist*, 8 September 2001.
76 Ibid.
77 *The Times*, 23 July 2001.
78 M. Douglas and C. Isherwood, *The World of Goods*, Allen Lane, London, 1979; A. Appadurai (ed.), *The Social Life of Things: Commodities and the Politics of Value*, Cambridge University Press, Cambridge, 1986; D. Miller, *Material Culture and Mass Consumption*, Basil Blackwell, Oxford, 1987/1994; D. Miller, *Modernity: An Ethnographic Approach*, Berg, Oxford, 1994; D. Miller (ed.), *Acknowledging Consumption*, Routledge, London, 1995.

79   *Sunday Times*, 25 August 2002.
80   Ibid.
81   *Time*, 23 July 2001.
82   Ibid.
83   Ibid.
84   *Global Business*, December 2003.

2 Increasing demand

1   C. Campbell, *The Romantic Ethic and the Spirit of Modern Consumption*, Basil Blackwell, Oxford, 1987.
2   *China's Foreign Trade*, February 2003.
3   Yan Yunxiang, 'The Politics of Consumerism in Chinese Society', in T. White, *China Briefing 2000*, M.E. Sharpe, New York, 2000, p. 186.
4   Linda Chao and Ramon Myers, 'China's Consumer Revolution: the 1990s and beyond', *Journal of Contemporary China*, Vol. 7, No. 18, 1998, p. 360.
5   Douglas and Isherwood, op. cit.
6   Chao and Myers, op. cit., pp. 353–4.
7   Ibid., p. 353.
8   Ibid., pp. 353–4.
9   *The Economist*, 12 October 1996.
10   Wu Yanrui, *China's Consumer Revolution: The Emerging Patterns of Wealth and Expenditure*, Edward Elgar, Cheltenham, 1999, p. 26.
11   E.P. Lozada, 'Globalised Childhood? Kentucky Fried Chicken in Beijing', in Jun Jing (ed.) *Feeding China's Little Emperors*, Stanford University Press, Stanford, CA, 2000, p. 117.
12   Ibid.
13   Yan Yunxiang, 'Of Hamburger and Social Space', in D. Davis (ed.), *The Consumer Revolution in Urban China*, University of California Press, Berkeley, CA, 2000, p. 205.
14   Ibid; *Business Beijing*, August 1998.
15   Chao and Myers, op. cit., pp. 355–6.
16   Ibid., p. 355.
17   Wu Yanrui, op. cit., p. 13.
18   Chao and Myers, op. cit., p. 358.
19   Wu Yanrui, op. cit., p. 14.
20   Chao and Myers, op. cit., p. 358.
21   R. Burgess, Zhu Liwei and Ran Yuan, *Chinese Urban Household Expenditure Analysis 1986–1990*, STICERD, London School of Economics, London, 1996.
22   Wu Yanrui, op. cit., p. 82.
23   Ibid.
24   Davis (ed.), 2000, op. cit., p. 4.
25   Ibid.
26   Ibid.
27   *Independent*, 31 December 1995.
28   Davis (ed.), 2000, op. cit., p. 4.
29   Lu Hanlong, 'To be Relatively Comfortable in an Egalitarian Society', in Davis (ed.), 2000, op. cit., p. 134.
30   Wu Yanrui, op. cit., pp. 82–3.
31   Lu Janlong, op. cit., p. 137.
32   *The Times*, 7 March 1998.
33   *Beijing Scene*, 21 September 1996; Catherine Meek, 'Consumption to Consumerism', MA Thesis, SOAS, University of London, 1993.
34   Ying Hong, 'The Pleasures of Shopping', *Women of China*, Beijing, 1 August 1993, p. 36.

35 Ibid.
36 B. Schmitt, 'Who is the Chinese Consumer?' Speech, China–Europe International Business School (CEIBS), Shanghai, 4 October 1996.
37 T. Ambler and M. Witzel, *Doing Business in China*, Routledge, London, 2000, p. 135.
38 Ying Hong, op. cit.
39 Schmitt, op. cit.
40 Ibid.
41 Ambler and Witzel, op. cit., p. 128.
42 Schmitt, op. cit.
43 *The Economist*, 10 August 1996.
44 Schmitt, op. cit.
45 Lu Hanlong, op. cit., p. 134.
46 Li Xiuqin, 'A View of Beijingers' Shopping', *Business Beijing*, 1 November 1995.
47 D. Rice, *The Dragon's Brood: Conversations with Young Chinese*, Harper Collins, London, 1992, pp. 88–9.
48 Li Xiaojiang, 'Gaige yu Zhongguo Nuxing qunti yishi de juexing' (Economic Reform and the Awakening of Women's Consciousness) in Shehui Kexue Zhenxian (Social Science Battleground), 4, 1998, pp. 300–10. Translated in C. Gilmartin, G. Herschatter, L. Rofel and T. White, *Engendering Women: Women, Culture and the State*, Harvard University Press, Cambridge, MA, 1994, pp. 360–82.
49 Schmitt, op. cit.
50 Rice, op. cit., p. 116.
51 Ibid., pp. 83–112, 158–82.
52 Chen Xiaomei, Occidentalism as Counterdiscourse: Heshang in Post-Mao China, *Critical Enquiry*, No. 18, Summer 1992, pp. 686–712.
53 Mayfair Yang, *Gifts, Favours and Banquets: The Art of Social Relationships in China*, Cornell University Press, Ithaca, NY, 1994; Yan Yunxiang, *The Flow of Gifts: Reciprocity and Social Networks in a Chinese Village*, Stanford University Press, Stanford, CA, 1996.
54 *The Economist*, 2 August 1997.
55 Studwell, op. cit., p. 132.
56 Wu Yanrui, op. cit., p. 85.
57 Ibid., p. 81.
58 Ibid., p. 83.
59 Ibid.
60 Ibid., p. 81.
61 Ibid., p. 83.
62 Davis (ed.), 2000, op. cit., p. 18.
63 *The Economist*, 9 March 1996.

3 Weakening demand

1 *China's Foreign Trade*, February 2003.
2 Davis (ed.), 2000, op. cit., p. 8.
3 *Transitions* (World Bank, Washington, DC), May–June 2002.
4 *Independent* (London), 31 December 1995.
5 *Newsweek*, 1 December 1997.
6 *Independent*, 31 December 1995.
7 *The Economist*, 8 June 1996.
8 Ibid., 28 September 1996.
9 *Far Eastern Economic Review*, 26 November 1998.
10 Ibid.
11 Ibid.
12 Ibid.

13 Ibid.
14 Ibid.
15 Ibid.
16 *China Daily*, 3 January 1999.
17 Lu Hanlong, op. cit., p. 137.
18 *Far Eastern Economic Review*, 14 October 1999.
19 *Independent*, 31 December 1995.
20 *Far Eastern Economic Review*, 26 November 1998.
21 Ibid.
22 Studwell, op. cit., p. 155.
23 *Independent*, 31 December 1995.
24 *Far Eastern Economic Review*, 26 November 1998.
25 *China Daily*, 10–16 December 1995.
26 *The Economist*, 28 September 1996.
27 *Newsweek*, 1 December 1997; *Sunday Times*, 3 October 1999; *China Daily*, 14 September 2000.
28 *Independent*, 25 January 1998.
29 *China Daily*, 30 October 1992.
30 *The Economist*, 2 January 1999.
31 Ibid.
32 Ibid.
33 *China Daily*, 30 October 1992.
34 *The Economist*, 2 January 1999.
35 Ying Hong, op. cit.
36 *The Economist*, 25 January 1997, 19 June 1999.
37 *Independent*, 28 November 1998.
38 Ibid.
39 *The Economist*, 25 January 1997.
40 *Independent on Sunday*, 25 January 1998.
41 *Time*, 30 June 1997.
42 *Independent on Sunday*, 25 January 1998.
43 Ambler and Witzel, op. cit., p. 131.
44 *Independent on Sunday*, 25 January 1998.
45 Ibid.
46 Ibid.
47 *Around Beijing*, 1 January 1999.
48 Ambler and Witzel, op. cit., p. 142.
49 *The Economist*, 28 September 1996; Studwell, op. cit., pp. 91, 155.
50 Ibid., pp. 127, 155, 224.
51 *The Economist*, 28 September 1996.
52 *Time*, 30 June 1997.
53 *Far Eastern Economic Review*, 26 November 1998.
54 Ibid.
55 *The Economist*, 25 September 1999.
56 *Around Beijing*, 1 January 1999.
57 *China Daily*, 24 November 1997.
58 Ibid., 7 January 1999.
59 *The Economist*, 25 January 1997.
60 *Business Weekly* (Beijing), 10–16 December 1995; Davis (ed.), 2000, op. cit., p. 2.
61 *Far Eastern Economic Review*, 14 October 1999.
62 Studwell, op. cit., p. 276.
63 *The Economist*, 28 March 1998.
64 *Far Eastern Economic Review*, 26 November 1998.
65 *The Economist*, 24 October 1998.

66 *Sunday Times*, 3 October 1999.
67 Ambler and Witzel, op. cit., p. 54.
68 *The Economist*, 28 September 1996.
69 *Far Eastern Economic Review*, 26 November 1998.
70 *The Economist*, 24 October 1998.
71 Ibid., 2 June 1998.
72 *China Daily*, 10–16 December 1995.
73 *The Economist*, 12 October 1996.
74 *China Daily*, 10–16 December 1995.
75 Davis (ed.), 2000, op. cit., pp. 6, 26.
76 *The Economist*, 2 January 1999.
77 Ibid., 25 September 2005.
78 Chao and Myers, op. cit., p. 354.
79 *The Economist*, 24 October 1998.
80 *Far Eastern Economic Review*, 26 November 1998.
81 Ibid.
82 *Business World*, 3 December 2001.
83 Teng Ssu-yu and J.K. Fairbank, *China's Response to the West: A Documentary Survey 1839–1923*, Harvard University Press, Cambridge, MA, 1967.
84 Rice, op. cit., p. 116.
85 *The Economist*, 29 April 1995.
86 Ibid., 9 March 1996.
87 Ibid., 25 January 1997.
88 Ibid., 25 September 1999.
89 Ibid., 2 January 1999.
90 Ibid., 25 September 1999.
91 Ambler and Witzel, op. cit., p. 150.
92 Ibid., pp. 151–2.
93 *China Daily*, 6 January 1999.
94 Ibid.
95 Ibid.
96 *Sunday Times*, 15 January 1995.
97 *China Daily*, 6 January 1999.
98 *Sunday Times*, 15 January 1995.
99 Oliver Yeo, *Consumer Behaviour in China: Customer Satisfaction and Cultural Values*, Routledge, London, 1994.
100 Ambler and Witzel, op. cit., pp. 71–3.
101 Ibid., pp. 33–5.
102 *International Herald Tribune*, 25 September 2000.
103 Ibid.
104 Ibid.
105 Ibid.
106 Ibid; *Newsweek*, 7 May 2001.
107 *Far Eastern Economic Review*, 26 November 1998.
108 Ibid.
109 *Far Eastern Economic Review*, 5 October 2000.
110 Ibid.
111 *China Business Review*, May–June 2004.
112 Ibid., 26 November 1998.
113 *The Economist*, 2 August 1997.
114 Ibid., 25 September 1999.
115 Ambler and Witzel, op. cit., pp. 17, 55.

4 Elite lifestyles

1   *China Business Review*, March–April 2003.
2   Chinese Academy of Social Sciences (CASS), *Social Stratification in China, Social Sciences in China* (Beijing), Special Issue, Spring 2002.
3   *The Economist*, 29 April 1995, 2 June 2001.
4   Ibid.
5   *Sunday Times*, 27 September 1998; *Far Eastern Economic Review*, 26 November 1998; *China's Foreign Trade*, February 2003.
6   *The Economist*, 20 March 2004.
7   *China International Business*, April 2003.
8   J. Gamble, 'Consuming passions', *China Review*, Summer 1999, p. 14.
9   *Business Beijing*, November 1995.
10 *China International Business*, April 2003.
11 *Wenhui Bao* (Shanghai), 11 October 1993.
12 *China International Business*, April 2003.
13 *Renmin Ribao* (People's Daily) Beijing, 20 November 2003.
14 *China International Business*, April 2003.
15 Ibid.
16 Ibid.
17 *The Economist*, 20 March 2004.
18 *China International Business*, April 2003.
19 Ibid.
20 Ibid.
21 *The Economist*, 16 August 2003.
22 *China Business Review*, Jan–Feb 2001.
23 *Guardian*, 8 November 2004.
24 *International Herald Tribune*, 29 December 2005.
25 *China International Business*, 1 April 2003.
26 *Newsweek*, 29 June 1998.
27 *The Economist*, 1 January 1999.
28 *Far Eastern Economic Review*, 26 November 1998, 7 October 1999.
29 Ibid., 26 November 1998.
30 Ibid., 7 October 1999.
31 Ibid., 12 December 2002.
32 Ibid., 20 November 2003.
33 Ibid., 7 October 1999.
34 Ibid., 19 October 2000.
35 *The Economist*, 18 April 1998.
36 Ibid.
37 Ibid., 30 September 2000.
38 Ibid.
39 *Far Eastern Economic Review*, 26 November 1998.
40 Ibid., 13 November 2003.
41 Ibid., 7 October 1999.
42 *Newsweek*, 9 October 2000.
43 Ibid; *China Business Review*, July–August 2004.
44 Ibid.
45 Ibid.
46 *Sunday Times*, 30 May 2004.
47 *Newsweek*, 9 October 2000.
48 *The Economist*, 11 October 2003.
49 *Far Eastern Economic Review*, 7 October 1999.
50 *The Economist*, 21 June 1997; *Asahi* (Tokyo), 26 October 2000.

51 *The Economist*, 15 March 2003.
52 *Independent on Sunday*, 16 February 1997.
53 *Beijing This Month*, October 2001.
54 Ibid.
55 *Far Eastern Economic Review*, 26 November 1998.
56 Ibid., 5 October 2000.
57 Ibid., 12 December 2002.
58 Ibid., 13 November 2003, 20 November 2003.
59 *Beijing This Month*, September 2002.
60 *Far Eastern Economic Review*, 7 October 1999.
61 Ibid., 14 October 1999.
62 Ibid., 12 October 2000.
63 Ibid., 13 November 2003, 27 November 2003.
64 *China Business Review*, March–April 2005.
65 *The Economist*, 5 October 2002.
66 Ibid.
67 Ibid.
68 *Far Eastern Economic Review*, 24 June 2004.
69 *International Herald Tribune*, 11 November 2005.
70 *The Times*, 3 September 2005.
71 *Daily Telegraph*, 1 August 2005.
72 *China Daily*, 22 November 1999.
73 *China Business Review*, March–April 2005.
74 *Far Eastern Economic Review*, 12 October 2000.
75 *International Herald Tribune*, 19 January 2005.
76 *Far Eastern Economic Review*, 14 October 1998, 21 October 1998.
77 Ibid.
78 Ibid.
79 *The Economist*, 2 August 2003.
80 *Far Eastern Economic Review*, 14 October 1998.
81 *The Economist*, 22 July 2000.
82 Ibid., 5 October 2000.
83 *Far Eastern Economic Review*, 7 October 1999, 14 October 1999.
84 Ibid., 12 December 2002.
85 *China Business Review*, March–April 2005.
86 *Far Eastern Economic Review*, 7 October 1999.
87 Ibid., 19 October 2000.
88 Ibid., 20 November 2003, 27 November 2003.
89 Ibid., 14 October 1999.
90 Ibid.
91 *China Daily*, 21–7 November 1999.
92 *Business Beijing*, January 1999.
93 *Far Eastern Economic Review*, 12 October 2002, 20 November 2003.
94 Ibid., 7 October 1999, 14 October 1999.
95 Ibid., 19 December 2002.
96 Ibid., 5 October 2000.
97 Ibid., 11 October 2001.
98 Ibid., 27 November 2003.
99 Ibid., 7 October 1999.
100 Ibid., 26 November 1998.
101 Ibid., 7 October 1998.
102 Ibid., 14 October 1999.
103 Ibid., 7 October 1999.
104 Ibid., 12 December 2002.

105 Ibid., 27 November 2003.
106 Ibid., 4 October 2001.
107 Ibid., 5 December 2002.
108 Ibid., 1 April 2004.
109 *International Herald Tribune*, 20–21 June 1998.
110 *The Economist*, 5 October 2002.
111 *Sunday Times*, 18 January 2004.
112 *Financial Times*, 11–12 October 2003.
113 *The Economist*, 19 January 2002.
114 Ibid; *Sunday Times*, 4 June 2000.
115 Sun Liping, 'Re-accumulation of Resources: The Background of Social Stratification in China in the 1990s', *Social Sciences*, Spring 2002, pp. 63–5.
116 Ibid.
117 Ibid., p. 59; *China International Business*, April 2003.
118 Sun Liping, op. cit., p. 64.
119 *China Daily*, 2 September 2002.
120 Sun Liping, op. cit., pp. 63–5.
121 Ibid; *The Economist*, 2 June 2001.
122 Ibid., 25 May 2002.
123 *China Daily*, 2 September 2002.
124 Liu Xin, 'Strata Consciousness in Transformation-Era Urban China', *Social Sciences*, Spring 2002, pp. 81–9.
125 *Time*, 7 September 2005.
126 *The Economist*, 5 March 2005.
127 *China Daily*, 29–30 October 2005.
128 *Financial Times*, 5 February 2003.
129 Ibid., 24 June 2004.
130 *The Economist*, 20 March 2004.
131 *Sunday Times*, 2 November 2003.
132 Ibid.
133 *The Economist*, 26 March 2005.
134 *China's Foreign Trade*, February 2003.
135 *The Economist*, 20 March 2004.
136 Ibid.
137 *Business Beijing*, February 2003.
138 *Newsweek*, 21 June 2004.
139 *The Economist*, 20 March 2004.
140 Ibid., 19 June 2004.
141 Ibid., 20 March 2004.
142 Ibid.
143 *Business Beijing*, February 2003.
144 *The Economist*, 23 April 2005.
145 Ibid.
146 *The Economist*, 4 June 2004.
147 Ibid., 19 June 2004.
148 Ibid.
149 *Sunday Times*, 7 March 2004.
150 *Newsweek*, 21 June 2004.
151 *The Economist*, 20 March 2004.
152 *Renmin Ribao* (People's Daily), 16 August 2004.

5 An urban conundrum

1 *The Economist*, 20 March 2004.
2 Ibid; National Bureau of Statistics Communiqué, *China Quarterly Chronicle*, June 2005, p. 481.
3 *The Economist*, 2 June 2001.
4 Ibid.
5 *Far Eastern Economic Review*, 7 November 2002; Sun Liping, op. cit.
6 *The Economist*, 30 September 2000.
7 Ibid.
8 *Far Eastern Economic Review*, 20 February 2003.
9 *International Herald Tribune*, 31 December 1997.
10 Ibid.
11 *The Economist*, 30 September 2000.
12 *Independent*, 16 June 1998.
13 *Beijing Review*, 3 April 2003.
14 D. Solinger, 'Labour Market Reform and the Plight of the Laid-off Proletariat', *China Quarterly*, June 2002, p. 304.
15 Ibid.
16 Xinhua (New China News Agency), 15 July 2002, 21 July 2002, 13–14 September 2002.
17 *The Times*, 19 March 2002.
18 *International Herald Tribune*, 3 June 1999.
19 *The Economist*, 10 January 2004.
20 Ibid.
21 Ibid.
22 *The Economist*, 8 April 2000.
23 *Time*, 30 June 1997.
24 *International Herald Tribune*, 3–4 April 1999.
25 Solinger, op. cit., p. 321.
26 A. Hussein, 'Living in the City', *China Review*, Spring 2000, p. 11.
27 Solinger, op. cit., p. 321.
28 Ibid., pp. 321–2.
29 *China Daily*, 16 July 1994.
30 Solinger, op. cit., p. 317.
31 Ibid.
32 Xinhua (New China News Agency), 6 April 2002.
33 Solinger, op. cit., pp. 315, 318.
34 *China Daily*, 25 March 1998.
35 Solinger, op. cit., p. 318.
36 *Renmin Ribao* (People's Daily), 29 April 2002; *China Daily*, 21–27 November 1999; *Guardian*, 7 March 2002.
37 Xinhua (New China News Agency), 13 April 2003.
38 *Far Eastern Economic Review*, 7 November 2002.
39 Ibid; Xinhua (New China News Agency), 26 October 2002.
40 *The Economist*, 20 March 2004.
41 Ibid.
42 Ibid.
43 Ibid.
44 *China Daily*, 11 September 2000.
45 *The Economist*, 20 March 2004.
46 Ibid., 1 March 2004.
47 Ibid., 20 March 2004.
48 *China Daily*, 31 December 2005.

49   *The Economist*, 20 March 2004.
50   Ibid.
51   Ibid.
52   *Time*, 30 June 1997.
53   *Independent*, 18 December 1998.
54   *The Economist*, 21 November 1998.
55   Solinger, op. cit., pp. 308–9.
56   Ibid., p. 309.
57   Ibid., pp. 308–9.
58   Ibid., p. 304.
59   *Time*, 30 June 1997.
60   Ibid.
61   Ibid.
62   *Independent*, 23 December 1994.
63   *Sunday Times*, 19 October 1997.
64   *The Times*, 30 June 1997.
65   *Sunday Times*, 19 October 1997.
66   Ibid.
67   *International Herald Tribune*, 7 April 2000.
68   A. Kernen, 'State Employees Face an Uncertain Future: the predicament in Northeastern China', unpublished ms., p. 2.
69   Ibid.
70   *The Times*, 6 June 2001.
71   *Far Eastern Economic Review*, 10 June 2004.
72   *Time*, 30 June 1997.
73   *Far Eastern Economic Review*, 9 January 2003.
74   *The Economist*, 11 October 2003.
75   *Guardian*, 12 November 2004.
76   *The Economist*, 20 March 2004.
77   *Observer*, 20 March 2005.
78   *The Economist*, 30 September 2000.
79   *China Economic Review*, June 2002.
80   *The Economist*, 20 March 2004.
81   Ibid.
82   *China Daily*, 29 December 2005.
83   *China Economic Review*, June 2002.
84   Ibid.
85   Ibid.
86   Xinhua (New China News Agency), 19 November 2003.
87   *Renmin Ribao* (People's Daily), 26 July 2003.
88   Hussein, op. cit., p. 9.
89   *Independent*, 23 December 1994; *The Economist*, 2 June 2001.
90   *Renmin Ribao* (People's Daily), 20 October 2002; *Far Eastern Economic Review*, 7 November 2002.
91   *Renmin Ribao* (People's Daily), 20 October 2002.
92   Xinhua (New China News Agency), 7 September 2004.
93   *The Economist*, 20 March 2004,
94   *Independent*, 23 December 1994.
95   *Far Eastern Economic Review*, 7 October 1999.
96   *Time*, 30 June 1997.
97   *Independent*, 23 December 1994.
98   *Far Eastern Economic Review*, 7 October 1999.
99   *Financial Times*, 16 December 2003.
100 Xinhua (New China News Agency), 13 January 2003.

101 *International Herald Tribune*, 6–7 December 2003.
102 *Far Eastern Economic Review*, 7 November 2002.
103 Ibid., 9 January 2003.
104 World Agenda (BBC), April–May 2005.
105 *Daily Mail*, 13 April 2005.
106 *The Economist*, 5 March 2005.
107 *The Times*, 14 May 2005.
108 *Renmin Ribao* (People's Daily), 20 October 2002.
109 *Far Eastern Economic Review*, 7 November 2002.
110 Xinhua (New China News Agency), 23 November 2004.
111 *China Daily*, 1 July 2005.
112 Ibid., 29 June 2005.
113 *Hong Kong Standard*, 7 July 2004.
114 Ibid.
115 *Business Beijing*, February 2003.
116 D. Davin, *Internal Migration in Contemporary China*, Macmillan, London, 1998.
117 Xinhua (New China News Agency), 31 May 2004.
118 *Guardian*, 9 November 2004.
119 *International Herald Tribune*, 3 June 1999.
120 *China Daily*, 10 June 2000.
121 K.E. Broldsgaard, 'Institutional Reform and the Bianzhi System in China', *China Quarterly*, June 2002, pp. 362–5.
122 Ibid., p. 365.
123 *Beijing Review*, 3 April 2003.
124 Broldsgaard, op. cit., p. 385.
125 Ibid, p. 386; *Beijing Review*, 3 April 2003.
126 *The Economist*, 21 June 2003.
127 Xinhua (New China News Agency), 4 September 2004, 6 January 2005, 22 February 2005.
128 *The Economist*, 21 June 2003.
129 Ibid.
130 Ibid., 14 August 1999.
131 Ibid., 22 April 2000, 28 August 2001.
132 *China Business Review*, May–June 2004.
133 *The Economist*, 20 March 2004.

6 A rural impasse

1 *Beijing Review*, 20 February 2003.
2 Ibid.
3 Jiang Wenran 'Prosperity Based on Prosperity and Disparity', *China Review*, Spring 2004, p. 4; *The Times*, 6 March 2004.
4 *China News Bulletin*, 9 February 1998.
5 *Far Eastern Economic Review*, 1 April 2004.
6 Mei Zhang, 'Down on the Farm: The Problems of China's Rural Population', *East Asia@Sheffield*, May 2004, Issue No. 8, p. 13.
7 Chow and Myers, op. cit., pp. 353–5.
8 Ibid., p. 353.
9 *China Quarterly Chronicle*, June 2003, p. 587.
10 Ibid., March 2003, p. 270; *The Economist*, 27 September 2003.
11 *China Reform Daily*, 6 January 2000.
12 Zhang Wanli, 'Twenty Years of Research on Stratified Social Strata in Contemporary China', *Social Sciences in China*, Spring 2002, p. 52; Sun Liping, op. cit., p. 59.

13 *The Economist*, 16 January 1998.
14 Ibid., 4 May 2000.
15 *Yearbook of China*, State Statistics Bureau, Beijing 2001.
16 *Far Eastern Economic Review*, 10 June 2004.
17 National Bureau of Statistics Communiqué, 28 February 2003, *China Quarterly Chronicle*, June 2003, p. 587.
18 *China Business Review*, March–April 2003.
19 *Far Eastern Economic Review*, 10 June 2004.
20 *Hong Kong Economic Journal*, 6 December 2002.
21 *Beijing Review*, 20 February 2003.
22 Sun Liping, op. cit., p. 64.
23 *Business Weekly*, 18–24 February 2003.
24 *Far Eastern Economic Review*, 1 April 2004.
25 B. Robertson, 'China: Selling Out the Family Farm', *Far Eastern Economic Review*, July 2005, p. 49.
26 *The Economist*, 25 June 2005.
27 Ibid., 26 September 1998.
28 Xinhua (New China News Agency), 6 June 2002.
29 Ibid.
30 *Asiaweek*, 13 October 2000.
31 Ibid.
32 *The Economist*, 19 June 2004.
33 Xinhua (New China News Agency), 6 June 2002.
34 *China Daily*, 4 September 2002.
35 *The Economist*, 16 November 1996.
36 Ibid., 21 July 2001.
37 Ibid., 5 October 2002.
38 Ibid., 22 February 2003.
39 National Bureau of Statistics Communiqué 2004, *China Quarterly Chronicle*, June 2005, p. 489.
40 *Shanghai Daily*, 29 December 2005.
41 *The Economist*, 16 November 1996.
42 Lu Xueyi, 'China's Modernization Process: Urbanisation of Rural Areas', *Social Sciences in China*, Spring 2002, pp. 110–11; *The Economist*, 29 December 2005.
43 A. Saich, 'China Party/State and Societal Relations in Transition', Paper presented at Conference on China in Transition, Utah, 11–13 September 1998.
44 *China Daily*, 13 December 1999; *The Economist*, 27 September 2003.
45 *The Economist*, 9 April 2005.
46 *Newsweek*, 29 June 1998.
47 *China Daily*, 12 June 2000.
48 *The Economist*, 8 April 2000.
49 Xinhua (New China News Agency), 7 October 2002.
50 Ibid., 6 October 2002.
51 *China Daily*, 1 July 2005.
52 Xinhua (New China News Agency), 2 October 2002, 13 January 2003.
53 Ibid.
54 *China Business Review*, May–June 2004.
55 Ibid.
56 Xinhua (New China News Agency), 17 April 2002.
57 Ibid.
58 Jiang Wenran, op. cit., p. 13.
59 *Business Weekly*, 18–24 February 2003.
60 Jiang Wenran, op. cit., p. 13.
61 *The Economist*, 15 December 2001.

62 *Hong Kong Economic Journal*, 6 December 2002.
63 *The Economist*, 22 February 2003.
64 *China Perspectives*, No. 3, January–February 1996.
65 *Newsweek*, 1 February 1999.
66 Ibid.
67 *China Quarterly Chronicle*, March 2003, p. 270.
68 *China Business Review*, March–April 2003.
69 Yan Yunxiang, *Private Life Under Socialism*, Stanford University Press, Stanford, CA, 2005, p. 126.
70 *Guardian*, 10 May 2005.
71 *Far Eastern Economic Review*, 20 February 2003.
72 *The Times*, 6 March 2004.
73 *Far Eastern Economic Review*, 15 July 2004.
74 Ibid., 29 November 2001.
75 *The Economist*, 24 July 2004.
76 Ibid.
77 *Financial Times*, 30 September 2003.
78 Ibid.
79 *Newsweek*, 26 December 2005.
80 *Far Eastern Economic Review*, 4 May 2000; *The Economist*, 23 December 2000.
81 *China Business Review*, March–April 2004.
82 Ibid.
83 *The Economist*, 23 December 2000.
84 *Far Eastern Economic Review*, 4 May 2000.
85 *Renmin Ribao* (People's Daily), 13 March 2005; Xinhua (New China News Agency), 29 April 2005.
86 *Far Eastern Economic Review*, 29 April 2004.
87 Ibid.
88 Ibid
89 *China Business Review*, May–June 2004.
90 *Newsweek*, 1 February 1999.
91 *The Economist*, 29 September 2001.
92 Ibid.
93 *China Daily*, 12 July 2004.
94 Ibid., 5 September 2002.
95 Ibid.
96 Ibid.
97 *Business Weekly*, 18–24 February 2003.
98 *South China Morning Post*, 17 November 2004.
99 *China Daily*, 6 September 2001.
100 *Far Eastern Economic Review*, 1 April 2004.
101 Ibid.
102 *The Economist*, 26 February 2005.
103 *Renmin Ribao* (People's Daily), 6 December 2002.
104 *Far Eastern Economic Review*, 1 April 2004.
105 Ibid., 29 November 2004.
106 *Time*, 8 December 2003.
107 Jiang Wenran, op. cit., pp. 12–14.
108 Ibid., p. 13.
109 Cao Jinqing, *China Along the Yellow River: Reflections on Rural Society*, RoutledgeCurzon, London, 2005; D. Davin, 'Corruption Sows Bitter Seeds in Countryside', *Times Higher Education Supplement*, 3 June 2005.
110 Xin Dongwang, Villagers' Biographies: Oil Painting Collection, Shanghai Art Museum, 29 December–10 January 2006.

111 *China Quarterly Chronicle*, March 2004, p. 257, June 2004, p. 495, June 2005, p. 575.
112 Ibid., March 2003, p. 275.
113 *Far Eastern Economic Review*, 1 April 2004.
114 *Hong Kong Economic Journal*, 6 December 2002 in *China Quarterly Chronicle*, March 2003, p. 269.
115 Ibid.
116 *Far Eastern Economic Review*, 29 November 2001.
117 Lu Xueyi, op. cit., pp. 110–11.
118 *China Quarterly Chronicle*, June 2003, p. 589.
119 Ibid.
120 Ibid.
121 Ibid.
122 *Far Eastern Economic Review*, 1 April 2004.
123 Ibid., 27 February 2003.
124 Ibid.
125 Ibid.
126 Ibid.
127 Xinhua (New China News Agency), 7 April 2004.
128 *Renmin Ribao* (People's Daily), 6 December 2002.

7 Children first

1 K. Chan and J.U. McNeal, *Advertising to Children in China*, Chinese University Press, Hong Kong, 2004, p. 19.
2 Interview with James Chadwick quoted in Bernadine W.L. Chee, 'Eating Snacks and Biting Pressure: Only Children in Beijing' in Jun Jing (ed.), op. cit., p. 68.
3 Jun Jing, 'Food, Children and Social Change' in Jun Jing (ed.), op. cit., p. 1.
4 *China International Business*, September 2002, p. 16.
5 *Far Eastern Economic Review*, 26 November 1998; Jun Jing, op. cit., p. 18.
6 *Far Eastern Economic Review*, 26 November 1998.
7 Elisabeth Croll, 'Production versus Reproduction: A Threat to China's Development Strategies', *World Development*, Vol. 11, No. 6, 1983, pp. 467–81.
8 Xinhua (New China News Agency), 31 August 2002.
9 *The Economist*, 18 December 2004.
10 Ibid., 5 March 2005.
11 Chan and McNeal, op. cit., p. 98.
12 Jun Jing, op. cit., p. 2.
13 C. Milwertz, *Accepting Population Control: Urban Chinese Women and One-child Family Policy*, RoutledgeCurzon, London, 1997, pp. 121–49.
14 *China Daily*, 20 November 1999.
15 Chan and McNeal, op. cit., p. 8.
16 Chee, op. cit., p. 60.
17 Elisabeth Croll, 'A Study of Reproductive Management in East and Southeast Asia', *Asia-Pacific Population Journal*, June 2002, p. 16; *The Economist*, 5 March 2005.
18 D. Davis (ed.), op. cit., p. 19; D. Davis and J. Sensenbrenner, 'Commercialising childhood: Parental Purchases for Shanghai's Only Child', in Davis (ed.), 2000, op. cit., p. 76.
19 Zhao Bin and G. Murdock, 'Young Pioneers: Children and the Making of Chinese Consumerism', *Cultural Studies*, Vol. 10, No. 2, 1996, p. 206.
20 Jun Jing, op. cit., pp. 5–6.
21 Milwertz, op. cit., p. 196.
22 Davis and Sensenbrenner, op. cit., p. 59.
23 *Far Eastern Economic Review*, 26 November 1998.

24 *China International Business*, September 2002, p. 17.
25 *China Today*, 1 March 2003.
26 Chan and McNeal, op. cit., p. 140.
27 *Far Eastern Economic Review*, 26 November 1998.
28 S.K. Gottschang, 'A Baby-Friendly Hospital and the Science of Infant Feeding', in Jun Jing (ed.), op. cit., p. 161.
29 *Far Eastern Economic Review*, 26 November 1998.
30 Gottschang, op. cit., p. 179.
31 Ibid., p. 181.
32 Yuan Yuan, 'Chinese Baby, Foreign Food?, *China International Business*, September 2002, p. 12.
33 Ibid., pp. 12–13.
34 Ibid., p. 13.
35 *China International Business*, September 2002, p. 17.
36 Jun Jing, op. cit., pp. 18–9; *Business Weekly*, 1–4 April 2003.
37 Yuan Yuan, op. cit., p. 12.
38 Ibid.
39 M.B. Gillette, 'Chilidren's Food and Islamic Dietary Restrictions', in Jun Jing (ed.), op. cit., p. 73.
40 Lozada, op. cit., p. 130.
41 G.S. Guldan, 'Paradoxes of Plenty: China's Infant and Child Feeding Transition', Jun Jing (ed.), op. cit., pp. 37–8.
42 Ibid., p. 41.
43 *Sunday Times*, 3 August 1997.
44 Ibid.
45 *Far Eastern Economic Review*, 26 November 1998.
46 Ibid., 4 December 2003.
47 Ibid.
48 Ibid., 26 November 1998.
49 Davis and Sensenbrenner, op. cit., p. 67.
50 *Far Eastern Economic Review*, 4 December 2003.
51 Ibid., 26 November 1998.
52 Ibid., 4 December 2003.
53 Ibid.
54 Ibid.
55 Ibid.
56 *Guardian*, 8 November 2004.
57 Ibid., 20 October 2004.
58 Davis and Sensenbrenner, op. cit., pp. 71–2.
59 Ibid., p. 69.
60 Zhao and Murdock, op. cit., pp. 203, 210, 214.
61 Davis and Sensenbrenner, op. cit., p. 68.
62 *China Daily*, 18 June 2005; *Asian Wall Street Journal*, 17–19 June 2005.
63 Xiao Hong, 'Children's Books at War', *China International Business*, September 2002, p. 8.
64 Ibid.
65 Ibid.
66 Li Heng, 'Large Returns on Young Readers', *China International Business*, September 2002, p. 20.
67 Xiao Hong, op. cit., p. 19.
68 Ibid.
69 Li Heng, op. cit., p. 20.
70 Ibid., p. 21.
71 Ibid.

72 *China Daily*, 29 June 2005.
73 Ibid.
74 Ibid.
75 *International Herald Tribune*, 29 December 2005.
76 *The Economist*, 20 August 2005; *Sunday Times*, 21 August 2005.
77 *Far Eastern Economic Review*, 26 November 1998.
78 *Asia Tomorrow*, December 2004.
79 Ibid.
80 Zhao and Murdock, op. cit., p. 206.
81 *China International Business*, September 2002, p. 16.
82 Chen Weixian, op. cit., p. 22.
83 *Beijing Today*, 6 September 2002.
84 *China Today*, 1 March 2003.
85 *The Economist*, 24 September 2005.
86 World Agenda (BBC), April–May 2005.
87 *Beijing Review*, 25 June 2003.
88 *China Today*, 1 April 2003.
89 *Beijing Today*, 25 June 2003.
90 *China Tomorrow*, December 2004.
91 *China Quarterly Chronicle*, June 2004, p. 550.
92 *Times Higher Education Supplement*, 1 April 2005.
93 *21st Century*, Beijing, 5 September 2002.
94 Ibid.
95 Ibid.
96 *China Today*, 1 April 2003.
97 *Asia Tomorrow*, December 2004.
98 Ibid.
99 Chen Weixian, 'Education Goldrush', *China International Business*, September 2002, p. 22.
100 Ibid.
101 Ibid.
102 *Beijing Today*, 6 September 2002.
103 Ibid.
104 *The Economist*, 10 July 2005.
105 Peng Xizhe, 'Education in China', in Peng Xizhe (ed.), *The Changing Population of China*, Blackwell, Oxford, 2000, p. 124; *Times Higher Education Supplement*, 18 March 2005.
106 Committee of University Chairmen, Newsletter, UK, April 2003.
107 *21st Century*, Beijing, 5 September 2002.
108 Ibid.
109 *Times Higher Education Supplement*, 18 March 2005.
110 Ibid.
111 Chen Weixian, op. cit., p. 22.
112 Ibid.
113 *Far Eastern Economic Review*, 22 April 2004.
114 Ibid.
115 Ibid.
116 Ibid.
117 Peng Xizhe, op. cit., p. 123.
118 Chen Weixian, op. cit., p. 22.
119 Ibid., p. 23.
120 Ibid., p. 22.
121 Ibid., p. 23.
122 *Far Eastern Economic Review*, 1 October 1998.
123 *The Economist*, 29 March 2003.

124 *Sunday Times*, 2 September 2001.
125 *The Economist*, 29 March 2003.
126 Ibid.
127 *Far Eastern Economic Review*, 1 October 1998.
128 *China Daily*, 11 October 2001.
129 Peng Xizhe, op. cit., p. 125.
130 *Newsweek*, Special Issue 2003, p. 74.
131 Committee of University Chairmen, op. cit.
132 *The Economist*, 29 March 2003.
133 Committee of University Chairmen, op. cit.
134 *Times Higher Education Supplement*, 14 October 2005, 21 October 2005.
135 Guo Yuhua, 'Food and Family Relations: The Generation Gap at the Table', in Jun Jing (ed.), op. cit., p. 109.
136 Jun Jing, op. cit., p. 6.
137 *Beijing Lifestyle*, 13 March 1998.
138 Guo Yuhua, op. cit., p. 110.
139 Chan and McNeal, op. cit., pp. 9–11.
140 Ibid., p. 28.
141 *China Daily*, 29 June 2005.
142 Chan and McNeal, p. 31.
143 Chee, op. cit., p. 53.
144 Ibid., pp. 54–5.
145 Chan and McNeal, op. cit., p. 3.
146 Davis and Sensenbrenner, op. cit., p. 68.
147 Chan and McNeal, op. cit., p. 3.
148 Jun Jing, op. cit., p. 6.
149 Yan Yunxiang (2000), op. cit., pp. 212, 217.
150 Chan and McNeal, op. cit., pp. 6–7.
151 J. McNeal and Yeh Chyon-Hwa, 'Development of Consumer Behaviour Patterns Among Chinese Children', *Journal of Consumer Marketing*, Vol. 14, No. 1, 1997 (quoted in Chee, op. cit., p. 68).
152 J.L. Watson, 'Food as Lens: The Past, Present and Future Family Life in China', in Jun Jing (ed.), op. cit., p. 210.
153 *China Daily*, 13 June 2000.
154 Jun Jing, op. cit., p. 6.
155 Milwertz, op. cit., pp. 136–7.
156 S. Heins Potter and J. Potter, *China's Peasants*, Cambridge University Press, Cambridge, 1990, pp. 228–9.
157 Chee, op. cit., p. 60.
158 Ibid., p. 64.
159 Juliet Schor, *Born to Buy: The Commercialised Child and the New Consumer Culture*, Scribner, New York, NY, 2004.
160 Xinhua (New China News Agency), 10 October 2004.
161 *Sunday Times*, 3 August 1997.
162 *Asian Wall Street Journal*, 3–4 March 2000.
163 *Guardian*, 9 November 2004.
164 Ibid.
165 Ibid.
166 Ibid.
167 *China Daily*, 13 June 2000.
168 P. Aries, *Centuries of Childhood: A Social History of Family Life*, Vintage Press, New York, NY, 1962.
169 Davis and Sensenbrenner, op. cit., p. 72.
170 Chee, op. cit., p. 53.
171 Yan Yunxiang (2000), op. cit., p. 223.

8 Chasing youthful dreams

1 *International Herald Tribune*, 25 June 2004.
2 *Asiaweek*, 24 November 2000.
3 Ibid.
4 *Guardian*, 12 November 2004.
5 *Beijing This Month*, Issue no. 24, nd.
6 *Guardian*, 12 November 2004.
7 *Beijing This Month*, Issue no. 24, nd.
8 Ibid.
9 *Guardian*, 12 November 2004.
10 *Asiaweek*, 24 November 2000.
11 *Newsweek*, 16 July 2001.
12 *Independent*, 18 June 1997.
13 *Newsweek*, 16 July 2001.
14 *China Business Review*, July–August 2004.
15 *The Economist*, 14 February 2004.
16 *International Herald Tribune*, 25 June 2004.
17 *China Business Review*, July–August 2004.
18 *China Daily*, 11 October 2001.
19 Ibid.
20 *The Economist*, 12 June 2004.
21 *Beijing This Month*, Issue No. 24, nd.
22 Ibid.
23 *The Economist*, 3 September 2005.
24 J. Unger, 'Urban Families in the Eighties: An Analysis of Chinese Surveys', in D. Davis and S. Harrell (eds), *Chinese Families in the Post-Mao Era*, University of California Press, Berkeley, CA, 1993, p. 43; J.C.B. Leung, 'Family Support and Community-Based Services in China' , in I. Chi, N. Campbell and J. Lubber (eds), *Elderly Chinese in Pacific Rim Countries: Social Support and Integration*, Hong Kong University Press,, Hong Kong, 2001, p. 176; P. Kwong and Cai Guoxuan, 'Ageing in China: Trends, Problems and Strategies', in D. Phillips (ed.), *Ageing in East and Southeast Asia*, Edward Arnold, London, 1992, pp. 118–19.
25 Huang Zhijian, 'Lifestyles and Future Trends of China's Youth', *China Mail*, Vol. 8, No. 4, 1995, pp. 37–41.
26 Ibid.
27 *China Daily*, 11 October 2001.
28 Ibid.
29 Ibid.
30 *China Business Review*, July–August 2004.
31 *The Economist*, 14 February 2004.
32 Ibid.
33 Ibid.
34 Ibid.
35 *China Business Review*, November–December 2005.
36 *The Economist*, 5 March 2005.
37 Martin King Whyte, 'The Fate of Filial Obligations in Urban China', *China Journal*, No.38, July 1997, pp. 3–31; Martin King Whyte (ed.), *China's Revolutions and Inter-generational Relations*, Centre for Asian Studies, University of Michigan, Ann Arbor, MI, 2003.
38 Yan Yunxiang, 'Rural Youth and Youth Culture in North China', *Culture, Medicine and Psychiatry*, No. 23, 1999, pp. 77–97.
39 Yan Yunxiang, op. cit. (2003), p. 225.
40 Ibid., p. 226.

41 Yan Yunxiang (1999), op. cit., p. 82.
42 *Asia Tomorrow*, June 2005.
43 *The Economist*, 21 February 1998; ibid., 30 October 1999; Schmitt, op. cit.
44 *The Economist*, 21 February 1998; *Sunday Times*, 9 September 2001; *The Economist*, 22 December 2002.
45 Ibid., 21 February 1998.
46 *Sunday Times*, 9 September 2001.
47 *The Economist*, 21 February 1998.
48 *Newsweek*, 29 June 1998; *The Economist*, 22 December 2001.
49 Liu Xinwu, 'Fashionable Summer Yellow', in *One-Minute Stories*, Panda Books, Beijing, 1992, p. 30.
50 *International Herald Tribune*, 10 December 1999.
51 E. Honig and G. Hershatter, *Personal Voices: Chinese Women in the 1980*, Stanford University Press, Stanford, CA, 1988, p. 43.
52 *Time*, 17 September 2005; *Observer*, 18 September 2005.
53 *Newsweek*, 29 June 1998.
54 *Observer*, 4 December 2005.
55 *Time*, 7 May 2001.
56 *China Today*, 1 August 2002.
57 B. Hooper, 'Women, Consumerism and the State in Post-Mao China', *Asian Studies Review*, April 1994, pp. 74–5.
58 *Far Eastern Economic Review*, 26 November 1998.
59 Ibid.
60 *The Times*, 30 October 1999.
61 Ibid.
62 Ibid.
63 Ibid.
64 *The Times*, 20 September 2003.
65 Ibid.
66 *China Daily*, 11–17 June 2000.
67 Ibid.
68 *China Daily*, 13 December 1999.
69 Ibid.
70 *Financial Times*, 2 September 2004.
71 *Business Beijing*, 1 January 1999; *China Daily*, 21–27 November 1999.
72 *Daily Telegraph*, 5 August 2005.
73 *International Herald Tribune*, 10 December 1999.
74 *City Edition* (Beijing), 24 September–14 October 1999.
75 Ibid.
76 Ibid.
77 Ibid.
78 *Time*, 7 May 2001.
79 *Guardian*, 11 November 2004.
80 Ibid.
81 *The Times*, 14 October 2004.
82 *Strait Times* (Singapore), 25 May 2004.
83 Ibid.
84 Yan Yunxiang (1999), op. cit., pp. 78–83.
85 *China Daily*, 25 July 2005.
86 *Guardian*, 8 November 2004.
87 *Sunday Times*, 3 June 2001.
88 *Guardian*, 11 November 2004.
89 Ibid.
90 *Sunday Times*, 6 June 2005.

91 Ibid.
92 *China Today*, 1 August 2002.
93 *Far Eastern Economic Review*, 19 October 2002.
94 N. Baravonitch, *China's New Voices*, University of California Press, Berkeley, CA, 2003, pp. 120–1.
95 Ibid.
96 *China Pictorial*, 1 June 2004.
97 *Newsweek*, 29 June 1998.
98 *International Herald Tribune*, 12 May 2000.
99 *Guardian*, 11 November 2004.
100 *Sunday Times*, 21 August 2005.
101 *China Daily*, 25 July 2005.
102 Ibid.
103 Ibid.
104 Ibid.
105 *Beijing This Month*, no. 24, nd.
106 Baranovitch, op. cit., p. 18.
107 Ibid., p. 39.
108 *City Weekend* (Beijing), 31 August–13 September 2000.
109 Ibid.
110 Coral Lee, 'From Little Teng to A Mei: Marking Time in Music', *Sino-rama* 23(3) 2000, p. 44 (quoted in Baranovitch, op. cit., p. 46).
111 *China Pictorial*, 1 June 2004.
112 *The Economist*, 3 September 2005; *Guardian* 7 October 2005.
113 *City Edition* (Beijing), 29 October–11 November 1999.
114 Ibid.
115 *Newsweek*, 16 July 2001.
116 *Guardian*, 9 November 2004.
117 Ibid.
118 Ibid.
119 Ibid., 12 November 2004.
120 Ibid.
121 *Beijing Scene*, 10–16 December 1999.
122 Ibid.
123 *Newsweek*, 7 June 1999.
124 Ibid.
125 *Guardian*, 11 November 2004.
126 Ibid.
127 Ibid., 29 June 1998.
128 Ibid., 11 November 2004.
129 *Newsweek*, 30 July 2001.
130 Ibid., 29 June 1998.
131 Ibid., 30 July 2001.
132 Ibid., 29 June 1998, 30 July 2001.
133 Ibid.
134 Ibid.
135 Ibid.
136 Ibid., 3 December 2001.
137 Ibid., 7 June 1999.
138 Ibid.
139 *International Herald Tribune*, 12 May 2000; *Sunday Times*, 3 June 2001; *The Economist*, 11 August 2001.
140 *International Herald Tribune*, 12 May 2000.
141 *The Economist*, 11 August 2001.

142 *International Herald Tribune*, 12 May 2000; *Sunday Times*, 3 June 2001.
143 *Newsweek*, 3 December 2001.
144 *China Quarterly Chronicle*, December 2004, p. 1131.
145 Ibid.
146 *Newsweek*, 3 December 2001.
147 Ibid.
148 Ibid.
149 Ibid.
150 *Guardian*, 12 November 2004.
151 Ibid.
152 *Sunday Times*, 5 June 2005.
153 *International Herald Tribune*, 5 June 2001.
154 *The Times*, 15 February 2006.
155 Tom Doctoroff, *Billions: Selling to the New Chinese Consumers*, Palgrave Macmillan, Basingstoke, 2006.
156 *The Times*, 15 February 2006.

9 The greying generations

1 World Bank, *China 2020: Old Age Security*, World Bank, Washington, DC, 1997, p. 14.
2 *The Times*, 9 April 2004.
3 Xinhua (New China News Agency), 6 January 2005, 22 February 2005.
4 Leung, op. cit., p. 172.
5 *The Economist*, 26 February 2005.
6 *Sunday Times*, 16 May 2004.
7 *The Economist*, 10 August 2002.
8 Ibid.
9 *The Times*, 9 April 2004; *The Economist*, 10 August 2004.
9 *The Times*, 9 April 2004.
10 Ibid.
11 Ibid.
12 *The Economist*, 10 August 2002; *The Times*, 9 April 2004; *Sunday Times*, 2 May 2004; ibid., 16 May 2004.
13 *The Times*, 9 April 2004.
14 *The Economist*, 10 August 2004.
15 Ibid.
16 *Sunday Times*, 16 May 2004.
17 *The Times*, 9 April 2004.
18 Ibid.
19 *Sunday Times*, 2 May 2004.
20 *The Economist*, 26 February 2005.
21 Ibid.
22 Yan Hao, 'Still the Family: Old Age Support in a Chinese Village', Paper presented at Conference on Changing Asian Family, Singapore, 24–26 May 2004.
23 *China Daily*, 3 April 1998.
24 World Bank (1997), op. cit., p. 19.
25 *China Daily*, 28 June 2000.
26 World Bank (1997), op. cit., p. 19.
27 *The Economist*, 2 November 2002.
28 Ibid.
29 *China Daily*, 3 April 1998.
30 Leung, op. cit., p. 173.
31 World Bank (1997), op. cit., p. 16.

32 Ibid.
33 G. White and Shang Xiaoyuan, 'Social Security Reforms in Urban China', in G. White and Shang Xiaoyuan, *Issues and Answers: Reforming the Chinese Social Security System*, Institute of Development Studies, University of Sussex, Brighton, 1996, pp. 25–8.
34 W. Hurst and K. O'Brien, 'China's Contentious Pensioners', *China Daily*, June 2002, p. 349.
35 Ibid., p. 353.
36 Zhou Daming, 'On Rural Urbanisation in China' in G.E. Guldin, *Farewell to Peasant China: Rural Urbanisation and Social Change in Late Twentieth Century China*, M.E. Sharpe, Armonk, New York, NY, 1997, p. 17.
37 *The Economist*, 21 November 1998.
38 Hurst and O'Brien, op. cit., p. 348.
39 Wang Feng, Xiao Zhenyu and Zhan Jie, 'Privilege or Punishment? Retirement and Unemployment Among the Chinese Urban Elderly', in Whyte (ed.), op. cit., p. 65.
40 Ibid., p. 80.
41 *Far Eastern Economic Review*, 12 October 2000.
42 *Time*, 30 June 2001.
43 World Bank (1997), op. cit, p. 4.
44 Ibid., pp. 6–9, 40–5.
45 *The Economist*, 22 May 2004.
46 Hurst and O'Brien, op. cit., p. 349.
47 *China Review*, Summer 2000, p. 17.
48 *The Economist*, 22 May 2004.
49 Wang, Xiao and Zhan, op. cit., pp. 61–84.
50 Ibid., p. 65.
51 Ibid., p. 80.
52 Ibid., pp. 75–8.
53 Wang Ningjun, 'Insurance in China', *Women of China*, Beijing, 1 June 1993.
54 Li Wei, 'China's Fewer Births and Greater Prosperity Co-operation', *Women of China*, Beijing, 1 November 1993.
55 Chen Xinxin, 'Marriage and the Family in Rural and Urban China', *China Today*, March 2003, pp. 35–7.
56 Yan Hao, op. cit.
57 *The Economist*, 20 December 2003.
58 Ibid., 26 December 2003.
59 Ibid.
60 *Far Eastern Economic Review*, 4 May 2003.
61 *The Economist*, 20 December 2003.
62 *Far Eastern Economic Review*, 4 May 2003.
63 Ibid.
64 Yan Shenming and Iris Chi, 'Living Arrangements and Adult Children's Support for the Elderly in the New Urban Areas of Mainland China', in Chi, Chappell and Lubben, op. cit., pp. 216–17.
65 Chen Sheying, *Social Policy of the Economic State and Community Care in Chinese Culture*, Avebury, London, 1996.
66 Zhu Yong, 'A Research Report on the Reform of China's Social Welfare System', in G. White and Sheng Xiaoyuan, *Reforms in Chinese Social Assistance and Community Services in Comparative Perspective*, Institute of Development Studies, University of Sussex, Brighton, 1997, p. 26.
67 *Sunday Times*, 15 September 2002.
68 Ibid.
69 Hong Zhang, 'An Alternative to Family Caregiving for the Elderly: The Development of Institutional Care in Urban China', Paper presented at Conference on the Changing Asian Family, National University of Singapore, 24–26 May 2004, p. 2.

70 Ibid.
71 *Sunday Times*, 15 September 2002.
72 *Far Eastern Economic Review*, 12 October 2000.
73 *Independent*, 20 August 2000; *Far Eastern Economic Review*, 12 October 2000.
74 *China Daily*, 28 June 2000.
75 Whyte (1997), op. cit., p. 5.
76 Unger, op. cit., p. 43; P. Kwong and Cai Guoxuan, 'Ageing in China: Trends, Problems and Strategies', in Phillips (ed.), op. cit., p. 118–19; Leung, op. cit., p. 170.
77 Groeling-Che Hui-wen von 'A Trend Towards Individual Arrangements within the Urban Chinese Family in Asia', *The Role of the Individual vis-à-vis the Family, Society and the State in Asia and Europe*, An Asia–Europe Foundation Monograph, Ludwig Boltzman Institute, Vienna 2001, p. 42.
78 Unger, op. cit., pp. 40–2; Whyte (ed.), op. cit., p. 162.
79 Elisabeth Croll, 'New Peasant Family Forms in Rural China', *Journal of Peasant Studies* Vol. 44 (4), July 1987, pp. 469–99.
80 *The Economist*, 5 March 2005.
81 Hurst and O'Brien, op. cit., pp. 352–3.
82 Yan Yunxiang (2003), op. cit., p. 182.
83 Potter and Potter, op. cit., pp. 228–9.
84 Milwertz, op. cit., pp. 136–7.
85 Kwong and Cai, op. cit., p. 121.
86 Whyte (1997), op. cit., p. 7; Leung, op. cit., pp. 175–6.
87 Whyte (1997), op. cit., pp. 8, 11.
88 *The Economist*, 14 February 2004.
89 *Guardian*, 9 November 2004.
90 Whyte (ed.), op. cit., pp. 132, 168–88; Yan (2003), op. cit., pp. 180–1; Leung, op. cit., p. 177.
91 Zhang Lijia, 'China's Grey Peril', *China Review*, Summer 2000, p. 13.
92 Xinhua (New China News Agency), 24–25 October 2003.
93 Kwong and Cai, op. cit., p. 124.
94 *The Economist*, 21 November 1998.
95 *New York Times*, 17 October 2004.
96 *The Economist*, 26 February 2004.
97 *Far Eastern Economic Review*, 26 November 1998.
98 *The Economist*, 26 February 2004.
99 *Far Eastern Economic Review*, 26 November 1998.
100 Ibid.
101 Ibid.
102 *The Economist*, 21 November 1998.
103 Ibid., 26 February 2005.
104 *Far Eastern Economic Review*, 12 October 2000.
105 *The Economist*, 21 November 1998.
106 Kwong and Cai, op. cit., p. 124.
107 *The Economist*, 26 February 2005.
108 Ibid.
109 *Far Eastern Economic Review*, 26 November 1998.
110 Ibid.
111 *Time*, 20 June 2001.

10 Consumer confidence

1 *BusinessWeek* (Beijing), 3 December 2001.
2 *Business Weekly* (Beijing), 18–24 February 2003.

3 *BusinessWeek*, 3 December 2001.
4 Ibid.
5 *Business Weekly*, 20–26 November 2000.
6 Ibid.
7 Ibid.
8 *BusinessWeek*, 3 December 2001.
9 Ibid.
10 *Far Eastern Economic Review*, 4 December 2003.
11 Ibid.
12 Ibid.
13 *The Economist*, 23 April 2005.
14 Ibid., 29 October 2005.
15 Ibid., 14 September 2002.
16 Ibid, 1 August 1998.
17 *China Daily*, 12 September 2000.
18 *The Economist*, 25 May 2002.
19 *China Daily*, 5 January 1999.
20 *Far Eastern Economic Review*, 18 April 2002.
21 Ibid., October–December 1998–2002.
22 *Independent on Sunday*, 23 May 1997.
23 Ibid.
24 Ibid.
25 Ibid.
26 *Time*, 22 June 1998.
27 Ibid.
28 *Newsweek*, 14 December 1998.
29 *The Economist*, 10 January 2004.
30 *The Times*, 27 December 2003.
31 *Time*, 8 October 2003.
32 *The Times*, 27 October 2003.
33 *The Economist*, 2 August 2003.
34 *Asiaweek*, 24 November 2000.
35 *Shanghai Star*, 29 December 2005.
36 *Asiaweek*, 24 November 2000.
37 *Guardian*, 15 April 2005; ibid., 29 July 2005; *The Times*, 21 February 2006; *Guardian*, 22 February 2006.
38 *South China Morning Post*, 29 June 2005; Xinhua (New China News Agency), 14 February 2006.
39 Ibid., 1 July 2005.
40 *BusinessWeek*, 27 October 2003.
41 *The Economist*, 21 August 2004.
42 Ibid.
43 *Far Eastern Economic Review*, 19 December 2002.
44 *The Economist*, 28 May 2005.
45 Ibid., 21 August 2004.
46 *BusinessWeek*, 27 October 2003.
47 *The Economist*, 21 August 2004.
48 Ibid.
49 Ibid.
50 *China Daily*, 29–30 October 2005.
51 Xinhua (New China News Agency), 2 June 2005.
52 *The Economist*, 21 August 2004.
53 Elizabeth Economy, *The River Runs Black*, Cornell University Press, Ithaca, NY, 2004.

54 *Guardian*, 25 November 2005; *The Times*, 26 November 2005; *Observer*, 27 November 2005.
55 *Guardian*, 15 April 2005.
56 *South China Morning Post*, 1 July 2005.
57 *The Economist*, 12 August 2000.
58 *The Times*, 10 December 2005.
59 *Newsweek*, 14 December 1998; *Independent*, 12 November 1998.
60 *Newsweek*, 14 December 1998.
61 Ibid.
62 *The Economist*, 12 August 2000.
63 *Independent*, 12 November 1998.
64 *Newsweek*, 14 December 1998.
65 *Times Higher Education Supplement*, 29 October 2004.
66 *Newsweek*, 14 December 1998.
67 *International Herald Tribune*, 28 December 2005.
68 *Guardian*, 17 June 2005.
69 Ibid., 29 July 2005.
70 Xinhua (New China News Agency), 12 September 2002; *Hong Kong Economic Journal*, 6 December 2002.
71 *The Economist*, 11 September 2004.
72 Ibid.
73 Ibid.
74 Ibid.
75 Ibid.
76 *Gongren Ribao* (Workers' Daily), 8 April 2005.
77 Xinhua (New China News Agency), 17 April 2002.
78 *China Quarterly Chronicle*, September 2002, p. 797.
79 Xinhua (New China News Agency), 4 September 2004.
80 Ibid., 21 July 2002.
81 *China Daily*, 29–30 October 2005.
82 *The Economist*, 12 June 2004.
83 Ibid.
84 *Times Higher Education Supplement*, 15 April 2005.
85 *China Daily*, 25 June 2004.
86 Ibid.
87 *Shanghai Daily* 29 December 2005.
88 Ibid.
89 *Renmin Ribao* (People's Daily), 20 October 2002.
90 *Transitions* (World Bank), May–June 2002.
91 Ibid.
92 *The Economist*, 24 September 2005.
93 *Transitions* (World Bank), May–June 2002.
94 *The Economist*, 26 March 2005.
95 *China Economic Review*, July 2005.
96 *The Economist*, 21 August 2004.
97 Ibid.
98 Ibid.
99 Ibid., 19 November 2005.
100 *China Daily*, 5 August 2005.
101 Xinhua (New China News Agency), 1 July 2005.
102 *The Economist*, 19 November 2005.
103 *Newsweek*, 31 October 2005.
104 *China Business Review*, November–December 2004.
105 *Newsweek*, 31 October 2005; *The Economist*, 19 November 2005.

106 Ibid., 21 August 2004; Xinhua News Agency, 7 July 2005.

107 *China's Foreign Trade*, February 2003.

108 *Times Higher Education Supplement*, 1 April 2005; K. Willmann and Gunter Schucher, 'Facts about and Development in the Rural Education of the PRC', *China Aktuell*, Institut für Asienkunde, Hamburg, May 2005.

109 *China's Foreign Trade*, February 2003.

110 *The Economist* 24 September 2005.

111 Elisabeth Croll, *From Heaven to Earth: Images and Experiences of Development in China*, Routledge, London, 1994, pp. 116–34.

112 *Observer*, 6 November 2005.

113 *Sunday Times*, 4 June 2000; *The Economist*, 18 January 2003; Ibid. 25 September 2005.

114 *Far Eastern Economic Review*, 26 November 1998; 21 October 1999.

115 *The Economist*, 24 September 2005.

116 Ibid.

117 *South China Morning Post*, 29 June 2004.

118 *The Economist*, 24 September 2005; *China Quarterly Chronicle*, June 2005, p. 487.

119 *Far Eastern Economic Review*, 14 November 2002.

120 *The Economist*, 17 July 2004.

121 *Financial Times*, 6 July 2005.

122 *Business Beijing*, February 2003; *International Herald Tribune*, 26 May 2004.

123 Chen Chien-Hsun and Shih Hui-Tzu, *Banking and Insurance in New China*, Edward Elgar, Cheltenham, 2004, p. x.

124 *China Daily*, 15–16 February 2003.

125 Chen and Shih, op. cit., p. 63.

126 Ibid., p. 64.

127 *Newsweek*, 12 October 2000.

128 *Far Eastern Economic Review*, 12 October 2000.

129 Ibid.

130 Croll (1994), op. cit., pp. 3–14.

131 *Daily Telegraph*, 16 March 2005.

132 Sun Shuyun, 'Buddha's Back', *China Review*, Winter 2003, p. 21.

133 *The Times*, 20 May 2005.

134 Edward Tang, 'Secret Christians', *China Review*, Winter 2003, pp. 16–7.

135 *Wall Street Journal*, 2 June 2005.

136 Ibid.

137 *Washington Post*, 22 November 2003.

138 *China Review*, Winter 2003, p. 26.

139 *Wall Street Journal*, 2 June 2005.

140 *The Economist*, 6 November 1999.

141 Ibid., 1 May 1999.

142 Kate Westgarth, 'Filling the God-shaped Hole', *China Review*, Winter 2003, p. 23.

143 *The Economist*, 1 May 1999.

144 Ibid., 31 July 1999, 6 November 1999.

145 Ibid., 7 August 1999.

146 *International Herald Tribune*, 12 May 2000.

147 Ibid.

148 *The Economist*, 30 June 2001.

149 *China Daily*, 22 February 1997.

150 *Asiaweek*, 24 November 2000.

151 *International Herald Tribune*, 20 April 2001.

152 *Guardian*, 15 April 2005.

153 *The Economist*, 23 April 2005.

154 *Financial Times*, 11 November 2005.

11 Developing demand

1 *The Economist*, 9 March 2002.
2 *Renmin Ribao*, 21 February 2004; *Far Eastern Economic Review*, 1 April 2004.
3 Xinhua (New China News Agency), 16 April 2005.
4 *Renmin Ribao* (People's Daily), 13 May 2005.
5 *The Economist*, 11 September 2004.
6 Ibid., 21 August 2004.
7 *Transitions* (World Bank), May–June 2002.
8 *Financial Times*, 16 December 2003.
9 Xinhua (New China News Agency), 4 September 2004.
10 *China Business Review*, May–June 2004.
11 *Newsweek*, 29 August 2005.
12 Ibid.
13 Ibid.
14 Ibid.
15 *Newsweek*, 29 August 2005.
16 *BusinessWeek*, 28 March 2005.
17 *China Daily*, 29 June 2005.
18 Ibid.
19 *Sunday Times*, 5 December 2004.
20 *The Times*, 5 March 2005.
21 Xinhua (New China News Agency), 1 October 2003.
22 *International Herald Tribune*, 2 August 2005.
23 Xinhua (New China News Agency), 14 October 2003.
24 State Council Communiqué 7 September 2004, *China Quarterly Chronicle*, December 2004, p. 1130.
25 National Bureau of Statistics Communiqué for 2004, *China Quarterly Chronicle*, June 2005, pp. 487–8; *China Daily*, 26 October 2005.
26 Xinhua (New China News Agency), 26 July 2004.
27 National Bureau of Statistics Communiqué for 2003, *China Quarterly Chronicle*, June 2004, p. 573.
28 *Transitions* (World Bank), May–June 2002.
29 Ibid.
30 *Time*, 5 December 2003,
31 *The Economist*, 21 August 2004.
32 Xinhua (New China News Agency), 6 November 2003; *The Economist*, 30 July 2005; *Guardian*, 26 January 2006.
33 Ibid., 21 August 2004.
34 *Chinba Business Review*, November–December 2004.
35 *The Economist*, 19 November 2005.
36 *Newsweek*, 31 October 2005.
37 *China Quarterly Chronicle*, June 2004, p. 550.
38 Willman and Schucher, op. cit., p. 14; *China Daily*, 26 October 2005.
39 Ibid.
40 Ibid.
41 *Times Higher Education Supplement*, 1 April 2005.
42 *Newsweek*, 14 December 1998.
43 *The Economist*, 8 April 2000.
44 *Asiaweek*, 3 March 2000.
45 *China Quarterly Chronicle*, March 2004, pp. 253–4.
46 *Renmin Ribao* (People's Daily), 4 July 2005; *Guardian*, 15 February 2006.
47 *The Times*, 2 July 2005.
48 *China Daily*, 29 June 2005.

49 Ibid.
50 *Financial Times*, 25 June 2004; *South China Morning Post*, 25 June 2004.
51 *China Daily*, 29 June 2005.
52 *South China Morning Post*, 25 June 2004.
53 *The Times*, 28 December 2005.
54 *Guardian*, 28 December 2005.
55 *International Herald Tribune*, 30 August 2005.
56 *BusinessWeek*, 27 October 2003.
57 Ibid.
58 Ibid.
59 Ibid.
60 Ibid.
61 *Observer*, 6 November 2005.
62 Xinhua (New China News Agency), 2 February 2005.
63 *The Economist*, 22 October 2005.
64 Xinhua (New China News Agency), 5 July 2005.
65 *China Economic Review*, July 2005.
66 *The Economist*, 20 March 2004, 2 October 2004.
67 *Newsweek*, 13 December 2004.
68 Ibid.
69 *The Economist*, 2 October 2004, 6 November 2004.
70 Ibid., 8 April 2000; *International Herald Tribune*, 14 April 2004.
71 *The Economist*, 29 October 2005.
72 Ibid., 8 April 2000.
73 Ibid., 20 March 2004.
74 Ibid., 5 March 2005; CNN News, China, 1 July 2006.
75 Xinhua News Agency, 28 July 2004.
76 *The Economist*, 10 January 2004; 26 March 2004.
77 *Financial Times*, 9 December 2003.
78 *The Economist*, 10 January 2004.
79 *Asian Wall Street Journal*, 24 June 2003.
80 *Financial Times*, 24 June 2003; 9 December 2003.
81 *The Economist*, 10 January 2004.
82 *Far Eastern Economic Review*, 14 November 2002.
83 *The Economist*, 20 March 2004.
84 *China's Foreign Trade*, February 2003.
85 *BusinessWeek*, 13 December 2004.
86 Ibid.
87 Ibid.
88 *The Economist*, 5 June 2004.
89 J. Anderson, 'The Great China Bank Sale', *Far Eastern Economic Review*, September 2005, p. 9.
90 *Financial Times*, 7 December 2004.
91 *BusinessWeek*, 13 December 2004.
92 *The Economist*, 29 October 2005.
93 Ibid., 20 March 2004.
94 Anderson, op. cit., p. 10.
95 *The Times*, 10 December 2005.
96 Justin Lin, 'Changing China's Growth Model', *Far Eastern Economic Review*, October 2005, pp. 52–3.
97 *Far Eastern Economic Review*, 10 June 2004.
98 *Newsweek*, 26 December 2005.
99 Sun Liping, op. cit., p. 59; *Renmin Ribao* (People's Daily), 7 December 2004.
100 *China Business Review*, March–April 2003.

101 Xinhua (New China News Agency), 18 June 2005.
102 *China Business Review*, March–April 2003.
103 Ibid.
104 National Bureau of Statistics Communiqué, *China Quarterly Chronicle*, June 2005, p. 487.
105 Xinhua (New China News Agency), 18 June 2005.
106 Ibid.
107 Ibid.
108 *Beijing Review*, 20 February 2003.
109 Sun Liping, op. cit; *Renmin Ribao* (People's Daily), 16 August 2004.
110 *China Daily*, 29–30 October 2005.
111 *The Economist*, 5 March 2005.
112 *China Daily*, 30 December 2005.
113 *China Business Review*, May–June 2004.
114 Ibid.
115 *Newsweek*, 13 December 2004.
116 National Bureau of Statistics Communiqué, *China Quarterly Chronicle*, June 2005, p. 487.
117 Anderson, op. cit., pp. 22–3.
118 *The Economist*, 19 June 2004.
119 *Financial Times*, 5 February 2003.
120 *International Herald Tribune*, 3 September 2004.
121 *The Economist*, 20 March 2004; *The Times*, 11 February 2006.
122 Ibid.
123 *International Herald Tribune*, 1 April 2005.
124 Ibid.
125 *The Economist*, 23 April 2005.
126 Ibid., 4 June 2005.
127 Ibid.
128 *Far Eastern Economic Review*, 1 May 2004.
129 *Financial Times*, 18 May 2005.
130 Ibid.
131 *The Economist*, 24 December 2005.
132 *Financial Times*, 18 May 2005.
133 *Sunday Times*, 4 September 2005.
134 Ibid.
135 *China Business Weekly*, 31 October 2005.
136 *International Herald Tribune*, 18 November 2005.
137 *South China Morning Post*, 29 June 2005.
138 Ibid.
139 *Financial Times*, 18 May 2005.
140 Thorsten Veblen, *A Theory of the Leisure Class*, George Allen and Unwin, London, 1925.
141 Georg Simmel, 'Fashion', *American Journal of Sociology*, 62 (May 1957), pp. 541–58. (reprinted from *International Quarterly* 10, 1904).
142 *The Economist*, 20 November 2004.
143 *Shanghai Daily*, 29 December 2005.
144 *Far Eastern Economic Review*, 1 April 2004.
145 *Newsweek*, 19 July 2004.
146 Ibid.
147 C.K. Prahalad, *Bottom of the Pyramid: Eradicating Poverty through Profits*, Wharton School Publishing, Upper Saddle River, NJ, 2005.
148 Ibid., p. 1.
149 Ibid., p. 10.

150 Ibid., p. 11.
151 Ibid., pp. 207–40; *The Economist*, 6 November 2004.
152 Ibid.
153 *Newsweek*, 19 July 2004.
154 Ibid.
155 Ibid.
156 *Newsweek*, 19 July 2004.
157 *Time*, 30 June 1997.
158 *Financial Times*, 7 December 2004.
159 Ibid.
160 *International Herald Tribune*, 1 April 2005.
161 Ibid., 9 August 2005.
162 Ibid.
163 *Far Eastern Economic Review*, 20 February 2003.
164 *International Herald Tribune*, 3 September 2004; *China Business Review*, March–April 2005.
165 *The Economist*, 20 March 2004; *Financial Times*, 26 November 2005.
166 Ibid.
167 *Newsweek*, 3 December 2004.
168 Ibid.
169 *Renmin Ribao* (People's Daily), 26 August 2005; *Guardian*, 22 February 2006.
170 *Observer*, 24 May 2005.
171 *Financial Times*, 9 December 2004.
172 Ibid., 11 October 2005; *The Economist*, 19 November 2005.
173 *Renmin Ribao* (People's Daily), 13 May 2005.

Index

eBooks – at www.eBookstore.tandf.co.uk

A library at your fingertips!

eBooks are electronic versions of printed books. You can store them on your PC/laptop or browse them online.

They have advantages for anyone needing rapid access to a wide variety of published, copyright information.

eBooks can help your research by enabling you to bookmark chapters, annotate text and use instant searches to find specific words or phrases. Several eBook files would fit on even a small laptop or PDA.

NEW: Save money by eSubscribing: cheap, online access to any eBook for as long as you need it.

Annual subscription packages

We now offer special low-cost bulk subscriptions to packages of eBooks in certain subject areas. These are available to libraries or to individuals.

For more information please contact webmaster.ebooks@tandf.co.uk

We're continually developing the eBook concept, so keep up to date by visiting the website.

www.eBookstore.tandf.co.uk